GLOBALIZATION AND
THE STUDY OF EDUCATION

The *Yearbook of the National Society for the Study of Education* (ISSN 0077-5762, online ISSN 1744-7984) is published in April and September by Blackwell Publishing, Inc. with offices at (US) 350 Main Street, Malden, MA 02148-5020, (UK) 9600 Garsington Road, Oxford OX4 2ZG, and 155 Cremorne St., Victoria, Australia. Blackwell Publishing is now part of Wiley-Blackwell.

Information for subscribers

The Yearbook of the National Society for the Study of Education is published in 2 issues per year. Subscription prices for 2009 are: Premium Institutional: £99 (Europe), US$161 (The Americas), £99 (Rest of World); Prices are exclusive of tax. Australian GST, Canadian GST and European VAT will be applied at the appropriate rates. For more information on current tax rates, please go to www.wiley.com, click on Help and follow the link through to Journal subscriptions. The Premium institutional price includes online access to the current and all online back files to January 1st 1997, where available. For other pricing options, including access information and terms and conditions, please visit www.interscience.wiley.com/journals.

Delivery Terms and Legal Title

Prices include delivery of print journals to the recipient's address. Delivery terms are Delivered Duty Unpaid (DDU); the recipient is responsible for paying any import duty or taxes. Legal title passes to the customer on despatch by our distributors.

Each volume of the 108th Yearbook is available from the publisher for $40 a copy. For earlier volumes please contact Periodical Service Company, L. P., 11 Main Street, Germantown, NY 12526-5635 USA. Tel: (+518) 537-4700, Fax: (+518) 537-5899, Email: Psc@backsets.com or http://www.backsets.com.

Contact details

Journal Customer Services: For ordering information, claims and any enquiry concerning your journal subscription please go to interscience.wiley.com/support or contact your nearest office:
Americas: Email cs-journals@wiley.com; Tel: +1 781 388 8598 or 1 800 835 6770 (Toll free in the USA & Canada).
Europe, Middle East and Africa: Email: cs-journals@wiley.com; Tel: +44 (0) 1865 778315
Asia Pacific: Email: cs-journals@wiley.com; Tel: +65 6511 8000

MAILING: Journal is mailed Standard Rate. Mailing to rest of world by IMEX (International Mail Express). Canadian mail is sent by Canadian publications mail agreement number 40573520. **POSTMASTER:** Send all address changes to *Yearbook of the National Society for the Study of Education*, Blackwell Publishing Inc., Journals Subscription Department, 350 Main St., Malden, MA 02148-5020.

This journal is available online at Wiley InterScience. Visit www3.interscience.wiley.com **to search the articles and register for table of contents and e-mail alerts.**

Disclaimer: The Publisher, the National Society for the Study of Education and Editor(s) cannot be held responsible for errors or any consequences arising from the use of information contained in this journal; the views and opinions expressed do not necessarily reflect those of the Publisher, Society or Editor(s).

GLOBALIZATION AND
THE STUDY OF EDUCATION

108th Yearbook of the
National Society for the Study of Education

PART II

Edited by
THOMAS S. POPKEWITZ
FAZAL RIZVI

Distributed by WILEY-BLACKWELL MALDEN, MASSACHUSETTS

Table of Contents

PREFACE, *Thomas S. Popkewitz and Fazal Rizvi*. . . . .　1

CONTRIBUTORS. . . . .　4

GLOBALIZATION AND THE STUDY OF EDUCATION: AN INTRODUCTION,
Thomas S. Popkewitz and Fazal Rizvi . . . .　7

GLOBALIZING GLOBALIZATION: THE NEO-INSTITUTIONAL CONCEPT OF A
WORLD CULTURE, *Daniel Tröhler* . . . .　29

SCOPIC SYSTEMS, PIPES, MODELS AND TRANSFERS IN THE GLOBAL
CIRCULATION OF EDUCATIONAL KNOWLEDGE AND PRACTICES,
Noah W. Sobe and Nicole D. Ortegón. . . . .　49

POLITICS, GLOBAL TERRITORIES AND EDUCATIONAL SPACES,
Rosa Nidia Buenfil-Burgos . . . .　67

EDUCATION AND THE PRODUCTION OF GLOBAL IMAGINARIES:
A REFLECTION ON TEACHERS' VISUAL CULTURE, *Inés Dussel* . . . .　89

CAPITALISM, MODERNITY AND THE FUTURE OF EDUCATION IN THE NEW
SOCIAL CONTRACT, *Roger Dale and Susan Robertson* . . . .　111

GLOBALIZATION, INTERNATIONAL EDUCATION, AND THE FORMATION
OF A TRANSNATIONAL CLASS?, *Phillip Brown and Hugh Lauder*. . . . .　130

WITHER THE NEIGHBORHOOD? EDUCATION POLICY, NEOLIBERAL
GLOBALIZATION AND GENTRIFICATION, *Kalervo N. Gulson*. . . . .　148

GLOBALIZATION AND EDUCATION IN JAPAN, *Kentaro Ohkura and
Masako Shibata* . . . .　160

TRANSNATIONAL GOVERNANCE OF HIGHER EDUCATION:
ON GLOBALIZATION AND INTERNATIONAL UNIVERSITY RANKING LISTS,
Sverker Lindblad and Rita Foss Lindblad . . . .　180

OPEN EDUCATION AND THE OPEN SCIENCE ECONOMY, *Michael A. Peters* . . .　203

RESEARCHING EDUCATION POLICY IN A GLOBALIZED WORLD:
THEORETICAL AND METHODOLOGICAL CONSIDERATIONS, *Bob Lingard*. . . . .　226

GLOBALIZATION AS A SYSTEM OF REASON: THE HISTORICAL POSSIBILITY
AND THE POLITICAL IN PEDAGOGICAL POLICY AND RESEARCH,
Thomas S. Popkewitz. . . . .　247

GLOBAL MOBILITY AND THE CHALLENGES OF EDUCATIONAL RESEARCH
AND POLICY, *Fazal Rizvi* . . . .　268

Globalization and the Study of Education

Preface

Globalization is the type of phrase that Antonio Nóvoa (2002) has called planetspeak. It appears as an ubiquitous word that everyone "knows." It appears daily in the newspapers about the promise of progress that once was spoken about through the worldwide Church's redemption of the soul, or as the evil that will erode one's senses of national belonging. It becomes the watchword of both good and evil, or what is right about the new world of this millennial and what needs to be corrected in this world.

In one sense, globalization is a floating signifier continually filled with excesses of meaning. Globalization is a word that floats across contemporary literature to name cultural and economic changes that cross national boundaries, and to describe and explain these changes. When discussed in policies relating to schooling and teacher education, those changes are often seen as unproblematic. In a European Study of Educational Governance and Social Exclusion, for example, globalization appears to suggest a fatalism about society and schooling; that is, globalization is presented as a fact of life to which schools must simply accommodate through revisions to their curriculum and expectations about who the child is and should be. The Thatcher government vigorously proposed the thesis of TINA (There Is No Alternative) to globalization.

This book changes and gives critical attention to this naturalization and fatalism of globalization and schooling by subjecting current and past schooling to systematic investigations. The chapters in this volume argue that globalization needs to be understood in terms of multiple social processes, each of which are historically constituted, politically implicated and culturally calibrated. This implies the importance of understanding global processes through specific positionalities and perspectives, as well as the need to be theoretically self-reflexive.

While we can talk about globalization as an issue of contemporary life and schooling, it is important to recognize that the phenomena of worldwide connectedness and relations are historical and that there is a

1

need to differentiate current processes from those that preceded them and to provide adequate interpretations about what are distinctive features, characteristics, and politics in the contemporary era. This book seeks to explore what these might be. For example, it might be argued that the current practices of globalization are driven by revolutionary changes brought about by new information and communication technologies, leading to a kind of time-space compression never witnessed before. Or indeed, it could be suggested that while the authority of nation-states has not entirely declined, the global architecture of the system of nation-states is transformed, and that there are new ways in which states now work in a manner that is globally networked. This clearly affects the ways in which educational policies are developed and allocated to forge particular kinds of subjectivities in and through schooling.

This book then does not take any particular pre-determined position with respect to the origins, forms and effects of globalization in education, but subjects various theoretical possibilities to critical scrutiny. It refuses to take for granted either a skeptical position or indeed the position of a global enthusiast. It accepts the view that globalization is a transformative phenomenon that has complex origins, and that it is re-shaping the world in a range of contingent and locally specific ways. This raises numerous issues about educational policy and the work of schools. In exploring these issues, this book has five key objectives.

First, the book engages the question about what is different and distinctive from the past about the current situation that produces concerns with globalization.

This engagement of the present with the past enables a consideration of schooling itself as an invention of early processes of globalization, raising the important question about how and why the current context of schools and nations is being conceptualized as something "new" and different from the past.

Second, the volume speaks to the political and ethical issues of cultural differentiation, social inclusion, and exclusion in education. This encompasses the dynamics of global networks and patterns of global communication that have led to the "diasporization" of communities, and new patterns and practices of intercultural communication and exchange.

Third, it examines the interrelated economics, politics and cultures in which the global and local are being assembled and connected, such as through international comparisons and ranking lists and the new technologies of the Internet. This exploration raises a number of issues relating to new practices of educational governance, and to the ways in which the symbolic rhetoric of globalization is used to marketize and corporatize higher education in particular.

Fourth, it explores the politics of schooling embedded in its pedagogical practices and research, including the images and narratives of the teacher, the child, and education embodied in the pedagogy of schooling, such as how global images relate to educational imaginaries of children, politics, and the redemptive role of teachers.

Fifth, the volume examines the social locations and challenges of research in the study of education, such as intellectual and spatial locations of researchers in the context of globalization and post-national pressures.

Together, the chapters in this volume are largely exploratory, raising new questions about the historical origins of globalization and politics surrounding its re-shaping the study of education. Our goal is to open up discussion of globalization by challenging taken-for-granted assumptions and by re-framing issues so that a more productive response to it might become possible.

The contributors are among the leading international educational scholars to talk about the issues, dilemmas and problems in schooling that appear through the changing international contexts and social relations of the present. The volume brings educational studies into a conversation with different fields of studies to understand the changes occurring in contemporary life. The interdisciplinary qualities range from comparative and policy studies to visual culture, cultural sociology, post-colonial studies, economics and political economy, philosophy, and history, among others.

Thomas S. Popkewitz
Fazal Rizvi
Editors

REFERENCE

Nóvoa, A. (2002). Ways of thinking about education in Europe. In A. Nóvoa & M. Lawn (Eds.), *Fabricating Europe: The formation of an education space* (pp. 131–162). Dordrecht: Kluwer Academic Publishers.

Contributors

Phillip Brown, Cardiff University (UK). He has written, co-authored and co-edited 13 books, the most recent of which are *Education, Globalization and Social Change* (with Hugh Lauder, 2006) and *The Mismanagement of Talent: Employability and Jobs in the Knowledge Economy* (with Anthony Hesketh, 2004). *The Global Auction: The Broken Promises of Opportunity, Jobs and Rewards*, written with Hugh Lauder and David Ashton, is to be published in 2010.

Rosa Nidia Buenfil-Burgos, Center of Research and Advanced Studies (Mexico). She is the author of three books about the educational discourse of the Mexican Revolution; editor of three books on political debates and educational research; and author of chapters, articles and papers mainly about philosophical debates on education and recent educational policies in Mexico in the context of changes produced by globalization, postmodernity, and technologies.

Roger Dale, The University of Bristol (UK) He is the co-founder of *Globalisation, Societies and Education*, and Scientific Coordinator of the EU's Network of Experts in Social Science and Education (NESSE). His main research interests are in the governance of education, with a particular interest in European education policy. His most recent publication is *Globalisation and Europeanisation in Education* (2009, Oxford: Symposium), co-edited with Susan Robertson.

Inés Dussel is a researcher at the Latin American School for the Social Sciences (FLACSO/Argentina). She has authored six books and more than 60 chapters in books and articles in refereed journals. Her interests include theory and history of pedagogy, and the relationships between education and contemporary visual culture.

Kalervo N. Gulson, The University of British Columbia (Canada). His research is in critical policy studies and urban studies, focusing on how education policy pertaining to K-12 schooling reflects and constitutes the changing nature of contemporary cities. His current work examines connections between education markets, globalization, gentrification, and inequality in inner city areas of London, Sydney, and Vancouver.

Hugh Lauder, The University of Bath (UK). His publications include *High Skills: Globalization, Competitiveness and Skill Formation*; *Capitalism*

4

and Social Progress; and *Trading in Futures: Markets in Education*. He is also the editor of *The Journal of Education and Work* and a member of the Economic and Social Research Council (UK) Virtual College. He has served as an advisor to central and regional government agencies in the UK. His research interests include the relationship of globalization to national labor markets and educational systems in relation to higher education.

Rita Foss Lindblad, The University of Gothenburg (Sweden). Her research is focusing on the social organization of knowledge and learning in contemporary societies with a special interest in its political dimensions, where issues of gender, class, ethnicity and sexuality are important, as are issues of policies, educational systems, and their epistemic configurations. At present she is researching higher education and lifelong learning, where she gives special attention to governing technologies such as evaluations, assessments, and ranking lists.

Sverker Lindblad, The University of Gothenburg (Sweden). He is a member of the Steering Committee of the Centre for Globalization and Development. Lindblad was President of the European Educational Research Association and has been participating in research council work and coordinating and reviewing research and research programmes in Scandinavian and European contexts. Lindblad is researching educational systems and the governing of education in terms of comparative statistics, information systems, and professional knowledge.

Bob Lingard, The University of Queensland (Australia). He has written extensively on globalization and education policy processes, productive pedagogies and gender issues in education. He has been an editor of *Discourse: Studies in Cultural Politics of Education* for almost 20 years.

Kentaro Ohkura, St. Margaret's Junior College, Tokyo (Japan). His area of research includes studies of school and modernity and social inclusion/exclusion in education.

Nicole D. Ortegón, Loyola University Chicago (USA). Her research examines changing conceptualizations of mental health/illness in relation to education and society.

Michael A. Peters, The University of Illinois at Urbana-Champaign (USA) and Adjunct Professor at the School of Art, RMIT (Australia). He is the editor of *Educational Philosophy and Theory*, and two international e-journals, *Policy Futures in Education* and *E-Learning*. He has a strong research interests in distributed knowledge systems, digital scholarship and e-learning systems and has acted as an advisor to government on these and related matters in Scotland, New Zealand, South Africa and the EU. Two of his recent books are *Global Citizenship Education* and *Global Knowledge Cultures*.

Thomas S. Popkewitz, The University of Wisconsin-Madison (USA). His studies are concerned with the systems of reason that govern pedagogical reforms, research, and teacher education. His work has explored historically and comparatively the changing notion of the citizen and human agency in pedagogical reforms and sciences as they relate to issues of inclusion, exclusion, and abjection.

Fazal Rizvi, The University of Illinois at Urbana-Champaign (USA) and Adjunct Professor at the University of Melbourne and Deakin University (Australia). He has written on theories of globalization and education policy studies, issues of culture and identity in transnational contexts, and internationalization of higher education.

Susan Robertson, The University of Bristol (UK). She is currently coordinator of the Centre for Globalisation, Societies and Education, and founding co-editor of the journal *Globalisation, Societies and Education*. Her current areas of research are on processes of globalization and regionalization, and how these are being mediated in the education sector through ideological projects advanced by states and international organizations around ideas such as the knowledge-based economy, public-private partnerships, and spatializing strategies. She has written and lectured extensively on these issues with a view to raising the social justice implications of current education policies.

Masako Shibata, The University of Tsukuba (Japan). Her research interest currently focuses on teaching of war history inside and outside the school.

Noah W. Sobe, Loyola University Chicago (USA). His research examines the global circulation of educational practices and theories. He is the author of *Provincializing the Worldly Citizen: Yugoslav Student and Teacher Travel and Slavic Cosmopolitanism in the Interwar Era* (2008) and editor of *American Post-Conflict Educational Reconstruction: From the Spanish-American War to Iraq* (2009).

Daniel Tröhler, The University of Luxembourg. He is editor-in-chief of the *Zeitschrift für pädagogische Historiographie*. His research focuses on the comparative analysis of paradigmatic languages of education; comparative school history and curriculum studies; pragmatism; and contemporary discourses about school reform. His recent publications include methodological questions on history and theory of education and a comparative curriculum history. His *Languages of Education* is forthcoming.

Globalization and the Study of Education: An Introduction

THOMAS S. POPKEWITZ AND FAZAL RIZVI

Globalization has been in the forefront of public debates in recent decades. It was brought anew in the debates surrounding the current global financial crisis that have forced many to reconsider the idea of globalization and raise a number of new questions. To what extent has the current crisis been caused by the ways in which the possibilities of globalization have been interpreted and enacted? In what ways did the rhetorics of globalization unleash a range of practices that led many countries to abandon prudent regulatory systems of financial systems? Were global processes badly managed or was their very construction flawed? To what extent and how did the dominant construction of globalization re-shape not only economic activity but also other fields of human endeavor, such as education, and with what effects? How did the narratives of globalization become so ideologically dominant? Is it possible to imagine a different form of globalization that does not have such disastrous social consequences?

The essays in this volume are written against the backdrop of these urgent and profoundly consequential questions. If the global financial crisis makes us more aware that individual existence is not just bound by one's immediate environment and national contexts, how can the interconnectedness of ethics, politics and culture presupposed in the term globalization be interpreted, and its implications explored for educational policies and research, as well as for curriculum and teaching? What are different modes of interpreting and conceptualizing the study of education in these changing conditions? What "demands" on contemporary life are being produced by a focus on globalization and how are they different from those that have dominated twentieth century scholarship?

The chapters in this book consider some of the different paths taken in the study of globalization to de-parochialize our understanding of educational aims, processes and outcomes. They signal the need for a reflexivity that enables understanding the present and its particular conditions as they impact the school. Each chapter examines in its own

7

distinctive way the premise put forward in multiple ways (for example by Appadurai, 2001; Connell, 2007; Hacking, 2002; Popkewitz, 1998; Rizvi & Lingard, 2009; Wagner, 2001) that the traditional conceptions of social research and its territorial boundedness are challenged by the processes that are described by the term globalization.

Globalization as a Contested Notion

Globalization is a highly contested notion. It both describes a set of empirical changes and suggests a range of the conceptual "tools" required to interpret and respond to changes in contemporary events and schooling. It is used, in one important respect, to name shifts in patterns of transnational economic activities, with respect to the movement of capital and finance. It also refers to contemporary political and cultural configurations that are being fashioned and reshaped (Larner & Walters, 2004; Tomlinson, 1999). Its normative qualities are expressed as both salvation themes and fears through which governments, research communities, and civil society are to both interpret and imagine the possibilities of our lives.

In their highly influential analysis, Held and McGrew (2005) argue that while there are no definitive or fixed lines of contestation surrounding the globalization debate, at least three contrasting positions can nonetheless be identified. The *globalists*, they argue, view globalization as a real and significant historical development that has fundamentally altered all aspects of our lives. The *skeptics* deny this claim, and view globalization as a primarily ideological social construction that has limited explanatory value. Enthusiastic globalists such as Friedman (1999) argue that globalization involves a significant re-configuration of the organizing principles of economic activity and social life. In contrast, skeptics believe that the claims about globalization are based on various myths, and that the changes that are described are largely exaggerated, and indeed, there is nothing new about global changes, which have been occurring at least since the 1880s (Hirst & Thompson, 1997).

A third and different intellectual tradition undoes the opposition of realism or nominalism in philosophy and social theory. This position, found in different degrees among chapters in this volume, takes as its focus the need to make visible the particular cultural territories being generated under the banner of globalization. Studies of international relations and global politics, for example, can be traced as governed by changing rationalities about security, development, immigration and poverty, and the ethical governance of corporate practices (see, e.g., Larner & Walters, 2004). These rationalities are not merely discourses but generating principles that order what is seen, acted on, and thought about. They cross institutional practices as they are given expressions in concrete social programs, theories and systems of evaluation, such as in the new management techniques of benchmarks that circulate in governmental policies about social reform and school reforms.

It needs to be noted, however, that the lines of disagreement about the changes are not absolute. No one, for example, completely denies the significance of recent global changes caused by the revolutionary developments in information and communication technologies. Nor does anyone suggest that everything has changed, and that we live in a world that is unrecognizably different. Much of the debate centers instead on how to talk and think about the changes we are witnessing in the "transformation of dominant patterns of socio-economic organization, of territorial principles and of power" (Held & McGrew, 2007). Held and McGrew take a middle position between the globalists and the skeptics, whom they refer to as *transformationalists*, a perspective that suggests that globalization has an undeniably material form, for it describes social transformations resulting from growing flows of trade, capital and people, as well as ideas, images and ideologies. Globalization, they argue, describes new patterns of worldwide interconnectedness—the stretching of social relations and economic activities across national spaces and regions resulting in various complex networks of interaction.

One of the major intellectual tensions has to do with globalization as a reality to deal with, a way of thinking about an ideological construction, and/or as something about the in-between "spaces" of institutional relations and knowledge systems. On one layer are the arguments that adopt a critical realism, such as that of Dale and Robertson, who speak, in this volume, of globalization as the ever-expanding, ever-improving, ever-progressing set of relationships between the historically intertwined but essentially distinct trajectories of capitalism and modernity. A different interpretation of globalization is presented by Lingard in this volume. Lingard highlights the importance of political agency in the constitution global processes. He rejects the idea that texts are merely about interpretation, and argues against viewing policy discourse as a unidirectional command and instruction that constrains the possibilities for interpretation. In a third position, Buenfil-Burgos, drawing on post-foundational political theories, suggests that the real and "discursive" are in fact distinctions of philosophy that may have little materiality or usefulness for the interpretation of issues of globalization. She offers a notion of territory to understand the relation of material and ideological dimensions in which globalization is studied to consider the interaction of universal values and temporal qualities as they enter into contact with each other.

In each instance, there is an attempt to think about how the knowledge systems (texts and discourses), institutional practices, and social structures are intertwined, through patterns that are not bound to particular nations and the politics of these relations that potentially span the globe.

Globalization in an Historical Perspective: So What's New?

Globalization is a name given to the phenomena of the present to consider the effects, consequences, and causes of the changes occurring. What if this newness of globalization is not so new? In view of such a challenge, the question arises as to how we might think about globalization as an event through which to understand how it is given such currency as a descriptor and explanation for contemporary conditions, the qualities of people's lives, and the paths that are offered for salvation and redemption.

The "newness" of globalization in today's public discussion is consistently linked to capitalism and technologies associated with modernity through European periodization of trade, rapid communication, and price convergence. Yet this "newness" may be challenged historically. One can argue that globalization as a process is evident at least since the late fifteenth century. This process includes: steady trans-Pacific connections; global awareness through mapping; global transformative effects of the exchange of New and Old World crops and germs after 1492; flows of exotic objects, medicines, experts, religion, and dynastic genealogies; and ideas associated with universal power, including centralized states to sponsor and protect long-distance trade.

An incipient globalization related to the development of capitalism was already evident in the second half of the nineteenth century, along with the emergence of more consistent and coordinated practices of colonialism (Scholte, 2005). Under colonial regimes, globally integrated markets and financial systems were forged as it became possible to transport goods across vast distances, and as people were able to remain in touch with each other using new communication technologies such as the telegraph (Ferguson, 2006).

When historically examining arguments about global integration after 1950, it becomes clear that the forms of interaction in trade, investment, and tourism—with the exception of migration growth—have remained steady. Only in the 1990s did flows reach the per capita rates of the 1910s and late 1920s. The distribution between different regions has remained almost steady since the 1870s, with even more regional concentration in the most recent decades with the rise of the European Union, although there are specific changes in the growing role of East Asia and declines in Africa, Latin America, and the former Soviet bloc.

Further, capitalism was not and is not a monolithic structure, but has different trajectories of development and institutionalization in North America, South America, Asia, and Eastern and Western Europe (Boyer, 1996). Its emergence is further nuanced through a range of literature that has focused on the increasing transformations and entanglements during the past 150 years to alter the social-cultural, economic, and political patterns even in allegedly secluded places (Sachsenmaier, 2009). The emergence of capitalism in Japan, for example, entails the overlapping of militaristic, political/bureaucratic, and commercial elites in a state corporatism through which modes of production were assembled and connected. Ohkura and Shibata (in this volume) argue, for example, that Japanese internationalization and interdependency from the nineteenth century to the present entails multi-polarization. This interdependency is evident in the Ministry of Education's textbook writing policy concerning "Neighboring Countries" in the Far East, which signals Japan's own international economic position and the emergence of China and South Korea as economic centers.

It is also possible to locate other forms of globalization in and outside of Europe through different kinds of worldwide[1] flows, networks and connections; some literary, some religious, some purely military, and others political as in the creation of a world system of nations. One can think of the military conquests of Rome, the literary movements that spread Sanskrit, the making of the universal church in medieval times, the spread of Islam and Buddhism, and the establishment of the modern nation in the 1648 Treaty of Westphalia as embodying particular events and institutions that create worldwide interactions that carry semblances to what might be labeled today as globalization.

The spread of ideas about civil society, liberalism, and notions of democracy is often cited as another manifestation of globalization. This notion of the spread of ideas is intricately tied to the formation of capitalism and liberalism, and normatively inserts the West as its focal point in rating the degree of nations' progress in efforts to accommodate to "globalization." This view of globalization, however, functions as a mode of colonialization through its comparative formulations. Globalization becomes simply the spread of Western cultural and political traditions. A variety of case studies outside of the West, though, illustrates how indigenous traditions of social solidarity and tolerance have produced different possibilities and institutional forms, socio-political orders and value systems than those of Western models (Sachsenmaier, 2009).

We historically focus on the question of the newness of globalization for two reasons. What is important about the present is not the general proposition about globalization or the interconnections, spatial condensation, and differentiation through which the child and citizen are located. Rather, what is important are the particular differences and similarities with the past that require attention when we wish to consider the possibilities and limits of these changes in educational policy, research, and schooling. The changes cannot be taken for granted or assumed, but must be interrogated through rethinking the practices and study of schooling that are not bound by its territorial boundaries or instrumental tasks.

The point about the complexity of globalization relates not only to theoretical issues but also matters relating to the politics of theorizing. Often globalization appears to be a term that emerges from the West and is articulated through its categories and geopolitical centers. Yet as several chapters in this volume argue, there are politics and the political in the deployment of globalization as foci of interpretation. Lingard, for example, calls for de-parochialization of research through an epistemological diffidence that does not reinscribe the Global North and its epistemologies in its constructions of what constitutes globalization. In another paper in this volume Buenfil-Burgos, from a different theoretical position, also argues for rethinking the categories and distinctions through which the study of education is engaged. She suggests the problematization of globalization through considering the *imbrication*, that is, the *overlapping of edges* through which a systematic order is given visibility as a positivity in contemporary affairs.

In each of these two papers, and in some others, globalization is shown to represent an ideological formation embedded within a social imaginary that is re-shaping most aspects of our sociality. This perspective is consistent with the argument of Larry Ray in *Globalization and*

Everyday Life (2007) that globalization may have reconstituted the concept of the *social* itself, implying a new way of interpreting modernity—the principles generated to order how thought and action are ordered and imagined as "our" futures.

Globalization: (Re)Visioning/(Re)Constituting Conditions of Modernities

The suggestion that globalization is not entirely a new phenomenon does not imply that the current patterns of global interconnectivity and interdependence are not in fact significantly different, shaped by the profound technological developments in transport, communication and data processing that have altered our concepts of time and space. In earlier eras space was understood largely in terms of concrete localities. Mobility was limited, and for most individuals it was safer to stay in the same place. This is not the case any more, as Rizvi points out in this volume. He argues that global mobilities of people are no longer linear but dynamic and networked, and that this has highlighted the need to pay attention to the "transnational." Gulson has similarly suggested that the ways in which urban neighborhoods are not so much declining as becoming reconstituted through the processes of gentrification are linked to the global mobility of capital and people, within the framework of structures emerging out of a neoliberal imaginary.

It is however, not only people and capital that move but also ideas and ideologies. For most of human history it took time for ideas to travel from one place to another. Today, it is possible to send a message around the world instantaneously, giving rise to a globalized media, and making it possible to lift cultural meanings out of their original social context and transplant them in a radically different community. In her paper in this volume, Buenfil-Burgos explores the politics surrounding the movement of ideas. Arguing against the subsuming political traditions under the economic conditions related to contemporary neoliberal thought, Buenfil-Burgos considers globalization as having multi-directions of economic tendencies, cultural diversity and the intertwining and interdependence of political trends whose syncretic and hybrid conditions are given a commensurability between the heterogeneous.

In an important layer of contemporary literature, the transformations are associated with new patterns of interconnectivity and interdependence resulting in the inexorable integration of markets, nation-states, and technologies to a degree never witnessed before. Globalization, it is argued, enables investors and corporations in disparate locations to move money at the speed of light. This instantaneity of capital flows creates conditions for a complex range of financial interactions that leads to the reshaping of boundaries within national, cultural, and political spaces. A globally integrated system has thus emerged, becoming so large and complex that it cannot be adequately controlled by the existing institutions created in an earlier era to regulate international trade and flows of capital. And hence the financial crisis.

Global enthusiasts assume this economic system to be natural. Indeed, such an account of global processes treats them as historically inevitable, as a kind of juggernaut, with which people and nations simply have to come to terms, or negotiate as best they can. It is based on a politics of meaning that appears to seek to accommodate people and nations to a certain taken-for-grantedness about the ways the global economy operates and the manner in which culture, crises, resources, and power formations must be filtered through their universal logic. They thus "ontologize" the global market logic, creating global subjects who are asked to consider policy options through its presupposed conceptual prism, which revolves around such market principles as free trade, the production of profits through greater productivity, a minimalist role for the state, a deregulated labor market, and flexible forms of governance.

But what the global financial crisis has made clear is that this account of the term "globalization" is deeply ideological, implying certain power relations, practices and technologies, playing a "hegemonic role in organizing and decoding the meaning of the world" (Scharito & Webb, 2003). It contains an unmistakable ideological dimension filled with a range of norms, values, claims, beliefs and narratives which, while they are not always grounded in truth and are often inconsistent, are nonetheless sufficiently plausible to suggest historical accuracy. The debate about whether globalization is good or bad arguably takes place within an arena of ideology that, as Steger (2003, p. 96) points out, is "notoriously difficult to resist and repel because it has on its side powerful social forces that have already preselected what counts as 'real,' and that it therefore shapes the world accordingly." It is assumed that globalization of the economy in particular is inevitable and irreversible. It implies moreover that nobody is in charge of globalization and that it benefits everyone. Not surprisingly, therefore, the states that take this ideology of financial deregulation for granted simply take their eyes off the ball. There is thus now a belated call for a new regulatory system.

According to Manuel Castells (2000a), the new economy is knowledge-based, postindustrial, and service-oriented. Castells (p. 82) speaks of this economy as "informational": it is "organized around global networks of capital, management, and information, whose access to technological know-how is at the roots of productivity and competitiveness." These networks constitute "the new social morphology of our societies," which has substantially modified "the operation and outcomes in the processes of production, experience, power and culture." This has the consequence of making capitalism more fragmentary, as time and space are rearranged by the flows of multinational capital. Acquiring a new form, capitalism has extended its reach, and now, Castells argues, potentially shapes all aspects of human life and relations.

Recent developments in information and communication technology, especially satellite technologies, have revolutionized the circulation of ideas and information. There is an increasing global spatial proximity today that gives intimacy and connections in the immediacy of everyday life. It is now possible to transfer a large amount of money across national boundaries with the click of a computer key, and hold a meeting of the representatives of a transnational corporation from every continent without ever having them leave their offices. These developments have transformed the nature of economic activity, changing the modes of production and consumption. But they have also transformed personal relations through the internet, email, and "communities" of gamers that entail people around the world. As Harvey (1989, p. 7) points out, in the age of globalization time and space have become compressed in a number of ways, through faster communication, virtual contact, cheaper travel, and digitization. The capitalism of the present has clearly taken advantage of these possibilities, stretching the manner in which individuality is given expression across the whole globe.

Improved systems of communication and information flows, and rationalization in the techniques of distribution, have enabled capital and commodities to be moved through the global market with greater speed. The rigidities of Fordism, which emphasized standardization, mass production and predictable supply and demand chains, have been replaced by a new organizational ethos that celebrates flexibility as its foundational value, expressed most explicitly in ideas of subcontracting, outsourcing, vertically integrated forms of administration, just-in-time delivery systems and the like, producing niched products for a highly differentiated market.

This central idea about speed and flexibility of communication expressed in the literature on globalization is often expressed as the "liquidity of knowledge." The focus is on changing patterns of communication, flows, flexibility, and flux (mobility) of knowledge that move around all currents of society, and the nonmaterial structures and organizational forms that enable and facilitate that mobility.

The issue of communication is given explicit attention through the discussion of visual media in the chapter by Dussel. She argues that visual culture is not simply a repertoire of images but a set of visual discourses that position people and others in an assembly of social practices that give us the "the rights to look." Examining the visual discourse of "powerful images" by selected teachers in a Buenos Aires course, Dussel explores media as events in which there are networks in which teachers operate that shape and fashion the freedom of action; and the networks are historically related "in some yet to be determined way to the history of arts, technologies, media, and the social practices of display and spectatorship. . . deeply involved with human societies, with the ethics and politics, aesthetics, and epistemology of seeing and being seen."

In his chapter, Peters examines the epistemic and pedagogic possibilities of new media and technologies, which are now converging around discourses of "open access" and "open education." These discourses suggest not only new patterns of global interconnectivities and collaborations but also democratization of knowledge in the production and dissemination of new knowledge, implying new ways we might think about educational research and policies.

This focus again raises the question of locating the spatial and temporal qualities governing the present and the ways in which this has constituted the nature of the political in contemporary life. It also brings to the surface the importance of the historical. Ironically, Marx in the nineteenth century called the "annihilation of space by time as one of the conditions of modernity" (cited in Tomlinson, 1999). Sobe (in this volume) argues that the idea of knowledge as actively moving in all currents of society comes from a 1899 lecture by John Dewey in which he was comparing the turn of the twentieth century with previous times, drawing attention to the changing technologies of media, material structures, and forms by which ideas "move." And in fact the idea of actively moving knowledge was found in the sixteenth century, with one of its authors being burned at the stake for a heretical cosmogony that threatened what Dewey later called "the high priesthoods of learning."

Rethinking the Nation, Schooling, and the Governing of Political Spaces

One of the defining characteristics of schooling since the nineteenth century has been its focus on the nation-state. Whether emphasizing the internal institutional development of primary and secondary education or the relation of schooling to issues of democracy, equity and economic progress, the nation has been the center of attention. There is, however, a small sociological and historical literature that has run against this parochialism outside of the literature on globalism (see, e.g., Smeyers & DePaepe, 2008; Meyer, Kamens, Benavot, Cha, & Wong, 1992; Popkewitz, 2005; Steiner-Khamsi, 2004).

The rethinking of the nation and the global as it relates to schooling is evident when thinking about John Dewey and pragmatism. Often considered as an icon of present educational reforms of teaching, Dewey's writing can be read not only as about the turn of the twentieth century American progressivism and American progressive education. On one layer of analysis, Dewey's pragmatism was a historical project in reshaping the relation of the citizen and the nation, as expressed in the broader political and social movement of progressivism (Menand, 2001). But the changes in the U.S. embodied a worldwide circulation of ideas and programs bounded with political, economic, and social changes (Popkewitz, 2005). The New Educational Fellowship, for example, was a reform movement with representatives from 53 nations that embodied similar cosmopolitan dispositions in the construction of a modern schooling through inserting scientific principles in teaching, greater pedagogical relevance to children's lives, and the incorporation of psychology. The various cosmopolitan principles were, however, not the same, as they entailed different cultural theses about modes of life in different time/spaces. This can be understood through considering how Dewey's pragmatism traveled and was assembled, and then disconnected, in the salvation narratives of the Mexican Revolution, Chinese reforms to replace Confucian hierarchies, Turkish modernization of its peasantry, and Pan-Slavic education in Yugoslavia; as well as the placing of Dewey as antihero, an epistemological foreigner who violated the *geist* of the nation in Germany and the Catholic anti-enlightenment reforms in Brazil.

Further, our purpose is to think about the rationale of schooling as it interrelates with institutional and social practices without making a distinction between ideas, discourse, and nominalism in opposition to realism. Ideas are never merely ideas or discourses but cultural and social practices that respond to and make up things of the world. The different assemblies, connections, and disconnections that can be traced through the traveling of pragmatism were made possible through changes that transcended the local and the national, yet at the same time brought into the different pedagogical contexts of schools to link collective belonging through universalizing narratives about who the child is and should be. These effects were material and not the same in Brazil, Japan, Mexico, and the United States.

If we move to the broader discussions of globalization, this parochialism of the nation is no longer sustainable. Nation-states have defined the social and economic conditions under which people work, but they are no longer the sole arbiter of governing. Increasingly, if we examine the increase in global capital, in the form of transnational corporations (TNCs), it has become equally if not more important. In an era of flexible accumulation, TNCs are able to exercise an enormous amount of power and influence, especially in the least developed countries. Controlling economic activity in two or more countries, TNCs benefit from globalization by maximizing the comparative advantage between countries, profiting from differences in wage rates, market conditions, and related political and fiscal regimes.

Accordingly, states are no longer the only or even the major drivers of the global economy. However, the new capitalism still requires the help of national governments to sustain its accumulation strategies; and it needs to create social subjects sufficiently invested in its operations, as well as cultural practices predisposed towards its products and services. Far from becoming redundant in a globalized economy, the state is now required to play a crucial role in developing public policies favorable to the processes of global capital accumulation. In this way, global economic shifts are dialectically related to contemporary political and cultural shifts. The changing architecture of the state may thus be viewed as both an expression of, and a response to, global economic processes, and the cultural changes we are now experiencing are partly a product of, and partly a contribution to, the consumerism promoted by the global economy.

Over most of the 1990s, many social theorists argued that the exclusive link between the state and political authority was broken. They spoke of the demise of the state and maintained that sovereign states could no longer claim exclusive authority over their citizens and their territory; and those recent changes in the structure of the global economy, as well as international law, regional political associations, and institutional formations had altered the fundamental constitution of the state system. But such a view is fundamentally mistaken, for as Wood (2003, p. 140) has argued, while globalization has certainly been marked by a withdrawal of the state from its social welfare and ameliorative functions, it is impossible for global capitalism to dispense with many of the other functions performed by the state, such as security, social stability and infrastructural provisions that are essential for economic productivity. Global capitalism depends more than ever on "a system of multiple and more or less sovereign states." Nation-states are still required "to perform the administrative and coercive functions that sustain the system of property and provide the kind of day-to-day regularity, predictability, and legal order that capitalism needs more than any other social form."

This new set of relations of the state and international organizations is evident in the new management approaches. Several chapters in this volume refer, for example, to OECD's PISA, an international assessment of students' "practical" knowledge of science, mathematics, and literacy. These assessment tools are ways of creating new categories of equivalence across nations. In the European Union, for example, it can be argued that they provide a technology for creating a European identity in a scaled order that redefined the nation. If we look at the university, it is undergoing a transformation all over the world, within a context of both competition and collaboration (Rizvi, 2004). Lindblad and Lindblad (this volume) argue that new ranking systems perform as external assessments to order the quality of institutions into a hierarchy. The ordering system loops back into and enters the steering mechanism for the allocation of resources, and determinants of "quality" as a network of organizations supplement each other in different ways. Globalization is fostered through a soft governing in which external assessments and inputs create global positioning systems (Simons & Maschelein, 2008) that provide a constant location of institutions (and individuals) with global frameworks.

The above examples suggest that issues of the globalization of economic, political, and educational issues are inextricably linked. And so are issues of cultural formation and the role that education is expected to play in the new economy. Within the system of modern states, considerable cultural importance has been attached to education. Educational systems carry the narratives of the nation. In extensive studies of curriculum from the nineteenth century to the present, Meyer, Boli, Thomas, and Ramirez (1997) argue that there emerges a world systems (globalization) that in part can be studied through the formation of modern schooling and its relation to the nation. Gellner (1983) points out, further, that it was the mass educational systems that provided the common framework of understanding which enhanced the processes of state-coordinated modernization. Through the diffusion of ideas, meanings, myths, and rituals, citizens "imagined" the nation and filtered conceptions of their "other." Although education continues to serve this function, for many globalization theorists the nation-state can now be imagined in a number of different ways, and the lives of its citizens are now inextricably linked to cultural formations that are produced in faraway places.

However, these developments that accompanied modern schooling can be viewed in at least two ways. One is the world system argument of an increasing homogeneity in the internal workings of schooling; that is, there is an increasing consistency of what constitutes the curriculum and teaching of the school into the twentieth century. This global consistency, argued in multiple chapters in this book, requires theoretical perspectives and historical specifications to understand differences, divisions and heterogeneous modernities, rather than a single model of diffusion.[2] Again to return to the Japan study in this book, Ohkura and Shibata's analysis of the multi-polarization of reforms includes Western human capital theories of development and international measurements of OECD's PISA as "actors" transmogrified through connections with Japanese cultural and social practices.

Under the conditions of globalization, then, the assumption of discrete national cultural formations can no longer be taken for granted because there is now an ever-increasing level of cultural interaction across national and ethnic communities. With the sheer scale, intensity, speed, and volume of global cultural communication, the traditional link between territory and social identity appears to have been broken, as people can more readily choose to detach their identities from particular times, places, and traditions. The media and the greater transnational mobility of people have had a "pluralizing" impact on identity formation, producing a variety of hyphenated identities that are less "fixed" or "unified." This has led to the emergence of a "global consciousness," which may represent the cultural basis of an "incipient civil society."

What this discussion suggests is that global patterns entail complex dynamic processes that are constantly changing in light of new economic, political, and cultural as well as technological developments that embody hierarchies and divisions that are not equal. Some benefit more than others, but the relationship is not that of a flat world, as Friedman (2005) suggests.

Globalization: Knowledge, Cultural Flows and Assemblies

Earlier we explored the difficulty of periodizing globalization. We argued that the contemporary expressions of globalization embody a range of practices that include processes of colonialization (Rizvi, 2004). Indeed, colonialism sought to bring communities across vast distances into a singular political space, controlled and coordinated from a center. Patterns of global inequality date back to the sixteenth century and continue today through different forms than earlier, something we explore below.

The arguments over topological questions about colonialization and globalization explored previously have a different but complementary notion of power embodied in the systems of reason; that is, the historically generated principles about how judgments are made, conclusions drawn, rectifications proposed, and fields of existence made manageable and predictable. Colonialization, as postcolonial literature has continually demonstrated, is not merely about territory and local self-governance but also about the insertion of epistemological systems that order what is thought, done, and hoped for. These studies explore, for example, how the transportation of history into archives, the creation of museums, the use of statistical forms, and social science intersected in the administration and conduct of post-colonial nationalism in the second half of the twentieth century (see., e.g., Mehta, 1997).

To differentiate the issues of colonialization from earlier discussions, we now consider colonialization as embodied principles or systems of reason about what is "seen," talked about, and acted upon. But to speak about "reason" is to locate its rules and standards historically and not in ideas in and of themselves. The relation of the rules and standards of "reason" as they intersect with and through economic, governmental, and social forms is seriously debated in social theory—from Harvey's (1989) placing knowledge as an epiphenomenon to material conditions to Hacking's (2002) "historical ontology" that speaks about the inadequacies of the dualism of knowledge (discourse and texts) and "realism."[3]

This focus of reason as an "actor" is made more succinct in the topoi of current reforms about the lifelong learner, the knowledge society and the knowledge economy. These phrases give explicit attention to knowledge rather than brute force as central in the steering of conduct and the act of governing. The materiality of "reason" was embodied in the eighteenth century founders of the American and French Republics, who recognized that the citizen is not born but made. Central was education in the making of society by making the child the future citizenrequired by the modern liberal state.

The "materiality" of knowledge—that how we "think" is not merely thought—can be illustrated through European enlightenment discussions about *civilize* and *civilizations*, and by contemporary international testing of science, mathematics, and literacy. The notions of "civilize" and "civilization" instantiate that present knowledge and wisdom superseded the past. "To civilize" in these debates was to extend what is common, or should be, to all human beings. "Civilized" encompassed a politeness, refinement, and new manners and decencies between people (Passavant, 2000). The travel literatures of the Scottish philosophers, influential in the formation of U.S. schools in the nineteenth century, accounted for societies in the New World and Africa through their approximations to "the superior" European models (Jack, 1989, p. 194). Today, European and North American narratives of globalization embody a different polarization that freezes authoritatively, for example, the meaning of Europe through expurgating its "Others." Heins (2005), for example, examines leading German intellectual attempts to redefine the mission of Europe that criticize cultural essentialism and Eurocentricism; yet that criticism embodies a binary moral geography. The "orientalizing" is told through tropes of lawlessness and inhumanness. Europe is variously cosmopolitan, bearer of Enlightenment values, open to all. America is profane and Europe is sacred; America is selective, violent, and immature politically; Africa is suffering; the Middle East and the Balkans are powder kegs.

The very inscription of the notion of "new" in the context of globalization brings to the fore a way of thinking of colonization through the inscription of difference. The "new" embodied a particular continuum of the past/present/future that stabilized space to calculated change in the name of progress. The placing of human life and change in a regulated time freed people from theological restrictions through notions of actors, development and progress, and made possible the development of social sciences in the nineteenth century to plan society by planning people.

Raising the issue of the conceptualization of time and space is to point to the ways that something as seemingly simple as time moves as both a way of thinking and as the organizing of practices about what is known and acted on. If we examine the international ranking systems of nations that serve as global positioning devices (Simons & Maschelein, 2008), a particular continuum of time and stabilized spaces are produced. The models of modernity and its "advanced" civilization is framed by the theories and programs about knowledge of science and mathematics found in the curriculum. The teaching of school subjects, however, is not merely teaching about disciplinary fields. School subjects are an alchemy that translates and transforms subject content into practices to govern dispositions and actions related to the obligations of the citizen (Popkewitz, 2008). Lindblad and Lindblad's discussion of international ranking of higher education provides a way to think about organized knowledge production and the circulation of "ideas" governing possibilities through the ordering of social facts and structures about what matters in higher education. The technologies of monitoring, standards, benchmarking, and ranking are produced in multiple sites and assembled by international, governmental, and local organizations. The divisions have a homology to the past differentiations of the civilized from those not as advanced.

Further explored in the Popkewitz chapter are principles that exclusion and abjection are no longer talked about as "advanced" and "less advanced civilizations" in contexts of colonialization. The construction of distinctions and divisions is embodied in policies and research related to equality that recognizes particular marginalized populations for inclusion yet inscribes the child as different. The connections among inclusion, exclusion, and abjection are embodied, Popkewitz argues, in the system of reason that historically makes possible a comparative style of thought through which globalization is "seen" and acted on. He pursues these issues of inclusion and exclusion by first focusing on European and North American enlightenments notions of cosmopolitanism that link and differentiate individuality and societies. This historical analysis orients the discussion of contemporary European and U.S. policy and research. It embodies the globalized school, the child, the lifelong learner who lives in the knowledge society/knowledge economy, and the "other"—the child left behind, who does not "fit" into the envisioned future.

The questions of the "reason" embodied in today's conditions and the relations of time and space that it presupposes require a rethinking of the very problematics through which globalization and education is studied. Sobe, in this volume, for example, distinguishes between the possibilities and limits of different theories of globalization to suggest scopic systems that interrelate epistemological movements and the mechanism through which they become established and recontextualized. Buenfil-Burgos in another chapter also pursues the question of how to think about current conditions and their multi-directional economic tendencies: cultural diversity, intertwining traditions, and interdependence of political trends that produce syncretic and hybrid conditions and prospects.

Globalization and the Study of Education

The questions about globalization raised in this volume are not merely about policy, research, or knowledge. They are also about the practice of schooling that reaches into the everyday life of schools. In proposals for reforms in education. In the United States and elsewhere, globalization has become part of the "planetspeak" of school reform and the university's statement of mission. Globalization discourses speak of educational institutions preparing the individual for what is new, and of the future that will renew humanity. That preparation is for the knowledge society and the knowledge economy that knows no boundaries, expresses the citizen reborn through the imperative of general and universal commitments to humanity where allegiances are global—with hospitality to the other who is multicultural and multi-ethnic; with commitments to human rights that transcend the territorial boundaries of the nation. The salvation themes embedded in the narratives of globalization carry a double irony, embodying principles for governing the future in the present and to prepare for the global world through prescriptions designed to make the nation competitive and progressive in the new world system.

Collectively, the chapters make apparent the need to rethink the problems and problematics in the study of schooling. Analyzing the processes of education and thinking about the practices of schooling require examining the broader transnational and historical frameworks in which policies are formulated and programs realized. We have argued that the consideration of the particular implications and consequences of globalization are connected to economic factors and about *homo economicus*; yet at the same time, so as not to be reductive, we must consider the interactions in which transnational relations are performed and realized as specific historical events.[4] The categorical imperatives that separate and segregate the arenas of the social, the political, the economic, and the cultural, in order to locate descriptions and explanations, are effects of power. If we take the formation of the discipline of economics through the work of Adam Smith in the late eighteenth century, it was concerned with moral philosophy and the good of society, linked to individual self interest. The institutionalization of the American Economic Association at the turn of the twentieth century was initially designed to bring Christian values into social policy. The moral purposes of the discipline, however, were instrumentalized and its normative ordering subsequentially subsumed in utilitarian theories and methods. The very separation of the category of economics from the moral, social, and cultural instantiated political processes differentiated colonial populations in forming their administration (see Mitchell, 1988).

An exploration of these issues should not be construed as an argument against social science but as an indication of the need to rethink the classifications and ordering procedures that engage the study of schooling and its limits. If the discussion of colonialization is of any relevance, the separation of knowledge from the materiality of the world is tenuous, if not eliding of the political. The same applies to globalization.

The volume speaks to issues of globalization and the ways in which it demands a rethinking of educational knowledge, and also, by implication, educational practice. It asks how, and the extent to which, global mobilities of ideas, capital, and people are re-shaping the terrain of educational work; and how global networks are utilized in promoting a particular set of prescriptions for educational reform, and how these prescriptions are shaped through the global processes of knowledge circulation, transfer, and convergence. The chapters in this volume suggest that teaching these prescriptions is based on a particular historical assemblage of values, which while they benefit some communities more than others, are perhaps masked behind a legitimizing discourse of globalization. While the perspectives on globalization presented in this volume vary, what is common to them all is the conviction that globalization is a name given to the present that needs to be historicized, and the very naming of that present is not neutral but part of the problem of political and governing practices.

The volume is organized in three sections. The first is entitled *Globalization and Education: Different Outlooks and Problematics*. Its major concern is with exploring existing approaches and alternatives for theorizing and conceptualizing the study of globalization. Themes of interconnectedness and difference give substantive discussions of the worldwide changes occurring and the issues posed for the study of education. The second section, *Globalization: Effects and Possibilities*, provides analyses of specific contexts and characteristics of globalization and education. This section, like the previous one, illustrates how different conceptualizations cast different ways to "see" and think about the phenomena and the expression of the issues generated through the study of globalization. The final section *Globalization and Challenges for Educational Research*, grapples with issues of rethinking the legacies of late-nineteenth-century educational theories, research, and practices through the subject of the nation as well as the social, cultural, and epistemological assumptions for ordering the changes occurring. Along with the previous sections, these chapters provide ways of (re)visioning the commonsense about globalization, social changes, and education. While there are families of resemblance in the chapters of each section, there are also overlaps in the themes and arguments across the different sections. These overlaps also, we believe, reveal the strength of the contributing authors, who bring to bear a wide range of scholarship to the discussion of globalization and education.

NOTES

1. We use the term "worldwide" rather than "international" as many forms of globalization preceded the notion of nation.

2. For discussion of multiple modernities see Eisenstadt (2000) and Sachsenmaier (2009).

3. We have argued earlier and below that part of the inadequacy and thus the rethinking of the social and education sciences is the categorical separation of these different spheres of human life that are residues of nineteenth-century social theories.

4. The early use of the word was oeconomy, that in the seventeenth century referred to the prudent managing of the household that was not merely about its resources but also its moral qualities of conduct. We suggest this earlier usage to suggest that the reference to economic categories in school policy and research related to pedagogy, for example, quickly overlaps with cultural theses about who the child and family are and should be. This relation of the moral, the political, and the cultural to schooling is one of the elements of rethinking the social sciences that is becoming necessary in the current discussion about globalization.

REFERENCES

Appadurai, A. (2001). *Globalization: A public culture book*. Durham, NC: Duke University Press.

Boyer, R. (1996). State and market: A new engagement for the twenty-first century? In R. Boyer & D. Drache (Eds.), *States against markets: The limits of globalization* (pp. 84–116). New York: Routledge.

Castells, M. (2000a). *The information age: Economy, society, and culture, volume 1: The rise of the network society* (2nd ed.). Oxford: Blackwell Publishing.

Connell, R. (2007). *Southern theory: The global dynamics of knowledge in the social sciences*. London: Allen and Unwin.

Eisenstadt, S.N. (2000). Multiple modernities. *Daedalus, 129*(1), 1–29.

Ferguson, J. (2006). *Global shadows: Africa in the neoliberal world order*. Durham, NC: Duke University Press.

Friedman, T.L. (1999). *The Lexus and the olive tree: Understanding globalization*. New York: Farrar, Straus and Giroux.

Friedman, T.L. (2005). *The world is flat: A brief history of the twenty-first century*. New York: Farrar, Straus and Giroux.

Gellner, E. (1983). *Nations and nationalism*. Ithaca, NY: Cornell University Press.

Hacking, I. (2002). *Historical ontology*. Cambridge, MA: Harvard University Press.

Harvey, D. (1989). *The condition of postmodernity: An enquiry into the origins of cultural change*. Cambridge, MA: Blackwell.

Heins, V. (2005). Orientalising America? Continental intellectuals and the search for Europe's identity. *Journal of International Studies, 34*(2), 433–448.

Held, D., & McGrew, A. (Eds.) (2005). *The global transformation reader: An introduction to the globalization debate* (3rd Ed.) Cambridge: Polity Press.

Held, D., & McGrew, A. (2007). *Globalization theory: Approaches and controversies*. Cambridge: Polity Press.

Hirst, P., & Thompson, G. (1997). *Globalization in question*. Cambridge: Polity Press.

Jack, M. (1989). *Corruption and progress: The eighteenth-century debate*. New York: AMS Press.

Larner, W., & Walters, W. (Eds.) (2004). *Global governmentality: Governing international spaces*. London: Routledge.

Mehta, U.S. (1997). Liberal strategies of exclusion. In F. Cooper & A. Stoler (Eds.), *Tensions of empire: Colonial cultures in a bourgeois world* (pp. 59–86). Berkeley: University of California Press.

Menand, L. (2001). *The metaphysical club*. New York: Farrar, Straus and Giroux.

Meyer, J., Boli, J., Thomas, G., & Ramirez, F. (1997). World society and the nation-state. *American Journal of Sociology, 103*(1), 144–181.

Meyer, J.W., Kamens, D.H., Benavot, A., Cha, Y.-K., & Wong, S.-Y. (1992). *School knowledge for the masses and national primary curriculum categories in the twentieth century*. Washington, DC: Falmer Press.

Mitchell, T. (1988). *Colonizing Egypt*. Cambridge: Cambridge University Press.

Passavant, P. (2000). The governmentality of discussion. In J. Dean (Ed.), *Cultural studies and political theory* (pp. 115–131). Ithaca, NY: Cornell University Press.

Popkewitz, T.S. (1998). *Struggling for the soul: The politics of education and the construction of the teacher*. New York: Teachers College Press.

Popkewitz, T.S. (Ed.) (2005). *Inventing the modern self and John Dewey: Modernities and the traveling of pragmatism in education*. New York: Palgrave Macmillan.

Popkewitz, T.S. (2008). *Cosmopolitanism and the age of school reform: Science, education, and making society by making the child*. New York: Routledge.

Ray, L (2007). *Globalization and everyday life*. New York: Routledge.

Rizvi, F. (2004). Theorizing the global convergence of restructuring policies in education. In S. Lindblad and T. Popkewitz (Eds.), *Educational restructuring: International perspectives on traveling policies* (pp. 21–42). Greenwich, CT: Information Age Publishing.

Rizvi, F., & Lingard, B. (2009). *Globalizing educational policy*. New York: Routledge.

Sachsenmaier, D. (2009) The concept of multiple modernities and its neighboring fields. In J. Schriewer & H. Kaelble (Eds.), *La comparación en las sciencias sociales y históricas: Un debate interdisciplinar*. Barcelona: Editorial Octaedro.

Scharito, T., & Webb, J. (2003). *Understanding globalization*. London: Sage.

Scholte, J.A. (2005). *Globalization: A critical view* (2nd Ed.). New York: St Martin's Press.

Simons, M., & Maschelein, J. (2008). From schools to learning environments: The dark side of being exceptional. *Journal of Philosophy of Education, 42*(3–4), 687–704.

Smeyers, P., & DePaepe (Eds.) (2008). *The educationalization of schooling*. Dordrecht, The Netherlands: Sense Publishers.

Steger, M. (2003). *Globalization: A very short introduction*. Oxford: Oxford University Press.

Steiner-Khamsi, G. (Ed.) (2004). *The global politics of educational borrowing and lending*. New York: Teachers College Press.

Tomlinson, J. (1999). *Globalization and culture*. Chicago: University of Chicago Press.
Wagner, P. (2001). *Theorising modernity: Inescapability and attainability in social theory*. London: Sage.
Wood, E.M. (2003). *Empire of Capital*. London: Verso.

Globalizing Globalization: The Neo-Institutional Concept of a World Culture

DANIEL TRÖHLER

The history of education in relation to globalization is quite paradoxical. The first global phenomena of education emerged out of reactions against the Reformation in the late sixteenth century, when the Counter-Reformation Jesuits, or Society of Jesus, started to establish institutions of higher education, first in Europe and later in other parts of the world. Provided in architecturally standardized buildings, the Jesuit education was based on a standardized curriculum developed by international experts[1] and used standardized quality rating systems to assess students' achievement (see, for instance, Dainville, 1978). The historiography of education in relation to globalization can be called a paradox because it does not focus on this successful Counter-Reformation concept but rather, quite to the contrary, on the alleged spread of mostly secularized Protestant concepts. It is these Protestant concepts that—according to the historiographic accounts—have been diffused around the world since at least the end of the Second World War, constituting through a "cultural globalization" process a new "world culture" in which specific patterns of thoughts are brought about by transnational organizations and international experts. One definition of this process reads as follows: "Cultural globalization involves the worldwide spread of models or blueprints of progress and the networks of organizations and experts that transmit these logics of appropriateness to nation-states and other collectivities" (Suarez & Ramirez, 2004, p. 1). Educational expectations and organizations play a crucial role in this process. According to these interpretations, educational systems were the crucial means used in "developing the Western Europe model of a national society" (Ramirez & Boli, 1987, p. 3) that, even though transcended in the twentieth century, has not diminished the importance of education; quite the contrary.

"Globalization" is a concept that refers to an encompassing process with radical effects, similar to concepts such as Christianization, confessionalization, secularization, or modernization. All of these notions serve to indicate fundamental theories describing these encompassing processes. However, when describing processes of this amplitude, the description is always a construction, too. This construing description has its pitfalls. The main danger is linearizing and harmonizing the process, starting out from its alleged result: Christianity, schism, secularity, modernity, or the globalized world.[2] Following the normative preferences of the authors, these descriptions tell either a story of decline or a story of success. Famous stories of success were written, for example, by the British Whigs in the eighteenth and nineteenth century, depicting the past as an unavoidable and thus teleological progression towards always greater individual liberty and enlightenment, resulting in modern forms of liberal democracy, constitutional monarchy, and scientific progress—in other words, to the dominant ideology of Whiggism in England. In order to criticize this goal-directed, often hero-based historiography, the British historian Herbert Butterfield published the celebrated book *The Whig Interpretation of History* in 1931 (Butterfield, 1931) and, ever since, the notions of Whig history or Whiggishness have been used to criticize teleological accounts of the past to the present.

In the following I will focus on how globalization and education are addressed in research. More precisely, I will concentrate on only one dominant approach to analyzing globalization and its effects on education and also the educational role within globalization. Although my focus is quite narrow and apparently analytic, I still do not imagine that I am refraining from talking about globalization and education, for the international discussion about globalization is itself a part of the process.[3] Nevertheless, I wish to analyze a model that seems to provide a basically analytical account of globalization with respect to education, the model called sociological neo-institutionalism, and its concept of world polity or world culture. This is an area of research that emerged mostly at the Department of Sociology and the School of Education at Stanford University. These analyses have garnered a lot of attention, and they are broadly discussed and refined all around the world in a number of different academic disciplines.

Basically, using the example of the sociological neo-institutional contribution to globalization and education, I will demonstrate how difficult it is to analyze or describe the process of "globalization" without premises that first construe the topic itself that is going to be described. In other words, the analysis of encompassing historical processes such as "globalization" is already predetermined by general epistemological assumptions in the research design. These epistemological premises in sociological neo-institutionalism are—as I will argue—rooted in Max Weber's Protestant ethic thesis. This origin is particularly juicy for neo-institutionalism, for its sociological paradigm is the result of a critical examination of Max Weber's theory of institutions. My thesis is that, with the background of Max Weber's Protestant ethic thesis, sociological neo-institutionalism interprets globalization as a more or less linear process, and the analysis becomes thus a part of the grand narrative of Protestantism itself.[4] I will demonstrate my thesis in four steps. First, I depict sociological neo-institutionalism and its contribution to the analysis of globalization. In the second part of the chapter I discuss the problems of analyzing historical processes. In the third part I show how linear constructions of a global history frame our view of the institutions of education, and finally I discuss how we can deal with the problem of analyzing globalization without construing it at the same time.

Education and the World Culture Thesis of Neo-Institutional Sociology

About 30 years ago the educational discourse was confronted with a conceptual distinction developed at the Department of Sociology at Stanford University on the basis of studies of educational establishments. The distinction reformulates Max Weber's concept of the institution by differentiating "institution" from "organization." The inspiration for this distinction was borrowed from a model developed in organizational psychology, the notion of "loose coupling," which describes the relation between the formal structures of and the inner activities within an organization (Glassmann, 1973; Weick, 1976). When this model, developed within organizational psychology, was looked at from a sociological point of view, the idea arose that these formal structures of an organization (such as the school) are a result of adjustment processes. These adjustment processes are interpreted to be triggered by institutionalized social and cultural expectations in order to provide the organization with legitimacy—in other words, to allocate the required resources to the organization. The loose coupling model in sociology thus describes the fact that these formal structures of organizations are not tightly linked to the practices of production of the organization. These inner activities are believed to have—regardless of public legitimacy—a logic of their own in terms of effectiveness and efficiency (Meyer & Rowan, 1977, pp. 341–343, 361; see also Meyer & Rowan, 1978, pp. 79–81). Historical case studies in education endorse the idea that the phenomenon of loose coupling is not only not a disturbing factor but quite on the contrary also a constitutive factor of an educational organization; indeed, attempts to connect formal structures and inner activities tightly can lead to an annulment of the organization (Bosche, 2008; Tröhler, 2009b). In other words, cultural expectations are mirrored in the formal structures and procedures of organizations such as schools, whereas the inner activities such as teaching are hardly affected by these organizational strategies—much to the chagrin of educational reformers.

Shortly after having presented this fruitful and, to a certain degree, non-historical sociological interpretation of the loose coupling model, the authors started to expand it. At first glance, the expansion was primarily geographical, for now global (rather than local or national) tangible structures of education were analyzed. But the expansion of the model was not only geographical, for it aimed at explaining long-term processes. The expansion became historical. The analysis of these processes in the period of the last 150 years led the scholars to posit the growth and enactment of a world culture, in which the world has become an "international society" or a "world polity" (Boli & Thomas, 1997; Meyer, 1980). They argued that, since at least the middle of the nineteenth century, a rationalized world institutional and cultural order has emerged which consists of universally applicable models that shape states, organizations, and individual identities (Meyer, Boli, Thomas, & Ramirez, 1997, p. 173). In order to write this kind of history of the emergence of a world culture, the authors relativize the traditional assumption according to which the school systems of the nation-states of nineteenth-century Europe, on the one hand, and the global structured schools of today, on the other hand, are incompatible to a large degree. In a paper on historical and comparative education, Meyer and Ramirez (2000) claim that as a rule the functionality and singularity of the national education systems of the nineteenth century are overestimated to a large degree. They point to a lot of transnational similarities, despite the fact that the national education systems became institutionalized in the national societies based on nationalistic agendas (see also Ramirez & Boli, 1987).

This historical and comparative interpretation led to the conclusion that the nation-states, these "imagined communities" (Anderson, 1983) with their educational systems as core means of these constructions, did not emerge mainly from "internal" ideas but rather were framed by "cultural principles exogenous to any specific nation-state and its historical legacy" (Meyer & Ramirez, 2000, p. 115) that exert pressure on the national educational systems. Due to this pressure, Meyer and

Ramirez continue, the national educational systems are not as much tied to new and very different idiosyncrasies of social realities as they are homogenized by common aims and projects of development and by shared technological visions to achieve the aims (p. 116). The process of homogenizing and standardizing became faster through technological means and organized international networks of communication: "The professionalization and scientifization of education greatly speeds up worldwide communication and standardization, just as the latter clearly facilitates the former. These processes reciprocally influence and strengthen each other" (p. 118). They are described to be isomorphic in the results (p. 127), fostering the worldwide formal adjustment of the national educational systems.

The leading ideology of this transnational process was accompanied by universalization of the notion of development. Whereas for a long time the concept of "development" was applied primarily to the so-called Third World states in order to outline their duties toward the First World, in the 1970s development became the core concept of modernity par excellence. In other words, all countries had to develop in order to guarantee global survival (Hüfner, Meyer, & Naumann, 1987, pp. 194–197).[5] Therefore, the cultural self-understanding of modernity is the permanent task of continuous self-development, a task that depends heavily on education, or the educational system. Although doubts have been raised about the connection between the establishment and development of the educational system and the economic, social, and political development, belief in this connection has become accepted all over the world (Chabbott & Ramirez, 2000). In other words, the world society requires both the nation-state and its overcoming in the age of globalization (Meyer, Drori, & Hwang, 2006), whereas belief in the agency of the educational system has been handed over from the ideal of the national to the global society without being altered in its importance.

Globalization is defined here as the "diffusion of cultural practices and commodities—from consumption of media like TV programs and Hollywood movies to norms like human rights and environmentalism" (Drori, Meyer, & Hwang, 2006, p. 11), which in turn exposes a need for adjustment in the single national societies. Meyer et al. (1997) state:

World-society models shape nation-state identities, structures, and behavior via worldwide cultural and associational processes. (. . .) As creatures of exogenous world culture, states are ritualized actors marked by extensive internal decoupling and a good deal more structuration than would occur if they were responsive only to local, cultural, functional, or power processes. (p. 173)

According to sociological neo-institutionalism, the world society is primarily a cultural phenomenon that arose historically, and international organizations such as the United Nations, the United Nations Educational, Scientific and Cultural Organization (UNESCO), or the World Bank founded in the wake of the Second World War have played a crucial role in establishing this globalized culture:

The colossal disaster of World War II may have been a key factor in the rise of global models of nationally organized progress and justice, and the Cold War may well have intensified the forces pushing human development to the global level. (Meyer et al., 1997, p. 174)

The crucial epistemic question remains as to whether processes like globalization can be described analytically at all, or how far sociology or history themselves contribute to the construction of their own object that is allegedly simply being described.

Sociology and the Temptations of History

Complementary historical and sociological explications of developments of organizations such as schools are not only academically desirable but also a desideratum of educational policy and of all efforts that are subsumed in the notion of school development. However, the complementary harmony between history and sociology has been from its beginnings more wishful thinking than artifact, if we only think of Émile Durkheim's Preface to his journal *Année Sociologique*, in which he evaluated the academic character of history with the standards of sociology:

History can be an academic discipline only to the extent that it explains, and it can explain only by comparing. (. . .) But then, from the moment it compares, history becomes indistinguishable from sociology. (Durkheim, 1898, p. III; freely translated here.)

The great interest of sociology in history is no coincidence, for history provides an inexhaustible potential of empirical facts. However, Durkheim's hierarchy in terms of academic standards is problematic, because sociology is tempted to argue historically, but not to use standards developed in academic history but rather its own standards.

Sociological neo-institutionalism relies largely on such an historiography, namely, on the historical reconstruction in Max Weber's study, published first as essays in 1904 and 1905, *Die protestantische Ethik und der "Geist" des Kapitalismus* (*The Protestant Ethic and the Spirit of Capitalism*) (Weber, 1930)—a prime example of a history construed by a rather a-historical sociology of religion. In this eminent study Weber transposes the German Lutheran concept of *Beruf* (*occupation*) into English Calvinism and by that creates a peculiar Lutheran interpretation of Anglo-Saxon Calvinism. It is this Lutheran/Calvinist amalgam that led to Weber's dilemma in religion policy, for despite his deep sympathy with Luther, Weber showed more respect for the Calvinist culture. The main theoretical problem with this blending is that Luther and German Evangelical Protestantism insist on a dualistic, two-kingdom doctrine. According to the doctrine, in the one kingdom Christ rules through word and sacrament, mercy and forgiveness are practiced, and there are no differences among people. In the other kingdom, in contrast, the Emperor reigns with the sword, and there is no mercy and no equality. But to Luther the worldly kingdom still has a purpose in that, namely, the prince curbs the evil in men—even if through violence, peace is established, and thus conditions are created for proclaiming the Gospel (Luther, 1523/1983, pp. 41–44). Logically, ideas like political participation, which is a core characteristic of the Baptist church and of Congregationalism, are foreign to Lutheranism. This political indifference of Lutheranism makes it understandable that, whereas Weber focused on the Anglo-Saxon Calvinist theory of work, he neglected its political theory of participation. Indeed, this culture is not inherent in original Calvinism but was developed by the English Baptist and Congregationalist sects in the seventeenth century in the light of the dominant Anglican Episcopal Church in which the suppressed Protestant sects had to fortify the role of the community and the concept of participation.[6]

To date the sociological research has hardly recognized that Weber's Lutheran interpretation of Anglo-Saxon Calvinism has eclipsed one core element of the latter, namely, the fundamental local democratic culture, and by doing so it has at the same time prescinded the alleged lone Calvinist citizen. This Weberian pattern seems to stand in the background of the (re-)construction of the idea of a world culture, too. For if neo-institutional analysis presumes that the nation-states of the nineteenth century were less unique and much more exposed to transnational pressures than one would think, the question arises as to where the transnational or universal ideas originate.

Neo-institutionalists address this task by going back to the time that is usually labeled the Renaissance, a cultural epoch superseding what are called the Middle Ages and breaking the path to modernity.[7] Again, it is Max Weber who provides the starting ground, namely, Weber's thesis of the rationalization of the world.[8] In an article on "Ontology and Ratio-nalization in the Western Cultural Account," Meyer, Boli, and Thomas (1987), with their concept of "world culture" in mind, understand the structuring of daily life as following standardized and impersonal rules; these rules constitute the social order as a means to achieve collective aims such as progress and justice. In this respect, Meyer, Boli and Thomas (p. 20) interpret the establishment of a world culture as a matter of a millennium project of the Western world, in which actors and actions are examined through universal lenses that are hardly rec-ognizable as general rules and that are very effective precisely because they are hard to recognize (p. 19).

In the same way that Max Weber argued, Meyer et al. (1987) state that the beginning of this development is situated in first universal structure to exist, namely, in the Western church:

> The institutions of the West devolve from Western religion and the church at least as much as they are built up by the strategies of subunits. (. . .) The frame derives directly from the Christian church and the invisible conceptual 'Kingdom of God' that the earthly church organization was supposed to rep-resent in an imperfect way. (p. 23)

It is interesting to see what the authors mean by the "Western religion and the church" that allegedly were at the origin of the millennium project. Obviously, the authors are in a dilemma. On one hand they foster the idea of an early global idea, and on the other hand they identify the Reformation (of all things) in the first quarter of the six-teenth century as the initial point of this peculiar development towards world culture. This, in turn, means seeing (church) schism as the begin-ning of a process of global standardization. Against that background, the historical source is blurred rather than identified. On one hand, a date is named that lies some years *ahead* of the Reformation, namely, "perhaps 1500" (Meyer et al., 1987, p. 23), when according to the authors the church had been "transnational" and able to comprise a multitude of cultures symbolically. The church had been universalistic in its duty to bring "the way, the truth, and the life" to the whole of humanity. On the other hand, the authors emphasize that the "power of the Word" had been extremely important in the church's evangelic attempt, which as a matter of fact would unmistakably be a Protestant interpretation; the holistic Catholic universalism of the late medieval times (or very early modern period) is being interpreted through Protestant lenses. What remains to be analyzed is: through the lenses of *which* Protestantism?

According to sociological neo-institutionalism, it was the expansion of Christianity that had prepared the way for the dissemination of universalistic ideologies with highly legitimated, boundary-less polities. It is precisely within this process that the modern "cultural" culture with its crucial means of the education system arose (Meyer et al., 1987, p. 23). In an article co-authored with Ronald Jepperson, Meyer argues how within the expansion, the development, and the secularization of Christianity the concept of agency altered. In the beginning, agency was ascribed to transcendent powers, and little by little it was transferred to society and the individual person as the "authorized agency" (Meyer & Jepperson, 2000, pp. 101f.). Here it is interesting that the authors, in only two pages, jump from the alleged universal world of "perhaps 1500" with its feudal system, to the ideology of technical progress and the sacred meaning of the nation-state in the nineteenth century with its educational system, and then to Bretton Woods and the founding of the World Bank, one of the crucial transnational organizations in the process of globalization. Here they leave little space for alternative concepts and counter-movements, and do not trace the questions as to how in a universal culture the idea of a nation-state became possible, how the school became the church of the (sacred) nation in the nineteenth century, and how the different denominations influenced the cultural understandings of the school systems (Meyer et al., p. 23). According to Ramirez and Boli (1987), "despite much variation in level of industrialization, class structure, and political regime, the ideological and organizational responses [mass education] of the various countries to challenges to state power were strikingly similar" (p. 9). This, of course, is a matter of the level of interpretation. At a very abstract global macro level, this interpretation might be convincing, and it fits in nicely with the idea of a global vision of universalism spreading around the world.

It is significant that an examination on a more meso level challenges the persuasiveness of this global interpretation. A comparison between the upper secondary education curricula in Prussia and Switzerland in the nineteenth century reveals a different picture. First, there appear to be striking transnational similarities with regard to both the formal differentiation of the upper-secondary education into types and the development of the curriculum (focusing mainly on the introduction of modern foreign languages). However, another picture appears if methods of historical contextualization are used. First, the contextualization of the curriculum within the overall organization of the school system raises doubts as to whether the similarity between the two countries is more than only quantitative on a very abstract level. The second contextualization of the overall organization of education within cultural convictions not only makes this even more doubtful but also reveals fundamental differences rooted in different political convictions, such as monarchism and republicanism (and German Lutheranism and Swiss Calvinism). The result of the comparison shows that, despite some formal similarities, the establishment of foreign language education in Switzerland and Prussia could not have been more different (Tröhler, 2009a). The point is that by abstracting from all cultural idiosyncrasies, it cannot be really surprising that a school is a school and that therefore they all appear to be similar.

The Linear Construction of a Global History and the Institutions of Education

The religious history serving the construction of the neo-institutional account of globalization is little differentiated and does not discuss explicitly the church schism of the sixteenth century, even though it is focused *on* the Reformation, and it does not pay sufficient attention to the different denominations within Protestantism and their respective development. The neo-institutional interpretation of Calvinism with the sacred individual as agent (besides the organization and the nation-state) is owed to Max Weber's Lutheran interpretation of Calvinism. When the authors of this interpretation start their historical account at "perhaps 1500," they do not claim that the globalized world culture in fact arose *out of* the Western church. It becomes evident that they are talking about Protestantism, more precisely about Calvinism that had become transformed in seventeenth-century England—in other words, the line of Calvinism that was already Weber's focus and to which he attributed the Lutheran concept of profession. Meyer and Jepperson (2000) refer explicitly to "Anglo-American" Protestantism without precisely distinguishing it from a "German and Scandinavian" tradition; they simply state that this latter tradition is "more corporate," while the Anglo-American tradition is supposed to be more individual (p. 108).

The fact that Anglo-American Calvinism and Lutheranism differ greatly in the idea of the political order and the concept of the citizen is not considered at all. Still today, *Bürger* in German means something completely different from "citizen" in U.S. American, as perplexed scholars in international comparative citizenship education have to admit. And whereas in some countries small efforts in citizenship education are very effective, in other countries, such as Germany, few of the desired effects are achieved, despite high investments. The low results are hard to explain: "Whether they are rooted in culture, history, or some aspect of schooling is not evident" (Hahn, 1999, p. 247). Neglecting these fundamental religious/cultural distinctions, Meyer and Jepperson (2000) believe in American individualism, losing sight of the fact that local democracy is the ideological counterpart of this individualism, setting boundaries to excessive individual liberalism—an ideological source, by the way, that stood at the beginning of the educational philosophy of pragmatism. The social culture emerging from this ideology was not least appreciated by Max Weber when he visited the United States in 1904. Weber's wife, Marianne Weber, wrote that her depressive husband recovered when he shared the social culture in the United States: "Weber could hardly wait for the landing procedures and customs inspection; he strode from board ship with long, bouncing steps—leaving his faithful companion behind—like an eagle set free that can finally take to the sky" (Weber, 1950, p. 318; freely translated here). And then, describing the culture: "The whole magic of memories of youth lies alone just in this time of life. Lots of sports, pleasant forms of social activities, endless intellectual stimulation, and long-lasting friendships are the yields, and especially, far more so than our students, they are trained in the habit of work." And at the end of their American travels, she reported: "This faithful companion sometimes has the feeling that she is bringing home a man who has recovered, who has become conscious of a slowly gathered stock of strength" (p. 345; freely translated here).

However, despite his personal experiences, Weber continued to interpret Calvinism as essentially individualistic without paying attention to its democratic local basis, and neo-institutional sociology seems to follow this crooked interpretation by defining this model as the basis of the American liberalism that eventually became successfully disseminated around the world after Second World War and that dominates contemporary world culture. In it the agent as that "abstract, rather contentless, entity in social space" is being legitimated (Meyer & Jepperson, 2000, p. 109). In accordance with Max Weber, the neo-institutional interpretation identifies an isolated individual as the result of Calvinist Protestantism having become the rationalized agent of the globalized process. However, by following a Lutheran interpretation of Anglos-Saxon Protestantism and its triumphant history, the historical account becomes itself part of this Whig history.

It is true, of course, that the democratic dimension in Anglo-Saxon Calvinism is universal in terms of its religious foundation, but the point is that this universal claim is foreseen to be materialized locally. Within this tradition, democracy is embodied locally, and the local traditions are distinguishable and, precisely, not standardized. But like any other fundamental theory about historical processes, the neo-institutional reconstruction of globalization pays little attention to challenging concepts, cultural idiosyncrasies, and the contingency of the process, for the glory of making complexity look logical. Weber's philosophy of history is rewritten and expanded in order to explain the emergence of a world culture, ignoring the taken-for-granted assumptions, the culturally anchored convictions, in other words, the institutions of the localism that *nota bene* had been the topic of the early neo-institutional studies with which this area of research was able to become established. This may be the reason why little attention is paid to the tensions between a global culture and a local culture, each of them sharing expectations about schooling. The fierce reactions to PISA in Germany, for instance, are due to a cultural clash between the national taken-for-granted assumptions about education and the transnational agenda of an international organization such as the Organization for Economic Co-operation and Development (OECD) (Overesch, 2007; Weigel, 2004). And in Switzerland, where schools are governed by the individual cantons and the school laws have to be put to the ballot, educational reform proposals following an international agenda are turned down by the local or regional sovereigns. Recently, even a not really far-reaching attempt to harmonize (for the very first time) the duration and some basic aims of the elementary schools in Switzerland (HarmoS) was rejected by some of the Swiss cantons.

The organizational expressions of this locally defined democracy within education are the already local and regional school boards in the United States, in some provinces of Canada, and in Switzerland—thus, in those regions of the world dominated by a modified Calvinist religion.[9] It is these that make out of a state school a public school, a distinction that is usually not broadly recognized. It is this localism that reinforces the stability of the inner activities of organizations such as the school, or the grammar of schooling, as David Tyack and others have said (Tyack, 2003). If the school is primarily subject to the local public instead of to the centralized administration, the caution shown towards reforms is greater, because communal responsibility does not gamble lightly with proven quality. It is no coincidence that the transnational culture of experts conflicts with the local logic of school governance. The constant accusation that the local school boards are the major cause of failing reforms signifies the dramatic clash between the idea of an elite democracy and the local democracy, or between expertise and common sense.[10]

These local cultural expressions are not the focus of sociological neo-institutionalism. They seem to disappear altogether or to take the role of agents, losing their character of agency in the course of the globalization process. However, within the Weberian-inspired historical theory of rationalization and Weber's Lutheran interpretation of Calvinism, phenomena will be perceived to fit into the encompassing historical process leading to the world culture. The alleged empirical evidence of the processes that seems to be the source of the theory of globalization is itself a consequence of a universalized interpretation of Protestantism that has been taken for granted. The historical particularity has thus become a universality, a frame that would allow no empirical evidence to be different other than to support the general thesis of globalization. The (alleged) description of the object turns out to be, in the end, the construction of the object. Insofar as this (re-) construction serves the interpretation of the universalized self (perception), we can recognize a new example of Whiggism. Is there an alternative?

Research in Globalization and Education

It is not difficult to find evidence of pro and con arguments regarding the globalization thesis of sociological neo-institutionalism. Leaving cultural idiosyncrasies of the school systems aside, there *is* a history of globalization leading to a more or less homogenous world of education, and focusing in contrast on historical particularities raises doubts about this history. The French do center on political symbols in citizenship education, and the British do not (Hahn, 1999). However, this kind of argument might not pay attention to the main problem discussed here. The problem is how to deal with phenomena without being part of them.

Classical scientific epistemology used the word "objectivity" to surmount the problem, but we know today that paradigms not only suggest certain solutions of the problem but indeed actually construe the problem, and any successful paradigm will reduce history to its own success, widely ignoring other paradigms (Kuhn, 1962). As there seems to be no Archimedean point from which we can perceive the subject of inquiry objectively, the inquiry needs to address the researcher as well—not in order to eliminate the researcher's own world view and epistemological frame but in order to become aware of it. I see no other way than to historicize not only a topic but the construer of the topic as well. One of today's leading historians, Quentin Skinner, said not without reason that one of the big advantages of studying history is not only the acquisition of knowledge but also the acquisition of self-awareness: "To learn from the past—and we cannot otherwise learn at all . . . is to learn the key to self-awareness" (Skinner, 1988a, p. 67). "Doing history" is essentially the discovering of one's own standpoint. From a historiographic point of view, the critical question discussed in this chapter is not how do we explain our global hegemony historically, but why and how we ourselves help to construe a history framed as a triumphant history (or a history of decline). Discussing the quest that a historian should be able "to discount or set aside the fact that he or she holds certain beliefs to be true and others false," Skinner (1988b) answers: "I am sure no historian can ever hope to perform such an act of forgetting, and that in any case it would be most unwise to try" (p. 236).

The act of forgetting would be unwise because it would homogenize the researchers with their topic, in other words meld the construction of the object with the research on it; again, the result is then a form of Whiggish history. One way out of this dilemma was John Pocock's suggestion to analyze the languages in which topics are discussed. History, Pocock (1987) says, always deals with transmissions of "acts of speech, whether oral, scribal or typographical" that depend on "the conditions or contexts in which these acts are performed" (p. 19). In accordance with Saussure (2006), Pocock indicates that political actors have always depended (and still depend) on a *langue* to perform a speech act: "For anything to be said or written or printed, there must be a language to say it in; the language determines what can be said in it, but is capable of being modified by what is said in it; there is a history formed by the interactions of *parole* and *langue*" (Pocock, 1987, p. 20).

Political and educational languages are modes of thought; not political slogans or concepts, but specifically used rhetoric and vocabularies, and they are identified to be the ideological context of any political and educational *parole*. Two things are important. First, by virtue of their normative structures framing the actor's *parole*, languages are deeds: they construe in a normative way what is perceived as social reality. And second—and this refers again more to Thomas Kuhn—several *langues* always exist at the same time, whereas one is always dominant. In other words, every epoch has its dominant mode of perceiving, analyzing, and discussing political phenomena, and it also has alternative modes that just do not dominate. These dominances do not alter unless deep crises occur that cannot be described in an appropriate way by the dominant *langue*, thus making that solution seem to be impossible. At these moments people can resort to another *langue* that seems to describe the circumstances in a more appropriate way. The new *langues* then become dominant, without erasing the former dominant *langue* (Pocock, 1962, p. 195; Pocock, 1987, p. 21f.).

If we only take a look at the period from the eighteenth century to the present, we can distinguish a number of paradigms that could be labeled educational languages (see Tröhler, 2009c), but the number is certainly limited. These educational languages are closely connected to visions of justice, happiness, and progress, and to the idea of the child and the citizen. The oldest language that survived the transformations after the Renaissance—at least to a certain degree—is the classical republican language based on public virtues and political freedom. This classical language that was formulated by Aristotle or Xenophon was reinforced and modified first by Machiavelli (Pocock, 1975) and almost at the same time by the Swiss Reformation, that is to say, by Calvin and Zwingli, with their inestimable influence on the idea that social problems are to be solved primarily by education (Tröhler, 2008). The focus is on the citizen of the *polis* as a concept, including the political, religious, economical, and military aspect of life in *one* person. Another old language that survived the transformations of eighteenth century lies within the Augustinian and Neo-Augustinian tradition. This language was especially attractive for educational questions in the anti-Jesuit movement of Jansenism, which found its most important stronghold in the Parisian convent of Port-Royal, haven of many important authors such as Antoine Arnauld, Pierre Nicole, and Blaise Pascal, all of them self-identified as rigorous followers of St. Augustine (Carraud, 1992) and all of them focusing on the insignificance of human life. Many of these important authors were widely received in specific traditions of education, especially in the German concept of *Bildung*, that originated in Luther (Luther being an Augustinian monk) (Horlacher, 2004; Osterwalder, 2003, 2006). It is these two languages that got mixed by Weber unintentionally, for he believed his interpretation was an analysis of Calvinism. A third educational language is the child of the late eighteenth century, more precisely of the French Revolution. Having its roots in the early modern sciences in England, it was developed into a specific form of educational language by Condorcet or Destutt de Tracy after 1790 (Osterwalder, 1992). Unlike the two others, this language builds essentially on academic knowledge and the public rationality effectuated by this knowledge. The ideal human being is not the contemplative person having found peace in his inner soul, as in the Neo-Augustinian tradition, nor the fully virtuous patriotic citizen, as in the classical republican tradition, but rather an individual person that is interconnected with other persons by a social contract based on rational deliberation and decision.

The historical analysis of a process of globalization that will minimize the construing of the topic will have to analyze the adaptability of the single languages, their connection to religious and/or political languages, and the hybrid forms that they receive in specific historical constellations. Isomorphic structures will then not be the center of research but rather patterns of thoughts and the adventure of their cultural diffusion. And we should not forget that Christianity is not the dominant religion in the world, that Protestants make up not even 10 percent of the world population, and that Christianization is not only the story of the missionaries but also of those being evangelized, as Jacques Gernet (1985) showed in his wonderful book, *China and the Christian Impact: A Conflict of Cultures*. There is ample empirical evidence that the dominant culture in the world today is a dominant one among others, and that historical accounts of the triumphant story will cement the position only at the price of neglecting others.

AUTHOR'S NOTE

An earlier version of this paper was presented at the Institute of Sociology at the University of Zurich, May 9, 2007. I wish to thank Thomas S. Popkewitz for his amicable and stimulating help in shaping this chapter.

NOTES

1. The procedure was dogmatic and pragmatic at the same time. First, in 1586 a committee of six experts from Spain, Portugal, Scotland, Flanders, Holland, and Sicily developed a draft of a course of study, which was then sent for comments to teachers all over Europe. A reformulation of the course of study based on the feedback received was sent out again for annotations. The result of this consultation was the (probably most successful) global curriculum, the *Ratio atque Institutio Studiorum Societatis Iesu*, published first in 1599 and remaining unchanged until the nineteenth century. For further details, see Donnelly (2006).

2. Thomas S. Kuhn detected this tendency in the history of science. After a paradigm shift has occurred, Kuhn says, the protagonists of the new paradigm write histories of the paradigm as if science could have not taken any pathway other than to the new state of the art. In doing so, they neglect, suppress, and marginalize competing paradigms (Kuhn, 1962).

3. Globalization is not only discussed as a distinct topic in the Western sphere by Western intellectuals, but has also become a global phenomenon in the academic discursive performances themselves. See, for instance, Khondker (2000).

4. For one of the famous (postmodern) critiques of the grand narratives, see Lyotard (1979/1984).

5. As a matter of fact, the idea goes back to the Cold War in the 1950s, and it influenced educational notions, especially those of the World Bank and the OECD (see Tröhler, 2010).

6. See, more broadly, Tröhler (2006). Calvinism in Scotland, in contrast, was broadly enforced, so that Scottish Calvinism—Presbyterianism—was not forced to develop a fundamental theory of democratic participation.

7. When exactly the epoch of the Renaissance starts, and when it ends, is a matter of dispute. In contrast to art historian Jacob Burckhardt, the "father" of the notion of the "Renaissance," Burke takes the example of the supposed "end" of the Renaissance to show that it would be more accurate to think in terms of a dissolution of the various Renaissance arts—painting, philosophy, music, or architecture—that was successive but that varied in the speed with which it took place in the different European countries (Burke, 1987, p. 81). It is also impossible, Burke concludes, to speak of a clearly identifiable "start" of the Renaissance, which—according to Burckhardt's thesis—marked the end of the Middle Ages and recognized, for the first time, the person as an individual identity.

8. "By 'rationalization' we refer (conventionally) to the cultural accounting of society and its environments in terms of articulated, unified, integrated, universalized, and causally and logically structured schemes." (Meyer & Jepperson, 2000, p. 105, footnote 5)

9. In the mentioned provinces of Canada it was American settlers who brought the tradition of the school boards with them, for instance to Alberta. In Switzerland it was Zwinglianism, reforming Calvinism towards more democracy.

10. It does not occur without reason that educational policy makers, experts in think tanks, and professors attracted by the alleged opportunity to reform schools are irritated by the existence of local democratic control of the school and that they accuse the school boards of hindering reform and sustaining the persistence of the status quo. In the view of the expert-driven democracy emerging at the beginning of the Cold War, democracy works essentially not locally but as a form of competition among elites for votes, and therefore democracy is reduced to its procedural function of election. Not even high voter participation in elections was sought after, far from it: "That democracy is best, in which people participate least," was the general assumption of the expertise-driven democracy in the 1950s (quoted in Gilman, 2003, p. 48).

REFERENCES

Anderson, B. (1983). *Imagined communities: Reflection on the origin and spread of nationalism.* London: Verso.

Boli, J., & Thomas, G.M. (1997). World culture in the world polity. *American Sociological Review, 62*(2), 171–190.

Bosche, A. (2008). Loose coupling als konstitutives Element der Organisation von Schule: Das Fallbeispiel Haldenstein-Marschlins in der Schweiz des 18. Jahrhunderts. In M. Göhlich, C. Hopf, & D. Tröhler (Eds.), *Persistenz und Verschwinden. Pädagogische Organisationen im historischen kontext* (pp. 69–81). Wiesbaden: VS Verlag.

Burke, P. (1987). *The renaissance.* Atlantic Highlands, NJ: Humanities Press International.

Butterfield, H. (1931). *The Whig interpretation of history.* London: Bell.

Carraud, V. (1992). *Pascal et la philosophie.* Paris: Presses Universitaires de France.

Chabbott, C., & Ramirez, F.O. (2000). Development and education. In M. Hallinan (Eds.), *Handbook of the sociology of education* (pp. 163–187). New York: Kluwer Academic.

Dainville, F. de (1978). *L'éducation des Jesuites (XVI-XVIIIe siècles)*. Paris: Les éditions des minuits.

Donnelly, J.P. (2006). *Jesuit writings of the early modern period, 1540–1640*. Indianapolis, IN: Hackett Publishing Company.

Drori, G.S., Meyer, J.W., & Hwang, H. (2006). Introduction. In G.S. Drori, J.W. Meyer, & H. Hwang (Eds.), *Globalization and organization* (pp. 1–22). Oxford: Oxford University Press.

Durkheim, E. (1898). Preface. *Année Sociologique 1896–1897*, (1), I–VII.

Gernet, J. (1985). *China and the Christian impact: A conflict of cultures*. Cambridge: Cambridge University Press. (Original work published in French 1982.)

Gilman, N. (2003). *Mandarins of the future: Modernization theory in Cold War America*. Baltimore: Johns Hopkins University Press.

Glassmann, R.B. (1973). Persistence and loose coupling in living systems. *Behavioral Science, 18*, 83–98.

Hahn, C.L. (1999). Citizenship education: An empirical study of policy, practices and outcomes. *Oxford Review of Education, 25*(1/2), 231–250.

Horlacher, R. (2004). Bildung: A construction of a history of philosophy of education. *Studies in Philosophy and Education, 23*, 409–426.

Hüfner, K., Meyer, J., & Naumann, J. (1987). Comparative policy research: A world society perspective. In M. Dierkes (Ed.), *Comparative policy research: Learning from experience* (pp. 188–241). New York: St. Martin's Press.

Khondker, H.H. (2000). Globalization: Against reductionism and linearity. *Development and Society, 29*(1), 17–33.

Kuhn, T.S. (1962). *The structure of scientific revolutions*. Chicago: University of Chicago Press.

Luther, M. (1983). Von weltlicher Oberkeit, wie weit man ihr Gehorsam schuldig sei (1523). In H.-U. Delius (Ed.), *Martin Luther: Studienausgabe. Band 3* (pp. 31–71). Berlin: Evangelische Verlagsanstalt Berlin. (Original work published 1523.)

Lyotard, J.-F. (1984). *The postmodern condition: A report on knowledge*. Minneapolis: University of Minnesota Press. (Original work published in French 1979.)

Meyer, J.W. (1980). The world polity and the authority of the nation-state. In A. Bergesen (Ed.), *Studies of the modern world-system* (pp. 109–137). New York: Academic Press.

Meyer, J.W., Boli, J., & Thomas, G.W. (1987). Ontology and rationalization in the Western cultural account. In G.M. Thomas, J.W. Meyer, F.O. Ramirez, & J. Boli (Eds.), *Institutional structure: Constituting state, society, and the individual* (pp. 12–38). Newbury Park, CA: Sage.

Meyer, J.W., Boli, J., Thomas, G.W., & Ramirez, F. (1997). World society and the nation-state. *American Journal of Sociology, 103*(1), 144–181.

Meyer, J.W., Drori, G.S., & Hwang, H. (2006). World society and the proliferation of formal organization. In G.S. Drori, J.W. Meyer, & H. Hwang (Eds.), *Globalization and organization* (pp. 25–49). Oxford: Oxford University Press.

Meyer, J.W., & Jepperson, R.L. (2000). The "actors" of modern society: The cultural construction of social agency. *Sociological Theory, 18*(1), 100–120.

Meyer, J.W., & Ramirez, F.O. (2000). The world institutionalization of education. In J. Schriewer (Ed.), *Discourse formation in comparative education* (pp. 111–132). Frankfurt: Peter Lang.

Meyer, J.W., & Rowan, B. (1977). Institutionalized organizations: Formal structure as myth and ceremony. *The American Journal of Sociology, 83*, 340–363.

Meyer, J.W., & Rowan, B. (1978). The structure of educational organizations. In J.W. Meyer and Associates (Eds.), *Environments and organizations* (pp. 78–109). San Francisco: Jossey-Bass.

Osterwalder, F. (1992). Condorcet: Instruction publique und das Design der Pädagogik als öffentlich-rechtliche Wissenschaft. In J. Oelkers (Ed.), *Aufklärung, Bildung und Öffentlichkeit* (28. Beiheft der Zeitschrift für Pädagogik) (pp. 157–194). Weinheim: Beltz.

Osterwalder, F. (2003). Die Heilung des freien Willens durch Erziehung. Erziehungstheorien im Kontext der theologischen Augustinus-Renaissance im 17. Jahrhundert. In J. Oelkers, F. Osterwalder, & H.-E. Tenorth (Eds.), *Das verdrängte Erbe. Pädagogik im Kontext von Religion und Theologie* (pp. 57–86). Weinheim/Basel: Beltz.

Osterwalder, F. (2006). Die Sprache des Herzens. Konstituierung und Transformation der theologischen Sprache der Pädagogik. In R. Casale, D. Tröhler, & J. Oelkers (Eds.), *Methoden und Kontexte. Historiographische Probleme der Bildungsforschung* (pp. 155–180). Göttingen: Wallstein.

Overesch, A. (2007). *Wie die Schulpolitik ihre Probleme (nicht) löst. Deutschland und Finnland im Vergleich.* Münster: Waxmann.

Pocock, J.G.A. (1962). The history of political thought: A methodological enquiry. In P. Laslett & W. Runciman (Eds.), *Philosophy, politics and society (second series)*, (pp. 183–202). Oxford: Oxford University Press.

Pocock, J.G.A. (1975). *The Machiavellian moment: Florentine political thought and the Atlantic Republican tradition.* Princeton, NJ: Princeton University Press.

Pocock, J.G.A. (1987). The concept of a language and the *métier d'historien*: Some considerations on practice. In A. Pagden (Ed.), *The languages of political theory in early-modern Europe* (pp. 19–38). Cambridge: Cambridge University Press.

Ramirez, F., & Boli, J. (1987). The political construction of mass schooling: European origins and worldwide institutionalization. *Sociology of Education, 60*, 2–17.

Saussure, F. de (2006). *Writings in general linguistics.* Oxford: Oxford University Press.

Skinner, Q. (1988a). Meaning and understanding in the history of ideas. In J. Tully (Ed.), *Meaning and context: Quentin Skinner and his critics* (pp. 29–67). Princeton, NJ: Princeton University Press.

Skinner, Q. (1988b). A reply to my critics. In J. Tully (Ed.), *Meaning and context: Quentin Skinner and his critics* (pp. 231–288). Princeton, NJ: Princeton University Press.

Suarez, D.F., & Ramirez, F. (2004). *Human rights and citizenship: The emergence of human rights education.* CDDRL Working Paper, Stanford Institute for International Studies. Retrieved May 8, 2009, from http://cddrl.stanford.edu/publications/human_rights_and_citizenship_the_emergence_of_human_rights_education.

Tröhler, D. (2006). Max Weber und die protestantische Ethik in Amerika. In J. Oelkers, R. Casale, R. Horlacher, & S. Larcher (Eds.), *Rationalität und Bildung: Studien im Umkreis von Max Weber* (pp. 111–134). Bad Heilbrunn: Klinkhardt.

Tröhler, D. (2008). The educationalization of the modern world: Progress, passion, and the Protestant promise of education. In P. Smeyers & M. Depaepe (Eds.), *Educational research: The educationalisation of social problems* (pp. 31–46). Dordrecht: Springer.

Tröhler, D. (2009a). Between ideology and education: The curriculum of upper-secondary education. *Journal of Curriculum Studies, 41*, 393–408.

Tröhler, D. (2009b). Curriculum, languages, and mentalities. In B. Baker (Ed.), *New curriculum history* (pp. 97–117). Rotterdam: Sense Publishers.

Tröhler, D. (2009c). Beyond arguments and ideas: Languages of education. In P. Smeyers & M. Depaepe (Eds.), *Educational research: Proofs, arguments and other reasonings* (pp. 9–22). Dordrecht: Springer.

Tröhler, D. (2010, in press). Harmonizing the educational globe: World polity, cultural features, and the challenges to educational research. *Studies in Philosophy and Education, 29*.

Tyack, D. (2003). *Seeking common ground: Public schools in a diverse society.* Cambridge, MA: Harvard University Press.

Weber, M. (1930). *The Protestant ethic and the spirit of capitalism*. New York: Charles Scribner's Sons. (The first English translation was published by Unwin Hyman, London & Boston, 1930, based upon the second German edition of 1920. The first German "edition" was two essays published in 1904 and 1905.)

Weber, M. (1950). *Max Weber. Ein Lebensbild*. Heidelberg: Lambert Schneider. (First published 1926.)

Weick, K.E. (1976). Educational organizations as loosely coupled systems. *Administrative Science Quarterly*, *21*(1), 1–19.

Weigel, T.M. (2004). *Die PISA-Studie im bildungspolitischen Diskurs Eine Untersuchung der Reaktionen auf PISA in Deutschland und im Vereinigten Königreich*. Diploma thesis at the University of Trier. Retrieved May 12, 2009, from http://www.oecd.org/dataoecd/46/23/34805090.pdf.

Scopic Systems, Pipes, Models and Transfers in the Global Circulation of Educational Knowledge and Practices

NOAH W. SOBE AND NICOLE D. ORTEGÓN

The purported "liquidity" of knowledge is often posed as one of the defining characteristics of the present "age of globalization." Liquidity describes the present moment as one marked by flows, flexibility and flux, and it also can be invoked to define the here-and-now by suggesting contrasts and departures from earlier historical eras. A statement such as the following: "*Knowledge is no longer an immobile solid, it has been liquefied. It is actively moving in all the currents of society itself,*" would seem to have tremendous import for the study of education. This might, for example, cause us to think about the "pedagogies of dislocation" (Edwards & Usher, 2007) that accompany and are prompted by this seeming increase in the mobility of knowledge. It might also prompt us to consider not just the ways that distance education, overseas "satellite" campuses, and the internationalization of education systems represent new institutional configurations and *trans*-local social networks, but also how they emerge against the backdrop of fundamentally altered epistemic paradigms. These are, no doubt, important angles to consider in the study of education. However, our focus in this chapter will be on "educational knowledge"—the corpus of rationalized expertise, best practices, and outcome-oriented scientific problematizations of educational practice and school organization (Popkewitz, 2000). Educational knowledge, one can argue, has become as mobile and liquid as other forms of knowledge. Yet, here we propose to take a step back and focus our attention on what makes liquidity and flow possible: the material and nonmaterial structures and organizational forms that enable and facilitate the mobility of knowledge. An orienting premise of this chapter is that these structures and forms are domain-specific, and, thus, one needs specifically to look at the particular historical circumstances and configurations that sustain (and sometimes accelerate) the worldwide flows of educational knowledge.

One of the points of contention in the social science literature on globalization concerns the extent to which researchers need to rethink

49

the analytic tools used to study global phenomena (Rossi, 2008). This chapter proceeds by examining three different scholarly currents and their understandings of how and why ideas move. We attempt to assess what is offered by and what is obscured by the conceptual tools and modes of analysis used (1) by a line of scholarship in the field of comparative education (dating back to the nineteenth century but demonstrating some remarkable continuities over time) that examines "educational transfer"; (2) in more recent neo-institutionalist sociology work, again primarily housed in the field of comparative education, that discusses a "world culture of schooling"; and (3) in scholarship undertaken in recent years by anthropologists who look at the formation of global epistemic communities and the "scopic systems" that sustain these communities, specifically in relation to world financial markets.

To gain perspective on this problem, it is useful to remind ourselves that these present circumstances may not be as historically novel as they are sometimes presented. The quotation above, suggesting that knowledge is *now* actively moving in all currents of society, in fact comes from an 1899 lecture by John Dewey, who was comparing the turn of the twentieth century with previous times. Dewey spoke of a "high-priesthood of learning" that parceled out education "to the masses under strict restrictions." With Gutenberg, and later with the industrial revolution, he argued, all of this changed:

Printing was invented; it was made commercial. Books, magazines, papers were multiplied and cheapened. As a result of the locomotive and telegraph, frequent, rapid, and cheap intercommunication by mails and electricity was called into being. Travel has been rendered easy; freedom of movement, with its accompanying exchange of ideas, indefinitely facilitated. The result has been an intellectual revolution. Learning has been put into circulation. (Dewey, 1900/ 1990, pp. 17–18)

Dewey's gloss on the ways that technological advances spurred ideas into circulation directs attention to the mediality and material structures and forms by which ideas "move." In his account, it is inevitable that simply the increase in the quantity of printed matter has liberalized knowledge. Similarly, increased "freedom of movement" has facilitated the exchange of ideas. Though this notion is commonplace to the point of banality, some historical evidence of its significance might be drawn from Carlo Ginzburg's (1980) masterful analysis of the inquisition transcripts of a sixteenth-century miller from the Friuli-Venezia Giulia region of northern Italy. Domenico Scandella, known as Menocchio, was unusual in being literate and also being able to travel to Venice, where he purchased books, including Boccaccio's *Decameron* and possibly an Italian translation of the *Koran*. On the basis of this exposure to a wider world of ideas—and, Ginzburg pivotally argues, in a syncretic combination with a long-enduring oral, peasant culture—Menocchio articulated a heretical cosmogony that ultimately led to his being burned at the stake in 1599. The Catholic Church's great interest in where Menocchio acquired his ideas (which is, ironically, the same question pursued by Ginzburg the historian) is indicative of the threat that the circulation of knowledge has historically posed to what Dewey referred to as "high-priesthoods of learning."

Dewey's narrative of progressive expansion prompts us to pay attention to the multiplication of paper as well as to individuals' geographic journeys and whom and what they encounter. The case of sixteenth-century Menocchio reminds us, however, that not all ideas can necessarily be traced with the level of determinacy and certainty that a causes-style and influences-style (Newtonian) modeling of circulation would strive to deliver. The question of how and why ideas travel brings to the table a whole host of cultural, social, historical, political, economic, not to mention epistemological, issues. In the following sections we discuss a set of research traditions and attempt to discern how each explains (or would explain) the globalization of educational knowledge.

Globalizing Educational Knowledge as Strategic Learning

The question of how ideas, practices and institutional forms related to education cross borders has long occupied researchers in the field of comparative education. One of the key "father figures" of the field, Marc-Antoine Jullien de Paris (1775–1848), who proposed a science of education in a series of 1816 and 1817 publications, was deeply interested in how features of schooling could be transferred from one nation to another. Jason Beech (2006) argues that Jullien conceived of education as intrinsically independent from context; meaning therefore that an idea or ideas from nation X could be seamlessly "transported" to nation Y (for more discussion of the cosmopolitan features of Jullien's social science see, Sobe [2002]). In his *Plan for Comparative Education*, for example, Jullien asked about the extent to which the Bell-Lancaster monitorial method was used in different countries. In this schema, the sheer act of comparison facilitates the "borrowing" of ideas. A second "father figure" of the field, Michael Sadler (1861–1943), is famously posed as a counterpoint to Jullien's optimism regarding borrowing (for a similar, earlier contrast see, Ushinsky [1857/1975]). Sadler cautioned that educational reformers not "wander at pleasure among the educational systems of the world," and, invoking ideas of native acclimatization, he likened deliberate borrowing to picking flowers and expecting "that if we stick what we have gathered into the soil at home, we shall have a living plant" (as quoted in Bereday, 1964, p. 310). As this suggests, one of the key problematics of transfer has thus been the appropriateness/inappropriateness of the circulation, whether the moved educational knowledge "fit" or did not fit its new context. And, relatedly, this has generated extensive discussion in the field across the twentieth century on whether transfer should or should not occur.

Such debates notwithstanding, deliberate "transfer" and "borrowing" from elsewhere does appear to occur with relative frequency. And, regardless of whether comparative education researchers are involved in the design and execution of the movement, it is something they can study and analyze. Beech (2006) argues that scholars have tended to view educational transfer as following a certain trajectory where

(1) a local problem was identified; (2) solutions were sought in foreign educational systems; and (3) a "tested" institution or educational practice (that had worked or was believed to have worked) was adapted to the new context and then implemented. (p. 2)

As Beech notes, an important feature of transfer research is the specification of a chronological trajectory. Study-tours and other officially sponsored forms of travel to foreign countries are one of the key means by which improvement-oriented reformers can learn about ideas that have been "successful" (or not) and determine which ideas to transfer or avoid transferring to their homeland.

Social science modeling of educational transfer has become increasingly complex in the last decade (e.g., Phillips & Ochs, 2004; Rappleye, 2006). In this current of scholarship, the circulations of educational knowledge can be posited, for example, not as simply linear but as a circular process that can be viewed as a transfer "cycle" that witnesses multiple stages, interest-pursuing actors and varying levels of political deliberation, negotiation and compromise. As diligent social scientists, educational transfer researchers typically place a premium on understanding how agency and structure interact to limit and enable the mobility and liquidity of educational knowledge. One noted leader in the field of educational transfer studies, Gita Steiner-Khamsi (2004), has argued that transfer studies often implicitly rely on the existence of "social networks" to help explain how certain things appear "attractive" and how they "move," and she recommends making the analysis of social networks a more central feature of scholarship in the field. Nonetheless, despite the inclination towards examining the globalization of educational knowledge in relational and transactional terms, scholarship in this tradition does not view knowledge itself as "distributed" or taking on any special "networked" properties. In adherence to a longstanding tradition of Western thought, knowledge is still very much seen to take an epi-phenomenal form, even though it can be "actively moving" in different currents of society, as Dewey put it over a century ago. In this paradigm, knowledge is out there to be accessed and leveraged strategically by social actors in accordance with their prefigured interests.

Educational transfer lends itself to convenient analytic dichotomies or continua, in designations such as possible/impossible, desirable/undesirable, voluntary/involuntary, universal and abstractable/particular and context-bound. Some key presuppositions emerge from across the literature. One is that it is possible (and at times relatively straightforward) to distinguish between educational knowledge that is "inside" or "native" to a given setting and that which is "outside" or "foreign." A second is that in large part we can look to the "agency" of individuals and, though with less emphasis, to the agency of institutional actors to explain movement. A third is that despite the apparent "liquidity" of discourses, texts and ideas, they are more or less bound to have localized or indigenized forms. A fourth is that we can rely on a standard set of sociological explanations for why educational knowledge is rendered mobile. Educational transfers, thus, serve some sort of functional purpose—purposes that might include furthering the technologization or rationalization of society, preserving elite interests or contributing to elite formation, helping achieve social justice and social welfare objectives, or advancing nation-building or other collective identity projects.

As the above suggests, educational transfer studies tend to offer actor-centered explanations for why and how educational knowledge moves. They can also offer explanations for why consensus forms around particular strands of educational knowledge. Not all "mobile" educational knowledge is equal in terms of its reach, its force or its global acceptance, and researchers face the challenge of explaining why certain pieces of educational knowledge attain *trans*-local acceptance while others do not. Jullien (1816-7/1964) understood the perfection of educational systems to be tantamount to "a universal tendency toward a similar goal" (p. 36) and the comparative tables he proposed were to develop a universal, ideal model in education. Other comparative education scholars across the twentieth century have spoken of "absolute values" (Nicholas Hans) and of "general aims" (Joseph Lauwerys), and one enduring goal of certain sectors of the field has been to identify a model of schooling that can be shared globally. "Darwinian" notions of natural selection also govern the selection of best practices, suggesting that studies of transfer, simply stated, show us "what works" and "what doesn't." Thus, from a transfer paradigm, educational comparisons enable not only the movement of educational knowledge but also contribute to the formation of a global consensus on an ideal model of schooling. In contrast, the body of scholarship that we examine next argues that educational ideals themselves—the ideational, symbolic sphere, more than the "best" practices that can be identified on a technical level—are what *trans*-local consensuses on educational knowledge are built around.

Globalizing Educational Knowledge as the Movement of Cultural Models

The comparative education research literature that is grouped around neo-institutionalist sociology, and specifically scholars such as John Meyer and Francisco Ramirez of Stanford University, who discuss "world cultural models," offers a different set of tools and techniques for analyzing how and why educational knowledge is both mobile and moves. First, however, some background is necessary. Frequently, the starting point of this body of scholarship is to account "for a world whose societies, organized nation-states, are structurally similar in many unexpected dimensions and change in unexpectedly similar ways" (Meyer, Boli, Thomas, & Ramirez, 1997, p. 145). Meyer and his colleagues argue that power relations-based and functional rationality-based explanations for why different institutions across the globe are becoming increasingly similar or "isomorphic" fail to acknowledge the ways in which world culture exogenously informs states and societies. In their view, the "world models" that are diffused through global cultural and associational processes have become the causal motor for institutional isomorphism. Many states seem willingly to adopt world models, something that power relations-based theories seem unable to explain satisfactorily. Functional-rationalist theories, according to Meyer, are not very successful at explaining why many states and societies have a "loose coupling" between their formally espoused models/principles and the actual practices that can be observed.

Neo-institutionalist sociologists place greater explanatory power in world "cultural myths." For example, a functionalist-rationalist approach to the idea that education is a means to remedying social maladies (e.g., inequalities) would be deeply troubled by the questionable ability of schools to actually perform this capacity (for discussion of this in the context of post-conflict educational reform see, Sobe [2009a]). Instead, if we take the idea that education serves the betterment of society as a "common-sense world model" we have a better purchase on both the significance of policy actions and why their repeated endorsement is so important.

Ramirez and Meyer (2002) argue that world-level entities are "organizational carriers of the world educational order" (p. 95). International organizations and "rationalized others"—the sciences and the professions—are examples of world-level entities. In this vein, Colette Chabbott (2003) identifies international development organizations and international professionals as carriers of "packages of 'correct' principles, 'appropriate' policies, and 'best' practices to national governments and local nongovernmental organizations alike" (p. 2). These scholars argue that the current time period in particular is well suited to diffusing world models which are codified and publicized. The appearance and subsequent expansion of authoritative, legitimizing international organizations and rationalized others has dramatically increased the visibility of world models and their liquidity: "Rationalized others are now everywhere, in massive arrays of international associations and epistemic communities, generating veritable rivers of universalistic scientific and professional discourse" (Meyer et al., 1997, p. 162). Few international governmental organizations were in existence in 1940 and the League of Nations—forerunner of the United Nations—was effectively inoperative. Emergency relief organizations after both world wars and international public health campaigns of the 1930s and 1940s fostered faith in addressing international issues on an international scale (Chabbott). In the aftermath of World War II, an organizational pattern was established, with the United Nations and its affiliates, in which international discourses could achieve a heretofore unprecedented standardization and could advance a modernist agenda of progress, rights, and development. Meyer et al. argue that "world organizations are, thus, primarily instruments of shared modernity" (Meyer et al., p. 164). World-level entities circulate particular discourses and agendas on an international scale, and thus foster consensus on issues that warrant worldwide attention. International organizations, sciences and professions, and other rationalized others derive their expert and legitimizing identities through posturing themselves as impartial, rationalized parties that disseminate necessary universal knowledge. Through this process, particular knowledge is rendered "common-sense." Meyer et al. also argue that direct relationships between local actors and world culture enable the mobilization of world models. In the context of schooling, the authority of local educational actors is often validated globally. Through professional development and networking, local educational actors are familiar with the "latest word on curricular and pedagogical matters" and the "knowledge bases of world centers" (Ramirez & Meyer, 2002, p. 96). In this schema, *trans*-local educational knowledge is thus circulated locally through globally validated local educational actors (and organizations). It is also important in this schema that educational knowledge—like knowledge writ large—is seen as constructing subject positions and helping to constitute subjectivities (see, e.g., Meyer, 1987).

Meyer and his colleagues also direct attention to the importance of a globally recognized nation-state "template" that is validated by the United Nations and the other world bodies who determine whether nation-state "candidates" have appropriately formulated their claims for sovereignty, that they appropriately control a population and territory, and that they express the right objectives. General adherence to this template (for purposes of formal recognition) engenders *trans*-local consensus with regard to the qualities and/or characteristics of nation-states. Systemic maintenance of nation-state actor identity refers to the ways in which world society structures/organizations aid nation-states in "conforming" to the "proper" world model. This maintenance furthers institutional isomorphism and also generates the category of "pariah" states. A focus on cultural models offers an explanation for the strong advocacy power that nongovernmental organizations have in this milieu. As Chabbott (2003) documents, international government organizations rely on regional, national, and local nongovernmental organizations to "monitor the implementation of declarations and national plans of action at the national and local levels" (p. 10). Technological developments have fostered the networks between local nongovernmental organizations and international development organizations, facilitating consensus-building and institutional isomorphism (see also Riles, 2000). The Internet and assorted online technologies have made it easier to attract international attention in instances when governments fail to live up to (their own) commitments to human rights, democratic principles, environmental stewardship, etcetera. Conforming pressures can thus come into play at the nation-state level (as governments attempt to please international authorities) or at sub-national levels (as local entities appeal to supra-national institutions and pressures to force national governments to act as "proper" nation-states).

Comparative education research in the neo-institutionalist sociology tradition focuses both on the nature of the knowledge that is rendered mobile and what vehicles or "carriers" are responsible for moving it. In terms of the former, Francisco Ramirez notes that "the education reforms that travel most extensively have both a universalistic and rationalizing quality" (Ramirez, 2003, p. 249). These same qualities of universability apply to the carriers as well, whose authority (and capabilities) are bolstered by their very ability to act in a worldwide or international manner. As noted above, these carriers exist "in massive arrays of international associations and epistemic communities" (Meyer et al., 1997, p. 162).

A number of contrasts can be drawn with the comparative educational scholarship on transfer as we discussed it above. For one, the educational transfer literature does not consistently distinguish what is responsible for some kinds of educational knowledge being more "liquid" than others. Two, while both bodies of literature share an interest in change over time, the work of Meyer et al. is deliberately calibrated to capture general, broad-scale trends rather than to chart or document the specific movement of any particular element of educational knowledge around the globe. Interestingly enough, however, both strands of scholarship see the act of comparison itself as implicated in advancing the circulation of educational knowledge. The global reports that demarcate educational "winners" and "losers" via league tables and international rankings lend visibility, according to Ramirez and Meyer (2002), to world models themselves. In the transfer paradigm, enterprises such as TIMSS and PISA lend themselves to "what works" and "what doesn't work" kinds of policy discourses—and, once again, we see a revealing difference between these two areas of scholarship on whether the mobility of educational knowledge occurs more in a symbolic and cultural context, or in a practical, and immediate results-oriented realm.

Globalizing Educational Knowledge Outside of Networks

The third area of scholarship that we examine here in relation to explaining how and why ideas move is the work undertaken by Karen Knorr Cetina (Knorr Cetina, 2003, 2008; Knorr Cetina & Bruegger,

2002), an anthropologist who has devoted a great deal of attention to world financial markets and what it means for information to flow in networked and non-networked ways. In standard understandings of networks, the links between nodes function as "pipes" through which information and resources can pass. The passage of information between nodes serves immediate instrumental purposes and also the broader, coordinating purpose of holding the arrangement together. In this schema, one or more conduits can lead to a single node, thus enabling the creation of central nodes and of multiple collectives (hence the appellation "rhizomatic" that is so frequently applied to network configurations).

Knorr Cetina discerns a different organizational schema in the currency markets which she investigates. Unlike most other financial markets which are organized as centralized markets (as, for example, national/regional security, bond and commodity markets), foreign exchange is an over-the-counter market that inheres in inter-dealer transactions housed within global banking institutions. Knorr Cetina (2008) reports that currency traders have up to six computer screens in front of them, fully capturing their gaze, with "the market [composing] itself in these produced-and-analyzed displays to which traders are attached." These terminals "deliver the reality of financial markets, the referential whole to which 'being in the market' refers" (p. 71). According to Knorr Cetina, the relational idiom of "network" or "being networked" does not capture the totality and reflexive comprehensiveness of the projection and reality being composed in this instance. She proposes the concept of a *scopic system* to describe this structure:

Like an array of crystals acting as lenses that collect light, focusing it on one point, such mechanisms collect and focus activities, interests, and events on one surface. . . . When such a mechanism is in place, coordination and activities respond to the projected reality to which participants become oriented. . . . When such an ordinary observer constructs a textual or visual rendering of the observed and televises it to an audience, the audience may start to react to the features of the reflected, represented reality rather than to the embodied, pre-reflexive occurrences. (Knorr Cetina, 2008, p. 8)

Information that moves through a scopic system thus has considerably different effects than information that moves through networks. Against an embedding of circulation in social relations, Knorr Cetina's work suggests a way of seeing a global system that tends toward a single collective (as opposed to multiple collectives or "pluri-centered" clusters). Based on her ethnographic study of currency trading floors in

Zurich and New York, she proposes that the configuration of screens, content and options that traders confront compose a *global reflex system*. She uses this term to denote

a reflexive form of coordination that is flat (nonhierarchical) in character while at the same time being based on a comprehensive summary view of things—the reflected and projected global context and transaction system. (Knorr Cetina, 2003, p. 8)

Though Knorr Cetina does not rely upon notions of mediality in her analysis, the emphasis she places on technologies and the ways they interact with and transform human beings/human bodies actually returns us to the "new chapter of human history" that John Dewey narrated in 1899 and the emphasis he placed on what technology (of a different order) enabled and transformed. One of the recurring themes of some globalization discourses is that we could well stand on the threshold of new modes for setting learning into circulation.

What, however, do currency markets, scopic systems and global reflex systems have to do with the liquidity and circulation of educational knowledge? We are not (yet?) at the point where policy makers and education professors in Birmingham, Brasilia and Bangalore sit in front of screens that supply them with instantaneous educational research journal table of contents alerts, real-time MCAT score reporting, the RSS feed from the UNESCO International Institute for Educational Planning, and the online social network "status updates" or "tweets" of prominent Ministers of Education. Knorr Cetina's concepts and insights do however, provide us with some tools for thinking about projected realities (and the means of projection) as well as the importance of reflexivity in the constitution of global communities (whether they be a singular collective or multiple collectives).

To think through this we continue our panning back a century and look at World's Fairs and International Expositions as the Reuters/Bloomberg screens and the scopic and global reflex systems of their time. This will also help us to think about the extent to which, or ways in which, global educational assessment projects such as TIMSS and PISA, as well as present-day academic conferences, function scopically and reflexively.

One of the more important points to be drawn from Knorr Cetina's work is that one-worldness, i.e. notions of belonging to a single collective and inhabiting a singular "global reality," can be constructed in certain domains. The International Expositions and World's Fairs of the end of the nineteenth and beginning of the twentieth centuries served a similar function of constructing a singular global reality and projecting forth a modern future. Exhibits on schooling were a regular feature of these international expositions, some of which could attract tens of millions of visitors and sizeable foreign delegations. As Martin Lawn notes:

A major significance of exhibitions was that they provided systems of classifications, and the models needed to illustrate them, which materialized the comparative process. Objects were placed in relation to each other by increasingly standardized systems of rules of measurement. . . . So, through this exhibitionary prism, hierarchies were established in the signs and sites of progress and modernity. (Lawn, 2009, pp. 16–17)

The technologies of museum display and their accompanying norms of spectatorship (Sobe, 2007) can be seen, in Knorr Cetina's terms, as a scopic system. The exhibits and what Lawn appropriately calls their "systems of classification" did not simply supply visitors with modes of viewing and "lenses" for examining existing schooling practices. Rather, in modeling the future and establishing scores of comparative matrices, much as TIMSS and PISA do today, they brought visitors and exhibitors into what one might call a "house of mirrors" where projections reflected an anticipated or actual "reaction." An example of this is Spain's educational exhibits at the 1876 Centennial Exposition in Philadelphia. These exhibits not only reflected an effort to present Spain as the spiritual mother of the Americas, but also an attempt to mitigate the supposed perception that Spain was deficient and far behind other European nations in advancing the cause of popular education. The solution was to send neither charts nor devices nor building models but handsomely printed books, which, since they were printed in Spanish—the Spanish Ministry of Education explicitly strategized in advance—had the added advantage of (probably) being unreadable by the American jurors who would award the education exhibit prizes. And indeed, this proved to be successful, for at this fair Spain received 93 awards in the education section, the most of any country after the United States (Pozo Andrés, 2009, pp. 162–163). Thus, while the World's Fairs/Expositions did provide countries with a platform on which to display themselves, this was a platform set within the scopic system of international competition and comparison that was at the same time a system through which modernity was debated and enacted.

The great International Exhibitions of the end of the nineteenth and early twentieth centuries purported to present a comprehensive, encyclopedic survey of the world. And, despite the great swaths of territory and human experience that were excluded, these "exhibition-ary prisms" did much to construct the reality of a "single world" as an all-encompassing, texturally even sphere within which codified distinctions and standardized differences could be established (in reference to concepts like "civilization," "progress," and "modernity"). When we consider the way that these events functioned like a global reflex system, it becomes clear that if one accepts the neo-institutionalist sociologists' idea that "world cultural models" play an important role around the world today, one needs to go back farther than the close of World War II to find the genesis of an increasingly isomorphic global educational system.

International Expositions continue today (as a follow-up to the Beijing Olympics, China is hosting EXPO 2010 in Shanghai), though no longer do they play the same coordinating role on the global scene that they once did. In some domains, this kind of coordination now takes place via the flickering glow of computer and television screens. However, the fanciful image of a Reuters and Bloomberg service for teachers, administrators and educational policy makers that we discussed above seems rather unlikely. And, even though meetings of organizations like the American Educational Research Association (AERA) have become vast international affairs, it is unlikely that we will return to the exhibitionary complexes of World's Fairs in their turn-of-the-twentieth-century heyday. Nonetheless, we should attend to the ways that an AERA annual meeting is not simply a singular episodic event but is tied up with a massive scientific journal production effort. Several hundred sub-specialization networks are coordinated through face-to-face and electronic communication, and there are multi-directional efforts to raise the legitimacy and professional profile of educational research, both in the public eye and vis-à-vis other academic disciplines. In like manner, an event like the 1990 Education For All (EFA) conference in Jomtien, Thailand, with its extensive preparatory conferences, textual circulations and institutional coalition-building, seems very much to have worked to create a sense among participants (and those who have worked on EFA in the two decades since) of belonging to a single collective that inhabits one global educational reality. Attention should also be paid to the international conferences of "umbrella organizations" such as the World Council of Comparative Education Societies (WCCES), whose membership consists of national, regional and linguistic comparative education associations across the globe (Maseman, Bray, & Manzon,

2008). WCCES meetings can surely be understood in network terms, yet they also stand to be analyzed in terms of the extent to which they function as an array of crystals that collects and focuses light on one surface.

Knorr Cetina's work invites us to consider the scopic systems and global reflex systems that condition/enable the circulation of educational knowledge today. And, while her ideas certainly do not annul the possibility of fragmentation and multi-perspectivalism, they do stand in some contrast to the oft-cited "-scape" notions proposed by Arjun Appadurai (1990). They suggest that the comparative education endeavor, however, fractured and incomplete, is helping to create not multiversal but universal standards and systems of coordination. Lawn writes:

High modernity might have lost its capacity for modeling the education future, the state might have retreated from state building and globalisation might have dislocated the clear meanings of education, but once, the future was crystallised in the work of the exhibitions, museums and magazines of the nineteenth century. (Lawn, 2009, p. 11)

While we agree with Lawn that there is much to indicate that the globalization of our present day and age has troubled some of the "clear" meanings of education, the overlapping efforts under way (and we can think of educational researchers as well as the institutions and carriers discussed by Meyer, Ramirez and Chabbott) to craft a "global reality" within which it is possible to think comparatively about education systems suggest that there are still crystallizing prisms at play. These are prisms which, to paraphrase Knorr Cetina (2008, p. 8), focus activities, interests and events such that participants and bystanders (1) become oriented to an increasingly shared understanding of reality and (2) increasingly begin to react to the features of that reflected and represented reality rather than to embodied and lived pre-reflexive occurrences.

Conclusion

Flow Architectures of Educational Knowledge

One of the important themes that ran through each of the sections above concerned questions of reflexivity, recursive processes and how to take account of "conversational interactions" that are at once intense and diffuse. Transfer approaches to historically studying the circulation of ideas and practices have been faulted for a "reflexivity deficit" (Werner & Zimmermann, 2006) that, for example, makes it difficult to untangle situations where "movement" involves reciprocal, reversible, and multiple vectors. While there may be certain instances where inter-relationships are strictly two-sided, it is probably more the case that the circulation of educational knowledge takes place within dense, overlapping webs of relationships (for more on this see Sobe, 2009b). The paradigm of bilateral, diachronic analyses that characterize most transfer research does not automatically capture the complexity and multiplicity of these relationships, particularly the "house of mirrors" dimensions where multiple refractions of images of self and other infiltrate and pattern the circulation of educational knowledge, and, in fact, may well exceed the possibility of a relational analysis.

The argument that world cultural models prominently figure in the movement of educational knowledge around the globe allows us to see this movement as more than the result of strategic learning. By focusing on the various carriers of world-level ideologies and educational ideals, this strand of scholarship is also predicated on networks playing an important role, yet it too fails to capture the possible multiple vectors that might be in play as these world cultural myths are shuttled around the globe. Meyer and his colleagues do in fact recognize this. They acknowledge that their emphasis on the ways external world models regulate states' and societies' identities could be enhanced by a more complete model that took account of recursive processes and demonstrated the ways in which "states, organizations, and individuals also contribute to the content and structure of world culture" and world-cultural change (Meyer et al., 1997, p. 151). That being said, the world models that spread are considered to be relatively dynamic and generative of diversity. The implication is not that all educational systems are precisely the same but more that the ways in which they are different has become standardized according to whether they are "tightly coupled" or "loosely coupled" with world models.

Institutional isomorphism arguments rely on these global "models" to supply the content of the educational knowledge that moves and they tend to presume network-based distribution/dissemination mechanisms. In contrast to the idea of a substance-filled model, the idea of a "scopic system" describes a technology or mechanism that establishes the *mis-en-scène*—the overall context and "reality" within which ideas emerge and move. This contrast becomes more evident in Knorr Cetina's comments on networks and on the need to pay attention to things that network analyses cannot capture:

Networks are embedded in territorial space, and they do not suggest the exist-ence of reflexive mechanisms of projection that aggregate, recontextualize, and augment the relational activities within new frameworks that are analyti-cally relevant to understanding the continuation of activities. (Knorr Cetina, 2003, p. 8)

Turn-of-the-twentieth-century World's Fairs and exhibitions were undeniably sites of intense social networking and helped to move edu-cational knowledge between various nodes. Nonetheless, we argued above that exhibitions also functioned in some important non-network ways in projecting and drawing people into the recursive enactment of a global educational "scene."

In studying the globalization of educational knowledge, insights can be drawn from each of the three bodies of scholarship discussed above. However, we would argue that alongside analysis of the "currents" and "pipes" through which educational knowledge moves around the globe, it is critical to think about the "prisms" that crystallize and focus indi-viduals, actions, institutions, events, and interests on a "global educa-tional reality." Exhibitionary complexes that physically gather people together and produce recursive reams of text commemorating and ana-lyzing the occasions are no longer the key prisms they once were. The research challenge becomes one of ascertaining what prisms are at play in the globalization of educational knowledge today and of explaining how these prisms change over time. One might ask, for example, what kind of scopic functioning there is to the distinction between qualitative and quantitative research. What kind of global comparability does this commonplace division engender? What kind of collective might it be contributing to forming? Similar questions could be asked about con-cepts such as "educational stakeholder," "community-school partner-ship," and "data-driven decision-making." The point being not simply that educational knowledge moves and becomes global, end of story. Rather, it is that what moves is linked into certain projections of reality that then become carried forward in a continual unfolding.

REFERENCES

Appadurai, A. (1990). Disjuncture and difference in the global cultural economy. In M. Featherstone (Ed.), *Global culture: Nationalism, globalization and modernity* (pp. 295–310). London: Sage.

Beech, J. (2006). The theme of educational transfer in comparative education: A view over time. *Research in Comparative and International Education, 1*(1), 2–13.

Bereday, G.Z.F. (1964). Documents: Sir Michael Sadler's "study of foreign systems of education." *Comparative Education Review, 10,* 307–314.

Chabbott, C. (2003). *Constructing education for development: International organizations and education for all*. New York: RoutledgeFalmer.

Dewey, J. (1900/1990). *The school and society*. Chicago: University of Chicago Press.

Edwards, R., & Usher, R. (2007). *Globalisation and pedagogy: Space, place and identity* (2nd Ed.), New York: Routledge.

Ginzburg, C. (1980). *The cheese and the worms: The cosmos of a sixteenth-century miller*. Baltimore: Johns Hopkins University Press.

Jullien, M.-A. (1816-7/1964). *Jullien's plan for comparative education*. S. Fraser (Trans.). New York: Teachers College Bureau of Publications.

Knorr Cetina, K. (2003). From pipes to scopes: The flow architecture of financial markets. *Distinktion*, (7), 7–23.

Knorr Cetina, K. (2008). Microglobalization. In I. Rossi (Ed.), *Frontiers of globalization research: Theoretical and methodological approaches* (pp. 65–92). New York: Springer.

Knorr Cetina, K., & Bruegger, U. (2002). Global microstructures: The virtual societies of financial markets. *American Journal of Sociology, 107*(4), 905–950.

Lawn, M. (2009). Sites of the future: Comparing and ordering new educational actualities. In M. Lawn (Ed.), *Modelling the future: Exhibitions and the materiality of education* (pp. 15–30). Oxford: Symposium Books.

Maseman, V., Bray, M., & Manzon, M. (Eds.) (2008). *Common interests, uncommon goals: Histories of the world council of comparative education societies and its members*. Hong Kong: CERC.

Meyer, J.W. (1987). Myths of socialization and personality. In T.C. Heller, M. Sosna, & D.E. Wellbery (Eds.), *Reconstructing individualism: Autonomy, individuality and self in western thought* (pp. 208–221). Palo Alto: Stanford University.

Meyer, J.W., Boli, J., Thomas, G.M., & Ramirez, F.O. (1997). World society and the nation state. *American Journal of Sociology, 103*(1), 144–181.

Phillips, D., & Ochs, K. (2004). Researching policy borrowing: Some methodological challenges in comparative education. *British Educational Research Journal, 30*(6), 773–784.

Popkewitz, T.S. (2000). *Educational knowledge: Changing relationships between the state, civil society, and the educational community*. Albany: State University of New York Press.

Pozo Andrés, M. de (2009). The bull and the book: Images of Spain and Spanish education in the World Fairs of the nineteenth century, 1851–1900. In M. Lawn (Ed.), *Modelling the Future: Exhibitions and the materiality of education* (pp. 153–182). Oxford: Symposium.

Ramirez, F.O. (2003). The global model and national legacies. In K.M. Anderson-Levitt (Ed.), *Local meanings, global schooling: Anthropology and world culture theory* (pp. 239–254). New York: Palgrave.

Ramirez, F.O., & Meyer, J.W. (2002). National curricula: World models and national historical legacies. In M. Caruso & H.-E. Tenorth (Eds.), *Internationalisierung/ internationalisation* (pp. 91–107). Frankfurt am Main: Peter Lang.

Rappleye, J. (2006). Theorizing educational transfer: Toward a conceptual map of the context of cross-national attraction. *Research in Comparative and International Education, 1*(3), 223–240.

Riles, A. (2000). *The network inside out*. Ann Arbor: University of Michigan Press.

Rossi, I. (2008). *Frontiers of globalization research: Theoretical and methodological approaches*. New York: Springer.

Sobe, N.W. (2002). Travel, social science and the making of nations in early 19th century comparative education. In M. Caruso & H.-E. Tenorth (Eds.), *Internationalisation: Comparing educational systems and semantics* (pp. 141–166). Frankfurt am Main: Peter Lang.

Sobe, N.W. (2007). Attention and spectatorship: Educational exhibits at the Panama-Pacific international exposition, San Francisco 1915. In V. Barth (Eds.), *Innovation and education at universal exhibitions, 1851–2010* (pp. 95–116). Paris: International Bureau of Expositions.

Sobe, N.W. (2009a). Educational reconstruction "by the dawn's early light": Violent political conflict and American overseas education reform. *Harvard Educational Review, 79*(1), 123–131.

Sobe, N.W. (2009b). Entrelaçamentos e troca cultural na História da Educação: mobilizando John Dewey no período entre guerras [Entanglements and Intercultural Exchange in the History of Education: Mobilizing John Dewey in the Interwar Era]. *Revista Brasileira de História da Educação, 21*, 13–38.

Steiner-Khamsi, G. (2004). Blazing a trail for policy theory and practice. In G. Steiner-Khamsi (Ed.), *Global politics of educational borrowing and lending* (pp. 201–220). New York: Teachers College Press.

Ushinsky, K.D. (1857/1975). On national character of public education. In A.I. Piskunov (Ed.), *K. D. Ushinsky: Selected works*. Moscow: Progress Publishers.

Werner, M., & Zimmermann, B. (2006). Beyond comparison: *Histoire Croisée* and the challenge of reflexivity. *History and Theory, 45*, 30–50.

Politics, Global Territories and Educational Spaces

ROSA NIDIA BUENFIL-BURGOS

Introduction

The links between globalization and territory seem to constitute a productive matter to discuss, since one of the most visible processes we are witnessing at an existential level involves massive and multi-directed migrations from less developed places to others upon which hopes of better opportunities have been conferred, and this traveling has educational effects. People from rural areas go to cities, thousands of persons from Africa and Asia migrate to Europe (from Turkey to Germany, from Algeria to France, from India and Pakistan to the UK, and so on), especially from previous colonies to the countries that were the colonizer. In the American continent, massive circulation takes place from Latin American countries (Mexico, El Salvador, Guatemala, *inter alia*) to the United States, pursuing the so-called "American dream"; from different nations (mainly Asian but also from the Americas) people migrate to Australia in search of better opportunities. And the list never ends. This pilgrimage involves educational questions, concerning the identitary formation of migrants, that have been considered as border pedagogy (Aronowitz & Giroux, 1991; Giroux, 1991), or have been analyzed under the disciplinary outlook of social pedagogy (Nuñez, 1999), and have also been dealt with focusing on the schooling angle as a conflict involving cultural and curriculum adaptation.

Immigration has been studied as a result of the impoverishment produced by globalization (McDowell, 1996; Sassen, 1998; United Nations Development Programme, 1995). And the first questions arising at this point are simple: When do we date the beginnings of global migrations? What about historic resettlements (the historic pre-Christian Jewish migration, the Chinese, the Lebanese, and some others that started later at the turn of the twentieth century)? The post World War II inmigrations (e.g., the Israelite, the African *Pied Noirs* to France, and the list can follow). Is migration really just a result of economics?

Although the economic dimension of emigration should not be ignored, there are many more angles such as the religious, cultural, political, and ethnic facets of the process in need of scrutiny, and thus resources of intelligibility (e.g., concepts, logics, positions) to these ends also need to be discussed.

Rather than adding one more narrative about the contiguity of neoliberalism, globalization, and deterritorialization to the endlessly available journalistic stories, my argument in this chapter is that the *problematization* (Foucault, 1985; Howarth, 2000) of territorial movements in the process of globalization can provide important insights to understand some educational aspects of contemporary migration, especially if the theoretical ingredients involved in the political analysis of the signifying dimension of this process are articulated and discussed.

In order to develop my argument I organize this text in three sections. First, I will criticize the viewpoint that equates globalization with neoliberalism, revising different angles of the process. Once the complex movement is situated, I introduce the critique to an idea of territory tied to a topographic ground. Then I will present some aspects concerning the way in which both territoriality, understood as a signifying open-ended system, and the de-centering of the current approach to education as a schooling process entail a productive approach to some movements involved in globalization.

Why is this discussion worth having? The mere perception of our existential condition is not enough to understand and get involved in a favorable and constructive way.

1. Is Globalization Neoliberalism?

Discussing globalization in the nineties may have been seen by some as just another intellectual fashion that would be soon replaced by a new one. Nonetheless, the bold persistence of accelerated transformations, interconnections, and concerns on a planetary scale has challenged educators, social workers, intellectuals, and many other professionals in such a way that today it is morally and politically irresponsible to deal with these conditions with either improvised, ready-made prescriptions, or universalistic procedures which may not meet any specificity. In addition, the way in which one constructs the meaning of these existential conditions is strictly related to the responses one produces to deal with them. Globalization has been understood by some as a neoliberal imposition on the entire planet (Chomsky & Dieterich, 1995; Dieterich, 1997; Ianni, 1996), and today some still adhere to this approach (Heron, 2008). However, many contributions have been available since the 1980s that provide not only empirical data but also intellectual tools to understand and interpret globalization in a more complex way (Hirst & Thompson, 1996): from a politico-military perspective (Gilpin, 1987); from a cultural approach (García Canclini, 1996; Hall, 1991; Bhabha, 1996; Perlmutter, 1991); from a political standpoint (Gilpin, 1987); emphasizing educational aspects (Giroux, 1991; McLaren & Lankshear, 1994; Popkewitz, 2000; Schriewer, 1996; Stromquist & Monkman, 2000); focusing on migration (Bauman, 1996; Bhabha, 1996); and so on.

To start, one can genuinely question why liberalism has to be reduced to an economic prospect and a whole political tradition (including from Dewey to Rawls) should be subsumed under the former. Indeed, economic neoliberalism has achieved a great deal of attention for its massive influence on industrialized economies and the well-known dramatic effect it has had on underdeveloped areas; however, the commonplace of neoliberalism as "the cause of the misery we live today," repeated by well-intentioned intellectuals involves ignorance of the centuries of misery associated with different social, political and economic regimes. And even worse, this unquestioned commonplace conflates and absorbs an important political tendency into this already oversimplified and overstated economic outlook.

There is also a debate as to how globalization is to be dated. Some would claim that this process started with Marco Polo's traveling (Aznarrán, 2003); others will argue that it started during the Cold War years (Fürntratt-Kloep, 1997); and others have dated its beginning in the late 1980s (Petras, 2003; Schriewer, 1996). Much has also been said about globalization as the blurring of nation-states (as we knew them for a long time), and the emergence of a regional organization of territories (e.g., Rosenau, 1990).

In an attempt to confer some regularity on this dispersion of views, I distinguish three positions concerning the tendencies involved in this process: for some, globalization leads to the universalization, homogenization, integration, and centralization of a single political, linguistic, educational, economic or military view (Braudel, 1991; Gilpin, 1987; Harvey, 1989; Hinkelammert, 1997; McLuhan & Powers, 1989; Rosenau, 1990; Wallerstein, 1991); for others, it conveys fragmentation and heterogeneity (the atomization of political, religious, aesthetic, social or cultural particularity and individualism), including views of syncretism (Perlmutter, 1991), pastiche, and Babelism as effects of global exchange; and for yet others globalization can be understood as the unresolvable tension of these and other opposing tendencies (universalism/particularism, regionalization/fragmentation) (Robertson, 1990).

Elsewhere I have discussed the wide dispersion of meanings of globalization (Buenfil-Burgos, 2000a). On the one hand, in a genealogical gesture, one can trace back and find that it became a key signifier in the late eighties and the nineties; work by Wallerstein (1991), Braudel (1991) and McLuhan and Powers (1989)[1] pioneered the proliferation of writing on the subject, although, as the understanding of a process of planetary interconnection, it can be traced to a much earlier period. On the other hand, in an organizing gesture, I have grouped this area of dispersion into *family resemblance* (Wittgenstein, 1963) of three types. First, there is the view of an intrinsic connection between globalization, modernity, and neoliberal capitalism, albeit with some differences in terms of how "benefits" are anticipated. Either through the laws of history or the course of economies, it seems that there is a necessary implication connecting these three signifiers. In this view, the causal link between globalization and homogenization seems to be taken for granted. Second, globalization has been equated both with a neoliberal and a postmodern regime, and even with a post-socialist global capitalist society (Fürntratt-Kloep, 1997) that can be superseded by progressive anticapitalist global perspectives. Rationalism and Habermas's "non-distorted communicative action"[2] would play a key role in achieving these ends. In this view, the bonds between globalization and capitalism can be broken, but there are still residues of a logic of necessity retro-actively operating as the conditions of possibility for a "non-capitalist global village," as in Archer's (1991) "new object of sociology." Thus we can have "evil" capitalist globalization as a necessary condition for the emergence of an "emancipated" global village (Chomsky & Dieterich, 1995). Third, the dissociation of globalization from a universal, necessary tendency of history, and from mere cultural, economic, ethical, or political imperialization (either capitalist or post-capitalist) becomes acknowledged (Hall, 1991; Kawame & Gates, 1997; Perlmutter, 1991; Robertson, 1990). Cultural clash and integration, post-socialist political world repositioning, economic world reorganization, *inter alia*, are considered as historical conditions for globalization. Emphasizing the heterogeneous and differential character of social communities in the planet, globalization can be understood as a condition for contact among what is different.

If one conceptualizes globalization as contact and interconnectedness, an important dimension for understanding the re-signification of global policies in their particular instantiations can be grasped. Some years ago, drawing on various arguments displayed by Giddens (1990, p. 175), Robertson (1990, p. 22), Perlmutter (1991, p. 911), and Kawame and Gates (1997, p. xi), I adhered to the idea that globalization can be understood as interconnectedness (Buenfil-Burgos, 2000a, 2000b).

- We have interpenetration of economic tendencies, contact of cultural diversity, intertwining of many traditions, interdependence of political trends. This means acknowledging our contemporary existential situation as a multi-directed conditioning of the universal and the particular, the homogeneous and the heterogeneous; understanding that opposed tendencies such as fragmentation and integration, centralization and de-centralization interact with each other.

- Indeed interpenetration involves the production of syncretic and hybrid economic, cultural, educational, and political outlooks and prospects, as well as the contention of assorted fundamentalist positions fostering a mythical pure and uncontaminated identity.

- Interconnectedness, contact, and interlacing of the diverse does not occur without conflict, since our planet has unequal development in each realm and geopolitical area. Tension, encounter, friction, clash, and conflict (De Alba, 1989) are part of the process, and this can hardly be overlooked or concealed by wishful Enlightenment thinking. However, this does not amount to a pessimistic outlook, since the indeterminate character of the outcome of tension opens up the road to both authoritarian and democratic tendencies (whatever democratic may mean). Indeterminacy in this case means that since there is no *a priori* guarantee, those for one or the other option have to work hard to achieve it.

- Globalization can be associated with the prospect of some commensurability between the heterogeneous, that is, contact among the different. Lyotard's metaphor on the *archipelago* is appropriate to visualize this possibility, since it involves the "different islands" (e.g., cultures, values, and so on) which are separate and yet connected by the sea (i.e., language, in his metaphor, discourse in ours).[3]

I still adhere the key ideas above presented (i.e., interconnectedness, impurity). However, I am now more concerned with the intellectual resources we require to understand mobility—not only of populations (from one country to another), from one identitary trait to a new one, from one linguistic practice to a different one, from a familiar cultural regime to an unfamiliar one, from one schooling system (curriculum, institution, certificates) to a different one; but also mobility that does not entail a radical abandoning of the preceding social links, and a radical embracing of the new. This will be revisited below.

Let us take for instance, the well known cultural, judiciary, moral, and social dilemmas involved in the regulations of a country receiving a migrant whose culture considers marriage as something that parents have the right to arrange, and polygamy and woman-beating as legitimate practices. This migrant arrives in a country whose judiciary system embraces cultural diversity, respect for cultural alterity, and also basic gender egalitarian rights. Is it politically, morally, or culturally defensible to endorse either the migrant view or the local vision without falling into a fundamentalist or a xenophobic position? If one approaches the issue through the *globalization neoliberal* equation, or the globalization as mere imperialist imposition thesis, one may be targeting the wrong objective. Something similar happens when one tackles the problem as merely an economic matter. Crucially, one is barking up the wrong tree if one keeps understanding the issue as a dilemma, as an either/or question.

I now suggest it might be more accurate to focus on the ways in which a gradual and winding cultural combination takes place, erasing some previous traces, inscribing some new ones, and re-inscribing some that had previously been weakened. I am convinced that deepening the logics of *imbrication*,[4] displacement, and aporia, *inter alia*, we can produce intellectually productive resources that help us to understand and interpret, at an ontic level,[5] crucial aspects of the discursive and political dimensions of the processes of globalized migration and its educational effects.

Accordingly, this process increasingly becomes a matter of debate rather than a "mere intellectual fashion" that one has to take for granted, and in which the sedimented commonplace equating globalization and neoliberalism would be sufficient to inscribe our understanding and political view. It must be evident that responsible positions concerning this issue involve at least the problematization of these *topoi*, as a starting point.

2. Is Territoriality Fully Visible as a Topographic Category?

The many angles of our global scenario have been previously situated. However, in order to provide a reasonable argument it is futile to try and focus on a large variety of targets. Therefore, I will only concentrate on two questions, namely, territoriality as a complex signifying net, and its implications for education in our global condition; and leave the other angles for a different moment.

We all are well-informed about the multiplicity of problems surrounding the insertion of multiculturality into educational policies (McLaren & Gutiérrez, 1997; Popkewitz, 2000). We all are aware of the difficulties involved in educating migrant populations; and the paradoxical situation of someone who goes to a different country pursuing a dream and, as soon as they get into the "promised land," they start a nostalgic trip, or those whose national identity was secondary but became central at the very moment of stepping in the country of destination. These are not new challenges and were approached already in the early years of the twentieth century[6]; however, they need to be understood by means of new categories. Cultural and educational enigmas are poorly appreciated when migrants are conceptualized as people who have merely been displaced from one territory to another, and complex symbolic networks involved in and affected by this geographic circulation are not visualized.

To this end I will start problematizing the well-criticized and yet still alive anchorage of territory and geographic space (e.g., Barreda, 2001; Wilson, 2008). Already, in the seventies, Deleuze proposed the idea of deterritorialization and reterritorialization, indicating some crucial features: their signifying character, the fact that the two movements cannot be separated, the impossibility of restricting the process to the nation-state regime, and the rhizomatic form of its circulation (Deleuze & Guattari, 2004).

Conditions entailed by agrarian labor migration, for instance from Mexico to the United States, are about the vicissitudes of the trip from one territory to the other; however, for an educational approach, these are secondary once the migrant is already situated in United States land. Instead, cultural, political, legal and other dimensions are crucial for a successful insertion of the migrant in the new country. All these dimensions are represented by the migrant differently from the way they are represented by the natives receiving those migrants. Accordingly, representations are better understood by analyzing the signifying processes whereby they are constructed rather than by the geographic limits and features of the territories involved. In addition, these signifying movements involved in the construction of cultural and identitary representations do not take place in a unidirectional way, since the migrant may have an idealized image of what is to be found, or may be traumatized by the mere experience of an unknown language, may find a hospitable or an unfriendly a reception, and so on and so forth.

These conditions can be better approached with the help of the Deleuzian intellectual tools above mentioned.[7] Two points are important for my argument. The first is the move towards concentrating on the discursive/signifying dimension of territorial movements instead of its geographic or institutional substance. The second is the rhizomatic character of the way in which this signifying circulation takes place when representations are constructed. This *de-substantializing* move of the notion "territory" provides a fertile terrain for understanding a whole variety of conflicting political, cultural, linguistic, educational, aesthetic, and moral aspects of the identitary changes taking place at an ontic level (e.g., in migrating agents), if one takes up ideas such as those involved in the images of deterritorialization and reterritorialization. The second point focuses on the multidirected and unpredictable ways in which the values, representations, and images interiorized by the agents (both the migrant and the natives) circulate, get involved, combine, or collide.

The attempt to conceptualize the process this way involves some ontological positions, certain political logics, and a series of intellectual tools to arrive at the political and politics. This ontological position means: first, that the identity of agents, their culture and so on, is historical, changes in each context, and does not have an atemporal, fixed or universal essence; second, that this identity is discursively constructed and does not operate beyond some forms of signification, which are also situated (i.e., contextual); and third, that these identities involve the inclusion and exclusion (i.e., political character) of cultural, legal, and educational features, *inter alia*. This effort also involves some logics, such as hegemony (domination and persuasion), aporia (i.e., the productive character of tension), and overdetermination (a multiple, inexhaustible, and mobile sort of causality).[8] Finally, this attempt also involves concepts such as identification (i.e., the internalization of identitary images), articulation and antagonism (as the political processes involved in a hegemonic practice); and the social/symbolic ordering as an open-ended, failed, incomplete, and only partially and temporarily stabilized system (Butler, Laclau, & Žižek, 2000; Laclau & Mouffe, 1985).

When one is facing similar cultural and educational problems in different historical contexts, the resulting strategies are not necessarily the same. For example, when colonial authorities had neither produced the intellectual resources nor the international political and moral standards to cope with education for the colonies, their judg-

ment produced policies that would hardly be legitimate today considering the moral and political mandates that we have in the globalized
twenty-first century. This is why ontological positions are worth problematizing too.

The claim of an ontological position that is discursive, historical,
and political, entails the understanding of social reality as constructed,
and that one can have access to it as a signifying open-ended, imperfect,
temporarily stable system. This means that the existence of the "world
outside" (to use an expression dear to analytical philosophy) is taken for
granted; however, its social meaning (i.e., its objectivity) is not derived
from its mere existence, but socially constructed in time and space (i.e.,
in history) as seen in the example of the vaccination campaign. In
addition, this contextually conditioned construction entails power relations in the sense that the instituting process of all social convention
takes place through the inclusion of some features, norms, values, and
practices, and the exclusion of others in a social, epistemologic, and
political asymmetric condition of existence (i.e., historic and ontic).

As for the logics involved, *imbrication*, displacement, and aporia
seem to be convenient intellectual images to figure out these relations.
Taking again the example of migration, for instance from Turkey to
Germany, the cultural difference emerges as an unbridgeable conflict
when the possible connections are not visualized. However, a variety of
strategies take place that allow some basic common ground upon
which these connections can be constructed. Imbrication, the idea of a
systematic overlapping at the edges, suggests a resource for understanding that the universality conferred to one code, and the particularity assigned to another cannot be thought of apart from each other.
To visualize the way in which these cultural imbrications take place, it
is convenient to focus in the movements of signification and representations carried by these migrants. Displacement evokes the circulation
and mutual pervasion between significations from one symbolic site to
another, from one culture to another, thus inoculating its intensity in
different nodes (e.g., religion, clothing, manners, etc.) of a given socio/
symbolic network. However, these movements are not predictable;
they can be more or less fluid, reach a deadlock, and so on. Take for
instance the use of religious symbols in laic public schools, or inter-
rupting classtime for a religious service. This poses a new challenge
to our understanding particularly because it is not always possible to
find a fair-minded solution. Aporia suggests the fruitful and dynamic
character of an unresolvable tension between opposite forces, and,
differently from the Hegelian synthesis or the Aristotelian "middle

disposition," this very lack of resolution is what produces multiple intellectual and strategic alternatives. Thus, taking once more our example, one can imagine a variety of possibilities to analyze the signifying moves taking place in the cultural clash between native Germans and migrant Turks without reducing the problem either to a frontal opposition (xenophobia) or to an unconditioned acceptance of the alien culture.

These logics enable our understanding of frequent theoretical "dilemmas," such as the relationship between universality and particularity, in a way that goes beyond the ordinary "either/or" solution. The universal is colloquially understood as "something common to all particulars," but one seldom asks oneself how these universals came to be. Are they derived from a metaphysical entity (God or Reason)? Or are they the outcome of social agreement? From Rousseau's Social Contract onwards, universal values have been increasingly interrogated, the relationship between universality and particularity has become an issue and can no longer be taken for granted. Today, many consider universals to be an outcome of negotiations historically and geographically situated and no longer transcendental *a priori* (Laclau, 1996).[9] This brings to the fore the constitutive character of the political. This relationist position has an obvious family resemblance with post-foundationalism (Arditi, 1996; Critchley & Marchart, 2004), and involves the idea that all foundations, including "our universal values," are historically established, *ergo*, context-dependent, which means that there is no atemporal essence, but that all universal principles once were particular values which came to reach some universality. These universals, however, have to be defined in each specific context (be it within a wider or a narrower scope), and in our planet these contexts are heterogeneous and unequal.

Let us take for example the universality of literacy. In our global contemporary condition, one may recognize it as a human right, as a historic conquest of human beings, as the gate to Western civilization, and many other positive values. But let us imagine a remote Third World village in which a literacy campaign may be introduced as a progressive and liberating strategy while for a neighboring village the very same campaign could become (i.e., be understood, experienced, represented as) a repressive and colonizing practice (e.g., because their language is different from that which is fostered in the literacy campaign, or due to the political representatives implementing it). The possibility of these opposed values of the very same ontic process lets us see that: first, although Western values may displace themselves to different places, they imbricate with other values with which they can collide or condense; second, an unresolvable tension is produced when the contact does not condense different values; and third, that there is no privileged position from which our "senior brother" will pre-define how this literacy campaign will be appropriated/ signified/represented at each particular site.

Values may expand their area of influence as long as they dominate and persuade or articulate and impose on others their particularity as "the universal" (thus involving, of course, political relations, i.e., hegemony). From the political and imbricative character of universality I derive two ideas: first, globalization cannot be thoroughly understood as the mere homogenization of the planet under a universal direction; and second, global educational policies which are already an outcome of the contact between universalism and particularism are resignified when they reach particular sites of educational practices and agents (sites that are not merely physical *topo* but complex signifying/symbolic networks).

An example of this multi-directed contact and re-signification can be presented drawing from recent research concerning displacements of the signifier "educational quality" (López-Nájera, 2009).[10] It moves from particular national representatives that reach an agreement in an international agency (in this study, UNESCO) that is both echoed and resignified by other international agencies (in this study, the World Bank), thus acquiring universal status. National geopolitical scales thus reaching the position of particular instantiations of the universal. Already in this first move, a multiplicity of particularities are implicit, pervading and contaminating the universal outcome. UNESCO's construction of "educational quality" relies upon particular academic reports (both field and theoretical research), and its meaning is the result of a negotiation taking place under unequal political conditions.

In addition, its contact with national particularities also inscribes in "educational quality" a variety of meanings (as presented below) previously absent in the international agreement. In López-Nájera's research a subsequent displacement of the signifier is approached: from the national inscription as a constitutive ingredient of an educational reform (mandated by the Mexican Ministry of Education), to the appropriations made in Oaxaca State by both an officially legitimated educational project (MexeOax), and a freelance unsubsidized effort (PEBIIT). Educational quality has different meanings in each enunciator; however, some equivalencies can be found, namely in its imaginary functioning (i.e., as in its image of plenitude and salvation: Enlightenment in all cases; homologation and development in the financial agencies; the reduction of inequality by education for UNESCO; competitiveness at an international scale for the Mexican Education Ministry; emancipation by strictly invigilated education for MexeOax; and the inscription of indigenous culture in schooling, for PEBIIT.

These differences and equivalencies appear distributed asymmetrically in a sort of *family resemblance*. For instance, the World Bank and UNESCO differ on the references taken for the construction of this concept (the former derives from quantitative reports while the latter gets information from qualitative research); UNESCO and MexeOax share a pedagogic outlook (although the latter is concerned with a thorough assessment of achievement while the former is not); the World Bank and MexeOax share the fascination for measurement, but the latter also engages in a qualitative approach to community education; finally, the Mexican Ministry of Education and PEBIIT seem to share a weak interest in precision—in the former, educational quality occupies a nodal position structuring the reform as a whole, while in the latter it is only located in a strategic position without reaching a pivotal function.

Two points invoke attention here: universality and particularity are not separable, they are imbricated; and the displacement of the signifier is poorly understood as images of determination and "necessary and sufficient causality." The logic of overdetermination provides inspiring descriptions (in the Rortyan sense). Interpretations of mere imposition (UNESCO and the World Bank) impose their principles on national education reforms, and are far from observing the multiplicity of processes taking place. The movements of the signifier "educational quality" along different geopolitical scales shows the political and discursive operations that, without excluding, go far beyond an economic, schooling, or ideological unidirectional tendency.

This example enables us to deal with globalization as a process that has been constructed by the variety of meanings previously sketched in section 1, and also permits us to handle these significations, not as some being true and others false, but as a discursive construct entangled with power relations among international agencies, nation-states, governmental institutions, and local authorities (i.e., within different levels of universality and particularity of social relations). Thinking of the relations between different levels of generality and specificity brings us to the question concerning to what extent it can be possible that international global policies may be consider local conditions or not. This is, of course, an important aporia that has to be faced by any policy maker, and by all policy administrators, and it puts forward the very question of the universality and particularity of globalization. Some have dealt with this using the notion of *glocalization*, that is, living locally and thinking globally, thinking globally and acting locally (Robertson, 1990). However, to approach globalization in a deeper way, it is convenient to further consider the relationship between the particular and the universal .

3. Territoriality as a Signifying Open-Ended System and Globalization

For a better understanding of conditions and processes we witness today, such as the educational examples noted above, our intellectual resources require to be refined. The movement of deterritorialization and reterritorialization provides an interesting opportunity to do so (especially for understanding education in the global condition characterized by massive migrations and all that entails). The conceptual network within which it is inscribed, the logics involved (aporetic, interconnected, and mobile thinking), the integration with the ontological position already presented, and a series of concepts such as identification or hegemony produce an epistemological terrain susceptible of a certain political mode of observation.

I distinguished two crucial issues from the discursive/signifying dimension of territorial movements in addition to its geographic/ topographic or institutional substance. I now claim that the non-substantial character of deterritorialization and reterritorialization, its rhizomatic and open-ended structuration, and the codependence of its constituting movements also provide ontological and epistemological terrain for the reinsertion of this process into our understanding of contemporary globalization.

At this point one is able to revise some positions about globalization previously asserted. In speaking of interpenetration of economic tendencies, contact with cultural diversity, intertwining of many traditions, interdependence of political trends, it is possible to discern that the geopolitical flow does not entail a predetermined and unidirectional displacement of forces (cultural, political, and so on), but can be better understood as a rhizomatic circulation of forces. Thus domination and imperialization occur as much as hybridization, neutralization, and even contestation within the very conditions of their existence. Acknowledging our contemporary existential situation as a multi-directed conditioning of the universal and the particular, the homogeneous and the heterogeneous, and understanding that opposed tendencies such as fragmentation/integration and centralization/de-centralization interact with each other, entails a moral, political, and epistemic terrain for possibilities suggesting both the reproduction and the dislocation of a given social order.

If interpenetration has involved the production of syncretic and hybrid economic, cultural, educational, and political outlooks and prospects, rather than ignoring or just rejecting *tout court* these new formations, it seems convenient to examine how they have been assembled, what has been included and excluded in the process, and how they have been structured, since this seems to be the best argument against fundamentalist positions fostering a mythical pure and uncontaminated identity.

The political dimension (i.e., inclusion and exclusion, domination and persuasion, antagonism and articulation) involved in this interconnectedness, contact, and interlacing of the diverse enables our understanding of conflicts derived from both imperialistic moves and the unequal development on each geopolitical front. As already claimed, tension, encounter, friction, clash, and conflict are part of the process, and this can hardly be ignored or concealed by wishful Enlightenment thinking (of a reconciled society bonded by non-distorted communication). However, instead of a pessimistic outlook before this scenario, and considering the indeterminate character of the outcome of tension, an insightful examination of the means by which persuasion and domination (i.e., hegemonic practices) take place seems convenient to tackle the undesired effects and goals of the opposing forces involved in these conflicts. Since there is no *a priori* guarantee for one or the other force, more than one possibility is always present (Rorty, 1989).

Such possibilities can be visualized when one considers that different cultures, values, economic modes, political regimes, religions, and so on may be antagonistic, or just different; that they seem separate, and yet are always connected by language, art, telecommunication, and so on (as in the *archipelago* metaphor). Thus, rather than the "non-capitalist emancipated global village" anticipated by Archer (1991) or Chomsky and Dieterich (1995), globalization can be associated with the prospect of some commensurability between the heterogeneous, that is, contact between the different, that preserves diversity and heterogeneity.[11]

Once a dichotomic or disjunctive logic is criticized, and instead imbrication, overdetermination, and aporia, *inter alia*, inform our understanding, it becomes clear that contemporary migrations can only partially be grasped by economics, demography, and (pessimistic) political views. In contrast, a richer, more complex, and more fruitful analysis will be enabled with the help of other theoretical contributions.

Thus, for instance, the migrant from a poor rural Mexican village to rich rural areas or cities of the United States will be deterritorialized, in the sense of the signifying nets they will face and those they will leave behind (culture, family position, religious rituals, language and so on). This does not mean, however, a mere replacement of identitary positions[12]; reterritorialization is seen as a complex cultural and linguistic (i.e., symbolic) negotiation, and a combination involving asymmetric relations, that can be better understood by means of the logics of displacement, imbrication, aporia, and so on. When this migrant faces alternatives that go against each other, when his/her adherence to one choice entails the weakening of other equally attractive choices, or the transgression of previous moral principles, or the betrayal of former cultural convictions, what is at stake is why and how the agent makes this decision[13]; how and why an external/ objective image manages to convince, and identification takes place; how and why antagonistic options of identification at one level can coexist and overlap, constituting a new hybrid identitary formation. Neglecting this complexity frequently leads the educator (be it a researcher, a priest, a sports coach, or a schoolteacher) to keep hold of traditional "scientific" prejudices (such as the biological inferiority of women, one nationality, one race, and so on), practical commonsense (such as prize and punishment), and other strongly sedimented beliefs that provide poor understanding to our global contemporary educational conditions.

These processes involved in the formation of identity encompass what I suggest as the basis of all educational practice, since, considering the historicity of school education[14] and its exaltation from the Enlightenment onwards, the crystallized equation "education = school" results in a poor and limited representation of all the social-psychic movements (i.e., emotional, cognitive, intellectual, and so on) implicated in the shaping of citizen identity.

Long ago Dewey (1916), Gramsci (1971, 1981), and Freire (1970), among others, wrote about the variety of social spaces wherein the social agent is educated (i.e., identity formation), displaying the strategies, devices, relationships between those who educate and those who are educated, and the ideological, political, and social knowledge and links at stake. Fully recognizing the crucial status of the discussion concerning the huge variety of modes, contents, methods, principles, and values inscribed in non-schooling educational practices, and the negotiations involved in their instituting processes (i.e., what is included and excluded, and so on), I reluctantly have to postpone their examination for another time and place, and leave the problematization and a proper de-centering of educational spaces for a future writing. Nonetheless, I will anticipate here some points.

Problematizing the "education = school" equation may produce the de-centering and reactivation of the very signifier education in at least six dimensions: (1) the epistemological move from teaching to learning as the decisive point of education[15]; (2) the symbolic webs and spaces where formation takes place; (3) the acknowledgement of its open-ended, incomplete, and relational character; (4) the dimension related to the lack of an identitary essence operating as the very possibility of any identity formation (i.e., educational process); (5) the rhizomatic structure reticulating the signifying displacements within a variety of educational spaces; and (6) the epistemological, social, and political orientation inscribed in the knowledge to be taught and appropriated.[16] And this, no doubt, can provide intellectual resources for understanding education in a globalized planet.

Interweaving Arguments (A Sort of Conclusion)

Globalization is still associated mainly with sheer imperialism, neoliberalism, migrations due to economic reasons, and technological changes. No one can deny the chronological contiguity of these conditions; however, deriving a causal link from this ontic proximity, and reducing a complex and mobile set of issues to only these four or five phenomena, results in a poor approach to our contemporary global condition.

My claim is that the problematization (in a Foucauldian sense), as presented above, produces fertile intellectual foundations for the interpretation of contemporary movements, such as the educational issues involved in global migrations. My current thematization on globalization has still under consideration issues concerning the interconnectedness of our cultural environment, extending from military conflicts, environmental anxiety, economic impacts, scientific advances, identitary changes, and schooling homologation, to mutual gastronomic influence. This cultural interconnectedness involves a multiplicity of displacements and condensations which include, of course, the traveling of populations from one geographic site to another. These movements indeed presuppose an empirical existence; however, from this existence its meaning for agents is not irradiated, and our understanding as social scientists is not satisfactory if we only grasp its economic, demographic, schooling, or ethnic dimensions (which are important nonetheless). The vicissitudes suffered by migrants in their traveling and in their permanence in the hosting country are multiple and mainly painful, but from this there is no automatic derivation to the way in which it is represented by the agents: as a necessary sacrifice to reach some paradise (American dream, or whatever name it takes); or as the result of a colonization that has impoverished his home country; or as the compulsory path taken by all the youngsters of a village (without further political or economic consideration); or as the only means to get away from the asphyxiating parochial routine of a particular environment; or as flight from a military and oppressive regime; and thus the representations endlessly proliferate. The investigation of the identitary effects of these representations is crucial for our knowledge and informed inter-vention as educators, especially when we do not limit education to schooling but visualize the whole variety of practices, contents, and spaces whereby the agent is formed. Thus, my current interest in glo-balization has included educational angles concerning the identity for-mation of migrants (moving either from one country to another, or from rural to urban areas), considering cultural, linguistic, labor, and other skills that are learned because of migration.

Exploring concepts, logics, and a historical, discursive, and political ontology such as I have discussed above activates intellectual tools to approach at least three angles. First, the symbolic character of these movements (migration, deterritorialization and reterritorialization, cul-tural hybridization, and so on) operating in different kinds of agents, produces alterations which, if properly understood, may not be as only-destructive, unidirectional, and catastrophic as they have been characterized and treated. Second, the multidirected character of the displacements taking place in globalization (military, cultural, political, economic, demographic, educational, *inter alia*) in turn produces opposed tendencies in permanent tension; *ergo*, refutes the interpreta-tions that can only see the tendency to homogeneity, imperialism, neoliberalism, and the loss of identitary roots. And third, these the-oretical dispositives also activate intellectual devices to revise our very concept of education, and approach the multiplicity of educational spaces, modalities, and contents that have always formed the population's identities in processes of deterritorialization and reterritorialization, and seem to be exacerbated in our global condition (characterized by mobility, hybridity, and tension).

The historicization of migrations may provide a good argument against fundamentalism of all signs, offer a refreshing starting point to reconsider contemporary educational challenges, and also help toward a better understanding of contemporary globalization.

NOTES

1. According to the preface it was actually written between 1976 and 1984.

2. I must say now that I do not know Habermas's updated position on globalization. Here I retrieve Chomsky and Dieterich's way to put Habermas into their own construction. On the other hand, knowing Habermas's theory of non-distorted communicative action, one can be authorized to sustain the compatibility of the approaches (see Habermas & McCarthy, 1981; Buenfil-Burgos, 1997).

3. This presupposes a painful assumption: that there is no distortion-free communication, no transparent society, no final resolution of antagonisms, in short no final suture of the social. Accordingly, once the necessary tendencies of history and a quasi-transcendental reason are conceptually rejected, one has to face the responsibility of one's own decisions (see Buenfil-Burgos, 1997).

4. From the word "imbricate," understood as "lying lapped over each other, an overlapping of edges" in a systematic order.

5. I am borrowing the ontic/ontological distinction in Heidegger's (1978) idea of *Dasein*, which exists by realizing or ignoring its various possibilities, one of which is to inquire into the structure of its life and possibilities. The kind of understanding thereby gained is ontological. The ontic (*existentiell*) characteristic of *Dasein* is to be ontological (*existential*); it is important that its meaning is not simply given but is rather constructed. The ontic/ontological distinction is not a formal one; it is a distinction which actually organizes a human reality as such.

6. Just as an example, in Mexico there was an intense debate in the twenties and thirties as to how the more than 80 indigenous cultures were to be inscribed in national education policies. Going further back in history, although colonial authorities may not have produced the intellectual resources to name it as we do today or the moral and political mandates that we have in the twenty-first century, they nonetheless faced similar cultural and educational problems as we do now.

7. Deleuze's whole idea has been criticized for being apolitical (Žižek, 2003). Far from attempting any possible orthodox defense of Deleuze's ideas (I doubt he would even need this), my point is that a non-political, merely academic and thus partially relevant reading can be made of this approach (emphasizing its complex logic, its sophisticated conceptual net, and so on); however, political insights can also be produced in this reading (together with or beyond Deleuze himself), which may result in an extremely useful understanding of, for instance, contemporary global migrations.

8. The term "overdetermination" is borrowed from psychoanalysis, and taken as a theoretical tool. It involves two symbolic moves: condensation (i.e., the fusion of a multiplicity of representations in one), and displacement (the circulation or forwarding of symbolic force, energy, intensity, or meaning).

9. This should not be misunderstood as "the abyss of relativism," as foundationalists call it. The lack of an ultimate positive foundation of morals, science, the community, and so on does not amount to "anything goes" as Habermas (1987) bitterly accused postmodern thinking to be doing, such that the difference between repression and emancipation

is blurred. I very much agree with the arguments posed by Bernstein (1983), Rorty (1982), and Laclau (1988), *inter alia*, that relativism is a false problem posed by foundationalists (see Buenfil-Burgos, 1997).

10. The data collected involve documents from the late 1980s to 2006, issued by UNESCO, the World Bank, Education for All, the Mexican Ministry of Education, and two educational projects in Oaxaca (MexeOax and Pebiit), as well as some interviews with those who produce and/or endorse these documents and implement these projects.

11. Greater visibility of the processes involved in subjectivation is needed here to provide intellectual ingredients for a revisiting of migration, deterritorialization and reterritorialization, education, and identitary formation in a global condition, this time considering its historical or contextual quality, its symbolic character, its political and psychic dimensions, and its partial and neverending disposition.

12. I am taking up the critique of a notion of fixed, predetermined, centered, and full identity (Hall, 1996; Laclau & Mouffe, 1985; Žižek, 1989, *inter alia*). Considering that the subject is possible through successive identifications triggered by a constitutive lack (Lacan, 1960; Laclau & Zac, 1994; Žižek, 1989) both in the structure of which he/she is part and in the subject positions previously internalized, I adhere to Laclau's thesis that the subject is the distance between the dislocated and undecidable structure and the decision (Laclau, 1990, p. 30). Of course, "decision" here is not associated with any rationalistic frame but with a historicist (Nietzsche; Heidegger, 1978, *inter alia*) mode of understanding.

13. Ontologically speaking, "the decision has the character of a ground which is as primary as the structure on which it is based, since it is not determined by the latter; and if the decision is one between structural undecidables, taking a decision can only mean repressing possible alternatives that are not carried out" (Laclau, 1990, p. 30).

14. Before the emergence of schools as the institutions under whose responsibility the formation of the citizen was placed, there were, no doubt, many spaces and institutions in charge of these community duties. These institutions and practices did not disappear because the school was created.

15. Teaching is not to be reduced to school teaching. Two considerations: the best teaching strategy does not guarantee an appropriation from the one who is intended to be educated; and the internalization of knowledge, values, and so on may or may not be intentionally promoted and even triggered by a poor teaching strategy.

16. Here I refer to questions such as: For whom is this a proper moral value to endorse? According to whom is this a right theory to promote? Indeed, these questions involve a political and epistemological debate on the horizon of a critique of any foundationalist and totalizing conception of morals, knowledge, politics, and so on, and all decisions have to be taken bearing in mind the context of their implementation.

REFERENCES

Archer, M.S. (1991). Sociology for one world: Unity and diversity. *International Sociology*, 2, 131–147.

Arditi, B. (1996). The underside of difference. *Working Papers*, *12*, 1–29.

Aronowitz, S., & Giroux, H. (1991). *Postmodern education, politics, culture & social criticism*. Minneapolis: University of Minnesota Press.

Aznarrán, G. (2003). Respondiendo preguntas sobre la globalización. *Gest Terc Milen*, *5*(10), 77–82.

Barreda, A. (2001). Los peligros del Plan Puebla Panamá. In *Mesoamérica, los ríos profundos: Alternativas plebeyas al Plan Puebla Panamá*. México: Instituto Maya.

Bauman, Z. (1996). From pilgrim to tourist. In S. Hall & P. Du Gay (Eds.), *Questions of cultural identity* (pp. 18–36). London: Sage.

Bernstein, R. (1983). *Beyond objectivism and relativism*. Oxford: Basil Blackwell.

Bhabha, H. (1996). Cultures in between. In S. Hall & P. Du Gay (Eds.), *Questions of cultural identity* (pp. 53–60). London: Sage.

Braudel, F. (1991). *Escritos sobre la historia*. México: Fondo de Cultura Económica.

Buenfil-Burgos, R.N. (1997). Education in a postmodern horizon: Voices from Latin America. *British Educational Research Journal, 23*(1), 97–107.

Buenfil-Burgos, R.N. (2000a). Globalization, education, and discourse political analysis: *Ambiguity and accountability in research*. International Journal of Qualitative Studies in Education *13*(1), 1–24.

Buenfil-Burgos, R.N. (2000b). Globalization and educational policies in Mexico, 1988–1994: A meeting of the universal and the particular. In N. Stromquist & K. Monkman (Eds.), *Globalization and education: Integration and contestation across cultures* (pp. 275–297). Lanham, MD: Rowman & Littlefield.

Butler, J., Laclau, E., & Žižek, S. (2000). *Contingency, hegemony, universality*. London: Verso.

Chomsky, N., & Dieterich, H. (1995). *La sociedad global*. México: Joaquín Mortiz.

Critchley, S., & Marchart, O. (2004). *Laclau: A critical reader*. London: Routledge.

De Alba, A. (1989). Postmodernidad y Educación. Implicaciones epistémicas y conceptuales en los discursos educativos. In A. De Alba (Ed.), *Educación y postmodernidad* (pp. 129–175). México: CESU/UNAM y M.A. Porrua.

Deleuze, G., & Guattari, F. (2004). *A thousand plateaus*. London: Continuum.

Dewey, J. (1916). *Democracy and education*. New York: Macmillan.

Dieterich, H. (Ed.) (1997). *Globalización, exclusión y democracia en América latina*. México: Joaquín Mortiz.

Foucault, M. (1985). *The history of sexuality, Vol. 2: The use of pleasure*. New York: Harvester.

Freire, P. (1970). *Pedagogy of the oppressed*. New York: Continuum.

Fürntratt-Kloep, E. (1997). El derrumbe del "socialismo real existente" y la "globalización" como resultados de la "Guerra Fría." In H. Dieterich (Ed.), *Globalización, exclusión y democracia en América Latina* (pp. 27–49). México: Joaquín Mortiz.

García Canclini, N. (Ed.) (1996). *Culturas en globalización*. Caracas: CNCA, CLACSO y Ed. Nueva Sociedad.

Giddens, A. (1990). *The consequences of modernity*. Cambridge: Polity Press.

Gilpin, R. (1987). *The political economy of international relations*. Princeton: Princeton University Press.

Giroux, H. (1991). Democracy and the discourse of cultural difference: Towards a politics of border pedagogy. *British Journal of Sociology of Education, 12*(84), 501–519.

Gramsci, A. (1971). *Selections from the prison notebooks of Antonio Gramsci*. Q. Hoare & G. Nowell-Smith (Eds.). London: Lawrence & Wishart.

Gramsci, A. (1981). *La Alternativa Pedagógica*. Barcelona: Fontamara.

Habermas, J. (1987). *The philosophical discourse of modernity*. Cambridge: Polity Press.

Habermas, J., & McCarthy, T. (1981). *Theory of communicative action*, Vols. 1–2. Boston: Beacon Press.

Hall, S. (1991). The local and the global: Globalization and ethnicity. In A. King (Ed.), *Culture, globalization and the world system* (pp. 19–30). London: Macmillan.

Hall, S. (1996). Who needs identity? In S. Hall & P. Du Gay (Eds.), *Questions of cultural identity* (pp. 1–17). London: Sage.

Harvey, D. (1989). *The condition of postmodernity*. Oxford: Basil Blackwell.

Heidegger, M. (1978). *Basic writings from* Being and Time *(1927) to* The Task of Thinking *(1964)*. London: Routledge and Kegan Paul.

Heron, T. (2008). Globalization, neoliberalism and the exercise of human agency. *International Journal of Politics, Culture, and Society, 20*(1–4), 85–101.

Hinkelammert, F. (1997). América Latina y la globalización de los mercados. In H. Dieterich (Ed.), *Globalización, exclusión y democracia en América Latina* (pp. 113–131). México: Joaquín Mortiz.

Hirst, P., & Thompson, G. (1996). *Globalization in question: The international economy and the possibilities of governance.* Cambridge: Polity Press.

Howarth, D. (2000). Genealogy, power/knowledge and problematization. In Howarth, *Discourse* (pp. 67–84). London: Open University Press.

Ianni, O. (1996). *Teorías de la globalización.* México: Siglo XXI.

Kawame, A.A., & Gates, H.L. (1997). *The dictionary of global culture.* New York: Alfred A. Knopf.

Lacan, J. (1960). *Le séminaire, livre VII: Le transfert.* Paris: Le Seuil.

Laclau, E. (1988). Politics and the limits of modernity. In A. Ross (Ed.), *Universal abandon?* (pp. 63–82). Minneapolis: University of Minnesota Press.

Laclau, E. (1990). *New reflections on the revolutions of our times.* London: Verso.

Laclau, E. (1996). *Emancipation(s).* London: Verso.

Laclau, E., & Mouffe, C. (1985). *Hegemony and socialist strategy.* London: Verso.

Laclau, E., & Zac, L. (1994). Minding the gap: The subject of politics. In E. Laclau (Ed.), *The making of political identities* (pp. 11–39). London: Verso.

López-Nájera, I. (2009). *La calidad educativa entre lo global y lo local. El peregrinaje de un significante de plenitud.* MSc thesis, Centro de Investigación y de Estudios Avanzados, México.

McDowell, C. (1996). *Understanding impoverishment: The consequences of development-induced displacement.* Providence, RI: Berghahn.

McLaren, P., & Gutiérrez, K. (1997). Global politics and local antagonisms. In P. McLaren (Ed.), *Revolutionary multiculturalism: Pedagogies of dissent for the new millennium* (pp. 192–222). Boulder, CO: Westview Press.

McLaren, P., & Lankshear, C. (1994). *Politics of liberation: Paths from Freire.* London: Routledge.

McLuhan, C., & Powers, B.R. (1989). *The global village.* Oxford: Oxford University Press.

Nuñez, V. (1999). *Pedagogía social: Cartas para navegar en el nuevo milenio.* Buenos Aires: Santillana.

Perlmutter, H.V. (1991). On the rocky road to the first global civilization. *Human Relations 44*(9), 897–1010.

Petras, J. (2003). El imperio y los trabajadores: EU y América Latina. *Eseconomía, 3*, 5–17.

Popkewitz, T. (2000). Reform as the social administration of the child: Globalization of knowledge and power. In N. Burbules & C. Torres (Eds.), *Globalization and educational policy* (pp. 157–186). New York: Routledge.

Robertson, R. (1990). Mapping the global condition. In M. Featherstone (Ed.), (1990) *Global culture* (pp. 15–30). London: Sage.

Rorty, R. (1982). *Consequences of pragmatism.* Minneapolis: University of Minnesota Press.

Rorty, R. (1989). *Contingency, irony and solidarity.* Cambridge: Cambridge University Press.

Rosenau, J.N. (1990). *The study of global interdependence.* London: Frances Pinter.

Sassen, S. (1998). *Globalization and its discontents.* New York: The New Press.

Schriewer, J. (1996). Sistema mundial y redes de interrelación. La internacionalización de la educación y el papel de la educación comparada. In M. Pereyra et al. (Eds.), *Globalización y descentralización de los sistemas educativos* (pp. 17–58). Barcelona: Pomares-Corredor.

Stromquist, N., & Monkman, K. (Eds.) (2000). *Globalization and education: Integration and contestation across cultures.* Lanham, MD: Rowman & Littlefield.

United Nations Development Programme (1995). *People: From impoverishment to empowerment.* New York: New York University Press.

Wallerstein, I. (1991). *The lessons of the 1980s in geopolitics and geoculture*. Cambridge: Cambridge University Press.

Wilson, J. (2008). The new phase of the Plan Puebla Panama in Chiapas. *Bulletins of CIEPAC*, no. 562, 1–14.

Wittgenstein, L. (1963). *Philosophical investigations*. Oxford: Basil Blackwell.

Žižek, S. (1989). *The sublime object of ideology*. London: Verso.

Žižek, S. (2003). *Organs without bodies: Deleuze and consequences*. London: Routledge.

Education and the Production of Global Imaginaries: A Reflection on Teachers' Visual Culture

INÉS DUSSEL

Introduction

If there is a field in which the talk on globalization is strong, it is media studies. Since the early 1990s, many theorists have been arguing that the production of visual subjects is taking place through globally-owned and globally-broadcast media (Maharaj, 1994), and that the spread of "landscapes of images" generated by these global electronic media is providing the world population with "repertoires of images, narratives, and ethnoscapes"[1] that constitute a new "imagined community" which is replacing the declining national imaginaries (Appadurai, 1996, p. 35).

This movement has not ceased to increase at an appalling pace, due to the interface of digital culture and globalization (Mirzoeff, 2005, p. 2). Global imaginaries are now produced through instant messaging, social networking sites, and global TV channels that makes us all viewers of the same chains of images and sounds. The visual has come to dominate the scene of representation, in times where fluidity and flexibility are greatly valued. Nicholas Mirzoeff argues that we are primarily visual subjects, that is, people defined as agents of sight (regardless of our capacity to see) and as the objects of certain discourses of visuality (p. 3). In the same line, Arjun Appadurai, whose ideas on the globalization of culture are still inspiring new thoughts, stresses the role that imagination has in the production of a globalized world. "Because of the sheer multiplicity of the forms in which they appear (cinema, television, computers, and telephones) and because of the rapid way in which they move through daily life routines, electronic media provide resources for self-imagining as an everyday social project" (Appadurai, 1996, p. 4). We are living in a time of hybrid globalization, where we all communicate in "the new international visual Esperanto" (Mirzoeff, 2005, p. 2). The global visual imaginary becomes a central framework for making sense of the world, for attributing actions, for eliciting feelings of commitment or detachment.

This transformation has been made possible by a technological and cultural leap of great proportions. Gilles Lipovetsky, known for his sharp best-selling essays on culture, and Jean Serroy use the metaphor of "the global screen" to define what is new in our contemporary experience: "Videoscreens, miniaturized screens, graphic screens, nomadic screens, tactile screens: the new century is the century of the omnipresent, multi-form, planetary, multimedia screen" (Lipovetsky & Serroy, 2009, p. 10). They describe a "tremendous cultural mutation" that is placing screens everywhere and at any time: in shops and airports, in restaurants and cars, in subways and planes, in banks and in the streets. Their gloomy perspective makes them foresee that "the day may come in which whatever is not available on a screen, will not bear interest nor existence for many individuals; almost everything will be searched for and delivered on a screen. To be on a screen, or not to be" (p. 314).

In all this talk on global imaginaries and the predominance of the visual, the young generation seems to be the one in which this trend has the higher impact. Sociologist Ulrich Beck describes a "global genera-tion," made of a constellation or patchwork of different experiences of inclusion and exclusion, which is being shaped by global media (Beck & Beck-Gernsheim, 2009). Besides the literature on the "digital natives" (Prensky, 2001), generally celebratory of what young people are doing with global electronic media, there is another line of research that is trying to understand the multiple ways in which social networking sites, virtual worlds, multifunctional mobile phones, blogs and wikis are actu-ally producing capabilities and sensibilities (Knobel & Lankshear, 2008; Vasudevan & Campano, 2009) and the extent to which they are lined with more traditional forms of social grouping—nations, classes, eth-nic divisions, gender affiliations—or are producing new identities (Buckingham, 2007; Lundby, 2008; Tobin, 2004). But it should be noted that, in most educational literature, especially from continental Europe and Latin America, young people are seen as the "new barbarians" who endorse the mutation without hesitation (Baricco, 2008). What nobody denies is that global media are producing considerable effects on young people.

Less attention has been paid to teachers' relationship to contem-porary visual culture, and specifically about their own visual culture. In this chapter, I would like to focus on how they relate to these global visual discourses, in order to discuss their participation in the production of visual imaginaries. I will confront the argument that posits that teachers are totally opposed to the "mediatized children and youth," and completely alien to the language and imaginaries of electronic global media (Beltrán, 2009; Cabello, 2006). In the Latin American education field, this has meant that a certain moral superiority is built around teachers and school culture, which are seen as neutral or non-participant in the supposedly evil trends of omnipresent screens. Teachers seem to endorse these moral discourses which assume that they are the first line of the trench for the protection of culture against the barbarians, and feel uplifted in the midst of what they feel is a decline in their economic power and cultural capital (Dussel, Brito, & Núñez, 2007).

The discussion of the chapter will be organized around the results of a visual exercise performed during 2005–2007 in the context of courses on images and pedagogy,[2] attended by teachers and education students from different countries in Latin America. The exercise asked the participants to select one powerful image in culture. This deliberately ambivalent assignment was intended to elicit the "ideoscapes" and "mediascapes" (Appadurai, 1996, p. 353)[3] that teachers and education students value and embrace. I will argue that the "powerful images" selected by teachers give us many hints about the relationship between education and the production of global visual subjects. My point will be that, far from being totally alien or neutral, education, and educators in particular, have played a significant role in the production of visualities (or ways of seeing), and of visibilities (or maps and landscapes of the visible and the invisible). Since the late nineteenth century and early twentieth, schools and teachers have been crucial in the transformation of modern scopic regimes and in the production of particular kinds of visualities and visual imaginaries (what will later be described as "visual technologies of truth"). Is it possible that this longstanding participation in the production of the spectator and of the visible has come to an end with global electronic media? The visual discourse articulated by teachers in their selection of "powerful images" shows many interconnections and overlaps that should make us more cautious about their alleged exclusion of contemporary visual culture.

My focus will be on teachers' visual culture. When I use this term, I refer less to their images of teaching, of themselves, or of school space—such as the ones that have been studied by Fischman (2000) or Weber (1995)—than about their participation in a broader visual culture that makes them articulate a visual discourse about the world, about schooling and childhood, and about their own role in the discourse. In that respect, I am interested in analyzing the kinds of images that organize their perceptions of the world; the type of relationship they establish with them; and the senses of space and time that shape its configurations.

Also, I would like to make it clear that, following W.T.J. Mitchell, I will consider *visual culture* as a set of hypotheses "that need to be tested—for example, that vision is (as we say) a cultural construction, that it is learned and cultivated, not simply given by nature; that there-fore it might have a history related in some yet to be determined way to the history of arts, technologies, media, and the social practices of display and spectatorship; and (finally) that it is deeply involved with human societies, with the ethics and politics, aesthetics and epistemol-ogy of seeing and being seen" (Mitchell, 2002, p. 166). Thus, visual culture is not simply a repertoire of images but a set of visual dis-courses that position ourselves and others, and that are embedded in social practices, deeply tied to the institutions that give us the "rights to look."[4] My framework is mainly based on visual studies (Mirzoeff, 1999; Schwartz and Przyblyski, 2004), a cross-disciplinary field that introduces a reflection on visual practices and subjectivities. Instead of treating images as iconographic symbols, this field analyzes them as events, that is, as the effects of a network in which subjects operate and which in turn conditions their freedom of action (Mirzoeff, 2005, p. 11).

Teachers' Visual Culture and the Visual Culture of Schools: A Historical Overview

Why study teachers' visual culture? As John Prosser (2007) and many others have argued, schools and teaching can be productively read as visual texts and practices. But my concern in this chapter is slightly different. I would like to interrogate the relationship between teachers and visual culture, and not consider them as visual texts themselves.

Teachers and schools are often seen as dull objects, which lack the glamour and the charm of the "society of the spectacle" (Debord, 1995). They are generally considered as the opposite of contemporary visual culture. And, if one thinks of their relationship to electronic media, teachers—at least in Argentina—are probably in the lower quarter among educated professionals in terms of their access to and use of new technological devices.[5] Yet, their role in creating a common culture is not minor at all, and I would like to suggest that we need much more research to understand the ways in which schools and electronic media culture coexist and interact in the shaping of the dispositions and sen-sibilities of the new generation. Despite all the claims about the decline of schools as sites for significant learning,[6] schools are still the largest public institutions that promote some kind of common sense defined by a lettered culture. The visual education of the public is done by many agencies, and schools are not minor players in that field.

Moreover, schools, and teachers in particular, have been key in the transformation of modern scopic regimes (cf. Brea, 2007). Jonathan Crary has pointed to the epistemological and political changes that occurred in the eighteenth and nineteenth centuries that reorganized the positions of the observer and the observed, the relations between knowledge and power, the devices and institutional discourses that were implied (Crary, 1995). These changes, also examined by Bruno Latour (1994), opened up the possibility of a public sphere as an open and homogeneous social space in which one can move around and convey "without deformation" observations done at any point, from an exterior point of view, "objectively" (quoted by Boltanski, 1999, p. 29).

Far from being external or opposed to this culture of spectacle, schools were active participants in their shaping. Modern pedagogy, as represented by Pestalozzi and others, stressed the value of the education of perception and of the senses in terms of this "objective distance." In the visual education that was promoted, seeing was equated with knowing and believing. There was neither mediation nor opaqueness in the act of seeing; differences were thought of as abnormalities and pathological deviations. Not less important was the participation of schools in the organization of a social subject, the modern spectator, who was supposed to have at the same time impartiality (detachment, a distance between observation and action, mediated by reflection), and commitment, that is, an affective, sentimental or emotional investment needed to arouse political commitment in the public sphere (Boltanski, 1999, p. 33). "What particularly holds our attention in the character of the spectator is, on the one hand, the possibility of seeing everything; that is of a totalizing perspective of a gaze which has no single point of view or which passes through every possible point of view; and, on the other, the possibility of seeing without being seen" (p. 24). Adam Smith is a crucial figure here, as he analyzed how to reconstruct morality, and a morally acceptable politics, around the double figure of an unfortunate and an impartial spectator who observes him at a distance. The epistemological emergence of "aperspectival objectivity" and the scientific reason is interdependent with the political emergence of a public sphere based on a politics of pity that reconstructed social bonds on the premises of suffering and commiseration (Arendt, 1990). The distant look of the spectator, moved but yet detached, is crucial in this. What I would like to stress is that this looking from a distance implied a pedagogical process.

Pedagogy took many visual forms: object lessons, display cupboards in classrooms, school museums, charts and paintings in walls, blackboards, statues and school furniture and architecture, illustrated textbooks, organized field trips, school exhibitions, even dress codes and régimes of appearances (Dussel, 2001) were all ways of educating the ways in which students should look and the meanings they should construct around these visual experiences (Lawn & Grosvenor, 2005). Seeing was as important as the construction of meaning around what was seen. According to González Stephan and Andermann (2006), the "showing" was as important as the "telling": these visual pedagogical devices had everything to do with the emergence of "visual technologies of truth" that sought, at the level of a "generalized visual equivalence," to stabilize the forms and contents of the representation of the world (p. 9). These visual technologies of truth were also intended to produce particular bodily and aesthetic dispositions of the "educated subject," defined, simultaneously, as a national subject. Space (nation-state, in a hierarchical "concert of nations") and time (as the logical evolution of civilization) were considered stable, definite frames for pedagogy and for social action.

In recent times, modern spectatorship has been deeply transformed. The invention of technical means to preserve the memory of events, namely photography and later cinema, has implied a profound change in the relationship we establish with the past, with others, and with the world. As Susan Buck-Morss (2004) puts it, the twentieth century "distinguishes itself from all previous centuries because it has left a photographic trace. What is seen only once and recorded, can be perceived any time and by every one. History becomes the shared singularity of an event" (p. 23). But patterns of circulation have also changed. "Images circle the globe today in de-centered patterns that allow unprecedented access, sliding almost without friction past language barriers and national frontiers" (p. 2). Of course, they are produced in global relations that are "wildly unequal in regard to production capacities and distributive effects" (p. 2).

Another important transformation is the ruptures in these "visual technologies of truth" that were dominant until some decades ago. Angel Quintana (2003) has pointed to the emergence of a suspicious spectator, even cynical, who, after having been "educated" by many media scams, positions himself or herself in a locus of disbelief and skepticism towards media images. The digitalization of images, and the expansion of the possibilities of technically altering them, have spread this state of disbelief and cynicism. The paradox of contemporary visual régimes is that, despite this generalized suspicion at a rational level, there is an increasing value put on the emotions elicited by visual narratives. The régime of discourses has ceased to be organized by the idea of "truth" and is being rearticulated around the idea of "authen-ticity." The "visual technologies of truth" might be moving towards a more emotional ground, based on sensation and shock (Jaguaribe, 2007; Quintana, 2009).

Georges Didi-Huberman, in a beautiful essay on the nature of images and their "burning" (ephemeral, hot) quality, says that "never, it seems, has the image been imposed with such a force as in our aesthetic, technical, political, historical, daily universe. Never before has it shown such harsh truths; yet never it has lied to us so much, soliciting our trust; never it has proliferated so much, and never has it suffered as much censorship and destruction" (Didi-Huberman, 2006a, p. 13). The pre-dominance of images might, paradoxically, be having an effect of pro-ducing a "wounded imagination": "By giving us *too much* by the multiplication of images, we are incited to disbelieve in *anything* that we see, and finally to avoid looking at anything but what we have in front of our eyes" (p. 42). These two operations of excess and subtraction, the *too much* and the *nothing left*, are central for thinking about our contem-porary visual culture, about the blurred boundaries between the visible and the invisible.

An Exercise on Teachers' Visual Culture: Space, Time, and the Reconfiguration of Scopic Régimes

I would like now to move to the reflections on the visual exercise presented in the first part of this chapter. In a course on images and pedagogy with teachers from different Latin American countries, the participants were asked to choose a "powerful image," that is, an image that stands as significant in culture. Through an intentionally broad formula, the strategy intended to know which kind of visual materials and events were cited, and which definition of culture was at stake.[7] The notion of "powerful images" was taken from visual studies literature, defined as a perdurable image, a lasting visual composition. In the courses, there were some discussions on the semiotics of images and the history of art, and examples such as a series of foreshortened figures such as Rembrandt's *The Anatomy Lesson* to a picture of Che Guevara's death to recent recreations in paintings and installations were provided. The power of religious images was discussed, as well as the iconography of school textbooks.

The "powerful images" selected by the teachers and student teachers were, however, of a totally different quality. There were more than 170 images selected, and a gallery was organized to discuss the collection's meaning as a visual discourse on the world and on culture. Among the world-known pictures, there was the photo of the Biafra child dying of starvation taken in the late 1960s, Kevin Carter's Pulitzer Award picture of a Sudanese girl, and Nick Ut's picture a young girl escaping her village after a napalm attack (taken in 1972). Also, there were many pictures on war in the Middle East, pictures of 9/11 and the destruction of the Twin Towers, of Latin American children amidst garbage dumps, photos of political events of the 1970s, and some Benetton-like images of "living together" and "accepting difference" (white and black kids). Only two paintings were chosen as powerful images: Délacroix's *Liberty Leading the People* (1830), and a piece of Diego Rivera's mural *The Dictatorship* (1936). Most of the subjects that appear in the pictures are children, generally portrayed in the middle of ruins, war, or famine. There were six pictures of a woman holding a child, which refer back to the religious figure of the Madonna: Mother Theresa of Calcutta, Amina Lawal, an Albanian refugee, an Afghan woman, an Ashaninka (Peruvian ethnic group) woman in a refugee camp, and Shakira in the first volume of her "Oral Fixation."

As a Spanish film critic has said, "any image that is born as a proof of the world, ends up being a discourse on the world" (Quintana, 2003, p. 23). The series of images can be analyzed as a visual discourse that, in fact, has few dissonances and transpires a gloomy, sad atmosphere. As Paul Virilio says, there has been a movement from the "standardization of public opinion" to the "synchronization of public emotion" (Virilio, 2005, p. 29). The public emotion that Latin American educators seem to share is the feeling of defeat and tragedy: children in the ruins, wars, disappeared people, violence, and motherly love amid exile or social disintegration.

But probably its most striking feature is the absolute predominance of photojournalism in the type of images selected. The French cultural historian Françoise Choay has said that "photography is a form of monument adapted to the individualism of our era" (Choay, 2007, p. 16). Photojournalism provides the monuments of contemporary memory, and memory in return archives photos as its privileged material (Figure 1).

FIGURE 1
A Woman Shows the Picture of a Disappeared Relative in Ayacucho,
Perú, 1984
(Picture taken by Vera Lentz)

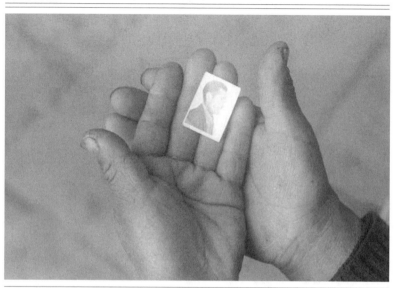

   The topics and icons that teachers use to speak this visual discourse
are provided by the visual Esperanto of global TV and media, which
constructs the self as a visual subject who can hardly imagine other ways
of representing the world than through those visual languages provided
by them. The "community of sentiment" does not work only at the level
of the nation-state, but promotes collective experiences of the mass
media (Appadurai, 1996, p. 8). One speaks of hunger and a Biafra boy is
envisaged, no matter how many closer examples could be found around
the corner of any street in Buenos Aires, Lima, or Bogotá. There is, as
Griselda Pollock (2008) has recently noted, a particular place held by
"Africa" in Western imagination that is still actively colonialist. Also,
Jacques Rancière has said in reference to similar images that "It is not
that we have seen too many suffering bodies, but that we see too many
bodies without a name, too many bodies that do not look us back, of
which we speak without offering them the possibility to speak back to
us" (Rancière, 2008b, p. 77). The African bodies are surfaces in which
this victimization continues to be constructed without giving them
names, histories, or a political quality. And this mode of enunciation

slides easily into Latin American images, with children portrayed as the utmost representatives of victims but also of hope and faith.

Most of the pictures are colored photographs, which acknowledge the shift in photojournalism from black and white to color in the last few decades, giving it more attractiveness and reality effect (Rosler, 2007). Also, most of the pictures are not assigned to a particular author. There are some exceptions, as in the photographs of Sebastiao Salgado[8] or the famous Kevin Carter picture of the Sudanese girl. In over 170 images, only two pictures were taken and posted by the participants, but only one of them (that portrays "the first day of school of my child") is strictly personal. At any rate, their exceptional quality says a lot about the primary sources and genres that this visual discourse uses in its modulations.

Photojournalism is consistent with the predominance of a hyperreal aesthetics that works as a mimesis of the reality produced by sensation-alist media (Jaguaribe, 2007). This hyperreal visual discourse seeks to produce a "shock of the real" and to elicit an effect of cathartic fright or horror in the viewer. The impact of the shock happens from the rep-resentation of something that is not necessarily extraordinary (there might be "daily occurrences of metropolitan life such as rapes, crimes, murders, struggles, erotic contacts"), but that is intensified and exacer-bated, in order to provoke a strong emotional resonance (p. 100).

This sensationalist aesthetics has many resemblances with W.T.J. Mitchell's analysis of the régime of images of the "war on terror" between 2001 and 2004—including Abu Ghraib's infamous pictures. "They are not images *of* trauma, but images designed to traumatise the viewer, especially those who identify with the victim. When propagated by digital reproduction and global circulation they produce a kind of effect quite different from the modern(ist) 'shock,' which had its thera-peutic, defamiliarising aspect. There is nothing like 'shock therapy' in the realm of trauma. These images are designed to overwhelm the viewer's defences, and that is why many of the news services that carried them on 1 April 2004 elected to *blur* them, rendering their contents almost unreadable" (Mitchell, 2008, p. 195).[9] Overwhelming emotion is one of the most frequent descriptors of the feelings that the gallery of powerful images arouses in the viewer (Figure 2).[10]

Another line of interpretation of this series of images has to do with the relationship to time and space that they produce. Not surprisingly, given that most images are photographs from the recent past, there is a predominance of the present, of the direct, of recent history which is hardly perceived as "history" in traditional terms and which appears, it

FIGURE 2
DEAD GIRL IN IRAQ
(Uncredited photographer)

could be said, as a "continuous present" punctuated by tragedies and social suffering. The perception of history seems to be flat—probably related to the sources of the images, more concerned with the direct impact than with complex relationships of causes and effects. As Martha Rosler says, the public "is increasingly used to TV and to the narrations of the real refracted through the distorted prism of sensationalism" (Rosler, 2007, p. 250). Time gets flattened; wars and tragedies become all the same, and they only differ in the intensity of sensations that they produce on our selves.

There is a paradox in these images, which purport to defy time and yet are ephemeral in their links to current events. It should be noticed that images always bring to us an anachronic time, a time-other, the presence of an absence that startles us before the unavoidable loss of the past (Didi-Huberman, 2006b). However, in this visual discourse, this anachronism is reduced to a visual cliché that actually revivifies and actualizes the past in a way that makes it no longer past. I will later argue that these images are also, at the same time, not exactly coeval to our time: the distance and the stereotyping prevent them to be part of our daily universe. It is probably a "no-time," a different kind of temporality, which does not rely on a sequential and chronological notion of time but which does not grant a place in the present either. Which kind of temporality does the "direct take" of TV and the Internet promote? Is it the same kind of present that was thought of when notions of lineal relationships between past-present-future were stable and clear? It is possible to suspect that it is not.

Regarding notions of space, there is the question of the locality of the images, and of the viewer. There is a remarkable spatial fluidity: the series refers to Albania, Iraq, Africa, as well as South America, in a selection that shows complex negotiations over the locality and perspective of the images. Is it a cosmopolitan humanism or is it something else? It seems that this spatial fluidity might be also part of the conflation of borders and contexts in global TV and media: it switches from one location to the other, and what the viewer finds in common is a journalist with a microphone denouncing something terrible that has happened, is happening, or is about to happen. Note, again, that in this set of actions the difference of verbal times becomes almost irrelevant.

The Spectacle of Suffering and the Sentimentalism of Denunciation

To understand further the locality of the images and of the viewer, it might be useful to understand them as part of a "spectacle of suffering," a mode of relating to others that puts in the first place a politics of pity that focuses on looking at other people's miseries, inaugurated by the French Revolution (Arendt, 1990). Arendt opposed a politics of pity (of commiserating with the poor, and doing it from a distant and external point of view, a spectator's point of view, which turns the unfortunate into a *victim*) to a politics of justice, which would focus on a logic of equivalence and rights. While I will not follow her lead, I believe it is important to keep this distinction in mind.

The global visual Esperanto spoken by teachers speaks about victims, people who can be looked at from a distance, and for whom one should feel compassionate and/or pitiful. The topics are well-known: war, famine, drought, immigration, persecution, solitude. Images are quite predictable, as the viewer has seen them a thousand or more times. In the series, there were almost no "happy" images. This might have several explanations, one of which redirects to the course itself and its own bias on a "progressive agenda" for educational change, which probably takes the viewer in the line of denouncing inequalities and political tragedies. But there might be an association with the melodramatic narratives that are prevalent in Latin American popular culture, from which teachers are not excluded. Carlos Monsiváis, a well-known cultural critic from Mexico, says that "in the Latin American tradition, the road to politics runs through melodrama." Melodrama is a "structure of understanding," a "unifying device for experience," and comes from the verbal blocks of nineteenth-century novels, the filmic melodrama, or TV's *telenovelas* (Monsiváis, 2006, p. 45). Contrary to Hollywood's happy ending movies where the cowboy saves the girl, it is very likely that in Latin American melodramas the girl dies right before her hero comes to her rescue (Figure 3).

Related to the gloomy atmosphere of the series, it is interesting to ask which kind of community is being shaped if we can only relate to others as sufferers, or encounter with others in their suffering. Mexican anthropologist Rossana Reguillo points to the role fear has in contemporary society, and the limits it poses for a more democratic organization of community life (Reguillo, 2005). There seems to be a correlation between these shocking and tragic images and the culture of fear, media saturation, and urban uncertainty (Jaguaribe, 2007, p. 110).

There is, however, an important point in the modern spectacle of suffering that should not be underestimated. Luc Boltanski remarks that the position of the spectator still calls us to take up sides: it is not acceptable for the modern ethical subject, at least not until recently, to say "that's how it is and I can't do anything about it." We (the modern ethical subject) should do something about it, at least report it, or donate money to charity. As Adam Smith noted, the public sphere is not just a space of reasonable debate, but it is also constituted by causes that mobilize effects. And "nothing promotes the formation of a cause more than the spectacle of suffering" (Boltanski, 1999, p. 30). These images advance a noble cause, and in that vein, they remain fully inscribed within the ethical domain of the modern subject.

The preferred topic to react to this cause, or to struggle for this cause, is denunciation. Most of the images that teachers picked can be

FIGURE 3
GIRL IN A GARBAGE DUMP, ARGENTINA
(Uncredited photographer)

put into this category: they are images for us to be indignant, angry, moved, shocked. When one becomes indignant with suffering, one denounces it. Denunciation can take the form of a single accusation (the "affair," like the Dreyfus affair, denounced in Zola's *J'Accuse*), or can take the form of a social revolt or a collective action. In both cases, the personal gets involved (indignation cannot be impersonal). Also, the discourses of science produce yet another kind of denunciation that establishes distance and detachment as the starting point; but these are not the preferred modes of denunciation taken by global TV and media, which fight for the implication of audiences and for getting more "real" and "closer" to the public (Quintana, 2003).

Denunciation has been critiqued for implying a comfortable position, a sort of inaction that makes the denouncer complicit with the suffering he or she is denouncing. It has also been said that the denouncer rejoices in the passion for denunciation, and does little for those who suffer. But what interests me in terms of the visual culture and the visualities it produces is that denunciation does not question the place of the spectator. The images in the teachers' powerful images are stereotypical images of children who suffer, mothers who suffer, people who suffer. *They* are the unhappy ones. It is up to *us*, teachers, pastoral missionaries (Popkewitz, 1998), to redeem their suffering through speaking it loudly. There is no logic of equivalence in this relation. Also, as Susan Sontag warned in one of her last essays, "no *we* should be taken for granted" when looking at other people's pain (Sontag, 2003, p. 23) (Figure 4).

Teachers also speak about suffering in other terms, those of sentimentalism. Boltanski, in the work on which I'm grounding these reflections, thinks of denunciation and sentimentalism as opposite and contradictory topics, but both seem to be present in the visual discourses that the teachers articulated, that, again, rely heavily

FIGURE 4

ASHANINKA WOMEN, FREED FROM A SHINING PATH CAMP BY THE MILITARY,
WAITING TO BE FED BY THE LOCAL GOVERNMENT, CUTIVIRENI, PERÚ, 1991
(Picture taken by Alejandro Balaguer)

on contemporary forms of TV narration. "In a topic of sentiment, the relation of spectator and unfortunate is real, authentic and thereby touching, when it is heart to heart, going from interiority to interiority" (Boltanski, 1999, p.81). In many photos, this sentimentalism takes the form of a melodramatic epic: the idea of surviving, of struggling, of love against tragedy, of mothers and children standing up against oppression.

The locality of the viewer as a distant spectator of several tragedies, also, becomes important. One can compare this series of images to Mirzoeff's (2005) reflections in his book *Watching Babylon*, where he describes watching the spectacle of the Iraq war from a gym on Long Island. In that event, the viewer puts the images of bombings and killings alongside SUVs, extended houses, and the no-place experiences of shopping at Wal-Mart and driving on highways. In that kind of visuality, the war seems one more episode of the spectacle of exercising imperial power: towards nature and landscape, towards material goods, towards foreign countries. The pleasure of seeing is tied, as in colonialism, to the pleasure of mastering. However, teachers in Latin America appear to be taking sides with the suffering, the unfortunate. There is a different epic involved in this set of images; probably sadder, more nostalgic, definitely not victorious. The images are the same, but the locality of the viewing makes a great difference to understanding the narratives in which they are inscribed.

To think about locality does not mean to reduce the image or the event of watching to a particular geographical context—on the contrary. Susan Buck-Morss says that "the force of the image occurs when it is dislodged from context. . . . Images are used to think. . . . They are not a piece of land. They are a mediating term between things and thoughts, between the mental and the non-mental. They allow the connection. To drag-and-click an image is to appropriate it, not as someone else's product, but as an object of one's own sensory experience" (Buck-Morss, 2004, p. 20).

That is why, she says, "The complaint that images are out of context (cultural context, artistic intention, previous contexts of any sort) is not valid. To struggle to bind them again to their source is not only impossible (as it actually produces a new meaning); it is to miss what is powerful about them, their capacity to generate meaning, and not merely to transmit it" (Buck-Morss, 2004, p. 23). These powerful images are such because they have been appropriated in different narratives, yet they still construct a discourse about the world that needs to be interrogated.

Teachers as Visual Subjects: Educational Imaginaries and the
Production of the Visible

There is another sense in which the locality of the viewer is important, and is related to the fact that these particular viewers are educators
(be it teachers or student teachers). It is not by chance that childhood
appears so significantly in these images. What is very telling is that
childhood is presented almost always surrounded by ruins. A wrecked
childhood, a childhood at risk of (or fully caught into) famine, war,
drought, exploitation, in a series that shows school as the repository for
hope. The prevalence of stereotypical images is appalling, and speaks
the extent to which the visual culture of teachers is almost exclusively
shaped by global media (and past pedagogies). As Spanish philosopher
Jorge Larrosa says, "real childhood might have been replaced by a series
of images about childhood. We would not relate to children, but to
representations about children, stereotypes about children, images
about children" (Larrosa, 2006, p. 134).

That images of schooling appears as the fountain of hope is not
surprising, given the redemptive ethos of teaching since the nineteenth
century (Popkewitz, 1998). But the other images that refer to "hope"
come directly from global advertising and include Benetton's multicul-
turalist icons of the black and white kids smiling at each other. This
representation of difference has been called "multicultural managerial-
ism" (Maharaj, 2002), as it fixes it into static components of cultural
essences and stereotypes.

Also, teachers are part of a school culture that values both sentimentalism and denunciation. In the visual discourse they articulate, one can
see the teachers' ethos that privileges the commitment to children and
to "the unhappy ones" (*les malheureux*), but at the same time feels that
the teacher's task in the world is to redeem others from their miseries.
The series of Madonnas appear to foster the notion of teachers as a
mother-like figure that care for children (Fischman, 2000). In that
respect, teachers' images also refer to the gendered culture of redemption that characterizes modern schooling. Children and mothers appear
repeatedly as part of a spectacle of suffering that combines the melodrama of media with the educational goal of salvation. Children can be
saved by mothers, or by their first-kin relatives, female teachers
(Figure 5).

In that series, there is an ironic twist (one of two in the larger
series) on the "true colors of Benetton": those of capitalism. As Erica
McWilliam (2002) has argued, teachers suffer from some kind of

FIGURE 5
THE TRUE COLORS OF BENETTON

"irony-deficiency", which is evident in the images that have been selected. The other ironic picture is the CD cover of Shakira. Also, it should be noted that Shakira and Benetton are the two only explicit pop-advertising icons that appear in this series. Probably, if the same question was posed to young people, the number of advertising images, and of images of their own production, would be much more significant than in the educators' selections.

Concluding Remarks

Throughout the chapter, I have intended to discuss the relationships between globalization and education through a particular lens: teachers' relation to contemporary visual culture. I have attempted to show that their visual culture is primarily shaped by global media, and that these media provide the material and the "tone" for the articulation of a visual discourse on the world. Globalization, then, has to be thought of also as a visual discourse that allows people to make sense of the world, to attribute actions, and configure sentiments and emotions.

The other point I have made is that schools and teachers are not alien to the world of new media, but are actively shaped by it. The visual discourse that educators articulate in this series of images shows particular notions of space and time and a particular sensibility (based on the sensationalist "shock of the real"). This sensibility redefines the modern ethical subject who looks from a distance in new terms, those of the hyperreal aesthetics of global media. Still, teachers are positioning themselves as distant viewers; and, despite all the talk of the interactive media consumer, it is very likely that schools are participating in the construction of a distant spectatorship for the new generation.

My third point is that globalization does not erase localities, but rather reconfigures them in new ways, as they are interwoven with new materials. When I speak of localities, I do not refer to a territorial space but rather to a constellation of practices that translate or modulate global discourses in peculiar forms. Latin American teachers' visual discourse has a spatial fluidity that is remarkable: they refer to European, African, Middle Eastern or South Asian events and say that they have impacted them profoundly. And they do it using the topics and the icons popularized by global media, overwhelmingly produced in the northern countries. Yet they modulate this discourse within a very peculiar narrative: sad, melodramatic, defeated, that is related both to their geopolitical location and to their own ethos as teachers (their views on children are remarkable in that respect). It is interesting to note this disjuncture between the global and the local (Appadurai, 1996).

Lastly, I would like to point out that my intention with this reflection on the powerful images selected by teachers has not been to censor their intentions or to dismiss their political commitment. Certainly, the topics chosen are moving, and I agree that something should be done about human suffering, inequalities, wars, injustice. But my point has been that this visual discourse, however morally superior it presumes to be, is complicit with the banality of images in present times. Being bombarded by terrible pictures does not make us any better on ethical or political grounds. Jacques Rancière says, in regard to the omnipresence of daunting images, that "the problem is not to know whether we have to watch some images or not, but to decide within which device of the sensible we may watch them" (Rancière, 2008a, p. 110) This shift towards interrogating the "devices of the sensible" would be a welcome one in the education realm, so critical of the morality of the global media and yet so available to reproduce many of its moral stances and its production of visual subjects.

NOTES

1. By "ethnoscapes," Appadurai refers to "the landscape of persons who constitute the shifting world in which we live: tourists, immigrants, refugees, exiles, guest workers" (Appadurai, 1996, p. 33).

2. "Identidades y pedagogía. Aportes de la imagen para trabajar en educación" (Identities and Pedagogies: The contribution of images to educational work), and, more recently, "Diploma en Educación, Imágenes y medios", both at Flacso/Argentina virtual campus. I have also done this exercise in workshops with teachers in different provinces in Argentina and in Mexico. It is a part of a project called Tramas, concerned with promoting debates and practices with the visual in schools (http://www.proyectotramas.org).

3. Again, landscapes of images that have to do with global electronic media and with concatenations of images more directly political and ideological, as defined by the author.

4. As Derrida says, more than one eye is needed so that a gaze appears; that it can only emerge when there is an interchange of looks, or even, of filiations; that we are raised within a "right to look" with its own authority, its own institutional authorities (those of Art—capital A—those of the spectator, those of the omniscient Lord, those of the oppressed servant; see Derrida and Fathy, 2004).

5. According to the Argentinean National Teaching Census, 2004, the percentage of use of computers at home among teachers was less than 35 percent. This might have changed significantly in the last few years, especially because of the overall expansion of internet access and personal computer ownership throughout different social groups.

6. See Dubet (2002) on the decline of the institutions; Duschatzky and Corea (2002) on the decline of schools.

7. I am aware of the methodological constraints that these exercises have, in terms of the projections done by researchers and the risks of over-interpretation. However, I would like to run those risks, as I believe that the analysis of the kind of visual discourses that emerges in this set of "powerful images" selected by teachers can also help us think about this "wounded imagination" that Didi-Huberman spoke about, about their configurations of space and time, about their construction of subject positions and knowledge about the world, and about the prevalence of certain aesthetic and ethical sensibilities.

8. It should be noted that the relationships between photojournalism and photographic pictorialism are increasingly tighter, as Didi-Huberman (2006a) and others underscore.

9. Interestingly, no participant included Abu Ghraib in their "powerful images."

10. While the teacher who selected the picture could not identify it, the original photograph is from Nabil El Jourana (or Al-Jurani), from Associated Press. The caption when it was originally published read as follows: "An unidentified Iraqi man holds an unidentified girl wounded after U.S.-led coalition air attacks over the southern Iraqi city of Basra, Saturday March 22, 2003. (AP Photo/Nabil El Jourana)"

REFERENCES

Appadurai, A. (1996). *Modernity at large: Cultural dimensions of globalization*. Minneapolis: University of Minnesota Press.

Arendt, H. (1990). *On revolution*. New York: Penguin Books.

Baricco, A. (2008). *Los barbarous. Ensayos sobre la mutación*. Barcelona: Anagrama.

Beck, U., & Beck-Gernsheim, E. (2009). Global generations and the trap of method-ological nationalism: For a cosmopolitan turn in the sociology of youth and genera-tion. *European Sociological Review, 25*(1), 5–36. doi:10.1093/esr/jcn032.

Beltrán, M. (2009). *Mediatizados. Encuentros y des encuentros entre la escuela y los medios.* Buenos Aires: Aique Educación.

Boltanski, L. (1999). *Distant suffering: Morality, media and politics.* G. Burchell (Trans.). Cambridge: Cambridge University Press.

Brea, J.L. (2007). Cambio de régimen escópico: Del inconsciente óptico a la e-image. *Revista de Estudios Visuales, 2*(4), 145–163.

Buck-Morss, S. (2004). Visual studies and global imagination. *Papers of Surrealism, 2,* 1–29. Retrieved June 28, 2009, from http://www.surrealismcentre.ac.uk/papersofsurrealism/journal2/acrobat_files/buck_morss_article.pdf.

Buckingham, D. (2007). *Beyond technology: Children's learning in the age of digital culture.* Cambridge: Polity Press.

Cabello, R. (Ed.) (2006). *Yo con la computadora no tengo nada que ver'. Un estudio de las relaciones entre los maestros y las tecnologías informáticas en la enseñanza.* Buenos Aires: Prometeo Libros-Universidad Nacional de General Sarmiento.

Choay, F. (2007). *Alegoría del patrimonio.* M. Bertrand Suazo (Trans.). Barcelona: Gustavo Gili S.L.

Crary, J. (1995). *Techniques of the observer: On vision and modernity in the nineteenth century.* Cambridge, MA: The MIT Press.

Debord, G. (1995). *The society of the spectacle.* New York: Zone Books.

Derrida, J., & Fathy, S. (2004). *Rodar las palabras. Al borde de un film.* A. Tudela (Trans.). Madrid: Arena Libros.

Didi-Huberman, G. (2006a). L'image brûle. In L. Zimmermann, G. Didi-Huberman, A. Rykner, K. Winkelvoss, M. Creac'h, & M. Pic (Eds.), *Penser par les images. Autour des travaux de Georges Didi-Huberman* (pp. 11–52). Nantes: Editions Cécile Defaut.

Didi-Huberman, G. (2006b). *Ante el tiempo. Historia del arte y anacronismo de las imágenes.* O.O. Fuentes (Trans.). Buenos Aires: Adriana Hidalgo Editora.

Dubet, F. (2002). *Le déclin de l'institution.* Paris: L'Harmattan.

Duschatzky, S., & Corea, C. (2002). *Chicos en banda.* Buenos Aires: Paidós.

Dussel, I. (2001). *School uniforms and the disciplining of appearances: Towards a comparative history of the regulation of bodies in early modern France, Argentina, and the United States.* Ph.D. dissertation, Department of Curriculum & Instruction. Madison, WI, University of Wisconsin-Madison.

Dussel, I., Brito, A., & Núñez, P. (2007). *Más allá de la crisis. Percepciones de profesores y estudiantes sobre la escuela media.* Buenos Aires: Fundación Santillana.

Fischman, G. (2000). *Imagining teachers: Rethinking gender dynamics in teacher education.* Lanham, MD: Rowman & Littlefield.

González Stephan, B., & Andermann, J. (Eds.) (2006). *Galerías del progreso. Museos, exposiciones y cultura visual en América Latina.* Rosario, Argentina: Beatriz Viterbo Editora.

Jaguaribe, B. (2007). *O choque do real. Estética, mídia e cultura.* Rio de Janeiro: Rocco.

Knobel, M., & Lankshear, C. (2008). *A new literacies sampler.* New York: Peter Lang.

Larrosa, J. (2006). Niños atravesando el paisaje. Notas sobre cine e infancia. In I. Dussel & D. Gutiérrez (Eds.), *Educar la mirada. Políticas y pedagogías de la imagen* (pp. 110–125). Buenos Aires: Manantial.

Latour, B. (1994). *We have never been modern.* C. Porter (Trans.). Cambridge, MA: Harvard University Press.

Lawn, M., & Grosvenor, I. (Eds.) (2005). *Materialities of schooling: Design, technology, objects, routines.* Oxford: Symposium Books.

Lipovetsky, G., & Serroy, J. (2009). *La pantalla global. Cultura hipermediática y cine en la era hipermoderna.* A. Prometeo Moya (Trans.). Barcelona: Anagrama.

Lundby, K. (Ed.) (2008). *Digital storytelling, mediatized stories: Self-representations in new media*. New York: Peter Lang.

Maharaj, S. (1994). 'Perfidious fidelity': The untranslatability of the other. In J. Fisher (Ed.), *Global Visions: Towards a New Internationalism in the Visual Arts* (pp. 28–35). London: Kala Press/Institute of International Visual Arts.

Maharaj, S. (2002). In other's words. Interview by D. Birnbaum. *Art Forum*. Retrieved June 30, 2009, from http://findarticles.com/p/articles/mi_m0268/is_6_40/ai_82800088.

McWilliam, E. (2002). Against professional development. *Educational Philosophy and Theory, 34*(3), 289–300.

Mirzoeff, N. (1999). *The visual culture reader*. New York: Routledge.

Mirzoeff, N. (2005). *Watching Babylon: The war in Iraq and global visual culture*. New York: Routledge.

Mitchell, W.T.J. (2002). Showing seeing. *Journal of Visual Culture, 1*(2), 165–181.

Mitchell, W.T.J. (2008). Cloning terror: The war of images 2001–2004. In D. Costello & D. Willsdon (Eds.), *The life and death of images: Ethics and aesthetics* (pp. 179–207). New York: Routledge.

Monsiváis, C. (2006). «Se sufre porque se aprende.» De las variedades del melodrama en Latinoamérica. In I. Dussel & D. Gutiérrez (Eds.), *Educar la mirada: Políticas y pedagogías de la imagen* (pp. 23–57). Buenos Aires: Manantial.

Pollock, G. (2008). Sin olvidar África: Dialécticas de atender/desatender, de ver/negar, de saber/entender en la posición del espectador ante la obra de Alfredo Jaar. In A. Jaar, et al. (Eds.), *La política de las imágenes* (pp. 91–131). A. Valdez (Trans.). Santiago de Chile: Metales Pesados.

Popkewitz, T.S. (1998). *Struggling for the soul: The politics of schooling and the construction of the teacher*. New York: Teachers College Press.

Prensky, M. (2001). *Digital natives, digital immigrants*. Retrieved June 30, 2009, from http://www.marcprensky.com/writing/Prensky-Digital-Natives-Digital-Immigrants-Part1.pdf.

Prosser, J. (2007). Visual methods and the visual culture of schools. *Visual Studies, 22*(1), 13–30.

Quintana, A. (2003). *Fábulas de lo visible. El cine como creador de realidades*. Barcelona: Acantilado.

Quintana, A. (2009). *Vers un art virtual? A l'ère du numérique, le cinéma est toujours une représentation du réel*. Paris: Ed. du Cahiers du Cinéma.

Rancière, J. (2008a). *Le spectateur emancipé*. Paris: La Fabrique Éditions.

Rancière, J. (2008b). El teatro de imágenes. In A. Jaar, et al. (Eds.), *La política de las imágenes* (pp. 69–89). A. Z. Madrid (Trans.). Santiago de Chile: Metales Pesados.

Reguillo, R. (2005). *Horizontes fragmentados: Comunicación, cultura, pospolítica*. Guadalajara: ITESO.

Rosler, M. (2007). *Imágenes públicas. La función política de la imagen*. J. Carrillo (Ed.), E. García Agustín (Trans.). Barcelona: Editorial Gustavo Gilli.

Schwartz , V., & Przyblyski, J. (2004). *The nineteenth century visual culture reader*. New York: Routledge.

Sontag, S. (2003). *Regarding the pain of others*. New York: Farrar, Straus & Giroux.

Tobin, J. (Ed.) (2004). *Pikachu's global adventure: The rise and fall of Pokémon*. Durham, NC: Duke University Press.

Vasudevan, L., & Campano, G. (2009). The social production of adolescent risk and the promise of adolescent literacies. *Review of Research in Education, 33*, 310–353.

Virilio, P. (2005). Cold panic. *Cultural Politics, 1*(1), 27–30.

Weber, S. (1995). *That's funny, you don't look like a teacher! Interrogating images, identity, and popular culture*. New York: Routledge.

Capitalism, Modernity and the Future of Education in the New Social Contract

ROGER DALE AND SUSAN ROBERTSON

Introduction

It is clear that we are entering a new and unknown world, where it seems that nothing can be predicted, except perhaps that it will be both in the short term rather uncomfortable and in the longer term quite different. This is at least as true of education as of any other area of organised human activity, and the fundamental concern of this chapter will be the changing role, nature, and place of "education" in twenty-first century societies.

We argue in this chapter that, against this framing, the ever-expanding, ever-improving, ever-progressing set of assumptions which have characterised education's historic tie to the development of the modern nation state are coming to an end, principally as a result of new developments in the relationship between the historically intertwined but essentially distinct trajectories of capitalism and modernity. Separately and together these two trajectories have been recast, rearticulated and recalibrated in ways that amount to a fundamental discontinuity with the era of modernity, in turn transforming the nature and role of education as we have come to understand it.

We will also suggest that these issues cannot be effectively understood through existing theoretical and methodological tools. As Santos (2002) puts it, we cannot solve the problems of postmodernity with the tools of modernity, not least because these are themselves rooted in the same basic assumptions that have shaped existing conceptions of education.

The main lens through which we intend to view and understand the nature of these changes is by focusing on the relationship between education and the social contract as the most effective means of developing what we have referred to elsewhere as a "zero-based" account of the nature and consequences of the current changes (see Robertson, Dale, Thrupp, Vaughan, & Jacka, 1997). Such an approach requires us to reconsider the fundamental purposes of education and their historic relationship with modernity. It is through its relationship with the social contract, which lies at the heart of the social imaginary of modernity (see Taylor, 2002), that the institutional relationship between education and modernity has been most extensively developed. It is here that we find conceptions of what education is for. Put at its simplest, what does society give to and expect from education? Crudely, what are we paying for when we agree to pay for education?

The way we proceed with this argument in the rest of the chapter is as follows. First, we will briefly elaborate on the theoretical basis of the argument: that what is leading to the perceived shortcomings of modernity in education is the tendential separation of the trajectories of capitalism and modernity. This essentially means that the institutions of modernity, including education as we have known it, no longer provide the "best possible shell" for capitalism in its current phase. We will then briefly discuss the methodological basis of the argument, before elaborating on the nature and importance of the social contract in modernity, specifying in particular the relationships among the market, citizenship, and the public sphere as its three key elements. The main body of the paper will be given over to discussions of how the place of education in society and its contribution to the social contract are being mediated and transformed through those three features. Our view is that this kind of analysis is critical as a condition for offering possibilities for the future direction of education in ways that might secures its emancipatory potential in the emerging social contract.

The "Discontinuity" Argument

The fundamental argument underpinning this chapter is that that the set of assumptions built around education's contribution to a modernist social contract built around continuous expansion, improvement and progress, along with the institutions associated with it, is coming to an end. Here we follow Boaventura de Sousa Santos in suggesting that it is crucial to the understanding of current global predicaments to distinguish between the trajectories of capitalism (as found currently in the form of neo-liberal globalisation) and modernity, and to examine the relationships between them. As he puts it, "Western modernity and capitalism are two different and autonomous historical processes . . . [that] have converged and interpenetrated each other." However, Santos suggests that those trajectories are now separating, in a "paradigmatic transition," and consequently "the socio-cultural paradigm of modernity . . . will eventually disappear before capitalism ceases to be dominant . . . partly from a process of supersession and partly from a process of obsolescence. It entails supersession to the extent that modernity has fulfilled some of its promises, in some cases even in excess. It results from obsolescence to the extent that modernity is no longer capable of fulfilling some of its other promises" (Santos, 2002, pp. 1–2). Underlying this is the problem that, in Santos's (2002) terms, while "Modernity is grounded on a dynamic tension between the pillar of regulation (which guarantees order in a society as it exists in a given moment and place) and emancipation . . . [and] the aspiration for a good order in a good society in the future[,]" (p. 2) . . . "what most strongly characterises the socio-cultural condition at the beginning of the century is the collapse of the pillar of emancipation into the pillar of regulation, as a result of the reconstructive management of the excesses and deficits of modernity" (p. 7). It is that tension between regulation and emancipation—to both of which education has been expected, at different times and places, by different bodies, to contribute—that has been, and currently remains, albeit in a trans-formed way, at the heart of struggles over the social contract and education's place in it.

The argument, here, then, is that it is to this tendential separation from capitalism more than to internal critiques around the end of grand narratives that we should look to explain the loss of confidence in modernity. In particular, the globalisation of the emergence of neolib-eralism, as the dominant form of capitalism, represented a new kind of challenge to modernity.

Neoliberalism is to be seen as a project and a programme rather than as a set of policies, or a process without agents. It emerged from, on the one hand, the "Fall of the Wall" in 1989, and with it the "End of the Cold War" and the removal of any alternative to Western capitalism, and on the other, the new technologies that made possible not only the rapid flow of finance around the globe, but the creation of new indus-tries and patterns of consumption. This was advanced through a vigor-ous round of negotiations and treaty-making activities such as the North American Free Trade Agreement (NAFTA) in 1991, the World Trade Organization (WTO) in 1995, and the expansion of the Euro-pean Union through the Maastricht Treaty (1993) and the Stability and Growth Pact (1999, which culminated in the Lisbon Declaration (2000). The key differentiating point about neoliberalism is that, unlike classical liberalism, it was not driven by a comprehensive opposition to all state activity; rather it worked *through* the state, in a process that Stephen Gill has called the "constitutionalisation of the neoliberal" (Gill, 2003). Harvey's (2005, p. 2) definition of neoliberalism is useful here: "a theory of political economic practices that proposes that human well-being can best be advanced by liberating individual entrepreneurial freedoms and skills *within an institutional framework characterized by strong private property rights, free markets and free trade.*" The italicized phrase is what matters most here; the dominant form of state regulation was to be one that removed controls from the market. And it has been those principles that have framed and underpinned the new social contract.

A Brief Methodological Excursus

Before moving on it will be important to indicate why and how we consider that our existing theoretical and conceptual tools, and our assumptions about the place of education in the world, can no longer be relied upon as guides to coming to terms with education in the remainder of this century. Those tools are themselves largely locked into the very theoretical assumptions of modernity that the nature of the current juncture requires us to challenge. We have attempted in a number of papers to indicate the nature and consequences of adhering to those assumptions, suggesting that they have become fixed in a series of theoretical and methodological "isms"; "ism" is used to suggest an approach to the objects that takes key elements of them as unproblematic and assumes a constant and shared meaning; they become "fixed, abstract and absolute" (Fine, 2003, p.465), or in other words as ontologically and epistemologically ossified. Those we specified were methodological nationalism, statism, educationism, and spatial fetishism (see Dale & Robertson, 2008; Robertson & Dale, 2008). Methodological nationalism essentially refers to the tendency to equate nation and society, with the national the taken-for-granted container of society. By methodological statism we mean the matching tendency to assume a that a common state *form*, typically that of postwar social democracy, is in place across the globe. In this context, it may be worth spelling out what we understand by "educationism" a little more fully. Educationism refers to the tendency to regard "education" as a single category for purposes of analysis, with an assumed common scope, and a set of implicitly shared knowledges, practices, and assumptions—though this should not be taken to imply that there is only one set of knowledges, etc., or one universally accepted representation of education. It occurs when education is treated as abstract, fixed, absolute, ahistorical and universal, when no distinctions are made between its use to describe purpose, process, practice, and outcomes. Particular representations of

education are treated in isolation from each other, and addressed dis-
cretely rather than as part of a wider assemblage of representations—for
there is no suggestion that the different representations of education
have anything in common with each other, or that the label is randomly
attached. Far from it, it is the recognition that there are crucial relationships between different representations of education that are being
occluded or disguised by the failure to distinguish between them that
makes it so important to identify and seek to go beyond educationism.
Finally, Brenner (2003, p. 38) sees spatial fetishism as involving "a
conception of social space that is timeless and static, and thus immune
to the possibility of historical change." The context now is globalization, yet its causal dynamics—in other words, "what difference does
space make?"—are absent. The global and globalization are thus inert
concepts; the container—context—is simply inflected with an adjustment of content, like a new product on the shelf.

The assumption/acceptance of such unproblematic conceptions of
the nation, the state, education systems, and the spatial geometry of
education constitutes an unproblematic set of lenses for understanding
the changes brought about by globalization, even as those changes
themselves radically alter and undermine the meaning of, and the work
done by, nation-states and education systems, thus thoroughly compromising their validity.

The depth of the penetration of these kinds of assumptions, and
their consequences for the social sciences and education, is summarized
in Ruggie's (1993) comments on what we are calling methodological
statism, as displaying "an extraordinarily impoverished mind-set
. . . that is able to visualize long-term challenges to the system of states
only in terms of entities that are institutionally substitutable for the
state" (p. 143).

One major consequence of such thinking is that it leads us to thinking about educational change in terms of the modification, however
radical, or repair of the existing system. Seeing the education of the
future as essentially continuous with the education of the present and
the past may be entirely justifiable and appropriate, but that has to be
demonstrated rather than assumed.

It also requires us to be aware of the crucial conditions of any such
endeavours. In particular, we need to be aware of what Roberto Man-
gabeira Unger (1998) refers to as "fetishisms"—"limits on our ability to
imagine and change society." These come in two types: *institutional*
fetishism, the "identification of institutional conceptions, such as rep-
resentative democracy, a market economy, and a free civil society, with

a single set of institutional arrangements"; and *structure* fetishism, "which finds expression and defence in an idea that opposes interludes of effervescence, charisma, mobilization, and energy to the ordinary reign of institutionalized routine, when, half asleep, we continue to act out the script written in the creative intervals" (p. 26). The first of these is especially important in this context, as it directs us to problematize not just those three key elements of the contexts of education but "education" itself.

At its simplest, this means asking not "how might we be doing education differently?" but "why are we doing education at all?" That is, in Unger's terms, it means interrogating the institutional *conception* of education as well as the institutional *arrangements* through which it is delivered This requires a double shift in our thinking, both from the association of education with a particular set of institutional arrangements (what will be referred to below as "the architecture of education" systems') and from a particular conception of what education is *for*.

Education and the Social Contract

Placing the question of the social contract at the centre of an investigation of fundamental changes in education is especially appropriate, since education has been a significant element of, and bearer of, the values and norms of modernity. The contribution of at least Western education—which has been widely diffused across the world—to the social contract has had at its heart the idea of the positive relationship between education and *progress*. Though the forms it has taken have varied, the social contract of modernity has emphasised the importance of individuals both as crucial to, and beneficiaries of, progress, of states and markets as its drivers, and of science and rationality as the means of achieving these ends. The link between modernity and education has been the focus of a group of theorists who advance the argument for a standardized world model of education, based on the principles of the Enlightenment, that applies equally to all nation states. First, as John Meyer (2001) puts it, "the two main goals of the proper modern national state—individual equality and collective progress—come together in an extraordinary worldwide wave of astonishingly homogeneous educational expansion" (p. 6). Elsewhere, Meyer and his colleagues have supplied compelling evidence of this homogeneous expansion that has come to include effectively all the countries of the world and certainly at a formal level (see Meyer, Kamens, & Benavot,

1992). Third, these theorists emphasize the importance of science, and the rationalization, "scientization" and professionalization of an ever increasing range of social issues and problems. These either cease to be subject to, or to be seen as beyond the capacities of, "local" interpretations and remedies.

All this has assumed that the more, and sometimes the more and better distributed, education, the better. And this has been the case effectively irrespective of the wide diversity of forms it has taken; educational provision is always justified in terms of the *improvements* it will bring about, to the point where it has often been seen as the chief "improvement mechanism" of societies, the means for remedying contradictions and problems of all kinds. This expansion of education's mandate has resulted in a changing conception of education that is very clearly, if rather distortedly, reflected in its arrangements.

These mechanisms have been increasingly incorporated into the mandate for education; the best example is probably the "babysitting/child-minding" function that is indispensable to the labor market and economy, but that could equally well be carried out through other social institutions, or by for-profit enterprises.

In order to begin to register more clearly what this might imply, in the next part of this paper we will elaborate on the three basic elements of the modern social imaginary as they have been highlighted by Lee and LiPuma, since these may be taken as framing more or less directly the social contract for education and as separately and collectively constructing the conception of education, and hence (in part, because of the accretion/attraction effect of education systems), particular sets of institutional arrangements. Lee and LiPuma (2002) refer to the social contract as something "in which individuals engaging in the reciprocal performative acts of promising and agreeing create a quasi-objective social totality that then governs their actions. The effectiveness of the social contract as a foundational ideology for Western modernity stems from the fact that its performative construction of collective agency is a crucial aspect not only of modern social imaginaries, but also of capital itself." They go on, "increasingly for the world as a whole, the public sphere, the modern citizen-state, and the market are the basic components of the social imaginary of modernity" (pp. 193, 194).

We intend to frame the remainder of this chapter using Lee and LiPuma's three elements of the social contract as a lens through which to view the changes taking place in education's relationship with the social contract. We aim to see the nature of what is changing in education by looking at how these parts of the social contract have changed/

are changing, and the implications for the changing nature of the social contract and of education's place within it.

A similar approach has been adopted by Magalhães and Stoer (2003), who advance the idea that:

> The nation-states that developed during modernity found in the conception of the social contract the ultimate legitimization of their tutelage over their subjects-citizens. Individuals gave up action on the basis of (what Rousseau referred to as) their "inclinations" and gave up their most immediate senses of belonging (ethnic, local) . . . that is, they gave up their sovereignty in order to endorse the nation-state. In compensation, individuals were guaranteed the maximum use of their capacities. These capacities are made up of each individual's talents, brought to fruition by the achievement obtained in the different contexts of state, community and market. Thus, the social value of individuals depends upon equality of opportunities in the exercise of their talents (concretized through schooling as both the instrument and the privileged place), upon the liberty to express entrepreneurial spirit on the market and upon fraternal participation in the community. (p. 54)

The Market and the Social Contract for Education

A useful way of approaching the nature of the relationship between education and the "market" component of the social contract is through Fourcade and Healy's (2007) extension of Hirschman's (1982) discussion of the relationship between markets and morality. Hirschman contrasted conceptions of markets as "civilizing," "destructive" and "feeble" in their effects on society. In the "markets as civilising," or "doux commerce," version, which Fourcade and Healy refer to as the "liberal dream," markets encourage personal virtues of honesty, integrity, trust, civilized and cooperative behavior, consumer sovereignty, and freedom in the public sphere, and provide incentives and opportunities for innovation. We might see a social contract based on this view of the relationship between market and morality justifying education as giving opportunities to all to advance on the basis of their talents. The public good it delivers is the aggregation of the private goods (exchange values) that the social contract enables to be accumulated. The second conception, referred to as the "destructive nightmare," in many ways inverts the claims of the liberal dream. Markets reduce justification for actions to the pursuit of self-interest. They are associated with competitiveness, corruption, and maximization of consumption; rather than allowing individuals to flourish, they commodify and dehumanize them.[1] The public good contributed by education here is essentially compensatory, seeking to provide the life chances that the market cannot provide for all. It is about combating social exclusion, and built-in barriers to access. It involves a conception of education as use value, for public as well as private benefit. The third view, of "feeble" markets, reverses the direction of the relationship between markets and morality as seen by both the liberal dream and the destructive nightmare, where markets shape societies, albeit in different directions. Feeble markets are the product of societies and cultures. It is such a view of the nature and consequences of markets that informs the world polity approach, for instance, where markets are essentially seen as expressions of the values of modernity rather than shaping those values.

It is also crucial to note that markets are always embedded in wider social institutions, and that it is the nature of those social—regulatory—institutions that frames the nature of the social contract. As we have seen, in a neoliberal era, the emphasis has been on minimizing the regulation of markets. However, it is also crucial to note two associated changes—registered in the ideas of methodological statism and methodological nationalism, respectively—to the embedding of markets in neoliberalism. On the one hand, the state is no longer the only regulator of markets; we now have multiple forms of private regulation, and self-regulation. On the other hand markets can no longer be (if they ever could) assumed to be either nationally based or nationally governed. At the same time, however, the idea of the social contract as nationally based remains a deeply rooted assumption.

If we consider the substance of these conceptions of market-morality relationships in education, we see that for the third quarter of the last century, certainly in Western Europe, the social contract for education was essentially informed by a "destructive nightmare" conception of the relationship between markets and morality. The job of education was to inoculate populations against the attitudinal and organizational dangers of the market, to display in its processes an alternative set of values, to protect against and compensate for the "destructive" characteristics of the market. The central thrust of the social democracy of that period was that a strong state was necessary to mitigate the inherent evils of the market. At the heart of the conception of the welfare state lay the idea of decommodification. Education's place in the social contract was central to this aim. It was to enable *all* children to develop *all* their capacities in full, in the face of a market logic that would limit and stunt them. The next stage saw a (fairly brief) flowering of a social contract informed by a strong version (at least in the Anglo-Saxon countries) of the principles of doux commerce—though the soubriquet "greed is good" perhaps contradicts the original appel-lation. All obstacles to individual attainment and progress were to be removed. Competition was the driver of success, in education and throughout society. This was followed by, and also contributed to, not so much a "softening" of the liberal dream, as what amounted to an inversion of the "feeble" market, shaped by and responsive to the range of social institutions, in the form of neoliberalism, which shaped those institutions to the forms and needs of the market. Seeing neoliberalism as involving the fusing of regulation and emancipation seems to us a very useful and pregnant way of understanding the current nature of the relationship between markets and other institutions of society. It does not so much resolve as dissolve and reconstruct the tensions between regulation and emancipation.

One major consequence of the changes in the institutional and agential regulation of the market (and especially the multiplication of its scalar bases) is that "the social contract of modernity [as] expressed [in] the exchange of local belonging for national loyalty" becomes difficult to sustain, since it assumed a national state with some degree of control over a national economy. In particular, the consequences of the separa-tion between economic and political citizenship have become more salient. In supranational organizations, such as the EU, it is essenti-ally economic citizenship that comes into the picture (see Dale & Robertson, 2006). However, possibly the most direct effect on educa-tion comes with the severing of its traditional links with labor markets. Though they have become much more international, it is still the case that while capital is mobile and international, labor is relatively immo-bile and nationally based.

It is also very important not to fetishize, or homogenize, markets. They take very different forms with very different effects. There is, for instance, a wide range of forms of public-private partnerships (see Robertson, 2007), while the dominant form taken by markets in edu-cation has been the quasi-market (see Le Grand & Bartlett, 1993). There may be no profit involved for state schools in quasi-markets, but the crucial point is that they encouraged "market-like" behavior in an area that had previously been regulated by state intervention, with, presumably, an eye to the effect on the social contract. Introducing competition among parents and among schools represented a signifi-cant undermining of the principles of the social contract in education. And from the other side of the contract, as it were, it is not necessarily the state that will provide these opportunities, but the market. As a result, as Magalhães and Stoer (2003) put it, "individual[s] becomes vulnerable to a form of social and cognitive injustice that conditions [their] very status as citizens" (p. 59).

Citizenship and the Social Contract for Education

In this section, we will discuss briefly four important shifts in the relationship between education and the social contract as they are mediated through the idea of citizenship. First, we will problematize the assumption that that relationship is necessarily mediated through the (political) form of citizenship, suggesting that the current conjuncture requires us to challenge that assumption. Second, we will consider some alternative bases of the social contract (as the basis of the production of well-being). Third, we will discuss the paradox of the heightened attention paid to citizenship education at a time when its traditional forms are being threatened. Finally, we will briefly consider the effect of new "populations" on the relationship between citizenship and education.

Put very simply, the basis of the social contract, in education as elsewhere, has been essentially one between state and citizen. This is not the place to go into extended discussions of what is meant by citizenship, or what it entails; but crucial to those definitions are that the relationship is both formal and reciprocal. One particularly effective elaboration of issues concerning citizenship has been provided by Jane Jenson, through the idea of "citizenship regimes"—"the institutional arrangements, rules and understandings that guide and shape concurrent policy decisions and expenditures of states, problem definitions by states and citizens, and claims-making by citizens" (Jenson, 2000, p. 55). She distinguishes four components of citizenship regimes. The second, third and fourth refer, respectively, to identification of those entitled to full citizenship status; the institutional mechanisms giving access to the state and the legitimacy of specific types of claims-making; and definitions of membership and identity. The first, and most important in this context, defines "the boundaries of state responsibilities and differentiate[s] them from those of markets, of families and of communities. . . . *The result is the definition of how to produce well-being, whether via the market, via the reciprocity of kin, via collective support in communities, or via collective and public solidarity, that is state provision and according to the principle of equality among citizens [which] establishes a place for citizenship*" (p. 55, emphasis added). What makes this so important is that it not only defines the boundaries of state responsibility but incorporates the definition of, and responsibility for, "the means of production and distribution of well being." This not only produces a definition

of citizenship that is crucial in this context, but at least equally importantly, directs us towards alternative sources and means of the production of well-being, specifically markets, families, and communities. The
production of well-being is not a "state-or-nothing" zero-sum game, as
it might have appeared historically, for instance in the definition provided by Magalhães and Stoer (2003). Put very simply, the social contract of neoliberal postmodernity does not place responsibility for the
production of well-being exclusively on the state (except as coordinator/
regulator of last resort, in education [see Dale, 2005, p. 40] as well as in
the banking sector), but on combinations of markets, communities,
stakeholders, and state. Equally important, this fulfils another tenet of
neoliberalism—that decisions about the production of well-being
should be based on commercial or technical, but as far as possible not on
political, principles and criteria (see also Robertson, 2009). So, as an
example of institutional fetishism, the crucial issue at stake here is not so
much "citizenship" but *the means of production and distribution of well-
being*, a distinction that has been obscured in the dominance of the
discourse of citizenship.

To move to our second question: once we recognize that citizenship
is one (albeit highly normatively and politically loaded) response to the
problem of the production and distribution of well-being, we are able to
open up that issue and ask what groups are involved in it as the "real"
issue, which we may see as basically one of representation in the social
contract around education. Who does it represent, and who is represented in it, and how?

This has been obfuscated rather than merely obscured in many
recent debates around the area. These debates have quite recent roots in
the simultaneous and equal distaste for both "state" (unresponsive
bureaucracy) and "market" (deregulated greed) solutions that emerged
in the aftermath of the decline of the social-democratic welfare state,
and the desire to find a "middle way" between state and market, less
harsh and more "human" than both.[2]

Two major types of partners in the production of well-being have
been distinguished in recent years—consumers and stakeholders. The
idea of "consumers" of education is not as strange as it would have
appeared 20 years ago. For better or worse, we have become accus-
tomed to the idea of the "privatization" of education, or education as a
"commodity." While we may not be sufficiently aware of the extent of
the activities generated in this area of commerce (for examples of the
truly amazing developments of private involvement in state education,
and of the development of "education industries," see Ball (2007) and

Meyer and Rowan (2007), it is well established that these are global industries that are to some degree regulated through global bodies such as the WTO's General Agreement on Trade in Services (GATS) (see Robertson, Bonal, & Dale, 2002). There has, however, been correspondingly little attention paid to the "producer-consumer" basis of the relationship of the social contract for education. It is quite distinct from, and not reducible to, the relationship between state and citizen as a basis for educational provision. The impact on pedagogic relationships of the introduction of the cash nexus has been very widely noted (we discuss the significance of the quasi-marketization of education in the next section), but here it is important to mention the form taken by the state-citizen relationship. At one level, it is reduced to that of consumer protection. One way it does this is by providing information for the (quasi-) market, through the collection of information and the production of means of comparing the meaning of that information. The state also provides protection, and sometimes redress, against rogue traders in education, as in other forms of trade. In particular, it assures quality and the credibility of qualifications (in most, if not all cases; one example is qualifications for IT technicians). At the same time, again as has been widely noted, states as quality controllers are in the position of defining that which they assure, in a sense of one-sidedly altering elements of the social contract that assumed mutual responsibility.

The term "stakeholder" is intended to act as an umbrella for an increasingly diverse and extensive array of concepts whose basis and focus is "thickening" relationships between states and their populations in various ways that seek to go beyond the relationships of formal political citizenship. On the one hand, formal citizenship is represented as too passive, as confining opportunities to participate in a society to voting in widely spaced elections. To oversimplify massively, "stakeholding" moves the relationship between state and citizen based on reciprocal responsibilities very much in the direction of the responsibilities of the citizen. This takes a very wide range of forms, from "active" (as implicitly opposed to passive) citizenship, to the need to foster social capital, and taking a stake in some aspect of the society. It seeks to extend the bases of citizen participation, in ways that vary from the hortatory, to the formal (for instance, at one extreme, "workfare"), to the use of targets and benchmarks (as we see in the case of the EU and its promotion of "civic competences" as key elements of it model of education). Other versions of this approach privilege "communities" as the appropriate level for citizen participation, or promote conceptions of ethical universals as alternatives to locally responsive social contracts.

We might see this as a reconstruction of the nature of citizenship, not related directly to either state or market, but part of a socially inclusive (Craig and Porter), communally active, self-responsible third sector which both leads to the embedding of such apolitical or even anti-political discourses as stakeholding and social capital, but on the other hand simultaneously exposes their intrinsically political nature. Newman and Clarke (2009) put this very well:

Enrolling community, civil society and voluntary organisations into the creation of economic and social development, social cohesion, and public well-being is not just a matter of finding functional substitutes for the provision of public services. Rather, popular resourcefulness is regarded as a source on non-state, non-political and spontaneous (if carefully tutored) value creation—from neighbourliness to civility, from cohesion to development. The double movement of displacing and de-politicising aspires to avoid conflict (or at least localise it and contain it in non-political locations) and to construct self-governing and self-provisioning agents (individuals, families/household, communities). (p. 177)

The changing nature of citizenship and its relation to the social contract also emerges in the apparently paradoxical flowering of "citizenship education," our third point. Indeed, "citizenship education" became part of the National Curriculum for England in 2002. It is as if we only need citizenship education when the original substance of citizenship has been eroded. We can see this at two levels. At a national level, it appears to be moving away from the "traditional" approach of "improving political literacy," that is, understanding the *rights* of citizenship granted in the social contract and how to make full use of them, towards replacing the state in its role as guarantor of social cohesion through an emphasis on stakeholding, responsibility, and active citizenship. Its focus is the practices of citizens defined as members of communities. It emphasises engagement and participation, and concerns skills and behaviors as well as knowledge and understanding (for stimulating accounts of the nature of citizenship education, approached from a Foucauldian perspective, see Pykett (2007, 2009a, 2009b). In these changes, we can see the scope of education's role in the social contract expand greatly, but its focus narrow.

One interesting feature of this development is that, as the nature and significance of national citizenship wanes (with the declining importance of national economies, for instance), so the focus on *global* citizenship and education waxes. Marshall (2003, 2005) suggests that the idea of global education originated essentially with the UN Declaration of Human Rights, addressing the need for a place in the curriculum for world studies, human rights, peace education and so on, in what might be seen as the reassertion of the discourses of modernity at a global rather than national scale. However, more recent approaches to global citizenship education appear to be constructed in response to the changes brought about by an increasing level of globalization, the impact of which is increasingly directly experienced at national level. The main pattern seems to be one of nationally-based responses, as nation-states perceive a need to respond to the changed condition of globalization and to shape their responses to the way it may impact on them. In education, this has been largely based on what might be called global education for, and as part of, national citizenship, reflecting a tacit recognition that the elements of the social contract are now no longer exclusively national. This involves "bringing the world into the classroom, where teachers teach from a world-centric rather than an ethno-specific or nation-state perspective" (Kirkwood, 2001, p. 10), or what Marshall (2005, pp. 83, 84) calls a "global gaze," a particular mode of recognizing the global reality "that appears to be required of both the student and the teacher during the teaching learning process."

The recognition of the significance of globalization, and the need to respond to it, takes us to the final part of our discussion of the consequences for education of the changing basis of the social contract. Globalization has, among others things, accelerated a movement towards recognizing the importance of *identity* in education. This had its origins in the break-up of the political-economic assumptions and their associated politics of decommodification and redistribution, and, especially with the neoliberal emphasis on the responsibility of individuals for their own success, it "created a space for the emergence of new voices and new claims" (Magalhães & Stoer, 2003, p. 54). The result of this, Magalhães and Stoer suggest, is that the reconfiguration of individual and collective citizenship moves beyond the nation-state, as

Individuals and groups, whose difference was . . . delimited, described and activated on the basis of a citizenship founded on the nation-state, have increasingly assumed difference, with the assumption of their own voice and voice itself. And they have done so going beyond the right of citizenship designed by modernity and beyond its moral(ity) and its politics of tolerance. . . . These differences, based on ethnic group, race, . . . sexual orientation, life style, . . . or religious preference, burst forth from the interior of western societies themselves. They are not a "threat" that the exterior has imposed; they arise, rather, from within as a new claim to sovereignty: the right to manage individual and collective life in accord with their own frames of reference . . . , bringing about a demand for a form of justice that is based not only on socio-economic but cultural differences. (Stoer & Magalhães, 2002, p. 700).

Thus, with the proliferation of different migrant groups and different lifestyles, citizenship "becomes thought of on the basis of difference, that is, on the basis of that which distinguishes and not on the basis of that which promotes common characteristic" (Magalhães & Stoer, 2003, p. 57) (and which was the basis of the modern social contract). "The implications of this new multicultural form of citizenship are only now beginning to show themselves and instigate an urgent re-conceptualization of the concept of citizenship, of the rights and duties of social actors" (p. 57).

Conclusion

Our aim in this article has been to offer some ideas about how education might change over the early decades of this century in response to the major changes currently occurring in the world, which might be seen as symptoms (indeed, "morbid symptoms," as Gramsci [1971] referred to them, that occur when "the old world is dying and the new cannot be born") of the major "paradigm shift" that we see as having been set under way in the final quarter of the last century. In order to do this we have felt it necessary to step back from, and behind, the conceptions of education that have dominated our thinking for most of the last century, and consequently partially limited our vision of what education is, does, and might be. To register the nature, degree and direction of those changes, we chose to focus on the question "what is education for?" and to take education's relationship with the social contract as the benchmark against which changing responses to that question might be calibrated. We also chose to make the nature of the social contract, as a foundational ideology of modernity, the basis of that question. This was because modernity has been at the heart of the values, discourses, and practices of education from the renaissance to the Sputnik. It is also, along with capitalism, one of the pair of shaping elements of societies, to the point where all societies are now influenced by their two trajectories.

However, it is in the tendential separation between modernity and capitalism, especially in its neoliberal form, where we see the fundamental reality of the major changes that surround us, not least in education. The symbolic symptom of that separation is that the discourses and institutions of modernity may be ceasing to provide "the best possible" shell for capitalism in its current form.

In order to get a more precise sense of these changes, we examined, necessarily very superficially, changes in two elements of the social contract and what they might mean for education: the market and citizenship. We argued that, as produced through neoliberalism, the market undermines key elements of the social contract. In particular, as the state moves from guardian of a social contract where individuals gave up their sovereignty in order to endorse the nation-state and in return were guaranteed the maximum use of their capacities, to that of minimizing (though not necessarily weakening) its own role in favor of the extension of the market, all the key elements of the social contract were transformed. In the absence of the protective state, "the individual becomes vulnerable to a form of social and cognitive injustice that conditions its very status as citizen" (Magalhães & Stoer, 2003, p. 59).

In considering aspects of the relationship between education and citizenship, our first argument was that, in the present conjuncture, a focus on "citizenship" is misleading, because of the multiple meanings it has accreted in addition to its original place in the social contract. Instead, we suggested that what was taken as citizenship in the social contract could be more generically regarded as the "means of production and distribution of well-being." Furthermore, other bases of partnership in that enterprise, such as consumership and stakeholding, are becoming much more prominent, and both have significant effects on education.

Finally, we discussed two important consequences for citizenship of the wider changes we have been discussing. One was the paradox that as citizenship appears to decline in importance and significance we see a major new emphasis placed on citizenship education. The other was the consequences of the fragmentation of the idea and practices of citizenship, and the proliferation both of the nature of citizenship claims and of those making the claims. If this appears to take us a considerable distance from the conceptions of the social contract, the citizen, and their consequences for education that we put forward as the benchmark against which changes in education should be measured, then we shall have achieved our aims. It is, as ever, the nature and significance of the journey, and of the route taken, that can be significant in knowing where our next steps may take us.

NOTES

1. We see the contrast between the liberal dream and destructive nightmare interpretations of the relationship between markets and morality very clearly represented in arguments for and against private education.

128   CAPITALISM, MODERNITY AND EDUCATION

2. In a paper entitled "State, Market and . . . ?" on the topic of the "third sector" (the most useful umbrella term I could find) that I presented as part of a conference to celebrate the "year of the family," I distinguished 12 different "soft" alternatives to state and market. See Dale (1994).

REFERENCES

Ball, S.J. (2007). *Education plc: Understanding private sector participation in in public sector education*. London: Routledge.
Brenner, N. (2003). *New state spaces: Urban governance and the rescaling of the state*. Oxford: Oxford University Press.
Craig, D., & Porter, D. (2004). The third way and the third world: Poverty reduction and social inclusion in the rise of 'inclusive liberalism'. *Review of International Political Economy, 11*(2), 387–423.
Dale, R. (1994, December). Locating "the family and education" in the year of the family. Keynote address to Australia and New Zealand Comparative Education Society conference, Melbourne.
Dale, R. (2005). Globalization and the rescaling of educational governance: A case of sociological Ectopia? In C.A. Torres & A. Teodoro (Eds.), *Critique and Utopia: New developments in the sociology of education* (pp. 25–42). Lanham, MD: Rowman & Littlefield.
Dale, R., & Robertson, S. (2006). Homo Sapiens Europaeus or Homo Atlanticus Quaestuosus? European learning citizen or Anglo-American human capitalist? The case of the UK. In M. Kuhn & R. Sultana (Eds.), *The European learning citizen* (pp. 21–45). Berlin: Peter Lang.
Dale, R., & Robertson, S. (2008). Beyond methodological "isms" in comparative education in an era of globalisation. In A. Kazamias & R. Cowen (Eds.), *Handbook on comparative education* (pp. 1113–1128). Dordrecht, the Netherlands: Springer.
Fine, R. (2003). Taking the "ism" out of cosmopolitanism. *European Journal of Social Theory, 6*(4), 451–470.
Fourcade, M., & Healy, K. (2007). Moral views of market society. *Annual Review of Sociology, 33*, 285–311.
Gill, S. (2003). *Power and resistance in the new world order*. New York: Palgrave Macmillan.
Gramsci, A. (1971). *Selections from the prison notebooks*. London: Lawrence and Wishart.
Harvey, D. (2005). *A brief history of neoliberalism*. Oxford: Oxford University Press.
Hirschman, A.O. (1982). Rival interpretations of market society: Civilizing, destructive, or feeble? *Journal of Economic Lierature, 20*, 1463–1484.
Jenson, J. (2000). Restructuring citizenship regimes: The French and Canadian women's movements in the 1990s. In J. Jenson & B. de Sousa Santos (Eds.), *Globalizing institutions: Case studies in regulation and innovation* (pp. 231–252). Aldershot, UK: Ashgate.
Kirkwood, T.F. (2001). Our global age requires global education: Clarifying definitional ambiguities. *Social Studies, 92*(1), 10–17.
Lee, B. & LiPuma, E. (2002). Cultures of circulation: The imaginations of modernity. *Public Culture, 14*(1), 191–213.
Le Grand, J. & Bartlett, W. (Eds.) (1993). *Quasi-markets and social policy*. London: Macmillan.
Magalhães, A.M. & Stoer, S.R. (2003). Performance, citizenship and the knowledge society: A new mandate for European education policy. *Globalisation, Societies and Education, 1*, 41–66.
Marshall, H. (2003). Review essay: Global education: A re-emerging field. *British Journal of Sociology of Education, 24*(3), 397–405.

Marshall, H. (2005). Developing the global gaze in citizenship education: Exploring the perspectives of global education NGO workers in England. *International Journal of Citizenship and Teacher Education*, *1*(2), 76–92.

Meyer, H.D., & Rowan, B. (Eds.) (2007). *The new institutionalism in education: Advancing research and policy*. Albany: State University of New York Press.

Meyer, J., Kamens, D., & Benavot, A. (1992). *School knowledge for the masses: World models and national primary curricular categories in the twentieth century*. Washington, DC: Falmer.

Meyer, J.W. (2001). *Globalization, national culture, and the future of the world polity*. Wei Lun Lecture, delivered at The Chinese University of Hong Kong, November 28.

Newman, J.E., & Clarke, J. (2009). *Publics, politics and power: Remaking the public in public services*. London: Sage.

Pykett, J. (2007). Making citizens governable? The Crick Report as governmental technology. *Journal of Education Policy*, *22*(3), 301–319.

Pykett, J. (2009a). Pedagogical power: Lessons from school spaces. *Education, Citizenship and Social Justice*, *4*(2), 102–116.

Pykett, J. (2009b). Personalization and de-schooling: Uncommon trajectories in contemporary education policy. *Critical Social Policy*, *29*(3), 374–397.

Robertson, S. (2009). Globalisation, education governance and citizenship regimes: New democratic deficits and social injustices. In W. Ayers, T. Quinn, & D. Stovall (Eds.), *Handbook of social justice in education* (pp. 542–553). London: Routledge.

Robertson, S., Bonal, X., & Dale, R. (2002). GATS and the education service industry. *Comparative Education Review*, *46*(4), 472–497.

Robertson, S., & Dale, R. (2008). Researching education in a globalising era: Beyond methodological nationalism, methodological statism, methodological educationism and spatial fetishism. In J. Resnik (Ed.), *The production of educational knowledge in the global era* (pp. 19–32). Rotterdam: Sense Publications.

Robertson, S., Dale, R., Thrupp, M., Vaughan, K., & Jacka, S. (1997). *A review of ERO: Final report to the PPTA*. Auckland: University of Auckland.

Robertson, S.L. (2007). Public-private partnerships, digital firms and the production of a neo-liberal education space at the European scale. In K. Gulson & C. Symes (Eds.), *Out of place: Contemporary spatial theories and the cartography of education policy* (pp. 215–232). London: Routledge.

Ruggie, J.G. (1993). Territoriality and beyond: Problematizing modernity in international relations. *International Organization 47*(1), 139–174.

Santos, B. de S. (2002). *Towards a new legal common sense*. London: Butterworth.

Stoer, S.R., & Magalhães, A.M. (2002). The reconfiguration of the modern social contract: New forms of citizenship and education. *European Education Research Journal*, *1*(4), 692–703.

Taylor, C. (2002). Modern social imaginaries. *Public Culture*, *14*(1), 91–124.

Unger, R.M. (1998). *Democracy realized: The progressive alternative*. London: Verso.

Globalization, International Education, and the Formation of a Transnational Class?[1]

PHILLIP BROWN AND HUGH LAUDER

Social class is "an active process, which owes as much to agency as to conditioning." (E.P. Thompson, *The Making of the English Working Class*, 1963, p. 9)

The idea that education is intimately linked to the reproduction of social class has a long pedigree. Through the theoretical contributions of writers such as Bowles and Gintis (1976), Bourdieu and Passeron (1977), and Collins (1979) it has been established that there are systemic educational inequalities: the children from professional middle class backgrounds are far more likely to succeed in the competition for credentials than those from the working class. But there has always been another element to theories of class reproduction which relate, broadly speaking, to character.[2] It is that education, as a classed institution, shapes or informs character by differentially creating or reinforcing the kinds of dispositions, attitudes, and cultural attributes necessary for entry into professional middle class occupations.

However, these theories of class reproduction were developed at a time when the key terms in theories of reproduction—education, social class, capitalism and nationalism—were all relatively stable. That is to say, the broad narrative was one in which there was a national, largely state system of education, which "certificated" students in terms of credentials and character for work in a capitalist economy which also structured the class system.

The key term here is "national," since it was assumed that class reproduction took place within national borders. However, the advent of economic globalization has raised the possibility, as suggested by Bauman (2002), that in an era of globalization the state is becoming separated from the nation because of the flows of people across borders, the loss of state power in guiding the economy, and the loss of what is perceived to be national cultures. This is of course an ambitious claim, yet in some areas Bauman's insight has resonance; one of these concerns the emergence of the international school system and international rather than state-certified forms of credential, like the International

Baccalaureate (IB), and an increasingly globalized higher education system. The international school system is not subject to any national system of control, and while elite universities in the English-speaking world, in particular, may be subject to national regulation, they act like private entities in attracting overseas students.

At the same time theorists have pointed to the creation of an international system of production of goods and services and of labor markets, in the latter case particularly for those with highly marketable professional skills (Reich, 1991). When these two new features of the global social and economic landscape are put together, it prompts the question of whether what we are witnessing is not so much the reproduction of class privilege but of the production of new educational pathways for the formation of a new global ruling class or set of elites. The recent history of globalization has created renewed interest in the possibility of a transnational ruling class (Faux, 2006; Robinson, 2004; Rothkopf, 2008; Sassen, 2005; Sklair, 2001).[3]

To ask this question is not to anticipate a clear or decisive answer. We are in the middle of what appears to be a fast-moving set of global educational and economic changes. Rather the purpose of the chapter is to raise a crucial issue. Although social class is about inequalities in life chances and about character, these are intimately related to who has power, how they gained it, and under what conditions, so the question we are focusing on concerns the ways that aspects of cultural and economic globalization may be fundamentally changing the nature of class and class reproduction. In this respect, international education can be seen as a kind of litmus test in interrogating the place of education, power, and ideology in a globalized economy.

In the following sections we detail the development of international education both with respect to character and credentials, and identify its putative links with elite higher education. How then might this educational path feed into global class recruitment? If we accept that significant aspects of class structuration develop out of economic relations, then clearly the plausibility of concepts like that of a transnational ruling class will depend upon global economic developments. Here there are two theoretically competing accounts of economic globalization which have a bearing on the issue of social class; the first relates to the ideology and practice of neoliberalism, which gives some plausibility to the emergence of a transnational ruling class, while the second sees economic globalization as fundamentally about imperialism—that is, a competition between nations for fundamental economic advantage across the globe (Callinicos,

2009). In this case the focus remains, as it has traditionally, on the construction of national class systems.

The International School System and International Qualifications

The international school system and its related credentials has a long history. However, it has been caught up in the processes of globalization described above. In 1964 there were estimated to be some 50 international schools; by 1995, there were over 1,000, and now there are approximately 2,700. This rise can be accounted for by the rapid increase in the numbers of global workers and the emergence of middle class elites in developing countries with the funds available for private international education. Canterford (2009) reports that, in his sample, over 50% of the students attending international schools were nationals in the country where the schools were located. There has been a significant debate about the nature and definition of international schools because there is a wide variation in their organization. However, our concern is with those that attract international and indigenous elites and who demand considerable fees for the education they offer. Research by Macdonald (2006) has shown that the average international school fee, per annum, is between US$6,429 and US$10,451, with the highest recorded being US$54,264. These are substantial sums.

In relation to questions of social class there are two elements to international education, as with national education systems, that are noteworthy: the production of character (including the question of language), and that of credentials.

An Education for "Character"?

One of the major debates within the international school system has turned on the question of how international education should relate to both global and national communities. It is not only that the schools stand outside the national systems of their host countries, but also that, in a sense, those students who are drawn from expatriate communities are seen as developing identities that do not relate to any particular national context. In other words, as the number of children in expatriate communities rises a new form of identity is being constructed which relates to and informs the nature of international schools.

Useem (1976)—who coined the term "third culture kids" (TKCs)—was the first to research the needs of American internationally mobile young adults. Finding there were commonalities in experiences of repatriation to their passport countries, Useem found that

Although they have grown up in foreign countries they are not integral parts of those countries. When they come to their country of citizenship (some for the first time) they do not feel at home because they do not know the lingo or expectations of others—especially of those their own age. Where they do feel most themselves is in that interstitial culture, the third culture, which is created, shared and carried by persons who are relating societies, or sections thereof, to each other. (Quoted in Langford, 1998, p. 29.)

In more recent times the issues relating to TCKs have been identified in a wider cohort of internationally mobile students from other nationalities, who due to their parents' occupations have spent a significant amount of their developmental years living in one or more countries outside of their passport country. This has given rise to the term "global nomads" (Sachaetti, 1993) who are "members of a world-wide community of persons who share a unique cultural heritage. While developing some sense of belonging to both their host culture[s] and passport culture[s] they do not have a sense of total ownership in any" (quoted in Langford, 1998).

Several studies on the experiences of TCKs and global nomads have identified a range of characteristics they have in common. These include multilingualism, cross-cultural awareness, and a range of related skills such as diplomacy, flexibility, patience, and tolerance (Kilham, 1990; Langford, 1997). However, they also refer to the ability to be self-sufficient, including characteristics such as independence, maturity, and the ability to cope in a crisis (Stuart, 1992).

"Character" and the Demands of the Global Labor Market

How then are we to understand the relationship between the characteristics of TCK students and the global labor market? In order to explore this question it is illuminating to compare the characteristics of the "ideal type" TCK/global nomad with the attributes sought for key workers in high-end managerial and research and design positions. Drawing upon interviews carried out by Brown, Lauder, and Ashton (2010) with HR personnel within a range of transnational corporations (TNCs) across diverse industries, a number of core competencies were identified as important. These were firmly rooted in the importance of "soft skills" such as interpersonal and communication skills, teamwork, nuanced understanding of multiple cultures, and a flexible adaptable outlook. Such requirements are neatly encapsulated in an interview with HR managers at an electrical TNC in Korea:

To be a global manager, [requires a person] . . . to be a kind of a cultural translator. I think this really requires a lot of the softer skills that have not been a traditional focus of Korean management. And I think that is something that we have to become more sophisticated about you know being a little bit more nuance in your interactions, just being more, being more aware and again being more flexible and not you know you hear the old adage you know treat others as you would like to be treated. It is treat others as they want to be treated and I think that just by learning more so it is not just going to a country and being the, you know the tourist, but really you know empathising.

In order to be able to relate to multiple national cultures, it was apparent that the culture and identity of the TNC was of fundamental importance. This was reflected in attributes sought in staff such that they could engage with multiple cultures while maintaining a commitment to the distinct culture of the corporation. This was explained in an interview with a global bank in Beijing:

This kind of people is not only very capable for the softer skills for leadership, communication, interpersonal and something like that but also the people who knows very well our company and our culture because for [X bank] it has already 140 years history and why we can run so smoothly because we have the core culture inside.

In one sense we might interpret these views as a straightforward correspondence between the student characteristics of TCKs and the way they are fostered within international schools and the "third culture" of TNCs. For example, an HR executive for a leading electronics TNC commented: "X is really a company with a very strong culture, globally. It doesn't mean you are US, or UK, or China, we have this consistent culture." Another electronics HR manager spoke of the common values that were necessary: "You can't have a different set of . . . value system or a code of conduct in India different than Europe, it, it's the same across the globe." A banking TNC HR manager spoke in similar terms: "The organisation is attempting really is to fuse together cultures . . . hopefully they'll absorb the best of each."

We consider this evidence suggestive. There are always debates about the nature and possibilities of correspondences between education and capitalist work (Cole, 1988). However, in these cases, TNCs may be able to articulate what they see as desirable qualities at a certain level of abstraction. Whether they are able to identify potential recruits with any precision is another matter. As Alvesson (2001) has noted, there is considerable ambiguity in both the qualities that are required for knowledge work and a considerable amount of impression management in judgments that are made about such workers. Moreover, while at one level it is surprising that HR managers seek the same qualities and skills, despite different cultural locations, there may nevertheless be different cultural interpretations of what these qualities and skills mean in practice.

Nevertheless, however these terms are understood, what these data point to is the search within TNCs for professional workers with a new cultural identity and forms of cultural competence—a consequence of a new form of global commercial organization.

Where the evidence of links between education and professional global workers is perhaps clearer is with respect to the teaching of English. It is the current *lingua franca* of global commerce and, as Lai and Byram (2006) have argued, it is key to the positional competition for education and credentials in East Asia. It is important to see that being bilingual or multilingual is not just a matter of acquiring a set of skills, it is a matter of confidence in being culturally conversant: in the current global era, it can be argued, it is a form of cultural capital and a significant element of identity.

The majority of international schools teach in English. Research by Canterford (2009) suggests that 95% of schools in his sample actively recruited teachers for whom English was their mother tongue because it was also the language of instruction. Given the comments above we can assume such schools will be at a premium for those that can afford them.

International Credentials

What is the evidence that the IB does indeed deliver a "gold standard" credential that opens doors to higher education? While general data on the destinations of international school students is not available, Matthews (1998) found that 89% of students from his sample of international schools went to university—with the majority going to the United States. This is a high proportion of school students who subsequently attend university. Canterford's (2009) study reinforces this point. In his sample, 94% of the schools stated that the USA or the UK featured as one of the top three destinations for higher education.[4]

These data, when combined with the cost of attendance at international schools, suggests that the emergent international education system does indeed cater for two kinds of elite: the children of professional global workers, and those from national elites who also buy into these schools. In turn they gain access to English-speaking universities, typically in North America and Britain. While this establishes the possibility that a global elite education system is being constructed, more data are needed to show that those from international schools are more likely to attend the globe's elite universities. It is certainly what many international schools claim.

What makes this possible and constitutes a crucial further part of the development of an educational path into the global elites is the commodification and internationalization of higher education (Marginson, 2006). The combination of global league tables for universities, coupled with an international flow of students prepared to pay for higher education, has fundamentally changed the nature of positional competition, because while it was once national it now has a very significant global dimension.

The significance of this global dimension can best be seen in the way that leading TNCs recruit from elite universities and the way these universities respond. The construction of social class is often seen as a one-way street from educational credential into the job market, but this does not address the question of why some universities are seen by leading corporations as more desirable than others.

Recruitment and the TNC-University Reputational Relationship

If we turn to the recruiting practices of these elite TNC companies utilizing the data from the study previously cited (Brown et al., 2010), it is apparent that transnational companies increasingly benchmark leading universities around the world. At the top end of the value chain, companies tend to target a small number of globally ranked universities and business schools for their international programs. A leading investment bank targets just eight business schools including Columbia, Wharton, Harvard, and INSEAD. While a lot of the business in based in London, only one of the eight is in the UK. As one HR manager put it:

We look at our tier ones [universities] and our tier twos and they're the ones that we say, okay, we're going to proactively go and we're gonna do presentations, we're gonna sponsor the hockey club . . . the very limited scholarship money we have we'll point in that direction. Everything that's going to enhance our brand at those universities then we'll do.

Leading transnational corporations gravitate towards the global elite of universities because they are believed to have the best and brightest students. It is difficult to understand what underlies this view but it seems that the reputations of these elite institutions not only relate to the credentials they offer but also that they stand proxy for a series of desirable characteristics that TNCs seek.[5] This view is actively promoted by leading universities because higher education has become a global business. The branding of universities and faculty members is now integral to the organization of academic enquiry. Claims to world-class standards depend on attracting "the best" academics and forming alliances with other elite universities elsewhere in the world, while recruiting the "right" kinds of students. Universities play the same reputational games as companies, because it is a logical consequence of market competition.

At the same time recruiting from these universities enhances TNCs own brand reputation, in that they are recruiting those recognized as the brightest and best. The issue of recruiting to enhance the brand of the company extends to the highest levels. One of our finance inter-viewees had an international reputation in relation to banking in China, and when he was recruited by a Western bank it made headlines in the financial sections of the papers in China.

By choosing to fish in such a small pond for talent, companies are strengthening the barriers to entry. It is as if they are putting a sign out, "Those who are not at internationally recognized universities need not apply." What may be considered extraordinary about this strategy is that despite the demand for increased numbers of young managers who can work across the globe, they remain focused on recruiting from the elite universities in each country. And here our data suggest that TNCs use the same strategy in each country, so that, for example, in China they will recruit from those universities considered amongst the very best.

Our data only relate to leading TNCs. There are clearly other global employers such as NGOs about which there is little data regard-ing their recruitment practices. However, what our data do show is that there is a clear path from elite universities into the high-end segments of the global labor market.

So far we have identified elements of a global educational path from international schools through to elite universities and into the labor market. And here we should stress that the evidence is incomplete. What we are witnessing is a set of possibilities, signs that a path is under construction. What then of the idea that this path might lead to the creation of a transnational ruling class as has been suggested? In order to understand the reasoning behind this literature we need first to examine developments in economic globalization. Here we can distin-guish between two phases.

The Changing Nature of Global Economic Competition

Phase 1: The Neoliberal Global Order

The most recent round of economic and political globalization can be dated from the 1980s under the administrations of Reagan and Thatcher. In her history of that period Patricia Marchak (1990) notes that the drive to open up economies to market forces was matched by their extension across borders. This could be seen as a response to the recession of the early 1980s, in which national trade union movements were seen as stifling innovation and wealth creation. By further opening borders to market forces, the strength of trade unions would be weakened while national corporate champions, particularly in the United States, could establish new markets and sources of profitability. The move to spread neoliberalism across borders was based, as Marchak's scholarship shows, on detailed planning exemplified by the work of the Trilateral Commission. This Commission, established by David Rockefeller in 1973, represented the international business elite and advanced "a general programme for achieving a liberal integrated world economic system, secure from protectionist disruption and domestic upheaval" (Ferguson & Rogers, 1980, p. 785).

Throughout the 1990s and early 2000s this program seemed to be working smoothly, at least on the surface. There were significant differences between the early round of imperialism debated by socialists and the current form of globalization which posed the question of whether the power of the nation-state was eroding. In turn this raised the possibility of a transnational ruling class.

Two major developments during the neoliberal global phase stand out. First, the emergence of transnational corporations: the United Nations estimates that there are around 64,000 transnational companies, a rise from 37,000 in the early 1990s. These transnational companies comprise parent enterprises and foreign affiliates which vary in size and influence. The foreign affiliates of these companies generated approximately 53 million jobs around the world (see UNCTAD, 2005). General Electric had the largest foreign assets in 2003, with 330 enterprises in the United States and over 1,000 foreign affiliates.[6]

The key role that these firms play in shaping the global economy is reflected in the fact that a third of global trade is due to intra-firm activities where components, products, services, and software are sold between affiliates within the same company. Equally, it is estimated that over 60% of the goods exported from China in 2005 came from foreign-owned firms that had moved manufacturing plants to increase profit margins (Stewart, 2005). This extraordinary expansion raises fundamental questions about the power of TNCs independent of nation-states, about the outlook of these organizations, and about the personnel that manage them.

There is little doubt that during the neoliberal era TNCs exerted great pressure on states, particularly in the conditions they demanded in return for their substantial capacity for investment. For nation-states, attracting investment is a crucial aspect of job creation. But it has also been well documented that TNCs can exert downward pressure on wages and job conditions through the threat to move location if workers do not accept the conditions offered (Brown et al., 2010). But TNCs have also played a crucial role in the rise of the East Asian economies, especially China. As one leading Chinese economist has put it, "China has been a big schoolroom and the multinationals our teacher" (quoted in Brown et al., 2010). He meant by this that, through TNC investment, China was catching up rapidly in the development and use of new technologies and in the structuring of organizations.

We have used the term TNC advisedly, because what we have witnessed over this period is the move from multinational companies (MNCs), which remained rooted in their home countries, to TNCs, for which their country of origin has less influence on their commercial decision-making. In turn this suggests a change in the outlook and allegiances of their senior managers. Such an outlook does imply the possibility of a transnational class.

The second major feature unique to the neoliberal phase of globalization turned on the development of multilateral agencies under the "Washington consensus." These agencies—the World Bank (WB), the International Monetary Fund (IMF), and the World Trade Organization (WTO)—helped to orchestrate in various ways the development of global trade and especially the activities of the TNCs. Williamson (1990) defined the pillars of this consensus as "prudent macroeconomic policies, outward orientation and free market capitalism" (p. 20). Central to this orientation was a rejection of state intervention, trade liberalization, privatization, and deregulation. In the light of subsequent events this policy platform may bring, at best, a wry smile to the reader. Nevertheless, what it did was to build an ideological and policy bridge between the key national players, TNCs, and the multilateral agencies, in a range of relevant areas including education (Rizvi & Lingard, 2006; Robertson, Bonal, & Dale, 2006).

It is on the basis of these developments that neo-Marxist scholars posited the development of a global ruling class. In neo-Marxist theories, in order for a class to be formed it must have a common basis in the means of production: for the ruling class, by either owning or organising production, and for the working class, by selling their labour to the owners and organizers of production. The rationale for arguing that we now have a global basis for production is that transnational corporations have indeed created a global form of production (Robinson, 2004). And there are grounds for believing such a transnational ruling class has emerged. As Will Hutton (2008) notes:

Every January, Zurich airport plays host to a peculiar migration when around 150 Gulfstream private jets touch down. The superclass is arriving for the World Economic Forum in Davos . . . A Gulfstream carries a mere eight passengers in extraordinary opulence; reclining leather armchairs, polished wood panelling and the latest high definition TV. They cost $45 million each and $1.25 million to service for each 500 hours in the air.

At Davos, the notion of a transnational ruling class appears to crystallize. Most fundamentally, growth in the global economy encourages the development of stateless elites whose allegiance is to global economic success and their own prosperity rather than the interests of the nation where they are headquartered. "As one prominent chief executive at Davos put it to Lawrence Summers (who now holds a key economic position in President Obama's administration), 'We will be fine however America does'" (*The Financial Times*, 29 April 2008).

But the annual meeting at Davos includes not only the owners and organisers of global production but also politicians and key policy makers. This suggests that the classical Marxist account given by Robinson (2004) needs extending. Sklair (2001) has argued that a theory of a transnational ruling class would need to include: TNC executives; politicians; high-level national and multilateral agency bureaucrats who are active in formulating global economic rules; professionals who act as consultants and operate think tanks seeking to influence global policy; and those involved in global trading, media and advertising. The extension of the transnational ruling class in this way implies that politicians and bureaucrats, for example, are active in the construction of the rules and processes of globalization as well as the organisation of production. This is intuitively plausible; if we take the World Trade Organization (WTO), for example, it is clear that its bureaucrats have actively helped to establish the rules of the present form of economic globalization.

It is significant that for Sklair (2001) the ideology that legitimizes the transnational class is that of neoliberalism, which privileges individual freedom within the market and elevates the market to the key organizational principle of society. In relation to globalization, market freedom is applied to the breaking down of trade barriers to enable powerful transnational corporations (TNCs) to extend their markets. In this sense there appears to be a coherent logic behind the idea of a transnational ruling class: they have a common objective position in terms of global production, they have common interests, and they have a common ideology.

There have been many theoretical critiques of neo-Marxist conceptions of class, and we shall return to these theoretical questions at the end of this chapter. The more immediate point is that while the notion that a transnational ruling class was plausible for the first 20 years of this round of economic globalization, more recent events suggest it is now less so. There are two reasons for this: the emergence of China and India as nationalistic economic superpowers, and the advent of the present economic crisis which has fundamentally challenged the neoliberal consensus and shifted economic power decisively towards East Asia.

Phase 2: The Emergence of China and India and the Global Economic Crisis

There are three features to the rise of these nations that are significant. Firstly, both nations see their entry into the global economy as a means of furthering national interests and in doing so they are responding to what they see as the neocolonialism of Britain and America. In a sense the form of the global economy from these perspectives are not so different from that viewed by socialists at the turn of the nineteenth century.

In China, the backdrop for this nationalism can be seen as the "century of humiliation" lasting from the mid-nineteenth to the mid-twentieth century before the rise of communism (Henderson, 2008; Wu, 2008). During this time the Chinese lost wars to Britain and Japan. How this century is understood as a central narrative is a matter of debate but there is little doubt that Chinese sensitivities about their past has driven their global ambitions. Indeed Henderson has argued that a new Global-Asian era is being ushered in with China at its centre.

In India there is a similar sense of overcoming a colonial past. As one owner of an Indian multinational company put it: "For years, globalization is something that the west did to the rest. Now the boot's on the other foot" ("Is This the Indian Century?" *The Guardian*, March 29, 2008). And this nationalism also has an element of the empire striking back. When the Tata conglomerate bought Jaguar and Land Rover, *The Times of India* rolled out the headline, "Tatas Rule Britannia," and on its front page, "It took a company from a former colony to come to the rescue of a beleaguered British brand" (reported in "Is This the Indian Century?"). The irony is that it was the decline of economic nationalism in the West and the advent of neoliberalism with respect to the role of TNCs and free trade agreements that has helped the rise of economic nationalism in Asian countries.

Secondly, it is no longer the case that these economies are merely the world's factory or call centers. Their processes of innovation are making them significant players in the world economy.

It is now becoming clear that Chinese companies are developing low-cost innovation strategies that threaten Western-based TNCs. As Zeng and Williamson (2007) note, "The cost-innovation challenge presented by Chinese companies is disruptive because it strikes at the heart of what makes many businesses in high-cost countries profitable" (Zeng & Williamson, p. 2). Why? Because just as politicians in the West think the antidote to the challenges of globalization is to upskill workers, so companies see moving up the value chain as the route to sustained competitiveness. The Chinese response is to innovate by moving up the value chain at costs far lower than their Western rivals.

With the strength of the yuan and the vast currency reserves China has accumulated, major foreign TNCs are being bought up or bought into in order to develop Chinese knowledge capacity. These include, for example, a stake in Barclays and the buying of MG Rover. Germany is a particular focus for China and here their interest appears to be in the Mittlestand engineering companies which have been the engine of German wealth creation. So concerned is the German government that it is considering the possibility of legislation to protect strategic German companies from mergers and acquisitions.

In India a similar story can be told. As part of our research into the skill strategies of TNCs, we interviewed senior policy makers in Delhi (Brown et al., 2010). Here we heard a similar account of the way Indian companies are buying up major Western companies in the way Tata purchased Jaguar and Land Rover from Ford. As one of our interviewees, a senior policy maker, in Delhi, noted:

Our pharmaceutical companies want to buy companies up outside, partly because of the trademarks that they hold, etc., but more because of the market access it gives them. And our manufacturing companies, particularly in automobile forging units are wanting to buy up a major German company.

... Because the costs of producing are high overseas, the Indian investors see an opportunity of taking it over, initially produced there, and introduce an Indian management style and maybe in the course of time relocate here.

Finally, countries like the United States and Britain are deeply indebted to China and the other East Asian nations that have accumulated US dollars. This has led not only to substantial Asian investments in the major global corporations but has announced the arrival of countries like China and India through their pressure to be included in the major economic fora representing national and global interests. As of May 2009, the United States had $1.4 trillion dollars worth of debt, rising by $1 billion a day. As James Fallows has noted, "every person in the (rich) United States has over the past 10 years or so borrowed about $4,000 from someone in the (poor) People's Republic of China" (Fallows, 2008).

Notwithstanding the irony of this state of affairs, the implications of the bailout of the American and British financial and motor sectors again point in the direction of national fixes for global problems. It is, after all, the taxpayers in these countries who will pay the bill for these debts.

In effect, this second phase of globalization looks significantly different from the first. In the former it seemed that the TNCs and multilateral agencies would see a decline in the significance of the nation state, as hyper-globalists like Ohmae (1990) had predicted, while in the latter phase the locus of power seems to have swung back to the nation-state.

Conclusion

We appear to have returned to a situation similar to that prior to World War I in that economic globalization looks more like a competition among nations. In this case, as Callinicos (2009) has reminded us, the more apt description of what we are witnessing is imperialist competition between major national economic powers, rather than economic globalization. If this is the case, then the account of how education and social class relates to economic globalization or imperialism looks rather different.

The emergence of China and India as economic powers and the national bailouts of the American and British banking sectors by taxpayers in those countries challenge the plausibility of theories of global ruling classes or indeed elites.[7]

However, before deciding that recent economic developments suggest a return to an imperialist competition for global advantage, there are two points to be made. First, economic globalization today is fundamentally different to that at the turn of the twentieth century. This is because, as well as the competition between nations, there are global institutions such as TNCs and non-governmental organisations (NGOs), that exert considerable influence on national economies, as we have seen. What we appear to have is a mosaic of global power and privilege that is part nationally based and part transnationally based. However, where power and privilege lie in any given context remains to be investigated.

In turn this suggests that we need a far more nuanced account of education and social class in the current phase of economic globalization. On the one hand we have to consider the routes from education through to the senior positions in transnational companies, and on the other the educational routes to elite positions in national state and private enterprise organizations. In this chapter we have drawn attention to the role of international education and elite universities in the process of developing access through character and credentials to TNCs. However the processes of recruitment to national and transnational elites are not distinct. The hierarchy of global universities may enable strategies that enable movement between national and transnational elites. For example, we were told in our research on TNCs skill strategies that in China attendance at a university such as Beijing then enabled students to gain places in Ivy league colleges to undertaken postgraduate work in the United States. This is a case of a national portal being used as an access route to universities of elite standing in the English-speaking world, which in turn may enable access to both national and transnational corporate elites.

Since education is closely involved in recruitment to these national and global elites, we need a theoretical account of class that considers both economic and cultural aspects of the recruitment process. As we have attempted to show, such an account would have to examine both the cultural formation of character in the present form of economic globalization as well as the economics of production and the labor market which generates the present national and transnational class structures. In particular, what is required is an understanding of the ways cultural and economic capital combine within educational, economic and political fields to produce advantage and exclusion within a global context (Devine, Savage, Scott, & Crompton, 2005). In effect, what we need is an account of social class that encompasses Marx's mill owners and Weber's Chinese literati.

At the heart of the shifting power dynamics we have identified, the issue of which groups come to shape our destinies remains. This is why questions of education in relation to social class will endure. In this context, the developments in international education provide something of a litmus test in seeing how education can be related to global class or elite formations in the present period of globalization. In this sense international education and a commodified global higher education system constitute elements in a complex and evolving set of education and class relations. It can be conjectured that these educational institutions may well provide access to elite positions in TNCs and NGOs. Given the increasing number of global workers as reflected in the almost exponential expansion of international schools and the intensifying positional competition for credentials, we can expect this sector to grow in significance as a route to power and privilege.

NOTES

1. This paper is a development of a series of papers related to the issues discussed here. These include: Brown (2000), Lauder (2006), and Brown and Lauder (2009).

2. How "character" is constructed is also a matter of different theories. See, for example, Bowles and Gintis (1976), Collins (1979), and more recently the approach developed by, for example, Popkewitz (2009) for the ways in which educational practices and discourse "construct" children.

3. There is of course a sense in which the reproduction of educational inequalities and privilege is always being re-created even within national contexts as labor markets and cultures change. Yet here we seem to be dealing with genuinely novel phenomena, hence the emphasis on production rather than creative forms of reproduction.

4. It should be emphasised that while the IB was intimately linked to the philosophy of international schools, an unintended consequence of its development has been that it is rapidly being adopted within national school systems. By 2020 it is estimated that two and half million students across the globe will be studying for the IB; this number far exceeds students attending international schools (Bunnell, 2009). In September 2007, of the 2,511 schools that now offer one or more of the IB programs, 38% are found in North America, and the majority of these are state schools.

This then points to an important distinction between the experience of attending an international school, which may foster the culture of global nomads, and the use of the IB qualification, which may in some way be grafted onto national systems. In turn this points to two different types of positional competition: the global, as represented by international schools, and the national. In this latter case it seems that local elites clearly see the IB as a way of gaining access to both national and global elites. In the case of state schools, what we may be seeing is the adoption of global credentials, such as the IB Diploma, in order to counter the advantage that credentials like the IB may have given private international schools. The development of IB schools within national systems also raises questions about whether those attending these schools can gain an advantage within the national positional competition for credentials. In other words, it may be that IB credential holders may gain access to national professional middle class jobs, if not those relating to the global economy.

5. For a discussion of the concept of reputation in relation to universities see Brown and Hesketh (2004) and Strathdee (2009).

6. UNCTAD (2005), Appendix A, pp. 267–268. These figures exclude TNCs in the financial sector.

7. In turn this economic crisis leads to a questioning of Bauman's view as to the separation of the national from the state.

REFERENCES

Alvesson, M. (2001). Knowledge work, ambiguity, image and identity. *Human Relations*, *54*(7), 863–886.

Bauman, Z. (2002). *Society under siege*. Cambridge: Polity Press.

Bourdieu, P., & Passeron, J. (1977). *Reproduction in education, society and culture*. Thousand Oaks, CA: Sage.

Bowles, S., & Gintis, H. (1976). *Schooling in capitalist America*. London: Routledge & Kegan Paul.

Brown, C., & Lauder, H. (2009). *The political economy of international schools and social class formation*. A report prepared for the Faculty of Education, Deakin University.

Brown, P. (2000). The globalisation of positional competition. *Sociology*, *34*(4), 633–653.

Brown, P., & Hesketh, A. (2004). *The mismanagement of talent*. Oxford: Oxford University Press.

Brown, P., Lauder, H., & Ashton, D. (2010). *The global auction: The broken promises of education, jobs and incomes*. New York: Oxford University Press.

Bunnell, T. (2009). The international baccalaureate in the USA and the emerging culture war. *Discourse: Studies in the Cultural Politics of Education*, *30*(1), 61–72.

Callinicos, A. (2009). *Imperialism and global political economy*. Cambridge: Polity Press.

Canterford, G. (2009). *Segmented labour markets in international schools*. Ed.D. thesis, University of Bath, UK.

Cole, M. (1988). *Bowles and Gintis revisited: Correspondence and contradiction in educational theory*. Brighton: Falmer Press.

Collins, R. (1979). *The credential society: An historical sociology of education and stratification*. New York: Academic Press.

Devine, F., Savage, M., Scott, J., & Crompton, R. (2005). *Rethinking class, culture, identities and lifestyle*. Basingstoke: Palgrave.

Fallows, J. (2008). The $1.4 trillion question. *The Atlantic*, Jan/Feb. Available at http://www.whitehouse.gov/omb/budget/fy2009/pdf/hist.pdf.

Faux, J. (2006). *The global class war*. New York: John Wiley & Sons.

Ferguson, T., & Rogers, J. (1980). Another trilateral election. *The Nation*, June 28.

Henderson, J. (2008). China and global development: Towards a global-Asian era? *Contemporary Politics*, *14*(4), 375–392.

Hutton, W. (2008). Feeble government lets the superclass soar over the rest of us. *The Observer*, May 4.

Kilham, N. (1990). World-wise kids. *The Washington Post*, February 15, B5.

Lai, P.-S., & Byram, M. (2006). The politics of bilingualism: A reproduction analysis of the policy of mother tongue education in Hong Kong after 1997. In H. Lauder, P. Brown, J. Dillabough, & A.H. Halsey (Eds.), *Education, globalization and social change* (pp. 490–504). Oxford: Oxford University Press.

Langford, M.E. (1997). *Internationally mobile pupils in transition: The role of the international school*. MA dissertation, University of Bath.

Langford , M.E. (1998). Global nomads, third culture kids and international schools. In M. Hayden & J. Thompson (Eds.), *International education: Principles and practice* London: Kogan Page.

Lauder, H. (2006). International schools, education and globalisation: Towards a research agenda. In M. Hayden, J. Levy, & J. Thompson (Eds.), *Research in international education* (pp. 441–449). London: Sage.

Macdonald, J. (2006). The international school industry. *Journal of Research in International Education*, 5(2), 191–213.

Marchak, M.P. (1990). *The integrated circus: The new right and the restructuring of global markets*. Montreal: McGill-Queens University Press.

Marginson, S. (2006). National and global competition in higher education. In H. Lauder, P. Brown, J.-A. Dillabough, & A.H. Halsey (Eds.), *Education, globalization and social change* (pp. 893–908). Oxford: Oxford University Press.

Matthews, M. (1998). *The ethos of international schools*. MSc dissertation, University of Oxford.

Ohmae, K. (1990). *The borderless world*. London: Collins.

Popkewitz, T. (2009, forthcoming). Numbers in grids of intelligibility: Making sense of how educational truth is told. In H. Lauder, M. Young, H. Daniels, M. Balarin, & J. Lowe (Eds.), *Educating for the knowledge economy?*. London: Routledge.

Reich, R. (1991). *The work of nations*. New York: Simon and Schuster.

Rizvi, F., & Lingard, B. (2006). Globalization and the changing nature of the OECD's educational work. In H. Lauder, P. Brown, J.-A. Dillabough, & A.H. Halsey (Eds.), *Education, globalization and social change* (pp. 247–276). Oxford: Oxford University Press.

Robertson, S., Bonal, X., & Dale, R. (2006). GATS and the education service industry: The politics of scale and reterritorialization. In H. Lauder, P. Brown, J.-A. Dillabough, & A.H. Halsey (Eds.), *Education, globalization and social change* (pp. 228–246). Oxford: Oxford University Press.

Robinson, W.I. (2004). *A theory of global capitalism*. Baltimore: Johns Hopkins University Press.

Rothkopf, D. (2008). *Superclass: The global power elite and the world they are making*. New York: Little, Brown.

Sachaetti, B. (1993, April). The global nomad profile. Paper presented at *The Global Nomad: The Benefits and Challenges of an Internationally Mobile Childhood*. Conference, Regents College, London.

Sassen, S. (2005). New global classes: Implications for politics. In A. Giddens & P. Diamond (Eds.), *The new egalitarianism* (pp. 143–170). Cambridge: Polity Press.

Sklair, L. (2001). *The transnational capitalist class*. Oxford: Blackwell.

Stewart, H. (2005). The west sees red. *The Observer*, June 12.

Strathdee, R. (2009). Reputation in the sociology of education. *British Journal of Sociology of Education*, 30(1), 83–96.

Stuart, K.D. (1992). Teens play a role on moves overseas. *Personnel Journal*, 71, 72–78.

United Nations Conference on Trade and Development (UNCTAD) (2005). *World investment report: Transnational corporations and the internationalization of R&D*. Available at http://www.unctad.org/wir.

Useem, R.H. (1976). Third culture kids. *Today's Education*, 65(3), 103–105.

Williamson, J. (1990). What Washington means by policy reform. In J. Williamson (Ed.), *Latin American adjustment: How much has happened?* (pp. 7–38). Washington, DC: Institute for International Economics.

Wu, G. (2008). From post-imperial to late communist nationalism: Historical change in Chinese nationalism from May Fourth to the 1990s. *Third World Quarterly*, 29(3), 467–482.

Zeng, M., & Williamson, P. (2007). *Dragons at your door: How Chinese cost innovation is disrupting global competition*. Boston: Harvard Business School Press.

Wither the Neighborhood?
Education Policy, Neoliberal Globalization
and Gentrification

KALERVO N. GULSON

This chapter is part of broader ongoing attempts to demonstrate that shifts in educational policy can be understood as mutually constitutive with the changing nature of contemporary cities, including changes in urban policy (see, e.g., Gulson, 2007a, 2007b, 2008). In this chapter I want to explore one aspect of these broader attempts, namely the relationships between education policy, globalization, and the notion of the neighborhood. To do this I am going to briefly propose that the neighborhood has been deemed as relatively insignificant within certain discourses of globalization, and then use the chapter to try and argue that the neighborhood retains significance not despite but *through* neoliberal globalization as played out in the connections between gentrification and education markets.

The understanding of neighborhood from which I am going to depart is one commonly linked to Harvey's (1989, 1993) reading of place. This mainly constitutes the neighborhood as a bounded and closed place with a stable homogeneous community. This tends to associate the neighborhood as reactionary, inferring stasis and tradition, as compared to the dynamism and innovation of globalization (see Massey, 1993, 1994; May, 1996). Within this framing, the significance of neighborhoods as places for the generation, contestation, and negotiation of social relations can be seen to wither in the face of the overwhelming logics of the dominant "social imaginary" (Rizvi & Lingard, 2009) of globalization.

To start to posit another way of understanding the neighborhood, in the first part of the chapter I identify how globalization, as pertaining to cities and education policy, has come to be represented by the political economy and philosophy of neoliberalism. In the second part of the chapter, I sketch out the rationalities of neoliberalism relating to education and urban policy, noting for the purposes of illustration the phenomena of education markets and neoliberal urban policy underpinning "third-wave" gentrification. Based on the connections between gentrification and education markets, I conclude the chapter by suggesting that the neighborhood is not *withering* in the face of neoliberal globalization; rather, it is being *reconstituted* according to the logics of the market. It is this idea of reconstitution that also provides the possibility of thinking about the neighborhood through a politics of place (Massey, 2005), and as such as a site of contestation and potential reinvention.

Globalization, Cities and Public Policy

In the late twentieth century, globalization arrived in the field of educational studies in a flurry of discourses about global flows of capital and knowledge; about space-time compression, homogenized identities and hyper-mobile subjects; and about the ramifications and veracity of these discourses for re-thinking the purposes of education and the provision of schooling, higher education and lifelong learning. It has become the pre-eminent way of explaining late twentieth century life, yet it is also subject to intense critique for the normative assumptions underpinning the dominant ideas of globalization (e.g., Dale, 2000; Green, 2002; Gulson, 2007c; Henry, Lingard, Rizvi, & Taylor, 2001; Usher, 2002). In this chapter I focus on links between globalization, cities, and policy. I locate my discussion somewhat differently than accounts ranking cities according to their position as nodes of economic, social, political, and cultural power (e.g., Knox, 1995), and also those accounts that create an analytical category of global city (e.g., Sassen, 1991). What tends to be common to these accounts of globalization and cities is an emphasis on capital that somewhat overdetermines everyday life. Conversely, a discourse of globalization and cities that I think is useful for the purposes of this chapter is transnational urbanism (Smith, 2001, 2003), a cultural-geographic metaphor denoting how transnational communications and social practices "'come together' in particular places at particular times and enter into the contested politics of place-making, the social construction of power differentials, and the making of individual, group, national and transnational identities, and their corresponding fields of difference" (Smith, 2001, p. 5). Within this construct globalization concerns issues of power, where meaning is contested and negotiated and unfolds in place, that is "articulated with other places in translocal communication circuits, and spread out across societies and national borders" (Smith, 2001, p. 3).

This articulation of globalization can be applied to the emergence of a global public policy realm. As Rizvi and Lingard (2009) suggest, there are notable similarities in policy shifts across nations, including educational policies, whilst there is also a need to consider their mediation "at the national and local levels by particular historical, political and cultural dynamics" (p. 3). Similarly, in urban policy, Cochrane (2007) notes that while there is some evidence of an urban global policy phenomenon, often spread through policy borrowing and traveling attached to think tanks advocating certain policy prescriptions, it is less clear how this unfolds in urban settings. Furthermore, while the mediation of the global at the local level is significant, what is also important is recognizing how "constructions of the 'global' and the 'local' are discursively and practically constructed 'positionalities' that are appropriated and deployed by specific social forces at particular times; globalization and localization are thus spatial and cultural metaphors embedded in historical time" (Smith, 2001, p. 2). If this is so, then, Smith argues, it is most useful to examine networks of power, to see how the "global" and "local" are constituted and reconstituted.

In this chapter I want to examine these networks of power by looking at technologies of the state that are deployed under, and through, neoliberalism. I thus wish to connect globalization to neoliberalism, and to see neoliberal globalization (Rizvi & Lingard, 2009) as a conjunction in order to posit that other constitutions of globalization are possible. Additionally, as I move to discussing neoliberalism I am also cognizant of the dangers of what Said (1983, cited by Reynolds, Rizvi, & Dolby, 2009) has called "traveling theory." Following Said, these authors point to the need to understand the productive movement of ideas, while also being cautious concerning theoretical appropriation as such:

[T]he movement of ideas is never unimpeded and always involves "processes of representation and institutionalization different from those at the point of origin" (Said, 1983, p. 226). [Said] urges caution—the need to specify the kind of movements that are possible. (pp. 363–364)

It is thus that I want to be careful to identify the genesis of neoliberalism within predominantly North American, and to lesser extent UK, sets of ideas and policy frames, and note that neoliberalism might apply differently to major cities in the global South like Lagos (see Davis, 2006). With this caveat, the next section is in part heuristic as it moves back and forth between a political economy and philosophy of neoliberalism.

Neoliberalism, Marketization and Policy

Neoliberalism is commonly equated with the decline, or perhaps more accurately, the rejection of the Keynesian welfare state, and the ascendance of "Chicago School" economics, leading to the legitimacy of free trade and market competition as the organizing principles of a global economy and policy enactments within, across, and between nation states. Neoliberalism may denote the role of the state in the maintenance of the market whilst also paradoxically withdrawing from (at least rhetorically) and also deforming the operation of the market (see Harvey, 2005). Neoliberalism is thus more than the replacement of the state with markets, or markets as self-creating or self-regulating (Peck, 2004); it is conceivably the very *marketization of the state*. As Brown suggests:

[t]he neo-liberal formulation of the state and especially specific legal arrangements and decisions as the pre- and ongoing condition of the market does not mean that the market is controlled by the state but precisely the opposite, that the market is the organizing and regulative principle of the state and society (Brown, 2003, para. 11).

Thus, the role of government is still significant for the conception and enactment of neoliberal projects, and in this way market rationality enters realms that were previously deemed to be incompatible with the economic (Burchell, 1996). In the late twentieth and early twenty-first centuries incarnations of neoliberalism reconfigured the role of the individual in the nation-state, whereby citizenship became consumerism, particularly in relation to public services, in which there is now a consumer/producer rather than a client/service relationship (Peters, 2001). Rose (1996) suggests that governmentality characterizes these deployments of a marketized political rationality, and should, as such, "be analyzed in terms of the strategies, techniques and procedures through which different authorities seek to enact programmes of government in relation to the materials and forces to hand and the resistances and oppositions anticipated or encountered" (p. 42).

In this chapter I am interested in the marketization of education and the city, and the role of policy as a significant meso-level technology between the state and the citizen. Education and urban policy sit as part of what Peck and Tickell (2002) assert is "the deliberate stretching of the neoliberal policy repertoire (and its associated rhetorics) to embrace a range of extramarket forms of governance and regulation" (p. 390). Through education and urban policy the state steers from a distance (Rose, 1996), with the reconfiguring of the relationship between the individual and the state requiring the self-actualization of the subject as the entrepreneurial self (Peters, 2001). At the same time, as opportunity arises—such as increased capacity to choose schools or choose where to live—the responsibility for success and failure is shifted away from a shared responsibility of state and citizen. The entrepreneurial self, while opportunistic, also "carries responsibility for the self to new heights: the rationally calculating individual bears full responsibility for the consequences of his or her action no matter how severe the constraints on this action, for example, lack of skills, education, and childcare in a period of high unemployment and limited welfare benefits" (Brown, 2003, para. 15). Policy provides some of the conditions of these possibilities, yet steering at a distance does not necessarily result in the intended outcome for perhaps, as Wilson (2004) contends, "[n]eoliberal governance . . . is not prior to situated individuals and collectivities but creations from their ongoing initiatives within deeply textured social and political life" (p. 773). Neoliberal policy thus may be an intervention into and instigation of differing relations, and an important mediation between the state and the individual within education and the city. Following the idea "that it is in cities and city-regions that the various contradictions and tensions [of neoliberalism] . . . are expressed most saliently in everyday life" (Jessop, 2002, p. 452), in the next section I look at the connection between neoliberal education policy, in relation to markets, and neoliberal urban policy supporting gentrification.

The Manifestation of Neoliberal Policy: Education Markets and Gentrification

Neoliberal education policies, including the encouragement and introduction of education markets, have been implemented to varying degrees across the globe, from New Zealand to France, from Greece to Chile (see Forsey, Davies, & Walford, 2008), though most of the research on markets has been UK and US centric. Blackmore (2000) argues that during the 1990s the governments of England, New Zealand, Australia, and Canada implemented neoliberal policies in education, including "marketization in the form of increased competition and public choice" (p. 381). This ascendance and consolidation of market forms has been tied to processes and practices of global policy sharing and the development of a global educational field (Ball, 1998; Rizvi & Lingard, 2009). In relation to K-12 schooling these global market rationalities enable parents to become choosers of schools, shift the function of inner city schools from being providers of education to

selectors of students, and encourage certain types of standardized outcomes framed by increasingly stringent mechanisms of accountability
and transparency.

These neoliberal educational policy directions parallel urban policy
directions in the mid to late 1990s. Cochrane (2007) outlines two
aspects of neoliberalism in relation to urban policy. The first is the
manifestation of the "free market" in the built environment, represented by mega-projects such Olympic Games venues. The second is
the management of difference in cities, notably the addressing of
inequality. Issues of justice, such as racism and poverty, have been
subjugated to an emphasis on the efficiency of the city. What is significant for Wilson is that "[n]eoliberal rhetoric is thus 'intertextual', speaking about policy but equally about other things, for example, 'the free
and unhampered individual agent,' 'the urban underclass,' 'an aging and
out-of-step urban economy,' 'the unproductive and civic-draining
poor,' 'the restless and mobile ghetto,' and 'the undisciplined immi-
grant'" (Wilson, 2004).

This neoliberal rhetoric as policy assertion is exemplified in relation
to gentrification as a global phenomenon. Lees, Slater, and Wyly (2008)
open their book titled *Gentrification* with a statement about gentrification as "the transformation of a working-class or vacant area into
middle-class residential and/or commercial use" (p. xv). Historically,
gentrification has at its heart class displacement, and Smith (1996, p. 39,
cited in Lees & Davidson, 2005, p. 1166) contends that gentrification
"is no longer about a narrow and quixotic oddity in the housing market
but has become the leading residential edge of a much larger endeavour:
the class remake of the central urban landscape." On the one hand
gentrification is concerned with the consumptive practices of gentrifiers
in so-called global cities like London and New York, where cosmopolitan elites, those especially of the professional managerial class, live in
residential enclaves that are more connected to similar neighborhoods
in similar cities, than to adjacent neighborhoods (Atkinson & Bridge,
2004). Atkinson and Bridge suggest that these elites "live in the neighborhood equivalent of a city-state. . . . [G]entrifiers form a residential
class who share an identity shaped by locational preferences, stage in the
lifecycle, occupation and a social network that crosses national boundaries" (p. 10).

On the other hand, the policy underpinnings of gentrification
pertain to what is termed neoliberal urbanism, or "third wave gentrification," as a "new amalgam of corporate and state powers and practices"
(Smith, 2002, p. 443). Neil Smith evokes an image of the middle class as

a disease, with neoliberal urban policy and third-wave gentrification creating "new landscape complexes [that] now integrate housing with shopping, restaurants, cultural facilities . . . open space, employment opportunities—whole new complexes of recreation, consumption, production, and pleasure, as well as residence" (2002, p. 443). The language adopted by urban policy makers to describe this type of gentrification is "urban regeneration," a term encapsulating an inclusive scope. This inclusivity is part of promoting gentrification as a necessary and benevolent intervention into decaying, dilapidated cities, where gentrification will create new social mixes. And as such "a 'socially mixed' community will be a 'balanced' one, characterized by positive interaction between the classes" (Blomley, 2004, p. 88). By creating a social mix, Byrne (2003, p. 422, cited in Lees et al., 2008, p. 205) argues:

. . . gentrification can ameliorate the social isolation of the poor. New, more affluent residents will rub shoulders with poorer existing residents on the streets, in shops, and within local institutions, such as public schools. Such newcomers may exhibit possibilities of social mobility and a determination to secure adequate public services that provide existing residents with role models.

However, as Ley and Dobson (2008) have noted, this both overestimates the agency of the "newcomers" and the willingness of those existing residents to accept being positioned as deficient to the new middle classes. Furthermore, this also assumes that gentrifiers are all part of a politically progressive, "pioneer" class with a concern for the area in which they live. For gentrifiers, "[h]ow much, and if at all, they invest in their 'neighbourhood' are increasingly matters of choice" (Butler, 2007, p. 172, citing Blokland, 2003).

Schooling has long been a central aspect of this urban investment and differentiation, with good schools marketed to potential home buyers in particular areas of the city. Every real estate sign out in front of a house with a reputable public school nearby is sure to point out this fact. In Australia, the UK and North America, choice of residence for the middle classes has been closely related to the strength of schools, with resultant "post-code segregation." The significance of schooling in understanding the city is also evident when considering how the benefits of "urban regeneration" and social mixing are argued to play out in the educational arena. The most pervasive assumption underpinning neighborhood renewal programs and their relation to education is that increasing the social mix in disadvantaged urban areas will result in more socially mixed schools. Leaving aside the deficit positioning of poor and/or students of color in these schools (Lipman, 2008) and that a social mix in a school in a similar manner to a neighborhood does not equate with social mixing (whatever that may denote) (Reay, 2008), as Lupton and Tunstall (2008) critique, the argument for socially mixed neighborhoods is that "[s]tudents of different backgrounds will in theory be spread more evenly around the school system, such that those who are most disadvantaged are not concentrated in the least advantaged schools" (p. 105).

However, education markets can dislocate or displace the neighborhood school, a complicating factor that can be exemplified through looking at school markets in the UK. In 1980 the Conservative government introduced the Education Act and in 1988 the Education Reform Act, each of which outlined market-oriented education policies that continued throughout the Blair and Brown Labour governments. One such suite of education policies concerns school choice, which allows parents to enroll their children in any public school. More specifically, parents nominate preferred schools, and if there are more student applicants than school places then decisions on admissions are made by either the Local Education Authority or individual schools (see West & Hind, 2007). Local education authorities have the difficult job of being required to provide parental choice of schools, whilst also being cognizant of the ostensive social cohesion role of neighborhood public schools.

One consequence of school choice is that certain schools become residualized, with reputations as difficult schools, "ethnic schools" and "working class schools," and as such liabilities in a market, with middle class parents then fleeing these "sink schools." Schools that are deemed to be "failing," on the basis of examination results or low student numbers or both, are closed (see, e.g., Gulson, 2007a; Robson & Butler, 2001). What this means for neighborhoods and schools is that gentrifying parents may well live in one neighborhood and send their child(ren) to a school in a different neighborhood. Thus, the existence of middle-class people in an area, with children, does not always mean active participation in schools, nor necessarily displacement of working-class students from schools, though middle-class participation in previously "demonized" schools is well recorded (Ball, 2003; Butler & Robson, 2003). Even without clear displacement of students, school choice is nonetheless a fairly classic spatial problem—the modalities of school choice involve questions about the movement of students in and out of schools. In this sense, education markets, as neoliberal policy outcomes, pose a conundrum for the connection of schooling to neighborhoods, especially in trying to understand the role of gentrification in school stratification. Yet what is also important is that education markets are also local markets (Gibson & Asthana, 2000), and thus need to be understood in reference to neighborhood specifics.

That is, education markets challenge the idea, proposed by Byrne (2003) above, of local people mixing in a local school. The convergence of gentrification and education markets means "[e]ducation markets are now rivalling those in housing and employment as determinants of the nature, extent and stability of middle-class gentrification of inner city localities" (Butler & Robson, 2003, p. 157). For example, gentrification and schooling are both to a certain degree underpinned by notions of consumption, reputations, choices, and navigations and negotiations about where to live and where to send one's children to school. To provide a refrain to the discussion of neoliberalism above, these are issues of entrepreneurialism, opportunity, and responsibility.

Wither Not: On the Reconstituting of Neighborhood

As I identified in the beginning of this chapter, globalization can be seen to supplant embedded notions such as the neighborhood. As a way of starting to pose an alternative to this position, I outlined that globalization and cities can be understood not only in reference to the role of capital but also through ideas of transnational urbanism which point to the significance of power and meaning in the city (Smith, 2001, 2005). I was interested in the conjunction of globalization and neoliberalism, and considered how the policy aspects and political rationalities of neoliberalism reconfigure relations between the state and the individual through the marketization of education and cities. I think education policy, such as the creation of K-12 education markets, and its convergence with gentrification offers a means to understand the neighborhood articulation of this marketization.

Therefore, I wish to conclude this chapter by positing that the neighborhood withers not; rather, it retains significance *through* neoliberal globalization. It is reconstituted according to the logics of the market, where neighborhood is understood in the realm of personal preferences, as opportunity and responsibility about where to send children to school and where to live. Yet while acknowledging the dominant imaginary of neoliberal globalization, this idea of reconstituting the neighborhood can also be thought about through a politics of place. There is no utopia of equal relations here, for as Massey (2005) argues, "the challenge of the negotiation of place is always shockingly unequal" (p. 169), and thus the logic of the market is predominant.

Nonetheless, Massey (2005, citing Amin, 2002) suggests that what is important is to consider the politics of place as a politics without guarantees, in which "'[n]egotiation' here stands for the range of means through which accommodation, any always provisional, may be reached or not" (p. 154). Therefore, while the neighborhood is reconstituted through the logics of the market, the neighborhood as a site of contestation is also perhaps a place for other types of reinvention.

AUTHOR'S NOTE

Thank you to Fazal Rizvi for providing the wording relating to reconstitution and logics of the market. Thank you also for the feedback on earlier versions of this chapter.

REFERENCES

Amin, A. (2002). Ethnicity and the multicultural city: Living with diversity. *Environment and Planning A, 34*(6), 959–980.

Atkinson, R., & Bridge, G. (2004). Introduction. In R. Atkinson & G. Bridge (Eds.), *Gentrification in a global context: The new urban colonialism* (pp. 1–17). London: Routledge.

Ball, S.J. (1998). Big policies/small world: An introduction to international perspectives in education policy. *Comparative Education, 34*(2), 119–130.

Ball, S.J. (2003). *Class strategies and the education market: The middle classes and social advantage.* London: RoutledgeFalmer.

Blackmore, J. (2000). Big change questions: Can we create a form of public education that delivers high standards for all students in the emerging knowledge society? *Journal of Educational Change, 1,* 381–387.

Blokland, T. (2003). *Urban bonds.* Cambridge: Polity Press.

Blomley, N. (2004). *Unsettling the city: Urban land and the politics of property.* New York: Routledge.

Brown, W. (2003). Neo-liberalism and the end of liberal democracy. *Theory and Event, 7*(1). Available at http://muse.jhu.edu/journals/theory_and_event/v007/7.1brown.html. Accessed October 6, 2009.

Burchell, G. (1996). Liberal government and techniques of the self. In A. Barry, T. Osborne, & N. Rose (Eds.), *Foucault and political reason: Liberalism, neo-liberalism and rationalities of government* (pp. 19–36). Chicago: University of Chicago Press.

Butler, T. (2007). For gentrification? *Environment and Planning A, 39*(1), 162–181.

Butler, T., & Robson, G. (2003). *London calling: The middle classes and the re-making of inner London.* Oxford: Berg.

Byrne, P.J. (2003). Two cheers for gentrification *Howard Law Review, 46*(3), 405–432.

Cochrane, A. (2007). *Understanding urban policy: A critical approach.* Oxford: Blackwell Publishing.

Dale, R. (2000). Globalisation and education: Demonstrating a "common world educational culture" or locating a "globally structured educational agenda"? *Educational Theory, 50*(4), 427–448.

Davis, M. (2006). *Planet of slums.* London: Verso.

Forsey, M., Davies, S., & Walford, G. (Eds.). (2008). *The globalisation of school choice.* Oxford: Symposium Books.

Gibson, A., & Asthana, S. (2000). Local markets and the polarization of public-sector schools in England and Wales. *Transactions of the Institute of British Geographers, 25*(3), 303–319.

Green, A. (2002). *Education, globalisation and the role of comparative research.* London: Institute of Education, University of London.

Gulson, K.N. (2007a). Mobilizing space discourses: Politics and educational policy change. In K.N. Gulson & C. Symes (Eds.), *Education and the spatial turn: Policy and geography matters* (pp. 37–56). New York: Routledge.

Gulson, K.N. (2007b). Repositioning schooling in inner Sydney: Urban renewal, an education market and the "absent presence" of the "middle classes." *Urban Studies, 44*(7), 1377–1391.

Gulson, K.N. (2007c). With permission: Education policy, space and everyday globalisation in London's East End. *Globalisation, Societies and Education, 5*(2), 219–237).

Gulson, K.N. (2008). Urban accommodations: Policy, education and a politics of place. *Journal of Education Policy, 23*(2), 153–163.

Harvey, D. (1989). *The condition of postmodernity: An enquiry into the origins of cultural change.* Oxford: Blackwell.

Harvey, D. (1993). From space to place and back again: Reflections on the condition of postmodernity. In J. Bird, B. Curtis, T. Putnam, G. Robertson, & L. Tickner (Eds.), *Mapping the futures: Focal cultures, global change* (pp. 3–29). London: Routledge.

Harvey, D. (2005). *A brief history of neoliberalism.* Oxford: Oxford University Press.

Henry, M., Lingard, B., Rizvi, F., & Taylor, S. (2001). *The OECD, globalisation and education policy.* Oxford: Permagon.

Jessop, B. (2002). Liberalism, neoliberalism, and urban governance: A state-theoretical perspective. *Antipode, 34*(3), 452–472.

Knox, P.L. (1995). World cities in a world-system. In P.L. Knox & P.J. Taylor (Eds.), *World cities in a world-system* (pp. 3–20). Cambridge: Cambridge University Press.

Lees, L., & Davidson, M. (2005). New-build "gentrification" and London's riverside renaissance. *Environment and Planning A, 37*(1), 1165–1190.

Lees, L., Slater, T., & Wyly, E. (2008). *Gentrification.* New York: Routledge.

Ley, D., & Dobson, C. (2008). Are there limits to gentrification? The contexts of impeded gentrification in Vancouver. *Urban Studies, 45*(12), 2471–2498.

Lipman, P. (2008). Mixed-income schools and housing: Advancing the neoliberal urban agenda. *Journal of Education Policy, 23*(2), 119–134.

Lupton, R., & Tunstall, R. (2008). Neighbourhood regeneration through mixed communities: A "social justice dilemma"? *Journal of Education Policy, 23*(2), 105–117.

Massey, D. (1993). Power-geometry and a progressive sense of place. In J. Bird, B. Curtis, T. Putnam, G. Robertson, & L. Tickner (Eds.), *Mapping the futures: Local cultures, global change* (pp. 59–69). London: Routledge.

Massey, D. (1994). *Space, place and gender.* Cambridge: Polity Press.

Massey, D. (2005). *For space.* London: Sage Publications.

May, J. (1996). Globalization and the politics of place: Place and identity in an inner London neighbourhood. *Transactions of the Institute of British Geographers, 21*(1), 194–215.

Peck, J. (2004). Geography and public policy: Constructions of neoliberalism. *Progress in Human Geography, 28*(3), 392–405.

Peck, J., & Tickell, A. (2002). Neoliberalising space. *Antipode, 34*(3), 380–404.

Peters, M.A. (2001). *Poststructuralism, Marxism and neoliberalism: Between theory and politics.* New York: Rowman & Littlefield.

Reay, D. (2008). Class out of place: The white middle classes and intersectionalities of class and "race" in urban state schooling in England. In L. Weis (Ed.), *The way class works: Readings on school, family, and the economy* (pp. 87–99). New York: Routledge.

Reynolds, T., Rizvi, F., & Dolby, N. (2009). Racism and education: Coincidence or conspiracy? *British Journal of Sociology of Education, 30*(3), 359–371.

Rizvi, F., & Lingard, B. (2009). *Globalizing educational policy.* London: Routledge.

Robson, G., & Butler, T. (2001). Coming to terms with London: Middle class communities in a global city. *International Journal of Urban and Regional Research, 25*(1), 70–86.

Rose, N. (1996). Governing "advanced" liberal democracies. In A. Barry, T. Osborne, & N. Rose (Eds.), *Foucault and political reason: Liberalism, neo-liberalism and rationalities of government* (pp. 37–64). London: UCL Press.

Said, E. (1983). *The world, the text, and the critic*. Cambridge, MA: Harvard University Press.

Sassen, S. (1991). *The global city: New York, London, Tokyo*. Princeton: Princeton University Press.

Shaw, W.S. (2000). Ways of whiteness: Harlemising Sydney's aboriginal Redfern. *Australian Geographical Studies, 38*(3), 291–305.

Smith, M.P. (2001). *Transnational urbanism: Locating globalisation*. Oxford: Blackwell.

Smith, M.P. (2003). Transnationalism, the state, and the extraterritorial citizen. *Politics & Society, 31*(4), 467–502.

Smith, M.P. (2005). Transnational urbanism revisited. *Journal of Ethnic and Migration Studies, 31*(2), 235–244.

Smith, N. (1996). *The new urban frontier: Gentrification and the revanchist city*. London: Routledge.

Smith, N. (2002). New globalism, new urbanism: Gentrification as global urban strategy. *Antipode, 34*, 427–450.

Usher, R. (2002). Putting space back on the map: Globalisation, place and identity. *Educational Philosophy and Theory, 34*(1), 41–55.

West, A., & Hind, A. (2007). School choice in London, England: Characteristics of students in different types of secondary schools. *Peabody Journal of Education, 82*(2), 498–529.

Wilson, D. (2004). Toward a contingent urban neoliberalism. *Urban Geography, 25*(8), 771–783.

Globalization and Education in Japan

KENTARO OHKURA AND MASAKO SHIBATA

In this chapter, the authors contend that globalization in Japan is the gradual process in which Japan's positioning of *self* within international relations, which had formerly been dominated by the West, has changed. Accordingly, Japan's relationships with the West and the rest of the world, for example, Asia, have also been reviewed and modified. The argument is developed in the context in which Japan sees itself through its image of the international community. The so-called Westernization theme of Japan, and probably of other "catch-up" countries, is not as linear as before, and does seem to be more complex in this age of globalization. The dominance of the West in education and other fields has steadily been multi-polarized, and its decline has raised competition among countries around the world.

To examine the shift in Japan's positioning in the world and her consequent modifications in dealing with education, the chapter looks at the historical and contemporary dimensions of Japanese education. It first traces the processes of Japan's national political agenda of modernization and Westernization, before exploring the present dispute in education reform as a global event. Thus, the major arguments are twofold.

First, as part of the global community, Japan has adapted to the principle of interconnectedness and interdependency and recognized its importance. This is examined through the ways in which Japan has been dealing with her "troubled past" and her relationship with countries in the Far East which had fallen victim to Japanese imperialist expansion in the midst of her drive toward Westernization. The treatment of Japan's national history is directly reflected in the Japanese government's policy regarding the teaching of history.

Second, with the decline of Western dominance as the major change in the world climate, Japan problematized educational competitiveness among the people, which involves the association of education with human capital theory. The rise of a global economy makes it possible to identify those individuals who need to be economically productive and globally competitive, mostly children, and to recognize them as the future members of the nation through educational reforms. In this argument, the idea of educational reform is seen as a form of politico-cultural governance that is realized in the way in which the membership of individuals is shared through the ideals and concerns over child-rearing and school practices linked to principles of collective belonging and the future of the nation. Globalization, then, is not only about Japan's place in a broader set of international relations. It is also about the ways in which national belonging is being recreated.

Both of these aspects of Japanese education are the reflection of the positioning of Japan versus the West and the rest of the world, which has been changing in the context of globalization in politics, economy, and above all education.

1. Japan, the West and the World in the Modern Age

In an age of globalization, the end of national education systems is a matter of concern to educationists as well as educational policymakers. There is an increasing anxiety that the long-established recognition of the role of education may be jeopardized. It has been assumed in the West, and eventually in the rest of the world, that national education impinges upon the basis of national states and the assertion of their *raison d'être*. This assumption has a long history. From the era of Jullien de Paris, nation states have concerned themselves about the political, economic, and social implications of their education system. So has Japan.

"Catch-up country" had been an almost century-old *cliché* to locate Japan in the international community in the modern age. Becoming modern and recognized as such by the modern states proper had been a prime theme on Japan's political agenda. In the end, her quest for a modern *self* culminated in her aspiration for power and its legitimacy, and culminated in the expansion of the Greater Japanese Empire in line with nineteenth-century discourse of international politics. The momentum of Japan's expansion was based on the centripetal dynamics of Japan's passage towards the modern world (Dudden, 2005; Gann, 1984).

"Society has a center" and it is a *phenomenon*, said Edward Shils (1975, p. 3). The center is a single inclusive entity which governs society. It is also a governing minority, characterized by an *allegedly* superior quality to the rest (Aron, 1967, Chapter 5; Bauman, 1987). In other words, the legitimacy of the power derives from the assumptions of superiority and the successful assertion of these qualities by itself.

Therefore, the positioning of the centre can be a fact, but not a fixed being. It is verifiable through observation, impression, logic, intelligence and other kinds of human experience. The values and norms which are shared within the small governing body prevail in their spatial domination. In order to claim the universality of the values and beliefs, the center has an expansive tendency (Shils). This shared sense of universal values configures a nucleus of the legitimacy of the state as a governing body in modern political discourses. Territorial expansion and the articulation of its legitimacy was a dominant model of international discourse during the heyday of imperial colonialism. By the key tenet of the rule of law, the modern West had successfully claimed its domination at the center of the international community, some *fin de siècle* signs of its decline notwithstanding.

As the West colonized neighboring countries with consummate ease (Hobsbawm, 1987, 1994), the Sino-centric worldview had lessened its influence in the vicinity of China. Japan came to embrace *Datsu-A-Nyu-Ou-ron*, the idea of finding Japan's way out of "ill-fated" Asia and joining Europe, in order to survive Western encroachment in Asia (Koyasu, 2003, Chapter VI). It must also be noted that it was not only the material wealth of the West that overwhelmed nineteenth-century Japanese leaders. Niall Ferguson captures the temptation of the modern Western world:

What enabled the West to rule the East was not so much scientific knowledge in its own right. . . . Western dominance was also due to the failure of the Asian empires to modernize their economic, legal and military systems, to say nothing of the relative stagnation of Oriental intellectual life. (Ferguson, 2006, pp. lxvii–lxviii)

What attracted the Japanese were the "progressive" ideas of national polity and social organization cultivated in the civilizing process of the West.

At the outset of the modern system of Japanese education, Western learning was heavily emphasized in elite education, while the instillation of a strong sense of Japanese national identity had been paramount in every aspect of education for the public. Regardless of their family background, the academic elite—those who had successfully outlived a series of competitive entrance examinations through higher education —absorbed Western knowledge at the Imperial University in Tokyo, the first and apex institution in modern Japanese education. Until reaching a sufficient number of Japanese teachers, the government firstly relied on the teaching force of foreign experts at Tokyo. As a necessary operational cost, exceptionally high salaries were paid to those foreign teachers, much higher than that for Japanese professors and even that for some Cabinet members (Borton, 1955; Jones, 1985). Progress in this national political project of Westernization had often been demonstrated deliberately to the Western audience (Japanese Department of Education, 1876). Recognizing the validity of the "universal value" of Western civilization in the nineteenth-century world, the Japanese government understood that competition with the Western powers had to take place on Western terms.

2. Demise of the Empire and the Long Post-War Period

Japan's inclination to the West continued even after her own imperial dream resulted in misery. Arguably, Japan was even further predisposed to look to the West because of the collapse of the Empire. The reconstruction of the Japanese state was done by American ideals "through and through" largely based on the appreciation of these ideals by the Japanese leadership (Shibata, 2005). The Report of the United States Education Mission to Japan was praised to the skies by Japanese translators, who noted in the Preface that "The Report expresses the best, the soundest tradition of American democracy. . . . Japanese parents, teachers, educational administrators, and every single Japanese should read the Report three times so that they can find the future direction of current Japanese education" (Sugo, Miyahara, & Munakata, 1950). While a similar attempt in occupied Germany ended in "tragic failure" (Ziemer, 1946), the Allies succeeded in drastic reforms in Japan within the first half of the occupation's entire period (1945–1952), just before the rise of communism in East Asia.

The Allies' destruction and reconstruction of Japanese education, including the rewriting of national history, had gone hand in hand with the enthusiasm of leading Japanese educators and, to a lesser extent, policymakers. History is, in principle, treated as an important matter of state affairs, often before it is a subject of education (Foster, 1999; Nicholls, 2006; Seddon, 1987). History concerns the identity of the state, while its authority and legitimacy rest on the law (Bobbitt, 2002, p. 6). The treatment of national history, thus, has always been impinged upon by politics rather than "scientific" debates.

With the rise of communism in her vicinity, Japan was regarded and treated as an important ally by the United States. The victims of Japan's conduct of the war and colonial rule were disregarded within the Anglo-American scheme for the post-war politico-economic and military order in Asia. The Chinese and Indian idea of an Asian version of the Marshall Plan was shattered, and the recovery of the Japanese economy was put at the top of the agenda by the General Headquarters of the Supreme Commander for the Allied Powers, which acted as the "salesman" of Japanese products in post-war Asia (Shibata, 2008). In 1952, Japan rejoined the international community in terms of the Treaty of Peace with Japan in San Francisco, to which Korea and both Chinas (The Republic of China and The People's Republic of China) were not invited. The Greater Japanese Empire became "history," while the Imperial Household survived. Thanks to the alliance with the United States, Japan survived and prospered in the long post-war period (Dower, 1999; Gluck, 1992).

After the demise of the Greater Japanese Empire, fanatic attempts to revive the old imperial nationalism were doomed to be irrelevant (cf. Irokawa, 1985). At the same time, Japan remained indifferent to the concerns of Asian countries. A renewed notion of the *raison d'être* of the state was sought in the political treatment of the national past. In teaching and remembering Japan's conduct of the war in Asia, the Japanese government had and still has difficulty in coming to terms with the nation's war-related dark past. In the early post-war period, there were a few historians who wrote national history on their own terms as opposed to those of the government. Ienaga Saburo[1] (1913–2002) was arguably the most prominent amongst them. The 1962 edition of his book *Shin Nihon-shi [New Japanese History]* for upper secondary education failed to be authorized as a "textbook" by the Textbook Authorization Research Committee (TARC), the textbook examination body of the Ministry of Education. As Ienaga was asked to delete or revise "inappropriate" descriptions about the war, he filed a civil lawsuit against the government by requesting a compensation for the psychological damage he suffered from such heavy ministerial demand for revisions, and claimed the unconstitutionality of the system as it violated his freedom of expression. Between 1965 and 1997, he filed altogether three lawsuits and won a partial victory (cf. Nozaki, 2008). But, essentially, the Japanese judiciary ruled that the textbook authorization system was constitutional.

Markedly, however, during this period when Ienaga raised questions about the Japanese government's treatment of the war in history textbooks, the Chinese and the South Korea governments virtually remained silent. At least their voice was not strong enough to be heard nationwide by the Japanese public. As late as the 1980s, the debate about the teaching of the "troubled national past" became an international controversy in East Asia. The Japanese government had difficulty in dealing with this rather abrupt protest from the victims of the war. But the diplomacy of the Japanese government towards those neighboring countries has gradually changed in the context of global politics.

3. National History in Global Politics

The long post-war period was to end as the balance of power gradually changed in Asia. The United States seemed to be at risk, and its influence in Asia has declined politically, economically and militarily since the 1970s. The rise of Japan and other Asian countries as important parts of the global economy and politics increased interconnectedness and interdependency between Japan and her neighbors. China also intensified its attention to the treatment of the war from this period. It was also the time of the death of Mao Zedong (1893–1976), the gradual demise of hard-line communist policy in Beijing, and the consequent rise of Den Xiaoping (1904–1997). It was Mao's policy that the Chinese history of "national shame" under Japan's occupation was to be downplayed in public memory and education at least until China obtained international recognition as a great political and economic power (Mitter, 2003). Under Mao, Beijing had maintained a policy of appeasement for Japan deliberately before Japan's official choice of the People's Republic of China as "China" over the Republic of China in 1972. This policy was not indefinite and was changed by Deng. He began to highlight the history of China as the victim of Japan's invasion. China is no longer an outmoded old country for Japan.

The international community also expected Japan to shoulder responsibility commensurate with the growth of her economy. Japan began to demonstrate its commitment to the task, especially in Asia. This time, unlike the era of the Empire, the government's nationalist policy surfaced along with its awareness that Japan should stand on a more "friendly" footing in the international community than it had during wartime. In 1977, Prime Minister Fukuda Takeo made an epoch-making declaration in the Fukuda Doctrine, which demonstrated Japan's "heart-to-heart diplomacy" for Asian countries. This idea set out the basis of Japan's Official Development Aid (ODA) policy. Japan has enjoyed a dominant influence on the operation of the Asian Development Bank (Wan, 1995; see also "In Defense of 'Asian Values'," *Time*, March 16, 1998, p. 40). Assuring her power in Asia has been increasingly crucial for Japan, as new political geographies have been developing especially since the end of the Cold War. From this period, unlike the early post-war period, Japan has occasionally chosen a policy for East Asian regionalism over US-led Asia-Pacific international relations (Yoshida, 2004).

In the 1980s, the Japanese Prime Minister called for the "internationalization" of Japanese education. The Ministry of Education set forth a "Plan for Accepting 100,000 International Students by 2000." Through ODA, Japan has provided a large amount of financial aid for countries in Asia in education in the way of scholarship provision for overseas students on Japanese campuses. On the whole, the policy of the Japanese government for offering financial support in education and elsewhere allowed the country to establish an important pathway for the exercise of Japan's foreign policy in Asia. Thus, for Japan, "internationalization" no longer necessarily means Westernization. Instead, it means the multi-polarization of the center of the world. Asia has gained greater significance in Japanese diplomatic and educational policies than ever before.

Even on the politically sensitive issue of national history, the Japanese government has shown a policy shift in teaching about the war and colonial history. The shift has certainly been slow and occasionally indefinite. As known widely, especially through the "orthodox" view of the Western media about Japan's treatment of the past, some hard-line conservatives, including Cabinet members, have remembered the war as a justifiable act for the salvation of Asia from the yoke of the West (Season, 2005). Some have also argued that Japan had paid enormously out of its own pocket for the construction of modern institutions such as industry and education in Taiwan and Korea rather than having exploited them, as Japan's colonial rule ended long before Japan could take advantage of it, unlike the case of the centuries-long European rule of the rest of the world. The policy of the post-war Japanese government for the treatment of the war history has been greatly different from the deliberate policy for *Vergangenheitsbewältigung* of the Adenauer line maintained by the German government from the 1950s on. But however tardily, the Japanese government since the 1980s has clearly demonstrated its policy on the treatment of the national past, as shown in the displacement of those who articulated historical views opposed to governmental policy (cf. "Japan and its History: The Ghost of War-times Past," *The Economist*, November 8, 2008, p. 41).

As said earlier, the so-called history textbook controversy became an international political problem in East Asia rather abruptly three decades after the end of the war. In 1982, *Asahi Shimbun*, a major Japanese newspaper, and other Japanese and foreign media reported that the Textbook Authorization Research Committee requested a publisher to use the word *shinshutsu* [advancement] instead of *shinryaku* [invasion] to express Japan's war against China. Unlike the time of the Ienaga textbook case in the 1960s, this time the Chinese and South Korean governments promptly reacted to this report and voiced their official protest against the Japanese government's measure. Although afterwards *Asahi*'s report turned out to be not based on facts, the report triggered political controversies about the treatment of the war in Japanese history textbooks.

The reaction of the Japanese government to China and Korea was quite quick. Miyazawa Kiichi, the Chief Cabinet Secretary at the time, stated that the Japanese government would revise the textbook authorization guidelines to develop friendly and cooperative relations with neighboring countries. This "Neighboring Country Clause" became a new criterion for textbook authorization, and the Ministry of Education has been subject to due consideration for the treatment of history concerning Asia, especially the history of World War II. In the 1990s, leading politicians in Japan also began to evince a sense of guilt and remorse for the wartime suffering of neighboring countries. In 1993, Kono Yohei, the Chief Cabinet Secretary under the Miyazawa Administration (1991–1993), officially admitted governmental involvement in the organization of the wartime prostitution of Korean women. Prime Minister Hosokawa Morihiro (1993–1994) pronounced Japan's guilt in the war, and Prime Minister Murayama Tomiichi (1994–1996) of the Social Democratic Party Japan followed suit. The background of the series of changes in the treatment of the war was the death of Japanese Emperor Hirohito (1901–1989), whose responsibility for Japan's conduct of World War II had never been out of the political debates on the national past. His death certainly made the theme of the war a less heavy topic and eased a kind of taboo for public voice about Japan's war responsibility. On the whole, the focus of Japan's educational policy has gradually shifted to Asia. The idea of an East Asian Community has re-emerged, however, this time, a very different conception with a renewed view of the world. An enthusiastic inclination towards this idea prevails in the minds of Asian intellectuals as well (Okonogi, 2005).

4. Educational Reform as a Global Event

Education, as discussed above, reflects the way in which Japan positions herself in the changing terrain of the globe. Japan's policy for education has slowly but certainly been inclined to look at the relationship of interaction and interdependency. This reinterpretation of the global terrain, at the same time, intensified international competition and raised Japan's competitiveness in education. The idea that education is a powerful means for salvation of the nation is reaffirmed.

From a political standpoint, children, minorities, the poor. and even the aged, are to be rescued from the pitfalls of globalization and societal exclusion through education. This belief could be called the "salvation theme," a theme which suggests that those who are disadvantaged due to the advent of the global economy and globalization should be salvaged and turned into competitive, agentive, or at least average citizens of the country. This theme, taken from a humanitarian compassionate point of view, is represented in the slogan George W. Bush promoted, "no child left behind." The following discussion will then focus on the hopes and fears, which are discursively tied to the wealth of nations and future of the country, of Japanese teachers and guardians regarding the international comparison of test scores, and the development of the mental and physical skills of children. In other words, education helps the nation governed as a whole, by holding hopes and sharing fears for the new global order which is often realized in the relationship between international comparison of academic achievement and the national wealth. The governing process is to give recognition to agency in every student and to schooling founded upon humanitarian compassion and the salvation theme, as exemplified in the slogan "no child left behind." The agentive will is strengthened in the notions of liberal democracy and developmental psychology.

When schooling was seen to have a considerable effect on economic development in East Asian countries, human resource and capital approaches were predominantly behind this problematic movement (see "Education and the Wealth of Nations," *The Economist*, 29 March 1997, pp. 15–16). These approaches are often discussed along with the expansion of student enrolment in primary and secondary education and schooling as a means of stocking the labor force.[2] This expansion of mass education is called the "world revolution" in education and has been observed since 1950 in many parts of the globe and said to be promoted by governments (Kariya, 1995; Meyer, Ramirez, Rubinson, & Boli-Bennett, 1977).

As observed in the United States, Europe, and East Asia, including Japan, educational reform is part of this world revolution in education, and has spread over the parts of the world which have undertaken mass or popular education. As Benedict Anderson points out, the end of a war is a decisive moment when a country can restructure itself and become stronger, richer and better, or, in other words, to make "progress" in various fields (Umemori, 2007). In the case of Japan, its defeat in the Second World War was the point at which Japan realized its need for social improvements, including an educational system open to the masses, by adopting the American way of schooling as well as the system of liberal democracy (U.S. Education Mission, 1946). To help the nation progress, postwar Japanese translated works of American thinkers like John Dewey, and reinterpreted some of their ideas in the national curriculum (Ohkura, 2005). For instance, the concepts of individual growth, individual potentiality, and the community of learning are represented as Dewey's thoughts. Ideals of liberal democracy were also developed along with the expansion of educational opportunities in upper-level schools and higher education.

The popular reform of Japanese education was recognized as a global model when William J. Bennett, former U.S. Secretary of Education, declared the United States a "nation at risk." Bennett found "principles, emphasis and relationships in Japanese education that are compatible with American values, indeed that tend to embody American values (as well as many findings of educational research)" that Americans might borrow and adopt for themselves (Bennett, 1987, p. 69). Bennett further argued that the Protestant ethic gets reinscribed in neoliberalism (see the chapter by Tröhler in this book). That value seems, on the surface, similar to the Japanese idea that youngsters take responsibility for their own learning and work. Bennett observed that Japan's competitiveness was rooted in its educational system and its economy strengthened by parental engagement in education, student self-discipline, teaching of tradition, dedicated teachers, and an adequate number of school days (Bennett, 1987; Willis, Yamamura, & Rappleye, 2008).[3] It could be pointed out that Bennett used an "oriental" scheme, a particularly American commonsense view of education, that became his lens to define Japanese education. But in this age of globalization, this spectrum of globalization, that is, education transfer, is not merely one nation's acceptance of the preconceptions of the other in the reconstruction of its own national identity in education. The very construction of education is continually produced comparatively, a production in which the self incorporates the other in its principles of action. This identity search has been continuously repeated as international competitiveness and rivalries have heated up.

5. Hopes and Fears of Nations in Global Comparisons

The salvation theme of globalization is evident in educational reforms that embody a certain configuration of hopes and fears. In the case of American educational reform, one can find in the No Child Left Behind policy hopes with fears that certain numbers of American students do not meet the expected standards in studies under the ideal of equal educational opportunity for all. In recent Japanese educational reforms, in contrast, students are seen as facing the fears of the world in competitions in economy and education (even though they have always placed in the top ten in OECD tests). At the same time, there is hope for the empowerment of individuals with academic abilities and job skills for productive outcomes. Education is no longer expected to train them as followers of the elite class.

In Japan, it could be pointed out that the shift in governance in Japanese education is from a bureaucratic system to a system of individual self-responsibility, or an elitist to democratic system that entails new rules and standards of governing at a distance. The transformation of governing in the era of liberal democracy embodies self-management and collective allegiance to the nation simultaneously.

Since the Second World War, the Japanese Model of education has also been adopted in particular in former Japanese colonies and in the cultural sphere of Confucianism, East Asia and South East Asia, while these states made many changes in their educational reforms to gain wealth, and, more importantly, to nationalize and ethnicize themselves (Cummings, 1997; Shibata, 2006). By the time Japan climbed up the global economic ladder, Japanese education, which was once restructured under the supervision of American occupation forces (as noted above), was globally acknowledged and referred to by both the East and West for economic and nationalistic reasons. The weaknesses in Japan's model were also used to revalidate their own theories and practices in education. The cultural "uniqueness" of their education was essentialized by revealing the weaknesses of Japan's global model of education, which included centralized control by the state, inequality among minorities, school violence, and student bullying (Shields, 1989). Other critics pointed to the dehumanizing aspect of Japanese education, noting that "the goal of Asian education systems (and all authoritarian and totalitarian educational systems) is obedience" (Bracey, 1997, p. 21). These reactions against the Japanese model "had more to do with political development within" their countries "than realities within Japan itself" (Willis et al., 2008, p. 504). In education, policy makers could therefore reach beyond ethical and ideological differences, and forge agreement among the different cultures and ethnic groups in the population; that is, education is for all.

Japanese reformers look at their educational system with hopes and fears for their country in the hegemony of a global economy that is discursively bound by international comparisons of academic achievement as seen in the OECD Academic Surveys and the TIMSS tests. These international assessments led a former Prime Minister, Shinzo Abe, to call for the testing of all sixth and ninth graders in order to help ensure academic abilities appropriate to all students.[4] The Prime Minister explained the aim of education in a way similar to what Bennett stated in his report, that is, students must study to take responsibility for their future (Abe, 2006). Accordingly, it is believed that good academic ability ensures the rest of the student's life. Borrowing from themes in the Thatcherian reform of England, school must be thus accountable for what students learn and how teachers supervise their learning (p. 211).

It is widely believed, especially in human capital theory, that international comparisons of academic abilities are an indication of future national prosperity and produce workers who are knowledgeable and skilful in a global economy (Baker & Holsinger, 1997). International comparisons work to facilitate economic competitiveness in Japan as a whole. In addition, the discourse of international comparisons of academic abilities and economic competition in the world produces the salvation theme or humanitarian sentiment that no one is allowed to fall behind, that is, competitiveness is guaranteed if all learn and work hard together. The salvation theme as a by-product of this discourse creates boundaries, distinctions, and differentiations among those students who are destined to participate in global competitions as members of an individual nation.

No matter how successfully Japanese students attain this goal by performing well in the OECD's PISA and TIMMS, there is always some fear among those in the Japanese educational system of a widening gap in academic achievement between "haves" and "have-nots," and concerns about a correlation between academic attainment and cultural capital reinforced by family income or socio-economic class (Kariya, 2002; Mimizuka, 2007). Referring to the relationship between academic attainment and socio-economic status (or the cultural background) of student's family, social critics continually argue that students in low-income families are less likely to be motivated to study in school. They argue over the correlation between the student's aspiration for learning and the academic career of the parent (rather than insisting on the renewal of the curriculum and reexamination of school programs in terms of individual needs).

It is often said that the increase in national wealth in post-war Japan was largely brought about by America's expenditure of money in the Cold War and its monetary policy toward the Japanese yen until 1985. However, the ranking of educational achievements by nation seemed to more efficiently vitalize national interest, to stimulate national sentiments, and to bring the accountability system in school under popular control (and less authoritarian control). The value of education is continually placed in global terms that elide it national(istic) qualities. For example, Japanese reform is necessary, it is argued, in general terms about humanity, which is seen as not necessary in one's vocation, and for any child, or historically in the nation.[5] However, educational comparisons enable us to establish the boundaries and distinctions among people in many ways. Further, the comparisons recast the variation of test scores among the Japanese students into the problem of cultural capital as well as socio-economic status.

Another educational reform in Japan was undertaken in 1989. The content of the curriculum and the number of school days were reduced, which contradicted what Bennett once praised Japan for. In 2001, in OECD tests, Japan placed top in mathematics, and second in science among 32 nations, but the headline in a major Japanese newspaper was "Anxiety about Education Prevails in the World" ("Kyoiku fuan sekaijyu ni," *Asahi Shimbun*, July 21, 2002, p. 1). The newspaper article continued on with the line that Japanese universities and business circles stressed that more time be spared for school learning in order for nations to remain in standing with Asian and Scandinavian countries. These Eastern and Western countries reflect both sides of the same coin, namely, the education the Japanese always wanted. Eastern education represents intellectual, knowledge-based training while Western education suggests a liberal education centered on values and the meaning of life. The OECD comparison illuminates two different qualities in education, and prods Japan to see what is lacking in its own educational system so as not to be left behind in the international competition.

6. Body and Mind as National and Global Concerns

While educational reforms have targeted academic achievements in the name of rescuing the nation economically, the testing of physical strength involves another salvation theme in Japan. Some statistics indicate delays in the physical development of children that has been prominent since 1979 ("10dai wa nikutai kouha," *Asahi Shimbun*, October 10, 1990, p. 3). In responding to the statistics as problematic, developmental psychologists claimed that, although "it may be an exaggeration, the continued weakening of physical strength in children may result in developmental problems and that delay in development may eventually deter their will to work" (Kato & Kusaka, 1993). The argument was then made to point out that the development of the mind (in both reasoning and emotion) is likewise impeded by social ills, such as poverty, and cultural and moral corruption. In other words, the current environment desecrates the innate good of child development. The response of the psychologists represents the position of the field of Japanese psychology which perceives development as a lineal process of internal growth from immaturity to maturity encouraged by the unity of body and mind, which is fundamentally independent of social environment and action. Developmental psychology suggests for the Japanese Piagetian that the stages of cognitive features are similar among those youngsters in the same age cohorts (Azuma & Shigeta, 1992).[6] In assuming that an innate nature exists inside of a child, the role of education is expected to respect and to construct individuality based on this innateness (Yoda, 1977). This psychological assumption, nativism (in opposition to empiricism), is dominant in the way Japanese look at Japanese children, in particular from infancy to adolescence.

The field of psychology was largely recognized as an imported field of study from the West, but there was some groundwork which existed before its adaptation (NSKI, 1982). *Koukugaku* (Japanese ancient studies or Japanese philology), committed to investigating the ethnic and national origin of mentality, is the major conceptual framework used to understand psychology from the West. Thus psychology, as it developed as a field in Japan, was somehow conceptualized and tailored to the study of collective mentality rather than solely that of individual mind.

Health in mind and body came to be regarded as a social concern, and the development of both was seen to be secured through sports activities offered in the national program of education. A national survey of physical strength has been enforced since 1964 and renewed in 2000, randomly targeting citizens aged 6–59. In 2001, the Ministry of Education, Culture, Sports, Science and Technology (MECSST) announced a program for the encouragement of sports (*Sports shinko kihon keikaku*) as a national policy for the next decade. According to the national program, "sports is a global culture in responding to physical and mental needs of the human race" (MECSST, 2000). The national program stressed that a sense of solidarity and attachment with others is nurtured through sports activities and events. It is crucial to recognize here that sports bring benefits to society as well as to the individual.

Sports are meant no longer to be tied to personal qualities, but to signify the "hopes and dreams of the entire nation" and "international friendship and goodwill." The national program and its survey, analyzed and explained with the use of chronological charts and age cohorts of physical strength, reinforced the agentive desire for being average or like every other student (MECSST, 2000). This is what is found in the arguments of, for instance, Popkewitz (1998) and Fendler (2001). As Popkewitz points out, teaching is treated as a problem in psychology for normalizing students. Their success in education and work in Japan are conditioned on average body strength and normal development of the mind. Everyone is thus expected to be "average." In 2008, schools eventually required all sixth and eighth graders to take tests of strength in gripping, jumping, throwing, and running, and to participate in surveys of daily routine, food habits, and the frequency of exercise as parameters in strength and mind.

Sport activities are moreover recognized in the program as effective for helping the national economy, global understanding, and self-realization. In terms of the economy, they contribute to financially saving "us" and economizing medical expenses in the national medical insurance scheme. The program further refers to job openings made available through the opening of sport events. The program defines sports as a global culture, overcoming differences among people in languages and customs. Sport competitions, which are held under set rules, encourage communication among people regardless of gender, age, and/or handicap. Sports activities provide a variety of opportunities, the program explained, for the individuals to think about themselves and the way to live and participate in society. The significant relationship which is found in mind and body and developed through sports activities helps in the construction of the individual as a national citizen, a global citizen, and an individual.

Statistical surveys showed a continuous decline of students' physical strength even after the program was reviewed in 2006. According to the Ministry, the problem behind this was that physical education and sport activities were paid less attention in comparison to academic attainments. In response, the Ministry stated that all students would be required to participate in the national survey so that "parents can supervise the strength of their own children" ("Hatsu no zenkoku chosa," *Asahi Shimbun*, January 25, 2009, p. 27).

In terms of governing as a technology of the self, the national survey of physical strength and the sport programs promoted by the Ministry suggest two things to consider. One is that the survey and program encourage self-discipline in schools by holding them accountable to guardians and parents for the quality of education in physical development. Sports could be practiced for individual pleasure, but when physical strength is discussed in connection with sports in education policy, the gym teacher is expected to prove how s/he has helped to foster physical strength and a sense of togetherness. The other is that the survey made it possible for each student to compare his or her physical strength to the average physical strength of students in the region and the entire nation. Because the portfolio is provided to every fifth and eighth grader as a self-reference for body strength, it enables students to consider the appropriate physical strength for the age cohort they identify with. As the discussion on internationally ranked academic attainments suggested, physical strength and sports discussed in education are not only a matter of importance to the individual, but also to national and social interests.

It is notable that tests of physical strength and physical check-ups, enforced by Japanese schools, provide rules and standards for students, teachers, and parents to view health in mind and body as an educational as well as national problem. The Japanese can "see" students' development of mind and body as problematic throughout the examinations. Although health and strength are believed to be the sole interest of the individual, school as a device can make the individual condition publicly problematic. While having particular cultural and political qualities in Japan, this is happening worldwide. Schooling as a global phenomenon connects people through the problematization of health (e.g., schools closed because of swine flu outbreaks, but public transportation never stopped) and the academic achievement of each student.

7. Concluding Remarks

A discussion on globalization often opens debates on world society, regional integration, expanding markets, global networks, or human rights. However, globalization also makes comparison possible; Japan sees itself in relation to other countries. Globalization provides a conceptual lens with which to examine not only Japan and other nations, but also Japanese nationals in the past and the present. International comparisons in academic achievements illuminate the nation as a whole with fears in the present but hopes for the future.

Globalization changes the terrain of relationship among the states. With the recession of the West, Japan gradually began to reconsider her earlier foreign policy, which dominantly focused on her relationship with the United States. Instead, Japan began to recognize the politics of an economy of a multi-polarized world. As a consequence, though tardily, her policy for Asia has been modified, even in the treatment of the dark past.

The global economy and politics have further changed the feature. After the fall of the Berlin Wall, people and ideas began to go beyond earlier boundaries. Exclusive ideologies are no longer important for the assertion of the identity of national state. How individual national states act in the international community is no longer a simple linearity. The world is more complex than a simple division into the First, the Second and the Third Worlds. After the end of the Cold War, the idea and practice of cross-national educational interaction no longer merely demonstrate *national* interest as in former centuries, but represent a powerful political metaphor for the creation of a global civil society. Within new notions of communal boundaries, the vigor of educational interaction is no longer explicable in a linearity of power relationships.

For sure, society has a center. In almost all arenas in Japanese society, Westernization was a synonym for modernization and its major premise in modern terms. As in modern times, the agenda of educational policy for "reform" and "development," framed by a particular notion of progress in Western terms, maintains universal values and application in our era of global politics, economy, and culture. This time, however, within the context of interconnectedness and interdependency, national goals and concerns seem to be parallel with global goals and concerns in education as in the economy. Fears and hopes are shared on a global scale, and the relationship of interconnectedness and interdependency surfaces in the traffic of knowledge and human resources. As hopes and fears are shared by countries, the pursuit of the goals of a nation is seen on one side of a coin, and those of other nations on the other side of the same coin.

Notes

1. Japanese and Chinese names are shown in indigenous order, that is, family name first.

2. Their approaches were also connected to Confucian ethics in the region, and Asia's counter-approach against the Western development of manpower and the school system which resulted from the area's colonial experiences.

3. A number of American and Japanese scholars, including Ezra F. Vogel, Edwin Reischauer, Nobuo Shimahara, and Benjamin Duke, who traveled to each other's countries, paved the way to the recognition of Japanese education.

4. All public schools, except one local school district in 2007, and approximately 60% of private schools joined in. The Prime Minister recommended all private schools participate in the survey.

5. Mortimer J. Adler's Paideia Proposal is a good example taking this position, which is against competition in education.

6. Since the 1960s, Japan's cognitive psychologists, who emphasize the scientific method and computational theory, have taken the position in developmental psychology that maturity develops through the innate nature of the human being.

REFERENCES

Abe, S. (2006). *Utsukushii kuni e [Toward the country of beauty]*. Tokyo: Bungei Shunju.

Aron, R. (1967). *Main currents in sociological thought 2: Pareto, Weber, Durkheim*. Harmondsworth, UK: Penguin Books.

Azuma, H., & Shigeta, S. (1992). *Hattatsu shinrigaku handbook [Handbook of developmental psychology]*. Tokyo: Fukumura shuppan.

Baker, D.P., & Holsinger, D.B. (1997). Human capital formation and school expansion in Asia: Does a unique regional model exist? In W.K. Cummings & P.G. Altbach (Eds.), *The challenge of Eastern Asian education: Implications for America* (pp. 115–131). Albany: State University of New York Press.

Bauman, Z. (1987). *Legislators and interpreters: On modernity, post-modernity, and intellectuals*. Cambridge: Polity Press.

Bennett, W. (1987). Implications for American education. In C.H. Dorfman (Ed.), *Japanese education today* (pp. 69–71). Washington. DC: U.S. Department of Education.

Bobbitt, P. (2002). *The shield of Achilles: War, peace, and the course of history*. London: Penguin Books.

Borton, H. (1955). *Japan's modern century*. New York: The Ronald Press.

Bracey, G.W. (1997). On comparing the incomparable: A response to Baker and Stedman. *Educational Researcher, 26*(3), 19–26.

Cummings, W.K. (1997). Human resource development: The J-model. In W.K. Cummings & P.G. Altbach (Eds.), *The challenge of Eastern Asian education: Implications for America* (pp. 275–291). Albany: State University of New York Press.

Dower, J. (1999). *Embracing defeat: Japan in the wake of World War II*. New York: W. W. Norton.

Dudden, A. (2005). Japanese colonial control in international terms. *Japanese Studies, 25*(1), 1–20.

Fendler, L. (2001). Educating flexible souls. In K. Hultqvist & G. Dahlberg (Eds.), *Governing the child in the new millennium* (pp. 119–142). New York: RoutledgeFalmer.

Ferguson, N. (2006). *The war of the world: History's age of hatred*. London: Allen Lane.

Foster, S. (1999). The struggle for American identity: Treatment of ethnic groups in United States history textbooks. *History of Education, 28*(3), 251–278.

Gann, L.H. (1984). Western and Japanese colonialism: Some preliminary comparisons. In R.H. Myers & M.R. Peattie (Eds.), *The Japanese colonial empire, 1895–1945* (pp. 497–525). Princeton, NJ: Princeton University Press.

Gluck, C. (1992). The idea of Showa. In C. Gluck & S.R. Graubard (Eds.), *Showa: The Japan of Hirohito* (pp. 1–26). New York: W. W. Norton.

Hobsbawm, E. (1987). *The age of empire 1875–1914*. London: Abacus.

Hobsbawm, E. (1994). *The age of extremes: The short twentieth century 1914–1991*. London: Abacus.

Irokawa, D. (1985). *The culture of the Meiji period*. Princeton, NJ: Princeton University Press.

Japanese Department of Education (1876). *An outline history of Japanese education; Prepared for the Philadelphia international exhibition*. New York: D. Appleton and Company.

Jones, H. (1985). The Griffis thesis and Meiji policy toward hired foreigners. In A. Burks (Ed.), *The modernizers: Overseas students, foreign employees, and Meiji Japan* (pp. 219–253). Boulder, CO: Westview Press.

Kariya, T. (1995). *Taishu kyouiku shakai no yukue [Whereabouts of mass education society]*. Tokyo: Chuko Shinsho.

Kariya, T. (2002). *Kaisoka nihon to kyouiku kiki [Stratified society and education at risk]*. Tokyo: Yushindo.

Kato, Y., & Kusaka, S. (1993). *Hattatsu no shinrigaku [Developmental psychology]*. Tokyo: Gakujyutsu Tosho Shuppansha.

Koyasu, N. (2003). *"Asia" wa dou katararete kitaka: Kindai Nihon no Orientalism [How has "Asia" been interpreted: The Orientalism of modern Japan]*. Tokyo: Fujiwara Shoten.

Ministry of Education, Culture, Sports, Science and Technology (MECSST) (2000). *Sports shinko kihon keikaku*. Retrieved April, 17, 2009, from http://www.mext.go.jp/a_menu/sports/plan/06031014/001.htm, http://www.mext.go.jp/a_menu/sports/plan/06031014.htm.

Meyer, J., Ramirez, F., Rubinson, R., & Boli-Bennett, J. (1977). The world educational revolution, 1950–1970. *Sociology of Education, 50*, 242–258.

Mimizuka, H. (2007). Determinants of children's academic achievements in primary education. *Journal of Educational Sociology, 80*, 23–39.

Mitter, R. (2003). Old ghosts, new memories: China's changing war history in the era of post-Mao politics. *Journal of Contemporary History, 38*(1), 117–131.

Nicholls, J. (2006). Are students expected to critically engage with textbook perspectives of the Second World War? A comparative and international study. *Research in Comparative and International Education, 1*(1), 40–55.

Nihon no shinrigaku kanko iinkai (NSKI) (1982). *Nihon no shinrigaku [Japan's psychology]*. Tokyo: Nihon Bunka Kagakusha.

Nozaki, Y. (2008). *War memory, nationalism and education in postwar Japan, 1945–2007: The Japanese history textbook controversy and Ienaga Saburo's court challenges*. London: Routledge.

Ohkura, K. (2005). Dewey and the ambivalent modern Japan. In T.S. Popkewitz (Ed.), *Inventing the modern self and John Dewey* (pp. 279–299). New York: Palgrave Macmillan.

Okonogi, M. (2005). Nikkan kankei no atarashii chihei: "Taisei masatsu" kara "ishiki kyoyu" e [The horizon of Japan-Korean relations: From "structural frictions" to "shared consciousness"]. In M. Okonogi & D.-J. Chang (Eds.), *Sengo Nikkan kankei no tenkai [The development of the post-war Japanese-Korean relationship]* (pp. 1–9). Tokyo: Keiogijuku daigaku shuppankai.

Popkewitz, T.S. (1998). *Struggling for the soul*. New York: Teachers College Press.

Season, P. (2005). Reporting the 2001 textbook and Yasukuni Shrine controversies: Japanese war memory and commemoration in the British media. *Japan Forum, 17*(3), 287–309.

Seddon, T. (1987). Politics and curriculum: A case study of the Japanese history textbook dispute, 1982. *British Journal of Sociology of Education, 8*(2), 213–226.

Shibata, M. (2005). *Japan and Germany under the US occupation: A comparative analysis of the post-war education reform*. Lanham, MD: Lexington Books.

Shibata, M. (2006). Assumptions and implications of cross-national attraction in education: The case of learning from Japan. *Oxford Review of Education, 30*(5), 649–663.

Shibata, M. (2008). Asia ni okeru nihon no "rekishi-mondai": Sengo-kousou to kokusai-seiji-bunmyaku wo hikaku no shiten kara [Japan's "history problem" in Asia: An analysis in comparative perspectives about the post-war reconstruction policy and international political context]. In T. Kondo (Ed.), *Higashi-Asia no rekishi-seisaku: Ni-chu-kan taiwa to rekishi-ninshiki ["History policy" in East Asia: Japan-China-Korea: The dialogues and perceptions of history]* (pp. 210–229). Tokyo: Akashi Shoten.

Shields, J.J. (1989). *Japanese schooling*. University Park: Pennsylvania State University Press.

Shils, E. (1975). *Center and periphery: Essays in macrosociology*. Chicago: The University of Chicago Press.

Sugo, H., Miyahara, S., & Munakata, S. (Eds.) (1950). *America kyoiku shisetudan hokokusho yokai [The summary of the United States Education Mission Report]*. Tokyo: Kokumin Tosho Kankokai.

Umemori, N. (2007). *Benedict Anderson globalization wo kataru [Benedict Anderson talking about globalization]*. Tokyo: Kobunsha Shinsho.

U.S. Education Mission (1946). *Report of the United States education mission to Japan.* Submitted to the Supreme Commander for the Allied Powers. Reprinted in E.R. Beauchamp & J.M. Vardaman (Eds.), *Japanese education since 1945: A documentary study* (pp. 85–90). Armonk, NY: M.E. Sharpe.

Wan, M. (1995). Japan and the Asian Development Bank. *Pacific Affairs, 68*(4), 509–528.

Willis, D., Yamamura, S., & Rappleye, J. (2008). Frontiers of education: Japan as "global model" or "nation at risk"? *International Review of Education, 54*, 493–515.

Yoda, A. (1977). *Shin kyoiku shinrigaku jiten [New encyclopedia of educational psychology]*. Tokyo: Kaneko Shobo.

Yoshida, T. (2004). *East Asian regionalism and Japan*. Tokyo: Institute of Developing Economies (IDE) in APEC Study Center, JETRO.

Ziemer, G. (1946). Our educational failure in Germany. *American Mercury* (June), 726–733.

Transnational Governance of Higher Education: On Globalization and International University Ranking Lists

SVERKER LINDBLAD AND RITA FOSS LINDBLAD

1. Introduction

This chapter is about globalization in higher education and how "globalism" is playing a role in stimulating university transformation around the world. Our specific focus is on international university ranking lists. Such lists are being given increasingly more space and attention in the mass media and by governments as well as by supranational organizations and the universities themselves. There has also been an increase in the number of ranking lists, each one presenting somewhat different criteria and procedures for identifying ranking positions.

But do such ranking lists matter? And if so, what effects do they have on higher education? Marginson (2009, p. 11) argues that at least the policy effects of such lists are quite substantial:

Rankings function as a meta-performance indicator. The criteria used to determine each institution's position in the ranking system become meta-outputs that each institution places on priority, so that rankings begin to define "quality". . . . By shaping university and system behaviors, while standardizing the definitions of outcome and output, rankings begin to decide university mission and the balance of activity, externalizing part of university identity.

From this perspective, international ranking lists are considered to have transformative powers concerning the organization and quality of higher education institutions and their identity.

In this chapter we are dealing with a particular aspect of these possibly transformative powers as we consider international ranking as a specific technology of government, heavily related to the ongoing globalization of higher education. More precisely, we are describing and analyzing university ranking lists as instruments in transnational governance of higher education. By doing so, we also hope to put forwards arguments concerning principles of globalization and education, and to draw attention to a new mode of regulation.

Such transnational governance has the potential to structure and guide activities and interactions beyond, across, and within national territories and has the specificity of, on the one hand, crossing the boundaries of different nations and, on the other hand, taking place inside as well as outside these boundaries. Its governance and ordering powers are "soft" as well as "externalized," as they rely less on formal rules and formal hierarchies within organizations, and more on information and knowledge about the organization (cf. Ahrne & Brunsson, 2009). Technologies such as monitoring, standards, benchmarking, and rankings are some examples. Within the realms of higher education the ordering powers of rankings could be regarded, with respect to their present status, as utterances of constructed facts concerning different aspects of universities and their activities that might be—but just eventually might be—translated into the languages of such organizations and incorporated in their decision-making.

As mentioned, ranking lists are but one example of instruments of governing the ongoing processes of "transnationalization" in the world. Such transnationalization exists not only in the domains of education and higher education, but also in those of business and companies (Wedlin, 2007). While the transnationalization of business can be related to the deterritorialization of the flows of finance capital, or to the mobility of jobs and workforces, in education and higher education it could be related to new ways of organizing knowledge production and to processes such as those of policy borrowing (Steiner-Khamsi, 2004) or policy traveling (Lindblad & Popkewitz, 2004), which spread ideas over wide territories.

The different instruments or technologies of transnational governance can be expected to vary in the ways in which they work and to have specific characteristics within their own institutionalized spheres. Given this, our objective is to deal with the university ranking lists as tools in transnational governance of higher education.

This means that we, *first*, have to consider some characteristics about higher education systems, their transformations as well as their societal role and relations, in order to understand why international ranking lists "might matter" in the first place. A keyword here is "what might matter"—how potentialities might transform into stabilized social facts and structures. If a possible reason for rankings is to govern higher education in the processes of translating possibilities into facts and structures, we also have to consider, *second*, how these processes of translation can be understood in terms of transnational governance. And in order to capture some aspects of how international ranking lists can be understood as tools for transnational governance of universities, we also have to consider, *third*, "what" aspects of university activities different ranking lists are addressing.

2. Higher Education in Transition

The university is a community of teachers and scholars whose roots go back to the medieval period, and even earlier in China and the Middle East. It has survived—in its varieties—over the centuries by means of combinations of boundary work relative to the church, the state and different sectors and crafts within civil society, and by innovations in its modes of working and organizing (Ramirez, 2002; Rothblatt & Wittrock, 1993). From its early times to the times of the rise of the modern university and its dual missions of research and education, claims of autonomy and self-organized change, in combination with impartiality and an emphasis on the public good, have been vital in academic rhetoric. From this point of view, it is problematic for the state—or other sponsors—to steer higher education in more instrumental ways—the interrelation between higher education and society at large has always been interactive and thus also transformative in a double sense.

For better or for worse—and within the time spectrum we call modernity and postmodernity—higher education has retained its key position as *the* producer of public, formal, and "scientific" knowledge and learning. Even though the label of science is elusive in the sense that it refers to a gradually more and more diversified body of knowledge, it remains a signifier for knowledge that in all its different intellectual embeddings brings with it the hope, and eventual dangers, of new constructs of insights of the world in which we live, and new insights, models, and artifacts regarding how to live and interact within—and with—our constructions. This "scientification" of society means not only the importance of science for human life, but points to a situation where "society" and what is "social" have been absorbed into what is considered "scientific" (see Latour, 1988).

This also implies structural, societal, changes. Peter Drucker (1969) and Daniel Bell's (1973) early claims of the transition into times of a "knowledge economy" and "the post-industrial society," as well as the related and more commonly used label of a "knowledge society" (Böhme & Stehr, 1986), all give voice to the increased expectations and dependence on higher education and its achievements. Gibbons et al. (1994) and Nowotny, Gibbons, and Scott (2001), with their claims of a radical shift in the forms of knowledge production from Mode 1 to Mode 2—from more traditional and disciplinary form towards knowledge production organized around application-focused problems—belong to a group of studies that have maintained that the shift is worldwide, as is the tremendous expansion of the higher education system. From a world polity perspective this should be understood as a result of "loose coupling" (Brunsson, 1999; Drori, Meyer, Ramirez, & Schofer, 2003; Meyer & Rowan, 1977), meaning that the scientification of reality and its worldwide extension is, first, dependent on the institutional and cultural *authority* of science more than any particular set of scientific ideas or practices which, second, are variously incorporated in different places and practices. Thus, homogenization presupposes local variation.

Here we could talk about global tendencies across local varieties, which deeply engage the organization of the higher education nexus of research and education. For some, such as Slaughter and Rhoades (2004), this has meant "academic capitalism," for example, a situation where higher education institutions around the world now operate as marketers—creating new circuits of knowledge that link higher education to the new economy and thereby transform its mission from being in the interest of the public good to being in the interest of profit and markets. For others—scholars such as Whitley (2000), Kogan, Bauer, Bleiklie, and Henkel (2006) or Tomusk (2006), for example—the very same tendencies of increased marketing and homogenization seem highly varied. For Whitley, the degree of intellectual competition and fluidity is widely varied across academic fields and nations, and varies more between the sciences in the United States than in more homogeneously organized academic systems, such as that of Japan. For Kogan, changes of norms, identities and the authority structure of higher educations are shown to be less prevalent than formal changes of reforms, and Tomusk has concluded that very little of the efforts to establish the "European Area of Higher Education" (more commonly known as the Bologna Process) has been filtered down into individual universities and colleges.

However, the increased interest in rankings could most fruitfully be read from the perspectives of scientification, increased marketing, and competition in the higher education sector. Here, ranking could be regarded as a tool presenting qualities of scientific craft and rigor acceptable to a scientified society.

3. Transnational Governance in Higher Education

In tandem with the extensive transformation of the higher education system are changes emerging in the control and governing of higher education that are closely interrelated to the dynamics and effects of the expansion of the sciences and the scientification of social and political life. What are the sites of government of such large-scale, worldwide, and complex forms of activities as those of the sciences and the higher education system, and how are they to be governed?

The politics of research and higher education policy has always been a heatedly debated, and a highly costly, affair. However, for a long time it was also an affair with some worldwide consensus regarding the goals and principles of governing. The influence of the Vannevar Bush (Director of the United States Office of Scientific Research and Development from 1941 and scientific adviser to President Roosevelt and President Truman) "contract" between science and society from 1945 cannot be overerestimated. His report to President Roosevelt, *Science: The Endless Frontier* (1945), was long virtually paradigmatic not only for United States research and higher education policy, but for research and higher education policy worldwide. The view of science was a highly trustful one in terms of achievements (science with endless frontiers), but it was conditional; it was dependent on the autonomy of the scientific and academic elites and higher education institutions. The problem for governing as it was understood in those days was how to secure this autonomy, without giving in either to commercial interest or to losing the interest of applied research—for example, research with instrumental and practical value. The solution, "the contract," involved guarantees of scientific autonomy and increases in public funding of basic research in exchange for increased demands on science and the higher education institutions to perform research and learning for the benefit of social and national goals of well-being and welfare.

Many of the problems that motivated these arrangements of steering and regulating the relations between science, higher education, and society as a public good are, indeed, still with us. The interests and expectations are much the same, as is the problem of the costs. The differences between now and then are much related to localization, where "the endless frontier of science" has come to mean also "the endless frontier of its production"—meaning its global spread and transnational character. Governing is now an escalating problem in relation to increasing differentiation in higher education and to demands for more national resources for higher education in a field where international cooperation, and competition, have now transcended their national embeddings.

The relation between the higher education system and society is now one of co-production, or co-evolution, which also means that general trends in society not only can be expected to have bearings on higher education and the sciences, but can be expected to enroll them (Nowotny et al., 2001). This could be said to be the case for governing as well.

Djelic and Sahlin-Andersson (2006) noted that the growth of transnational interaction and regulation could be expected not only to go beyond state-to-state interaction and to include other actors such as social movements and business enterprises, but also to involve higher education as well as the symbolic signs of being "scientific." Such a shift from government to governance—from top-down governing processes in, for example, the state, to processes with a multitude of actors outside as well as inside the state—is related to a shift in regulatory mode. Simply stated, "hard" rules and coercion measures are being turned into, or complemented by, "soft" rules, for instance benchmarking and standards. Such a soft mode of regulation is crossing national as well as organizational borders.

Soft rules imply more interpretive leeway for those who are to "follow" the rules, and fewer threats of sanctions from those who "produce" these rules. In sum, we are getting changing fields of governance, where different actors and processes in different places are interacting and where ideas and instruments are traveling between and are being translated into different contexts. Stated otherwise, transnational governance is embedded into—shaped by as well as shaping—cultural and institutional contexts.

A soft mode of regulation is part of the organizing of outside organizations. In this context Ahrne and Brunsson (2009) posit that instruments such as membership definition, rules or procedures, monitoring measures, and sanctions constitute "fundamental elements of formal organisations, but they can also be used outside these" (p. 9). A soft mode of regulation often means that instruments in organizational decision-making are exported to or imported from other organizations. An organization that is importing instruments is incomplete, but its organizing becomes more complete with this import. By means of such importation and exportation, governance is achieved by a network of organizations supplementing each other in different ways.

Given the developments and characteristics presented above, it is necessary to conceptualize transnational governance as different from state-centered governing based on the complete organization of decisions and a hard mode of regulation. Djelic and Sahlin-Andersson (2006) argue for the use of a field perspective. They combine the institutionalist interest in space and relations—topographies of places, networks, and interaction—with institutional forces that constitute and structure systems or cultures of meaning. Such a combination produces a field of transnational governance. The notion of institutional forces is distinctive here, as they form activities and interests in ways that are conceived of as the "natural" way of doing things, often in a self-reinforcing way. By doing so, Andersson-Sahlin & Djelic argue, the institutional forces constitute the rules of the game in the transnational field. Important forces here are, for example, scientization and marketization, as well as democratization. In different ways such forces—sometimes in contradiction to each other—are at work in the making of transnational governance of higher education.

International university ranking lists are examples of such a soft mode of regulation in higher education. Ranking lists are produced outside universities—but sometimes based on information provided by them. There are no demands to be informed by them for decision in the universities. But they still might matter. The ranking lists have no force as such but might matter when considering institutional forces at work in the emerging field of transnational governance. Thus they might strengthen networks and positions in networks. Furthermore, for better or for worse, they are condensations of sets of different utterances on universities and their qualities in ranking numbers, giving a sense of comprehensibility and navigation avenues for different actors—sponsors, consumers, university boards, and managers, by producing the numbers in a ranking game. Since they are offers that you can resist, since they just might matter, they need to be conceived of as reliable, valid, and having legitimacy in the transnational regulatory field. To inform ourselves about this we will turn to the inner qualities of ranking lists in the next section.

4. International University Ranking Lists

The long history of universities stands in sharp contrast to the short history of university ranking lists. A starting point often mentioned is the regional *US News and World Report* ranking of American Colleges in 1983, though less elaborated rankings of higher education providers occurred before that (according to, for example, Stuart [1995]). Usher and Savino (2006) provide an overview of 16 university ranking lists and compare criteria used for ranking in the respective lists. Most lists focus on student choice in regional settings. The international university ranking lists are of recent origin, and over the last few years a number of ranking lists have emerged, and present their results mostly on an annual basis. Here, we will not deal with regional university ranking lists, such as the *US News and World Report*'s rankings (for a comparative presentation and discussion of four such lists in the United States, UK, Australia and Canada—for instance, concerning their validity and relevance—see also Dill and Soo [2005]), since we are interested in transnational aspects of higher education, and for this purpose international ranking lists seem to be best suited.

In Table 1 we present an overview of four international ranking lists—when they published their first list and the organizations that compile the lists. We also present the main criteria that are used for comparison and ranking. The ARWU list—often called the Shanghai list—is based on prizewinners and publication and citation studies. The Times Higher Education list (THE-QS) is also based on bibliometrics, but surveys among academics and employers play a vital part. The Webometrics ranking, based on a number of criteria concerning visibility on the Web using different kinds of search engines such as Google and Yahoo, was originally constructed in order to improve university presentation and publication on the Web.[1] The Professional Ranking of World Universities deals with the ability of universities to educate people to elite positions in leading international companies.[2] It is based on data from *Fortune* magazine.[3] Thus, it addresses relations between the academy and the economy in a very specific way, arguing that such positions are equivalent to getting Nobel Prizes in the academy.

In Figure 1 we present the results of these ranking lists, where higher education institution and nation are basic categories when presenting ranking positions. We present the 60 highest ranked universities or institutes in each ranking list.

First, we note that a small number of countries are players in the top international ranking game—a total of 24 nations. Thus, there are 170 countries that do not have any university in one of the top 60 positions in any of these ranking lists. This is further underlined by the fact that nine countries listed in the figure cover 90% of the possible top positions. Second, we also note a strong overall Anglo-Saxon dominance in the lists. The Webometrics list is the one that most dominantly presents Anglo-Saxon universities, followed by the ARWU list, where rather

TABLE 1

Overview of FOUR INTERNATIONAL RANKING LISTS: START YEAR, RANKING CRITERIA AND RANKING ORGANIZATION

University Ranking List	Start Year	Ranking Criteria	Ranking Organization
Academic Ranking of World Universities (ARWU)	2003	BibliometricsAlumni and staff prizewinners	The Shanghai Jiao Tong University
Times Higher Education—QS World University Rankings (THE-QS)	2004	Surveys on peer reputation, international attraction and employability Bibliometrics	Times Higher Education and Quacquarelli Symonds
Webometrics Ranking of World Universities	2004	Website visibility and web impact according to search engines	Cybermetrics Lab at the National Research Council in Spain
Professional Ranking of World Universities	2007	Chief executive officers in leading worldwide companies according to *Fortune* magazine	École Nationale Supérieure des Mines de Paris

FIGURE 1

HIGHER EDUCATION INSTITUTIONS AMONG THE FIRST 60 IN FOUR
INTERNATIONAL RANKING LISTS
(Number over Countries)

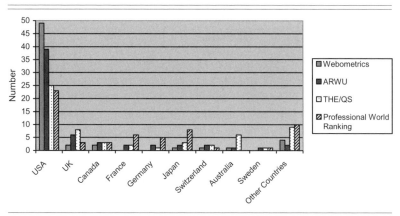

different tools are at work. The THE/QS list is a bit less United States dominated, and the Professional Ranking of World Universities actually has more universities outside than inside the United States in its ranking.

In the following sections we will focus on the ARWU and the THE-QS lists, since these frequently appear on the higher education agenda.[4]

Academic Ranking of World Universities: Shanghai Jiao Tong University Ranking List

The Shanghai list—or more precisely the Academic Ranking of World Universities (http://ed.sjtu.edu.cn/ranking.htm); the Shanghai Jiao Tong University ranking list, with the acronym ARWU—was a result of the Chinese government's political ambition to develop world-class universities in China. A number of universities were selected in 1998 to further develop these ambitions. This resulted in benchmarking activities, where different categories of United States universities were compared to Chinese top universities (Liu, 2009). A main task, according to the constructors of this list, is to identify and to analyze world-class universities in order to set up working goals and indictors for universities around the world to become world-class universities.[5] Based on this, the first Shanghai list of world-class universities was presented in 2003 and attracted considerable interest around the world.

In Table 2 we present the criteria and indicators for the Shanghai ranking list as well as their relative weight for the calculation of ranking positions of universities. Of importance in the construction are two things. First, what is used are specific measures of track records, that is, what is achieved in terms of prizes and publications. In sum, 90% of the ranking position is derived in that way. Second, these track records are mostly in the arena of science. Social scientists or educationalists as well as teachers and researchers in the humanities do not matter much here.

Information for ranking from other organizations such as publishers and bibliometric analysts is also important. Vital here are the services of the Thomson ISI (Institute for Scientific Information).[6] It is part of the Thomson Reuters Corporation, which offers different bibliographic database services such as measurements of citation impacts of different kinds.[7] In sum, the Thomson ISI services contribute 50% of the making of ranking lists. Taken together, the Shanghai list is based on a network of agents—the Chinese government and its Ministry of Education and the Shanghai Jiao Tong University, as well as the Thomson Reuters Corporation.

The presentation of the results of the ARWU ranking emphasizing measures of scientific qualities. It is claimed that there are no commer-

TABLE 2

CRITERIA AND INDICATORS AND THEIR RELATIVE WEIGHTS IN THE CONSTRUCTION OF A BASIS FOR COMPARING UNIVERSITIES IN THE SHANGHAI RANKING LIST

Criteria	Indicator	Weight
Quality of education	Alumni of an institution winning Nobel Prizes and Fields Medals	10%
Quality of faculty	Staff of an institution winning Nobel Prizes and Fields Medals	20%
	Highly cited researchers in 21 broad subject categories	20%
Research output	Articles published in *Nature* and *Science*	20%
	Articles in *Science Citation Index–Expanded, Social Science Citation Index*	20%
Size of institution	Academic performance with respect to the size of an institution	10%
Total		100%

Source: http://www.arwu.org/rank/2007/ranking2007.htm.

cial interests involved and that the criteria used are objective and the results open to inspection by other researchers.

The annual ARWU list was first presented in 2003 with considerable publicity in scientific as well as in political contexts. In the 2008 ranking (see Table 4 below) we find Harvard at the top, followed by Stanford and UC Berkeley. Cambridge is the first non-United States university, being fourth in rank. During 2003–2008 there is a seemingly stable pattern over the years in the top positions. We also note a stable ranking order in terms of political geography. The United States, in combination with "Oxbridge," occupies almost all the first 20 places—with a Japanese university in as number 19 in the 2008 ranking list. Going down the list there is less stability, however, often due to the fact that the objects for ranking are sparse, for instance Nobel laureates (recruiting a Nobel laureate to the faculty means a great deal for the outcomes of the ranking).

The collected data in the ARWU list are analyzed in terms of regional and geopolitical aspects concerning, for instance, the distribution of top universities across the world in relation to GDP and percentage of population. Below we present a glimpse of such analyses presented by ARWU:

- The United States has 54% of the top 100 universities, 27% of the GDP and 5% of the population of the world.
- The UK has 11% of the top 100 universities, 5% of the GDP and 1% of the population of the world.
- Sweden has 4% of the top 100 universities, 0.8% of the GDP and 0.1% of the population of the world.
- Russia has 1% of the top 100 universities, 2% of the GDP and 2.2% of the population of the world.
- China has 0% of the top 100 universities, 5.5% of the GDP and 20% of the population of the world.

This gives a clear message to the reader—top universities are unequally distributed across the world, and so is the GDP. However, this is not only considered as a fact but also something that can be dealt with in order to improve universities that do not now belong to the world elite. "World Class Universities is a dream for generations of Chinese. It is not only for pride, but also for the future of China" (Liu, 2009).

Given this way of framing the outcomes of the Shanghai list, a number of universities—in China and in other parts of the world—are putting forwards ambitions to become world-class universities and are presenting strategies and time schedules for achieving such goals

Times Higher Education—QS World University Rankings

The THE-QS ranking list (Table 3) was first published in the Times Higher Education Supplement in November 2004. The stated purpose of the THE-QS World University Rankings (2004) has been, from the start, to recognize universities as the multi-faceted organisations that they are, and to provide a global comparison of their success against the notional mission of remaining or becoming world-class (Jobbins, 2005).

The THE-QS list is 50% based on reviews—like net surveys—of academics and employers. This is to a large extent a measure of reputation of universities and their students. The track record (citation impact) in a more narrow sense contributes 20% to the total sum on which the ranking is based. Teaching quality is measured by dividing the number of students with the number of faculty staff. In addition, the THE-QS gives weight to the participation of international staff and numbers of international students as indications of academic quality.

The QS (Quacquarelli Symonds) mentioned here is an international company specializing in careers and developing information on higher education.[8] The QS formerly used the Thomson ISI services and now uses Scopus[9] for determining citation impacts. The QS also gathers information by providing surveys to the universities themselves as well as to academics and recruiters concerning university reputation and student employability.

TABLE 3
The CONSTRUCTION OF THE THE/QS RANKING LIST

Field	Method	Weight
Peer review	Survey of the QS Company to 5100 academics	40%
Recruiter review	Reviews of important international employers	10%
Citation Impact per paper	Number of citations of papers that university staff have published as measured previously by Thompson Web of Science and now Scopus.	20%
Staff-Student Ratio	This is based on the number of staff in relation to the number of students, where a higher rate is conceived of as higher quality.	20%
International attraction	The ability of the university to attract number of foreign students.	5%
International faculty	Measures the ability of a university to attract teachers from other countries according to QS.	5%
Total		100%

TABLE 4
UNIVERSITY RANKS IN THE ARWU LIST 2008 COMPARED TO THE
THE-QS RANKINGS
(First 30 universities in the ARWU list)

University	Country	Rank ARWU	Rank THE-QS
Harvard University	USA	1	1
Stanford University	USA	2	17
University of California—Berkeley	USA	3	36
University of Cambridge	UK	4	3
Massachusetts Institute Tech (MIT)	USA	5	9
California Institute Tech	USA	6	5
Columbia University	USA	7	10
Princeton University	USA	8	12
University of Chicago	USA	9	8
University of Oxford	UK	10	4
Yale University	USA	11	2
Cornell University	USA	12	15
University of California—Los Angeles	USA	13	30
University of California—San Diego	USA	14	58
University of Pennsylvania	USA	15	11
University of Washington—Seattle	USA	16	59
University of Wisconsin—Madison	USA	17	55
University of California—San Francisco	USA	18	-
Tokyo University	Japan	19	19
Johns Hopkins University	USA	20	13
University of Michigan—Ann Arbor	USA	21	18
University College London	UK	22	7
Kyoto University	Japan	23	25
Swiss Fed Institute Tech—Zurich	Switzerland	24	24
University of Toronto	Canada	24	41
University of Illinois—Urbana Champaign	USA	26	71
Imperial College London	UK	27	6
University of Minnesota—Twin Cities	US	28	87
Washington University—St. Louis	USA	29	60
Northwestern University	USA	30	33

The rankings in the THE-QS are less stable than the QS. Actually, the variation over time is somewhat of a mystery. For instance, how can the decline of UC Berkeley be explained—down from position 2 in 2004 to position 36 five years later?

The presentation of the 2008 ranking list by THE-QS was framed as a public event. The universities were informed of their positions by the THE-QS a few days before they were made public. Lots of comments from university people were published, and a "Globalisation of University" Conference took place just after the publication. An introductory question is:

Higher education is global: Where is your institution positioned? ...
Some 300,000 overseas students are currently in the UK spending £5 billion
annually on their education—what is your institution's strategy to fill this
audience's growing requirements? (http://www.timeshighereducation.co.uk at
2008-10-14)

Here the THE-QS put forward questions for universities to consider
how to attract overseas students. A number of reactions around the
world on the 2008 ranking are presented, including fears that the UK is
losing position in the ranking game.

Comparing University Ranking Lists

In Table 4 we present the 30 highest ranked universities in 2008
according to the ARWU list. We also present how these universities are
ranked according to the THE-QS list.

The ARWU (or Shanghai) list presents overwhelming ranking
results in favor of top United States universities. UK universities (Cambridge, Oxford, and the London University Colleges) are given somewhat more favorable positions in the THE-QS list. Furthermore, the
differences in ranking show that there are, even at the top level, inconsistencies between the two lists. The inconsistencies correspond to the
ways the lists are constructed. For instance, the employer reviews put
UK universities much more frequently in top positions (14 among the
30 highest ranked according to the employability criterion).

In Table 5 the Shanghai list and the THE-QS list are compared in
terms of ambitions, instruments, and outcomes, and also show the
different organizations that participate in order to make the rankings
possible.

We note here different ambitions with the ranking lists. The
Shanghai list is constructed to be a tool in the making of modern
top-class universities with an emphasis on science and scientific qualities, while the Times Higher Education list is constructed as an instrument for the modern entrepreneurial university operating in an
international as well as a national market. This is furthermore underlined by the rhetoric used when presenting and analyzing the ranking
results, in terms of making a world-class university as is the case is
in ARWU, or capitalizing on ranking positions as in THE-QS.
Thus, the two ranking lists in different ways emphasize two important institutional forces in a transnational regulatory field of higher
education—science and market.

TABLE 5
Comparing University Ranking Lists

Aspect	ARWU	THE-QS
Emphasis	A tool for modernizing universities based on qualities in science and technology innovations.	A tool for entrepreneurial universities to strengthen their position and as an information system for stakeholders
Participating organizations	Initiative by the Chinese government,the Shanghai Jiao Tong University,the Thomson Reuters Cooperation and the ISI Web of Science	The Times Higher Education, the QS Quacquarelli Symonds Limited,the Reed Elsevier publishing company, and Scopus.
Instruments	Collecting information on high status awards. Analysis of publications and their impact by means of Thomson ISI. Thin basis for comparisons.	Surveying reputation and employability by means of QSCollecting information from universities. Analysis of publications and their impact by means of Scopus. Somewhat broader basis for comparisons.
Outcomes	Rather stable rankings over years at the top. More unstable below top positions. Analyses of geopolitical and financial characteristics.	Rather unstable rankings over years even among the top positions. Sense-making of instabilities in positions.

These ranking lists are similar in they are constructed by means of the services of multinational companies. We can here talk about partnerships between ranking-list constructors and a set of international enterprises—the Scopus or the Thompson bibliometrical institutes, plus of course the case of the THE-QS (Quacquarelli Symonds operates globally from offices in Beijing, London, Paris, Singapore, Sydney, Tokyo and Washington DC). The Thompson Reuters Corporation ownership of Thomson ISI is a similar construction, as is the Reed Elsevier Company, where Scopus is located.

There are differences in the instruments—the Shanghai list is based on the universities' own research and the services of the Thomson ISI, while the THE-QS uses the services of QS and Scopus. The THE-QS uses commentaries in order to make changes understandable; instability is combined with good-reason essays on this instability. The Shanghai list is used for analyses of inequalities in the world, as well as in distributions of world-class universities around the world as we understand it, to change the current state of the art in higher education.

Controversies in University Ranking

Ranking lists are assumed to represent higher education and research institutions in ways that make it possible for laymen and politicians, as well as students and parents, to understand and compare qualities of different universities (e.g., Dunn, 2003). Thus, such representations are assumed to provide information about a world that seems to be incomprehensible and to make higher education transparent and possible to deal with by informed customers, or as decision-makers in and involving higher education. In order to matter in the governance of higher education, ranking lists have to be recognized as representing academic work and life in a trustworthy way.

However, in discourses on international ranking lists a number of problems are ventilated. We will give a short overview of controversial issues.

Cavallin and Lindblad (2006) analyzed the instruments for making university ranking lists and pointed to a number of problems in their construction as representations of academic qualities:

- The basis for ranking involves very thin descriptions of academic work life and performance. This leads to instability in ranking outcomes over years that are dubious, given that they represent large and complex organizations that use huge infrastructures in their work.
- A language problem is visible in ranking. Almost all top universities are working within an English-language domain. Universities in other linguistic contexts such as for instance French, German, Spanish, or Chinese are highly underrepresented.
- There is a privileging of certain scientific fields. Mathematics, natural sciences, medicine and technology are heavily emphasized, while the humanistic and artistic fields of knowledge and educational sciences, as well as large parts of the social sciences, are to a large extent underrepresented.
- A specific publication genre is favored in ranking lists—articles in peer-reviewed journals—while monographs and books and other ways of presenting research are more or less invisible in the making of ranking positions.
- Large universities with broad faculty coverage and large teaching tasks are disfavored compared to universities specializing in medicine, technology, or natural sciences.

Thus, what counts in university ranking is research in math, sciences, and medicine carried out in North America or Great Britain and published in peer-reviewed scientific journals.[10] Writing books in the arts or philosophy in French or Swedish does not matter much, and in the ranking game this kind of academic work is at a disadvantage, given that the number of articles and citations that matter are divided by the number of teachers and researchers.

Lack of consistency between ranking lists is another problem. Thus, Usher and Savino (2006) compared a number of ranking lists—often with a regional focus—and found a conglomerate of indicators and little consistency between national ranking systems:

> Intriguingly, however, there is absolutely no agreement among the authors of these indicators as to what indicates quality. The world's main ranking systems bear little if any relationship to one another, using very different indicators and weightings to arrive at a measure of quality. This suggests that the position of certain institutions in their national rankings is largely a statistical fluke—if another country's ranking system were used, a different result might emerge. (p. 3)

However, Usher and Savino note a consistency in outcomes with a few similar universities at the top, which we also noted in the previous section. They argue that there is a factor "X" at work—presumably a combination of traditional prestige, university resources and student recruitment—which make the top rankings plausible and stable.

Last but not least, there is a problem concerning the legitimacy of the networks producing university ranking lists (Lindblad, 2008). As is shown above, a constellation of private and public organizations are participating here. With what right are they—that is, QS or Reed Elsevier—participating in judging the quality of universities and thereby also taking part in the governing of higher education and research?

Criticisms like those presented above point in direction of an inbuilt conservatism in university ranking, where past victories and reputation, translated into ranking positions, are taken as indications of current prosperity as well as future progress (Marginson, 2009). This is indeed a most severe criticism—that ranking lists might matter in the governing to preserve tradition instead of innovation in higher education.

5. University Ranking Lists and Transnational Governance

We have presented here notions about higher education in flux, where transnational tendencies in governing are emerging in terms of networks and regulatory fields. These tendencies correspond to institutional forces such as marketization and scientification, which are making it plausible that ranking lists might matter as instruments in transnational governance of higher education. They are mapping universities and their positions relative to each other around the world, thus opening them up for international competition and cooperation. In several ways university ranking is a technology with ambitions to present university qualities in a transparent and accountable way in response to current demands on higher education governing. Such a technology in many ways appeals to the governance of higher education. It provides opportunities for soft regulation across national and organizational boundaries, informing many actors in different positions in the regulatory field of higher education.

As a governing instrument, ranking is very much in line with current transitions in higher education and new demands on higher education governance. This is further reinforced by the techniques applied, such as citation impact or measures of staff reputation, which are used in other higher education regulation as well. From this point of view, the potential success of international ranking listing is a product of our time.[11]

University ranking as a technology appeals to conceptions of science in its striving to be objective and precise, according to certain ways of understanding science. This can be understood as *scientification* of academic life appealing to different stakeholders inside as well as outside academia.

A vital ingredient in ranking is the construction of abstract indications of academic quality in terms of position. There is an economy of positions—and positions are assumed to be achieved by, for example, hard work and clever strategies. If ranking positions are considered by different agents as useful for determining the overall performance of universities in relation to each other, then they serve as information in academic capitalism, governing the governance. In a word, rankings have potential in terms of the *marketization* of higher education.

However, these indications of academic qualities are regarded as questionable in several ways: as being too one-dimensional—favoring certain aspects of academic work and disfavoring other aspects—and too inconsistent in their selection of indicators. As several critics have pointed out, such as Altbach (2006) there are serious deficits in the international ranking game that are quite apparent when considering their emphasis and when comparing positions in different lists and comparing positions over time in the same list. To base academic capitalism on ranking positions seems to be too risky an enterprise. From this point of view, university ranking is a higher education governance technology in need of *standardization*.

Thus, the EU is now supporting the development of another international university ranking list. Based on a criticism of existing university ranking lists with their geopolitical and language biases, the European Commission is now giving support to the development of a multi-dimensional global ranking system:

The new ranking to be designed and tested would aim to make it possible to compare and benchmark similar institutions within and outside the EU, both at the level of the institution as a whole and focusing on different study fields. This would help institutions to better position themselves and improve their development strategies, quality and performances. Accessible, transparent and comparable information will make it easier for stakeholders and, in particular, students to make informed choices between the different institutions and their programs.[12]

The European Commission has the ambition to provide the transnational field of higher education governance with an improved way of international university ranking, including different categories of academic work and comparing what is considered as comparable in academia. Within a couple of years another ranking system will be presented by a consortium of institutions and organizations from the Netherlands, Germany, Belgium, and France. Such a development is a result of international and transnational cooperation in order to produce a standardized instrument for transnational governance. The implications of such standardization of higher education need to be thoroughly analyzed and discussed in terms of governance and homogenization, as well as critical thinking and innovations in research.

So far, ranking is a technology offering a soft mode of regulation of higher education. So far, this kind of technology might matter only softly. But given ongoing tendencies in scientification, marketization and standardization, it might turn into "an offer that you cannot refuse," turning soft regulation into hard matters of fact.

NOTES

1. See here http://www.webometrics.info/about_rank.html.

2. http://www.ensmp.fr/Actualites/PR/defclassementEMP.html.

3. Considering *Fortune* magazine and the Global 500 list, see http://money.cnn.com/magazines/fortune/.

4. Parts of our analyses here are based on Lindblad (2008).

5. For presentation of reasons and ranking problems, see http://www.arwu.org/rank2008/ARWU2008FAQ(EN).htm.

6. See http://www.thomsonreuters.com/, where the following is stated: "The Institute for Scientific Information (ISI) was founded by Eugene Garfield in 1960. It was acquired by Thomson Scientific and Healthcare in 1992, became known as Thomson ISI and now as Thomson Scientific. It is a component of the multi-billion dollar Thomson Reuters Corporation." It presents itself: "We combine industry expertise with innovative technology to deliver critical information to leading decision makers in the financial, legal, tax and accounting, scientific, healthcare and media markets, powered by the world's most trusted news organization."

7. See http://thomsonreuters.com/products_services/science/academic.

8. See http://www.qsnetwork.com/, where it is stated that QS Quacquarelli Symonds was founded in 1990 and has become established as the world's leading network for top careers and education. "Our mission is to enable motivated people around the world to fulfill their potential by fostering international mobility, educational achievement and career development." See http://www.qsnetwork.com/about_qs/who-are-we.

9. Scopus is part of the Reed Elsevier Company. It presents itself as a world-leading provider of professional information and online workflow solutions in the Science, Medical, Legal, Risk Information and Analytics, and Business sectors. "Based in over 200 locations worldwide, we create authoritative content delivered through market leading brands, enabling our customers to find the essential data, analysis and commentary to support their decisions." See http://www.reed-elsevier.com/AboutUs/Pages/Home.aspx.

10. See here Archambault et al. (2005), Moed (2005) and Oppenheim (1997), who have compared the English evaluation system, Research Assessment Exercise (RAE) evaluations, based on citations; and Aksnes and Taxt (2004), who have done similar analyses in Norway. See also Bollen, Van de Sompel, Smith, & Luce, 2005 and van Raan (2005).

11. See, for example, European University Association Newsletter, No. 20, 5 December 2008.

12. http://ec.europa.eu/education/programmes/calls/3608/annex1_en.pdf.

REFERENCES

Ahrne, G., & Brunsson, N. (2009). *Complete and incomplete organisation* (Scores Reports 2009:2). Stockholm: University of Stockholm.

Aksnes, D.W., & Taxt, R.E. (2004). Peer reviews and bibliometric indicators. *Research Evaluation*, 13(1), 33–41.

Altbach, P. (2006). The dilemmas of ranking. *International Higher Education, 42*. Available at http://www.bc.edu/bc_org/avp/soe/cihe/newsletter/Number42/p2_Altbach.htm.

Archambault, É., Vignola-Gagné, É., Côté, G., Larivière, V., & Gingras, Y. (2005, July). Welcome to the linguistic warp zone: Benchmarking scientific output in the social sciences and humanities. Proceedings of the 10th International Conference of the International Society for Scientometrics and Informetrics (ISSI), Stockholm, Sweden. Stockholm: ISSI.

Bell, D. (1973). *The coming of post-industrial society: A venture in social forecasting*. New York: Basic Books.

Böhme, G., & Stehr, N. (1986). *The knowledge society: The growing impact of scientific knowledge on social relations*. Dordrecht: Reidel.

Bollen, J., Van de Sompel, H., Smith, J.A., & Luce, R. (2005). Toward alternative metrics of journal impact: A comparison of download and citation data. *Information & Processing Management*, 41(6), 1419–1440.

Brunsson, N. (1999). *The organization of hypocrisy*. Chichester, UK: John Wiley & Sons.

Bush, V. (1945). *Science: The endless frontier: A report to the president.* Washington, DC: U.S. Government Printing Office.

Cavallin, M., & Lindblad, S. (2006). *Världsmästerskap i vetenskap? En granskning av internationella rankinglistor och deras sätt att hantera kvaliteter hos universitetet.* Göteborg: Göteborgs Universitet Dnr G11 530/06.

Dill, D.D., & Soo, M. (2005). Academic quality, league tables, and policy: A crossnational analysis of university ranking systems. *Higher Education, 49,* 495–533.

Djelic, M.-L., & Sahlin-Andersson, K. (2006). *Transnational governance: Institutional dynamics of regulation.* Cambridge: Cambridge University Press.

Drori, G., Meyer, J., Ramirez, F., & Schofer, E. (2003). *Science in the modern world polity.* Stanford: Stanford University Press.

Drucker, P.F. (1969). *The age of discontinuity: Guidelines to our changing society.* New York: Harper & Row.

Dunn, D.D. (2003). Accountability, democratic theory, and higher education. *Educational Policy, 17*(1), 60–79.

Gibbons, M., Limoges, C., Nowotny, H., Schwartzman, S., Scott, P., & Trow, M. (1994). *The new production of knowledge: The dynamics of science and research in contemporary societies.* London: Sage Publications.

Jobbins, D. (2005). Moving to a global stage: A media view. *Higher Education in Europe, 30*(2), 137–145.

Kogan, M., Bauer, M., Bleiklie, I., & Henkel, M. (2006). *Transforming higher education: A comparative study.* Dordrecht: Springer.

Latour, B. (1988). *Knowledge and reflexivity.* London: Sage.

Lindblad, S. (2008). Navigating in the field of university positioning: On international ranking lists, quality indicators and higher education governing. *European Educational Research Journal, 7*(4), 438–450.

Lindblad, S., & Popkewitz, T.S. (2004). *Educational restructuring: International perspectives on traveling policies.* Charlotte, NC: Information Age Publishing.

Liu, N.C. (2009). The story of academic rankings. *International Higher Education Newsletter, 54*(2). Available at http://www.bc.edu/bc_org/avp/soe/cihe/newsletter/Number54/p2_Liu.htm.

Marginson, S. (2009). University rankings, government and social order: Managing the field of higher education according to the logic of the performative present-as-future. In M. Simons, M. Olssen, & M. Peters (Eds.), *Re-reading education policies: Studying the policy agenda of the 21st century.* Rotterdam: Sense Publishers.

Meyer, J., & Rowan, B. (1977). Institutionalized organisations: Formal structure as myth and ceremony. *American Journal of Sociology, 83,* 340–363.

Moed, H.F. (2005). *Citation analysis in research evaluation.* Heidelberg: Springer Verlag.

Nowotny, H., Gibbons, M., & Scott, P. (2001). *Rethinking science: Knowledge and the public in an age of uncertainty.* Cambridge: Polity Press.

Oppenheim, C. (1997). The correlation between citations counts and the 1992 research assessment exercise. *Journal of documentation, 53*(5), 477–487.

Ramirez, F. (2002). Eyes wide shut: University, state, and society. *European Educational Research Journal, 1,* 255–271.

Rothblatt, S., & Wittrock, B. (Eds.) (1993). *The European and American university since 1800: Historical and sociological essays.* Cambridge: Cambridge University Press.

Slaughter, S., & Rhoades, G. (2004). *Academic capitalism and the new economy: Markets, state, and higher education.* Baltimore, MD: The John Hopkins University Press.

Steiner-Khamsi, G. (Ed.) (2004). *The global politics of educational borrowing and lending* (pp. 201–220). New York: Teachers College Press.

Stuart, D.L. (1995). Reputational rankings: Background and development. In R.D. Walleri & M.K. Moss (Eds.), *New directions for institutional research No. 88: Evaluating and responding to college guidebooks and rankings* (pp. 13–20). San Francisco: Jossey-Bass.

Tomusk, V. (Ed.) (2006). *Creating the European area of higher education.* Dordrecht: Springer.

Usher, A., & Savino, M. (2006). *A world of difference: A global survey of university league tables.* Retrieved July 1, 2008, from http://www.educationalpolicy.org/pdf/World-of-Difference-200602162.pdf.

van Raan, A.F.J. (2005). Fatal attraction: Conceptual and methodological problems in the ranking of universities by bibliometric methods. *Scientometrics, 62*(1), 133–143.

Wedlin, L. (2007). The role of rankings in codifying a business school template: Classifications, diffusion and mediated isomorphism in organizational fields. *European Management Review, 4*(1), 24–39.

Whitley, R. (2000). *The intellectual and social organization of the sciences.* New York: Oxford University Press.

Open Education and the Open Science Economy

MICHAEL A. PETERS

Introduction

Openness as a complex code word for a variety of digital trends and movements has emerged as an alternative mode of "social production" based on the growing and overlapping complexities of open source, open access, open archiving, open publishing, and open science. Openness in this sense refers to open source models of scientific communication, knowledge distribution, and educational development, although it has a number of deeper registers that refer more widely to government ("open government"), society ("open society"), economy ("open economy") and even psychology (openness as one of the traits of personality theory). The concept and evolving set of practices has profound consequences for education at all levels. "Openness" has become a leading source of innovation in the world global digital economy, increasingly adopted by world governments, international agencies, and multinationals, as well as by leading educational institutions as a means of promoting scientific inquiry and international collaboration. It is clear that the free software and "open source" movements constitute a radical non-proprietarian (i.e., social) alternative to traditional methods of text and symbolic production, distribution, archiving, access, and dissemination. This alternative non-proprietary model of cultural production and exchange threatens traditional models of intellectual property and it challenges major legal and institutional means such as copyright currently used to restrict creativity, innovation, and the free exchange of ideas.

It is the argument of the chapter that the openness movement with its reinforcing structure of overlapping networks of production, access, publishing, archiving, and distribution provide an emerging architecture of alterative educational globalization not wedded to existing neoliberal forms. The open education movement and paradigm has arrived: it emerges from a complex historical background and its futures are intimately tied not only to open source, open access and open publishing movements but also to the concept of the "open society" itself which has multiple, contradictory, and contested meanings. This

203

chapter first theorizes the development and significance of "open education" by reference to the Open University, OpenCourseWare (OCW) and open access movements. The chapter takes this line of argument further, arguing for a conception of "open science economy" which involves strategic international research collaborations and provides an empirical and conceptual link between university science and the global knowledge economy.

MIT was one of the first universities to introduce OCW, announcing its intention in the New York Times in 2001. It formed the Open-CourseWare Consortium in 2005 and by 2007 had published virtually all its courses online.[1] The OCW Consortium advertises itself in the following terms, emphasizing one aspect of alternative educational globalization—the distribution and free exchange of course content, potentially a major source for the internationalization of curriculum:

An OpenCourseWare is a free and open digital publication of high quality educational materials, organized as courses. The OpenCourseWare Consortium is a collaboration of more than 200 higher education institutions and associated organizations from around the world creating a broad and deep body of open educational content using a shared model. The mission of the Open-CourseWare Consortium is to advance education and empower people worldwide through opencourseware.

On February 14, 2008 Harvard University adopted a policy that requires faculty members to allow the university to make their scholarly articles available free online. The new policy makes Harvard the first university in the United States to *mandate* open access to its faculty members' research publications and marks the beginning of a new era that will encourage other U.S. universities to do the same. The Harvard policy is a move to disseminate faculty research and scholarship and to give the University a worldwide license to make each faculty member's scholarly articles available globally. In effect the new policy establishes a global scholarly publishing system that allows scholars to use and distribute their own work, giving them greater control over these aspects of scholarly production. Harvard's open-access repository makes scholarly research available worldwide for free, while the faculty member retains the copyright of the article.

Harvard University is not alone. Both the National Institutes of Health (NIH) and the European Research Council have recently adopted similar open access mandates, putting pressure on other government agencies in the United States and elsewhere to do the same. In a clear sense this is the beginning of a mega-trend that will make intellectual research and teaching resources freely available worldwide and will encourage forms of education based on open source, open access, open archiving, and open publishing models, as well offering support for burgeoning initiatives like the Creative Commons project,[2] the P2P Foundation,[3] the Public Knowledge Project[4] (that supports Open Journal Systems), and the Open Knowledge Foundation,[5] to mention only a few.

While I focus on higher education in this context, it does not take much imagination to see the ramifications for the extension of the principles and architectures to K-12 and, indeed, to all levels of education from pre-school to university. What I call the "open education" paradigm (Peters & Britez, 2009) has strong connections to and is reinforced by what I call the "open science economy," a concept I tentatively and experimentally seek both to develop and explain in the second part of the chapter by investigating the political economy of global science and the global economics of science. The chapter begins with an account of the emergence of the paradigm of open education by reference to four major reports.

The Emergence of the Open Education Paradigm

What I now call simply "open education" has emerged strongly as a new paradigm of social production in the global knowledge economy. In the last year or so four major reports have documented existing developments and new tools and technologies, heralded the utopian promise of "openness" in global education (extolling its virtues of shared commons-based peer-production), and analyzed the ways in which it contributes to skills formation, innovation, and economic development.

The powerful Washington-based Committee for Economic Development (CED)[6] released its report *Open Standards, Open Source, and Open Innovation: Harnessing the Benefits of Openness* in April 2006, examining the phenomenon of "openness" in the context of today's digital economy; highlighting the key attributes of accessibility, responsiveness, and creativity; and commenting on the relevance of the three areas of open standards, open-source software, and open innovation. The report by The Digital Connections Council of the CED built on three earlier reports dating from 2001: *The Digital Economy and Economic Growth* (2001); *Digital Economy: Promoting Competition, Innovation, and Opportunity* (2001); and *Promoting Innovation and Economic Growth: The Special Problem of Digital Intellectual Property* (2004).[7] These reports emphasized intellectual property issues involved with file-sharing and peer-to-peer networks and the way that "heavy-handed enforcement of intellectual property rules and reliance on business practices designed for the trade of physical goods can stifle the collaboration and innovation that is vital to the growth of the digital economy." What is perhaps of greatest interest in the present context is the emphasis in the new report on what they call "open innovation"—new collaborative models of open innovation, originating outside the firm, that result in an "architecture of participation"[8] and to a lesser extent their definition of "openness." Here is what the report says about "open innovation":

Open innovation can be seen in the growing use of digital software tools tied to computer-controlled fabrication devices that allow users to design an object and then produce it physically. As the costs of these digital design tools decrease, users are able to innovate, breaking the model of manufacturers being the source of innovation and customers simply consuming them. The openness model, the antithesis of a "not invented here" attitude, encompasses not only manufacturers and users, but suppliers whose innovations should be welcomed by the companies they supply. (CED, 2006, Executive Summary)

The report goes on to mention "the extraordinary increase in peer production of digital information products" which are produced by individuals without any expectation of monetary gain and commenting that "sophisticated commercial firms are harvesting the benefits of openness." In this same context they mention the movement of "open science" promoted by the National Institutes of Health (NIH) and the model of open courseware on which they comment:

Advocates for more openness contend that openness will result in greater innovation than would be achieved by restricting access to information or allowing first creators to exert greater control over it. Such a belief in the value of tapping the collective wisdom is profoundly democratic.

As one can see, this set of statements makes a string connection between firm innovation, open education, and the emergence of the social mode of production (Benkler, 2006) which is based on the employment of social media and social networking as a means of freely exchanging ideas. In effect, the social mode of production names a new, third mode of production in the digitally networked environment that Benkler calls "commons-based peer-production," to distinguish it from the property-based and contract-based models of firms and markets. As he says: "Its central characteristic is that groups of individuals successfully collaborate on large-scale projects following a diverse cluster of motivational drives and social signals, rather than either market prices or managerial commands." Benkler explains "why this mode has systematic advantages over markets and managerial hierarchies when the object of production is information or culture": first, it is better at identifying and assigning human capital to information and cultural production processes ("information opportunity cost"), and second, "there are substantial increasing returns to allow very larger clusters of potential contributors to interact with very large clusters of information resources in search of new projects and collaboration enterprises" (Benkler, 2002).

In 2007 three substantial reports were released that reviewed open education as a movement and assessed its benefits: the OECD's *Giving Knowledge for Free: The Emergence of Open Educational Resources* (OECD, 2007); a project and report of Open e-Learning Content Observatory Services (OLCOS) entitled *Open Educational Practices and Resources* (OLCOS, 2007); and *A Review of the Open Educational Resources (OER) Movement: Achievements, Challenges, and New Opportunities* a report to the William and Flora Hewlett Foundation (Atkins, Brown, & Hammond, 2007). These three reports share similar emphases, each focusing on "openness" and the promise of the new technologies and their educational benefits. The OECD (2007) report focuses on four questions:

- How can sustainable cost/benefit models for open educational resources (OER) initiatives be developed?
- What are the intellectual property rights issues linked to OER initiatives?
- What are the incentives and barriers for universities and faculty staff to deliver their materials to OER initiatives?
- How can access and usefulness for the users of OER initiatives be improved? (pp. 3–4, Foreword)

The Executive Summary gives us a flavor of the potential of OE[9] and the utopian educational promise that graces these three reports:

An apparently extraordinary trend is emerging. Although learning resources are often considered as key intellectual property in a competitive higher education world, more and more institutions and individuals are sharing digital learning resources over the Internet openly and without cost, as open educational resources (OER). (OECD, 2007, p. 9)

The report then concerns itself with the following questions: What are open educational resources? Who is using and producing OER and how much? Why are people sharing for free? What are the provisions for copyright and open licences? How can OER projects be sustained in the long run? alongside a set of policy implications and recommendations.

The OLCOS report, by comparison, focuses on: policies, institutional frameworks and business models; open access and open content repositories; and laboratories of open educational practices and resources, warning against instituting open education within the dominant model:

OER are understood to be an important element of policies that want to leverage education and lifelong learning for the knowledge economy and society. However, OLCOS emphasizes that it is crucial to also promote innovation and change in educational practices. In particular, OLCOS warns that delivering OER to the still dominant model of teacher centred knowledge transfer will have little effect on equipping teachers, students and workers with the competences, knowledge and skills to participate successfully in the knowledge economy and society. This report emphasises the need to foster open practices of teaching and learning that are informed by a competency-based educational framework. However, it is understood that a shift towards such practices will only happen in the longer term in a step-by-step process. Bringing about this shift will require targeted and sustained efforts by educational leaders at all levels. (OLCOS, 2007, p. 12)

In Chapter 4, "Competences for the Knowledge Society," the OLCOS (2007) report opines that "priority must be given to open educational practices that involve students in active, constructive engagement with content, tools and services in the learning process, and promote learners' self-management, creativity and working in teams" (p. 37), and "introduces the idea of value chains of open educational content which emerge when teachers and students re-use available content and make enriched and/or additional material (e.g., use cases, experiences, lessons learned, etc.) available again to a larger community of practice" (p. 37). The report defines a competency-focused, collaborative paradigm of learning and knowledge acquisition where "priority is given to learning communities and development of knowledge and skills required for tackling and solving problems instead of subject-centred knowledge transfer." For the purposes of this paper and audience I quote further from the report:

We believe that, to acquire the competences and skills for personal and professional achievement in the knowledge-based society, the learner's autonomy, personal mastery and self-direction must be acknowledged and innovative approaches implemented that foster self management, communication and team skills, and analytical, conceptual, creative and problem solving skills. However, there is of course a huge difference between identifying required competences and operationalizing them for inclusion in the concrete practices of teaching and learning at different educational levels. (p. 39)

The report then lists the following skills of "digital competence":

- Ability to search, collect and process (create, organise, distinguish relevant from irrelevant, subjective from objective, real from virtual) electronic information, data and concepts and to use them in a systematic way;
- Ability to use appropriate aids (presentations, graphs, charts, maps) to produce, present or understand complex information;
- Ability to access and search a website and to use internet-based services such as discussion fora and e-mail;
- Ability to use ICT to support critical thinking, creativity and innovation in different contexts at home, leisure and work. (p. 39)

The report to The William and Flora Hewlett Foundation (Atkins, Brown, & Hammond, 2007) is perhaps the most comprehensive. It follows similar lines of investigation to the others, but frames the report in terms of Amartya Sen's work with the plan to develop "a strategic international development initiative to expand people's substantive freedoms through the removal of 'unfreedoms'." What is impressive about this report is not only the inventory of open education projects (the incubation of high-quality specialized open resources) but also its attempt to conceptualize the issues and to move to a new understanding of openness in terms of an ethic of participation (and the design of "open participatory learning infrastructure") that supports the role of technology in emphasizing the social nature of learning and its potential to address questions of the digital divide in developing countries.

There is much else that deserves attention in these reports. However, while they touch on conceptual issues to do with openness and document aspects of the contemporary movement of open educational resources, they do not provide a history of "openness" in education—it has a long, complex and significant history that influences conceptions of its wider purposes—or make the necessary theoretical links to the wider political literature (see Peters & Britez, 2009). The reports, it might be argued, are too wedded to a technological account of open education and to an engineering notion of information that blind them to the criticisms that have been and can be mounted against various conceptions of "openness," "information," and the "cybernetic society" based upon these ideas. To see the force of these criticisms, we need to understand something about the emerging political economy of global science and the economics of science.

The Political Economy of Global Science

The emerging political economy of global science is a significant factor influencing development of national systems of innovation, and economic, social and cultural development, with the rise of multinational actors and a new mix of corporate, private/public and community involvement. It is only since the 1960s, with the development of research evaluation and increasing sophistication of bibliometrics, that it has been possible to map the emerging economy of global science, at least on a comparative national and continental basis. The Science Citation Index (SCI) provides bibliographic and citational information from 3,700 of the world's scientific and technical journals, covering over 100 disciplines. The expanded index available in an online version covers more than 5,800 journals. Comparable "products" in the social sciences (SSCI) and humanities (A&HCI) cover, respectively, bibliographic information from 1,700 journals in 50 disciplines and 1,130 journals.

On a world scale it is now possible to get some idea of science distributions in terms of academic papers for the first time. An issue of the *UIS Bulletin on Science and Technology Statistics* (UNESCO, 2005), published in collaboration with the Institut National de la Recherche Scientifique (INRS) (Montréal, Canada), presents a bibliometric analysis of 20 years of world scientific production (1981–2000), as reflected by the publications indexed in the SCI. It indicates that:

In 2000 the SCI included a total of 584,982 papers, representing a 57.5% increase from 1981, when 371,346 papers were published worldwide. Authors with addresses in developed countries wrote 87.9% of the papers in 2000, a decrease from 93.6% in 1981. Developing countries, on the other hand, saw a steady increase in their share of scientific production: from 7.5% of world papers in 1981 to 17.1% in 2000. . . . Since 1981 the world map of publications changed significantly. North America lost the lead it had in 1996, and in 2000 produced 36.8% of the world total, a decrease from 41.4% in 1981. The opposite trend can be found in the European Union, which in 2000 published 40.2% of the world total, up from 32.8% in 1981. Japan went up from 6.9% to 10.7% in 2000. Collectively this "triad" has therefore maintained its dominance, accounting for 81% of the world total of scientific publications in 2000, up from 72% in 1981.

While sub-Saharan African publications remained stable at around 1% of the world total, and the share of publications from the Arab States increased from 0.6% in 1981 to 0.9% in 2000, and the Central Eastern European share remained stable around 3% of the world total, both the Newly Industrialised Countries (NIC) in Asia (a group that includes China) and Latin America and the Caribbean (LAC) increased their share significantly, from 0.6% of the NIC total in 1981 to 4.2% in 2000 (with China accounting for 85% of the publications, an increase from 63% in 1981), and 1.3% to 3.2% in LAC countries. The SCI covers biology, biomedicine, chemistry, clinical medicine, earth and space, engineering and technology, mathematics, and physics.

The *UIS Bulletin* concludes that the developed world share of publications has declined, while developing regions (Asia and Latin America) have expanded and Africa has stagnated. There is also clear evidence that there has been considerable growth in international collaboration. These bibliometric measures present a biased view in the sense that they do not take into account book citations, important for the humanities and social sciences, and they tend to favor English as the global medium of communication. Nevertheless, used with caution, as the UNESCO publication suggests, they can reveal some insights through trends regarding aspects of scientific production at global level.

Britain's one time Chief Scientist David A. King (2004) provides an analysis of the output and outcomes from research investment over the past decade. To measure the quality of research on national scales and to set it in an international context, he reveals the unevenness of world distribution of science and ascendancy of a group of 31 countries[10] that accounted for "more than 98% of the world's highly cited papers, defined by Thomson ISI as the most cited 1% by field and year of publication. The world's remaining 162 countries contributed less than 2% in total" (p. 311). His analysis reveals the overwhelming dominance of the United States (whose share has declined recently), the United Kingdom, and Germany, and the fact that "the nations with the most citations are pulling away from the rest of the world" (p. 311). He provides the following analysis:

The countries occupying the top eight places in the science citation rank order . . . produced about 84.5% of the top 1% most cited publications between 1993 and 2001. The next nine countries produced 13%, and the final group share 2.5%. There is a stark disparity between the first and second divisions in the scientific impact of nations. Moreover, although my analysis includes only 31 of the world's 193 countries, these produce 97.5% of the world's most cited papers. (p. 314)

And King goes on to draw the following conclusion:

The political implications of this last comparison are difficult to exaggerate. South Africa, at 29th place in my rank ordering, is the only African country on the list. The Islamic countries are only represented by Iran at 30th, despite the high GDP of many of them and the prominence of some individuals, such as Nobel prizewinners Abdus Salam (physics, 1979) and Ahmed Zewail (chemistry, 1999). (p. 314)

There are clear signs that architecture of global science is shifting, especially with the huge investment in research and the consequent growth of scientific publications in Asia. Adams and Wilsdon (2006) report that China's spending on research has increased by more than 20% per year, reaching 1.3% of GDP in 2005 and making it third in the global league table in research expenditure after the United States and Japan. Science budgets in India have increased by the same annual percentage, adding some 2.5 million IT, engineering, and life sciences graduates, 650,000 postgraduates, and 6000 PhDs every year.

The U.S. National Science Board's (2008) publication *Research and Development: Essential Foundation for U.S. Competitiveness in a Global Economy* charts the decline since 2005 of Federal and industry support for basic research, which accounted for 18% ($62B) of the $340B U.S. research budget in current dollars in 2006. The report comments:

Federal obligations for academic research (both basic and applied) and especially in the current support for National Institutes of Health (NIH) (whose budget had previously doubled between the years 1998–2003) declined in real terms between 2004 and 2005 and are expected to decline further in 2006 and 2007. This is the first multiyear decline in Federal obligations for academic research since 1982.

The report also clearly shows the declining competitiveness of U.S. science and technology: patents dropped from 55% in 1996 to 53% in 2005; and "basic research articles published in peer-reviewed journals by authors from U.S. private industry peaked in 1995 and declined by 30% between 1995 and 2005." The report goes on to say: "The drop in physics publications was particularly dramatic: decreasing from nearly 1000 publications in 1988 to 300 in 2005." The loss in U.S. share and its decline of science and technology "reflects the rapid rise in share by the East Asia 4 (comprising China, South Korea, Singapore, and Taiwan)."

The architecture of world science is changing rapidly. The United States needs a comprehensive strategy based on an understanding of the emergent globalization of science, the promotion of innovation through international collaboration and the global value chain, and the fostering of a world vision of open science that makes maximum use of Web 2.0 technologies, if it is to remain both competitive and responsive in the coming decades. The globalization of science, which in part takes place through new global architectures that promote scientific communication and collaboration, also in effect constitutes one form of the globalization of education, especially at the higher levels where PhD study takes place in the sciences as part of a scientific team contributing to a well-defined problem. There is a series of connections in this respect between globalization of science, the ways that the new social media promotes an ethic of participation and collaboration, and the globalization of education that utilizes the same soft architectures to encourage learning in distributed environments.

The Economics of Open Science

The Argument Concerning Digital Knowledge Goods

Knowledge as an economic good defies traditional understandings of property and principles of exchange and closely conforms to the criteria for a public good. In this sense it has been described as non-rivalrous, barely excludable, and not transparent:

1. Knowledge is non-rivalrous. The stock of knowledge is not depleted by use, and in this sense knowledge is not consumable; sharing with others, use, reuse, and modification may indeed add rather than deplete value.
2. Knowledge is barely excludable. It is difficult to exclude users and to force them to become buyers; it is difficult, if not impossible, to restrict distribution of goods that can be reproduced at no or little cost.
3. Knowledge is not transparent. Knowledge requires some experience of it before one discovers whether it is worthwhile, relevant, or suited to a particular purpose.

Thus, knowledge at the ideation or immaterial stage (considered as belonging to the realm of pure ideas) operates expansively to defy the law of scarcity. It does not conform to the traditional criteria for an economic good, and the economics of knowledge are therefore not based on an understanding of those features that characterize property or exchange and cannot be based on economics as the science of the allocation of scarce public goods. As soon as knowledge becomes codified or written down or physically embedded in a system or process, then it can be made subject to copyright or patent and then may be treated and behave like other commodities.

In so far as digital information goods approximate pure thought or the ideational stage of knowledge, they conform to knowledge as a global public good and can be considered to escape traditional understandings of property and principles of exchange. This is even more the case when information through experimentation and hypothesis testing (the traditional methods of sciences) can be turned into "justified true belief," the three conditions logically necessary for knowledge. The classical account of Western knowledge is the source of traditional epistemology dating from Plato's conceptual investigations in the dialogue the *Theaetetus* where Socrates considers a number of theories as to what knowledge is, the last being that knowledge is true belief that has been "given an account of." Epistemology normally draws the distinction between "knowing how" and "knowing that" (or propositional knowledge that is expressed in sentences, we would say today). It also considers counterexamples to the classical or three-cornered view of knowledge first suggested by Edmund Gettier in 1963.

In other words, digital information goods also undermine traditional economic assumptions of rivalry, excludability, and transparency, as the knowledge economy is about creating intellectual capital rather than accumulating physical capital. Digital information goods differ from traditional goods in a number of ways:

1. Information goods, especially in digital forms, can be copied cheaply, so there is little or no cost in adding new users. Although production costs for information have been high, developments in desktop and just-in-time publishing, together with new forms of copying, archiving, and content creation, have substantially lowered fixed costs.
2. Information and knowledge goods typically have an experiential and participatory element that increasingly requires the active co-production of the reader/writer, listener and viewer.
3. Digital information goods can be transported, broadcast, or shared at low cost, which may approach free transmission across bulk communication networks.
4. Since digital information can be copied exactly and easily shared, it is never consumed (see Davis & Stack, 1997; Kelly, 1998; Morris-Suzuki, 1997; Varian, 1998).

This analysis summarizes a large and growing body of literature that demonstrates that the traditional law of scarcity that governs supply and demand does not apply to digital information goods insofar as they approach the status of pure thought or the ideation stage of production of science. This analysis provides an understanding of global information and knowledge goods and the way in which ideas do not lose their value (or are not depleted) when used but that sharing may enhance the value of an idea, leading to its refinement and development. Symbolic and cultural goods that take the form of information and knowledge global goods often as digital goods therefore exhibit a different mode of development (see Marginson, Murphy, & Peters, 2009; Peters, 2007; Peters & Besley, 2006; Peters, Marginson, & Murphy, 2009).

Towards an Open Science Economy

The Mode of Open Production

Openness is a new mode of social production that has become a leading source of innovation in the world global digital economy and constitutes a radical non-proprietarian alternative to traditional methods of text production, dissemination, and distribution. In terms of a model of communication there has been a gradual shift from content to code in the openness, access, use, reuse, and modification reflecting a radical personalization that has made these open characteristics and principles increasingly the basis of the cultural sphere. So open source and open access has been developed and applied in open publishing, open archiving, and open music, constituting the hallmarks of "open culture." For some theorists, such as law professors Yochai Benkler and Larry Lessig, this symbolizes a new mode of social production and a form of cultural formation that represents an alternative to capitalist forms of globalization. As a number of economists have remarked (see the list above), this marks the emergence of global science and knowledge as a global public good that rests on an ethic of participation and collaboration based on the co-production and co-design of knowledge goods and services. As one author expresses the point:

The present decade can be called the "open" decade (open source, open systems, open standards, open archives, open everything) just as the 1990s were called the "electronic" decade (e-text, e-learning, e-commerce, e-governance). (Materu, 2004)

And yet it is more than just a "decade" that follows the electronic innovations of the 1990s; it is a change of philosophy and ethos, a set of interrelated and complex changes that transforms markets and the mode of production, ushering in a new collection of values based on openness, the ethic of participation, and peer-to-peer collaboration.

New forms of freedom are occurring in the fundamental shift from an underlying metaphysics of production—a "productionist" metaphysics—to a metaphysics of consumption as use, reuse, and modification. New logics and different patterns of cultural consumption are appearing in the areas of new media, where symbolic analysis becomes a habitual and daily activity. It is now a truism to argue that information is the vital element in a "new" politics and economy that links space, knowledge, and capital in networked practices. Freedom is an essential ingredient in this equation if these network practices are to develop or transform themselves into knowledge cultures.

The specific politics and eco-cybernetic rationalities that accompany an informational global capitalism comprised of new multinational "edutainment" agglomerations are clearly capable of colonizing the emergent ecology of public info-social networks and preventing the development of knowledge cultures based on non-proprietary modes of knowledge production and exchange.

Complexity as an approach to knowledge and knowledge systems now recognizes the development of both global systems architectures in (tele)communications and information and of open knowledge production systems that increasingly rest on the establishment of new and better platforms (sometimes called Web 2.0), the semantic web, new search algorithms, and new processes of digitization—social processes and policies that foster openness as an overriding value, as evidenced in the growth of open source, open access, and open education and their convergences that characterize global knowledge communities that transcend borders of the nation-state. I would argue that "openness" seems also to suggest political transparency and the norms of open inquiry, indeed even democracy itself, as both the basis of the logic of inquiry and the dissemination of its results. In other words, certain institutional forms are required to promote the organization of knowledge in order to enhance its free flow, the mode of open criticism, testing and validation characteristic of science-based institutions, and the non-ideological replication, trial-and-error ethos that typifies the scientific method consonant with an open community of inquiry.

The role of nonmarket and nonproprietary production promotes the emergence of a new information environment and networked economy that both depends upon and encourages great individual freedom, democratic participation, collaboration, and interactivity. This "promises to enable social production and exchange to play a much larger role, alongside property and market based production, than they ever have in modern democracies" (Benkler, 2006, p. 3). Peer production of information, knowledge, and culture enabled by the emergence of free and open-source software permits the expansion of the social model production beyond software platforms into every domain of information and cultural production.

Open knowledge production is based upon an incremental, decentralized (and asynchronous), and collaborative development process that transcends the traditional proprietary market model. Commons-based peer production is based on free cooperation, not on the selling of one's labor in exchange for a wage, nor motivated primarily by profit or for the exchange value of the resulting product; it is managed through new modes of peer governance rather than traditional organizational hierarchies. It is an innovative application of copyright, which creates an information commons and transcends the limitations attached to both the private (for-profit) and public (state-based) property forms.[11].

As the Ithaka Report *University Publishing in a Digital Age* (2008) reveals, these broad initiatives in open source, open access, open publishing, and open archiving are part of emerging knowledge ecologies that will determine the future of educational resources and scholarly publishing, challenging commercial publishing business models and raising broader and deeper questions about content development processes as well as questions of resourcing and sustainability. The new digital technologies promise changes in creation, production, and consumption of scholarly resources, including the development of new formats designed to allow integrated electronic research and publishing environments to enable real-time dissemination and dynamically-updated content, as well as alternative distribution models.

Open access means "putting peer-reviewed scientific and scholarly literature on the Internet, making it available free of charge and free of most copyright and licensing restrictions, and removing the barriers to serious research." Referring to Harvard University's recent new policy requiring faculty members to allow the university to make their scholarly articles available free online, Lila Guterman reports in *The Chronicle of Higher Education*'s News Blog,

Stuart M. Shieber, a professor of computer science at Harvard who proposed the new policy, said after the vote in a news release that the decision "should be a very powerful message to the academic community that we want and should have more control over how our work is used and disseminated."[12]

Open access has already transformed the world of scholarship. Since the early 2000s, with major OA statements starting with Budapest in 2002, the movement has picked up momentum and developed a clear political ethos. Harvard's adoption of the new policy follows hard on the heels of open-access mandates passed within months of each other at the National Institutes of Health (NIH) and the European Research Council (ERC). As one blogger remarked, "open archiving of peer-reviewed journal literature [is] now on an irreversible course of expansion," not only as U.S. universities follow Harvard's lead but also as open archiving makes learning material available to anyone, including students and faculty from developing and transition countries. Harvard's adoption of the open archiving mandate is similar in scope to the step taken by MIT to adopt OpenCourseWare (OCW) in 2001. These initiatives are examples of new strategies to establish knowledge cultures that will determine the future of scholarly publishing, the form and content of educational resources, and therefore also the future of innovation and research in the digital global economy.

Open Science Economy

In the emergent science system five forces are structuring the twenty-first century (open) science system: networks, emergence, circulation, stickiness (place), and distribution (virtual).

The decline of the U.S. economy relative to other world economies is facilitating the strengthening of science elsewhere. An evolving multipolar world economy is leading to multiple centres of science—the United States, the European Union, Japan, China, Russia, and possibly India. The increasing wealth of several of these societies is enabling them to lure back many younger scientists trained abroad in the world's leading institutions. In particular, China is moving towards an integrated system of national innovation, replacing state control with more enabling frameworks and focusing on improving the university and research systems. It is also stepping up the internationalization of research with collaborative networks across Europe, Japan, and United States. The predictions are that by the end of 2020 China will achieve more science and technological breakthroughs of great world influence, qualifying it to join the ranks of the world's most innovative countries. Some think that in 20 years global science will be driven by Indian scientists, with new interfaces in science and new rules, where new countries can contribute on an equal footing.

One thing is clear: the emergence of a globalized science system with the increasing globalization of research, science, engineering, and technology. The growth of China, India, and South Korea are changing the atlas of the world scientific knowledge system.

International research collaboration is becoming an important source of national comparative advantage and nations see the importance of tracking and analyzing global knowledge flows and transfers to determine national and regional collaborations. Increasingly, national science administrations use information technologies and bibliometrics in facilitating cross-border knowledge flows and also in analyzing citations, co-authorship, and collaborations, focusing on the development of new metrics systems including webometrics for the measurement of research impacts, growth, and distributions. What is even more marked is the increasing significance of new social networking and social media for Web 2.0 science and open-access publishing.

In this new "open science economy" there are significant advantages to smallness, both with the shift to international collaborative research and the virtual organization of global science teams. Teams produce more papers and receive more citations (see Wuchty, Jones, & Uzzi, 2007). Big science has built-in irreversible constraints, including bureaucratic, fragmented, communication difficulties and organizational rigidities. Now, science policy experts argue that excellence in science requires nimble, autonomous organizations—qualities more likely to be found in small research settings. Enhanced performance takes place through creation of several dozen small research organizations in interdisciplinary domains or in emerging fields. Small, flexible, specialized teams are seen to be the answer. Dozens of scientists who have made significant advances did so in organizations with fewer than 50 full-time researchers. In the past decade, Nobel prizes have been awarded to scientists for work done in relatively small settings: Günter Blobel (physiology or medicine), Ahmed Zewail (chemistry), Paul Greengard (physiology or medicine), Andrew Fire (physiology or medicine), Roderick MacKinnon (chemistry), and Gerhard Ertl (chemistry) (see Hollingsworth, Müller, & Hollingsworth, 2008). Many economists draw attention to the development of small, flexible, specialized teams in regional centers ("clustering").

Alongside national science systems, an increasingly complex transnational science is occurring. New research partnerships that are no longer solely state- and university-oriented are emerging. There is also spectacular growth of corporate multinational research, especially in new materials, biotechnology (genetics), pharmaceutics, and information technology—growth of private science, with shifts in funding regimes from public to private, state to global, big science to applied science, science to technology, and technology transfer. In this context a new role is emerging for humanities, performing arts, and social sciences as "soft" sciences and technologies concerned with new international values, legalities, global civic cultures, knowledge measurement, management, and public relations—the so-called "soft" programming architectures that encourage new forms of technology-led education on the basis of new architectures of participation and collaboration. There is also an emergence of global science and research organization and cultures—extra-national organizations, NGOs, UN initiatives, UNESCO, the European Science Foundation, and other international science-based organizations.

New models of open science are rapidly developing based on mode 2.0 with greater interdisciplinarity and "flattening" of geocentric science centers and knowledge flows toward global teams. Correspondingly there is a reversal from close-conduit peer review to open-source public scrutiny and increased use of open-source data analysis, management of large data bases, and sharing (bioinformatics). Science publishing has undergone a sea change with "changes in creation, production and consumption of scholarly resources"—"creation of new formats made possible by digital technologies, ultimately allowing scholars to work in deeply integrated electronic research and publishing environments that will enable real-time dissemination, collaboration, dynamically-updated content, and usage of new media," and "alternative distribution models (institutional repositories, pre-print servers, open access journals) have also arisen with the aim to broaden access, reduce costs, and enable open sharing of content" (Brown, Griffiths, & Rascoff, 2007, p. 4).[13] The new models of open science are to some extent in opposition or conflict with expanded protection of intellectual property. Open-source initiatives have facilitated the development of new models of production and innovation. The public and nonprofit sectors have called for alternative approaches dedicated to public knowledge redistribution and dissemination. Now, distributed peer-to-peer knowledge systems rival the scope and quality of similar products produced by proprietary efforts where the speed of diffusion of open-source projects is an obvious advantage. The successful projects occur in both software and open-source biology. Open-access science has focused on making peer-reviewed, online research and scholarship freely accessible to a broader population (including digitized back issues). Open science demonstrates an "exemplar of a compound of 'private-collective' model of innovation" that contains elements of both proprietary and public models of knowledge production (Von Hippel & von Krogh, 2003). Rhoten and Powell (2007) ask: "does the expansion of a patenting culture undermine the norms of open science? Does the intensification of patenting accelerate or retard the development of basic and commercial research?"

As *Scientific American* (Waldrop, 2008) acknowledges, the emergence of Science 2.0 generally refers to new practices of scientists who post raw experimental results, nascent theories, claims of discovery, and draft papers on the Web for others to see and comment on. Proponents say these open-access practices make scientific progress more collaborative and therefore more productive. Critics say scientists who put preliminary findings online risk having others copy or exploit the work to gain credit or even patents. Despite pros and cons, Science 2.0 sites are beginning to proliferate; one notable example is the OpenWetWare project started by biological engineers at MIT. Waldrop demonstrates that rich-text, highly interactive, user-generated, and socially active Internet (Web 2.0) activity has seen linear models of knowledge production giving way to more diffuse, open-ended, and serendipitous knowledge processes.

Open science economy plays a complementary role with corporate and transnational science and implies a strong role for governments. Increasingly, portal-based knowledge environments and global science gateways support collaborative science (Schuchardt et al., 2007; see, for instance, Science.gov & Science.world). Cyber-mashups of very large data sets let users explore, analyze, and comprehend the science behind the information being streamed (Leigh & Brown, 2008). The World Wide Web has revolutionized how researchers from various disciplines collaborate over long distances, especially in the life sciences, where interdisciplinary approaches are becoming increasingly powerful as a driver of both integration and discovery (with regard to data access, data quality, identity, and provenance) (Sagotsky, Zhang, Wang, Martin, & Deisboeck, 2008). National science review and assessment systems play a formative role in developing distributed knowledge systems based on quality journal suites in disciplinary clusters with an ever finer mesh of in-built indicators. Meanwhile economists argue that open source software can be an engine of economic growth (see David, 2003; Etzkowitz, 1997, 2003, 2008; Garzarelli, Limam, & Thomassen, 2008), and clearly the notion of open science economy is one of the leading sectors of the knowledge economy.

Concluding Observations

The open science economy constitutes a strong leading-edge development within the science and general knowledge economies based on different social and economic principles that can be referred to under the notion of the social mode of production. Paul A. David (2003) has described open science in terms that strongly contrast with industrial or knowledge economy models based on strong institutions of intellectual property:[14]

"Open science" institutions provide an alternative to the intellectual property approach to dealing with difficult problems in the allocation of resources for the production and distribution of information. As a mode of generating reliable knowledge, "open science" depends upon a specific non-market reward system to solve a number of resource allocation problems that have their origins in the particular characteristics of information as an economic good.

Elsewhere he writes: "Scientific and technological collaboration is more and more coming to be seen as critically dependent upon effective access to and sharing of digital research data, and of the information tools that facilitate data being structured for efficient storage, search, retrieval, display and higher level analysis" (David, 2005).

Open science has become an important part of the knowledge economy in advanced industrial societies. In part it has grown out of similar trends in alternative modes of creation, production, and distribution of information through the development of social media that has given rise to the movement of open education. Indeed these two parallel movements have only recently been seen as part of an emerging seamless whole that clearly links school to university, and education at these levels to open scientific research that depends on the same or similar norms of sharing and collaboration in open networked environments.[15] Some scholars have already warned how the commercialization of campuses threatens the development of the open science economy. John Willinski (2005), for instance, writes:

Are universities currently re-entering the world on the side of a greater openness among intellectual properties or are they getting in on a greater share of knowledge-based property rights? Up to this point, the universities have fostered open science, and advanced open source software, even if both originated off campus in large measure. With the more recent of these open initiatives—open access—it falls almost entirely to the universities and their faculty to take the lead. Universities "re-entering the world" with the intent to "serve the world" would do well to support faculty participation in open access archives and journals. Open access to research and scholarship would foster a global exchange of public goods. It would extend and sustain an open, alternative economy for intellectual properties. It would strengthen the links between open source software—which is vital to providing open access to research—and the university's long-standing tradition of open science. Given the encroachments, not to mention the temptations, of the knowledge business, this is no time to take the commonwealth of learning for granted. It falls to the members of that commonwealth to recognize and support the current convergence of open initiatives that represent dedicated efforts to ensure the future of that learning.

AUTHOR's NOTE

I would like to thank the editors, Tom Popkewitz and Fazal Rizvi, for a set of useful criticisms on an earlier version of this chapter.

NOTES

1. See the OCW website at http://www.ocwconsortium.org/.

2. See http://creativecommons.org/.

3. See http://p2pfoundation.net/The_Foundation_for_P2P_Alternatives.

4. See http://pkp.sfu.ca/.

5. See http://www.okfn.org/.

6. See the website http://www.ced.org.

7. Digital versions are available on their website at http://www.ced.org/projects/ecom.shtml.

8. See O'Reilly (2005) on Web 2.0 technologies, including "harnessing collective intelligence," "blogging and the wisdom of crowds," and "architectures of participation." As O'Reilly mentions, Mitch Kapor once noted that "architecture is politics." Participation is intrinsic to Napster, part of its fundamental architecture.

9. I prefer the term OE to OER because it embraces the notion of *practices* as well as the notion of sharing educational resources, and also because it gels with open source, open access, and open science (as well as open innovation).

10. The countries are: Australia, Austria, Belgium, Brazil, *Canada*, China, Denmark, Finland, *France*, *Germany*, Greece, India, Iran, Ireland, Israel, *Italy*, *Japan*, Luxembourg, the Netherlands, Poland, Portugal, *Russia*, Singapore, Spain, South Africa, South Korea, Sweden, Switzerland, Taiwan, the *United Kingdom* and the *United States*. (G8 countries are in italics.)

11. See, for instance, Michel Bauwens' P2P Foundation work at the P2P Foundation at http://p2pfoundation.net/3._P2P_in_the_Economic_Sphere.

12. See http://chronicle.com/news/article/3943/harvard-faculty-adopts-open-access-requirement.

13. See, for instance the *Journal of Visualized Experiments* at http://www.jove.com/.

14. See David's recent papers on the relationship between open software and economic growth at http://ideas.repec.org/e/pda76.html. On "The Historical Origins and Economic Logic of Open Science" see http://videolectures.net/cern_david_openscience/.

15. See, for example, the Prague-based Project of Open Science at http://www.otevrena-veda.cz/ov/index.php?p=o_projektu&site=ov_en, designed to increase the competitiveness of the Czech economy.

REFERENCES

Adams, J., & Wilsdon, J. (2006). *The new geography of science: UK research and international collaboration*. London: Demos.

Atkins, D.E., Brown, J.S., & Hammond, A.L. (Eds.) (2007). *A review of the open educational resources (OER) movement: Achievements, challenges, and new opportunities*. Available at http://www.oerderves.org/wp-content/uploads/2007/03/a-review-of-the-open-educational-resources-oer-movement_final.pdf.

Benkler, Y. (2002). Coase's penguin, or Linux and the nature of the firm. *The Yale Law Journal, 112*. Available at http://www.yalelawjournal.org/pdf/112-3/BenklerFINAL.pdf.

Benkler, Y. (2006). *The wealth of networks*. New Haven: Yale University Press.

Brown, L., Griffiths, R., & Rascoff, M. (2007). *University publishing in a digital age*. Retrieved October 14, 2008, from http://www.ithaka.org/ithaka-s-r/strategy/ithaka-university-publishing-report.pdf.

Committee for Economic Development (CED) (2006). *Open standards, open source, and open innovation: Harnessing the benefits of openness*. Available at http://www.ced.org/library/reports/36/204-open-standards-open-source-and-open-innovation.

David, P.A. (2003). The economic logic of "open science" and the balance between private property rights and the public domain in scientific data and information: A primer. Available at http://129.3.20.41/eps/dev/papers/0502/0502006.pdf.

David, P.A. (2005). Towards a cyberinfrastructure for enhanced scientific collaboration: Providing its "soft" foundations may be the hardest part. Available at http://129.3.20.41/eps/le/papers/0502/0502004.pdf.

Davis, J., & Stack, M. (1997). The digital advantage. In J. Davis, T.A. Hirschl, & M. Stack (Eds.), *Cutting edge: Technology, information capitalism and social revolution* (pp. 121–144). London: Verso.

Etzkowitz, H. (1997). The entrepreneurial university and the emergence of democratic corporatism. In H. Etzkowitz & L. Leydesdorff (Eds.), *Universities and the global knowledge economy: A triple helix of university-industry-government relations* (pp. 141–154). London: Continuum.

Etzkowitz, H. (2003). Innovation in innovation: The triple helix of university-industry-government relations. *Social Science Information, 42*(3), 293–337.

Etzkowitz, H. (2008). *The triple helix: University-industry-government innovation in action*. London: Routledge.

Garzarelli, G., Limam, Y.R., & Thomassen, B. (2008). Open source software and economic growth: A classical division of labor perspective. *Information Technology for Development, 14*(2), 116–135.

Hollingsworth, R.J., Müller, K.H., & Hollingsworh, E.J. (2008). The end of the science superpowers: Could the end of world dominance over research mark the passing of national science giants? *Nature, 454*(24 July 2008), 412–413.

Kelly, K. (1998). *New rules for the new economy*. London: Fourth Estate.

King, D.A. (2004). The scientific impact of nations: What different countries get for their research spending. *Nature, 430*, 311–316. Available at http://www.berr.gov.uk/files/file11959.pdf.

Leigh, J., & Brown, M.D. (2008). Cyber-mashups of very large data sets let users explore, analyze, and comprehend the science behind the information being streamed. *Communications of the ACM, 51*(1), 82–85.

Marginson, S., Murphy, P., & Peters, M.A. (2009). *Global creation: Space, connection and universities in the age of the knowledge economy*. New York: Peter Lang.

Materu, P.N. (2004). *Open source courseware: A baseline study*. Washington, DC: The World Bank. Retrieved January 7, 2008 from http://www.ictlogy.net/bibciter/reports/contacts.php?idc=728.

Morris-Suzuki, T. (1997). Capitalism in the computer age and afterward. In J. Davis, T.A. Hirschl, & M. Stack (Eds.), *Cutting edge: Technology, information capitalism and social revolution* (pp. 57–72). London: Verso.

National Science Board (2008). *Research and development: Essential foundation for U.S. competitiveness in a global economy. A companion to science and engineering indicators.* Available at http://www.nsf.gov/statistics/nsb0803/start.htm.

Open e-Learning Content Observatory Services (OLCOS) (2007). *Open educational practices and resources* Available at http://www.olcos.org/cms/upload/docs/olcos_roadmap.pdf.

O'Reilly, T. (2005). What is Web 2.0? Design patterns and business models for the next generation of software. *O'Reilly Media.* http://oreilly.com/web2/archive/what-is-web-20.html.

Organization for Economic Cooperation and Development (OECD) (2007). *Giving knowledge for free: The emergence of open educational resources.* Available at http://www.oecd.org/dataoecd/35/7/38654317.pdf.

Peters, M.A. (2007). *Knowledge economy, development and the future of higher education.* Rotterdam: Sense Publishers.

Peters, M.A., & Besley, T.A.C. (2006). *Building knowledge cultures: Education and development in the age of knowledge capitalism.* Lanham, MD: Rowman & Littlefield.

Peters, M.A., & Britez, R. (Eds.) (2009). *Open education and education for openness.* Rotterdam: Sense Publishers.

Peters, M.A., Marginson, A.S., & Murphy, P. (2009). *Creativity and the global knowledge economy.* New York: Peter Lang.

Rhoten, D., & Powell, W.W. (2007). The frontiers of intellectual property: Expanded protection versus new models of open science. *Annual Review of Law and Social Science, 3,* 345–373.

Sagotsky, J.A., Zhang, L., Wang, Z., Martin, S., & Deisboeck, T.S. (2008). Life sciences and the Web: A new era for collaboration. *Mol. Syst. Biol., 4,* 201.

Schuchardt, K., Pancerella, C., Rahn, L.A., Didier, B., Kodeboyina, D., Leahy, D., et al. (2007). Portal-based knowledge environment for collaborative science. *Concurrency Computation Practice and Experience, 19*(12), 1703–1716.

UNESCO (2005). What do bibliometric indicators tell us about world scientific output? *UIS Bulletin on Science and Technology,* Statistics Issue no. 2, September.

Varian, H.R. (1998). *Markets for information goods.* Available at http://people.ischool.berkeley.edu/~hal/papers/japan/japan.pdf.

Von Hippel, E., & von Krogh, G. (2003). Open source software and the "private-collective" innovation model: Issues for organization science. *Organization Science, 14*(2), 208–223.

Waldrop, M.M. (2008). Science 2.0: Great new tool or great risk? *Scientific American, 298*(5). Retrieved October 18, 2008, from http://www.sciam.com/article.cfm?id=science-2-point-0-great-new-tool-or-great-risk.

Willinski, J. (2005). The unacknowledged convergence of open source, open access, and open science. *First Monday, 10*(8). Available at http://firstmonday.org/htbin/cgiwrap/bin/ojs/index.php/fm/article/view/1265.

Wuchty, S., Jones, B.F., & Uzzi, B. (2007). The increasing dominance of teams in production of knowledge. *Science, 316,* 1036–1039.

Researching Education Policy in a Globalized World: Theoretical and Methodological Considerations

BOB LINGARD

Introduction

Globalization means that we have to reconsider the ways we do education policy analysis. This is because changes as a result of globalization have had an impact on policy and policy production in education. These changes include: the rescaling of contemporary politics (Brenner, 2004); the move from government to governance (Rhodes, 1997; Roseneau, 1997); and the effects of those processes on the object of education policy analysis, namely, policy and policy processes. These changes and their effects have implications for theory and methodology for doing education policy analysis.

The rescaling of contemporary politics relates to what some have called the move away from Westphalian politics, which were constructed around national sovereignty and political authority (Krasner, 2000). What we see today in the wake of the Cold War, collapse of the Soviet bloc and rise of a global economy is a post-Westphalian politics. This is a rescaling of politics, with new relations and agencies above the nation having political effects within nations, as well as some internal restructuring of the nation-state. Accompanying such rescaling is the emergence of a number of global fields, for example, a global education policy field (Lingard & Rawolle, 2009; Lingard, Rawolle, & Taylor, 2005).

Appadurai (2006) represents these two forms and different scales of politics through the descriptors "vertebrate" and "cellular." Westphalian politics were vertebrate, that is, bureaucratic and hierarchical in character, with political authority located within the nation, while post-Westphalian politics are more cellular, networked and horizontal in character, functioning across porous national borders. This does not mean the nation-state is no longer significant or powerless, but rather that it now has to function in different and globally strategic ways. As Dale (2006, p. 27) observes, "It seems to be widely accepted that states have at the very least ceded some of their discretion or even sovereignty to supranational organizations, albeit the better to pursue their national interests." The result of the transition is an overlay of Westphalian and post-Westphalian politics. So this rescaling of politics and reworking of nation-states provides the first reason why we need to rethink how we do education policy analysis today.

The second reason for rethinking education policy analysis is the move from government to governance (Rhodes, 1997; Roseneau, 1997). This refers to and is inclusive of the rescaling of politics outlined above, but is also used to depict various privatization pressures within the public sector (e.g., the emergence of public-private partnerships) and the effects of new public management, which is basically the importation of private sector management practices into the public sector. Taken together, these changes have resulted in a more polycentric, networked state with some privatization of policy and policy processes.

The third factor demanding a rethink of our theory and methodology for carrying out education policy analysis flows from the first two. A commonly accepted definition of public policy, including education policy, is that provided by Easton (1953), who defined policy as "the authoritative allocation of values." The rescaling of politics and the move to governance mean that each aspect of this definition has been challenged. These changes have affected the location of political authority, practices of allocation via a reconstituted state at the national level framed by a rescaled politics, and policy discourses, which while they often have their gestation in various global networks, are negotiated and rearticulated at regional, national, provincial, and local levels.

Purposes and Positionalities

There is no recipe for doing policy analysis in education. Rather, the appropriate approach to adopt will depend on the nature of the policy being analyzed (e.g., World Bank policy, national or provincial policy, school policy). The type of approach taken to policy analysis is also dependent on the site of production of the policy (e.g., international organization, department of education or a school), while the purposes of policy analysis are equally significant for the theoretical and methodological approaches to be adopted.

In the traditional policy literature a distinction is made between *analysis of* and *analysis for* policy (Gordon, Lewis, & Young, 1977). The former is the more academic exercise, conducted by academic researchers, seeking to understand why a particular policy was developed at a particular time, what its analytical assumptions are and what effects it might have. The latter, *analysis for* policy, refers to research conducted for actual policy development, often commissioned by policy makers inside the bureaucracy within which the policy will be developed, and is thus *ipso facto* more constrained as to theoretical framework and methodology and usually has a short temporal frame. Analysis of policy sets its own research agenda and does not take for granted the policy construction of the problem, which policy seeks to address. The first step in analysis of policy might be a critical deconstruction of the problem as constructed by the policy and of the context and history assumed and/or constituted by the policy. In contrast, analysis for policy takes as given the research problem as constructed by those framing policy and thus lacks a critical orientation. This binary should not be overstated, however, and perhaps the two types of analysis might best be seen as sitting at various points on an academic/applied education policy studies continuum (Cibulka, 1994). The analysis of/for binary implies different relationships between these two forms of policy research and actual policy, which we might see as an activist relationship geared to enhancing understanding or "enlightenment," as opposed to a more instrumental, "engineering" relationship geared to problem solving and sometimes legitimation (Trowler, 2003).

The focus of policy research can vary, from the analysis of the context of policy; of the construction of the problem which the policy addresses; of values articulated by the policy content; of policy production processes; of the information needed for policy making; of the policy actors and processes of advocacy; of policy allocation, dissemination and implementation; as well as policy evaluation and review. Given these multiple foci, issues relating to the positionality of the policy researcher and the significance of that positionality to policy analysis become important. The questions of who is doing the policy analysis and for what purposes, and within what context, are clearly relevant in determining the approach to be taken to policy analysis.

Positionality has four meanings. The first relates to the actual location of the policy researcher in respect of the focus of analysis. For example, contrast the positionings of the academic researcher, the doctoral student, the policy bureaucrat, and the commissioned researcher, and consider how such positioning frames the type of policy analysis conducted. The second meaning of positionality links to theoretical and political stance adopted by the policy researcher, which has implications for the intellectual resources brought to bear on the research topic, including theory and methodology.

Commissioned policy research, that is, research for policy, usually demands methodologies that often assume a kind of rationalist "engineering" model, involving a series of steps, from the specification of policy goals, an examination of the possible implementation strategies, a determination of the resources available for implementation, the selection of the most efficient strategies to realize the specified policy goals, to actual implementation. In this approach ends and means are separated, while the operational values of efficiency and effectiveness are considered paramount.

There is a third meaning of positionality in respect of policy research that is intimately linked to the features of globalization. Here positionality is taken to refer to the spatial location of the researcher, specifically national location, and the positioning of that nation in respect of global geopolitics, including location within the Global North/Global South divide. Spatiality has become a new focus of contemporary social theory and research in the context of the apparent time/space compression associated with globalization (Massey, 1994). Tickly (2001) has observed that the problem with much theorizing about globalization and education policy is that it fails to recognize the different positionings of different nations *vis-à-vis* international governmental organizations (IGOs) such as the World Bank, UNESCO, and the OECD. In developing their educational policy, donee countries in the Global South are, for example, much more constrained than those of the Global North.

It is important to recognize that positionality then may refer to the national location of the policy researcher, which has implications for the nature of the analysis done and the theoretical and methodological options available. Working with doctoral students from various nations of the Global South has made me very aware of this meaning of positionality in education policy analysis. Indeed, in many nations of the Global South the only extant education policy analysis is research commissioned by donor agencies such as the World Bank or the UK Department for International Development (DfID), with all the implications that result in relation to problem setting, theoretical frameworks, and methodologies.

The above discussion underlines the importance of taking a historical approach to understanding how globalization might affect policy processes. This point is well exemplified in respect of the postcolonial aspirations of many nations of the Global South and the role that education policy is expected to play in achieving those aspirations. Neglecting the history of their education systems—what Gregory (2004) calls the "colonial present"—will necessarily reduce the veracity and quality of the education policy analysis carried out. Colonial histories are necessary to an understanding of the education policy effects of globalization. In this way, the temporal location of the education policy analyst is the fourth aspect of positionality, which is important in the chronological consideration of what policies have preceded any given policy, and the extent to which the policy represents an incremental or a radical change.

Contemporary accounts of research methodologies in the social sciences stress the significance of reflexivity to quality research. Reflexivity demands transparent articulation of researcher positionality and the significance of this to data collection and analysis. Bourdieu (Bourdieu et al., 1999), for instance, have spoken of the need to reject "epistemological innocence." Such a rejection demands that researchers articulate their positioning within the research in terms of their value stances, their problem choice, and their theoretical and methodological frames. Bourdieu (2004, p. 94) thus sees the necessity of researchers "objectivating" themselves in order to deconstruct their "taken for granted" assumptions. Bourdieu's argument is that this is necessary to arrive at more trustworthy and justifiable accounts of the data.

Critical policy analysis not only explores the workings of political power and authority, but is also embedded within relations of power. As Foucault (1980) has suggested, every relation of power has an associated knowledge and every form of knowledge exists within relations of power.

Questions for Policy Analysis

The approach to policy analysis adopted here is located within what Jenny Ozga (1987) has called "policy sociology." Policy sociology is "rooted in the social science tradition, historically informed and drawing on qualitative and illuminative techniques" (p. 144). While historical understanding is important to policy analysis, policy sociology has been affected in a number of ways by globalization. For example, globalization effects an elision of a simple homology between society and nation in relation to what we call the *social*. As Massey (1994) has noted, globalization is social relations stretched out.

By way of an example: Burawoy and colleagues (2000) have investigated methodological issues arising from global shifts in relation to ethnography. They have suggested that there are three axes of globalization, namely "global forces," which refer to the large structural developments in respect of global capitalism, "global connections," which refer to the connections between local and global flows of people, and a "global imagination," which encapsulates how these structural changes and connections provoke the mobilization of meaning about globalization and the changes it has effected. In a sense, these axes of globalization provide a specific contemporary account of how the central problem of social theory, namely, the recursive relationships between structure and agency, might be reconceptualized and interrogated in the context of globalization.

Methodologically, much of the recent research conducted in the name of policy sociology has been "qualitative and illuminative." This is not to suggest, though, that policy sociology should simply reject quantitative methods; rather, for many empirical policy problems, quantitative methods can be appropriate. As Gale (2001, p. 382) has noted, "quantitative data can also prove illuminating, particularly when it is subjected to the methodological assumptions of critical social science." Fitz, Davies, and Evans (2006, p. 3) have argued that the difficulties and complexities associated with quantitative methods ought not mean the abandonment of such methods, a position adopted in this chapter, nor do such approaches have to be non-critical. In terms of methodology, what is needed is an appropriate fit between the research problem and the methods adopted, together with a historically informed reflexivity. The type and site of the policy, and the focus and purpose of analysis, are all important considerations to find the methodological fit. Ball (2008) has used the metaphor of a pragmatic tool box to suggest that methodologies should not determine the approach to education policy analysis, but that methodology should be framed in terms of research purpose and researcher positionality.

Policy sociology has multiple purposes, not only descriptive and analytical, but also normative and imaginative. Thus policy sociology should not only describe relations of power and processes through which policies are developed and allocated, but also point to strategies for progressive change which might challenge oppressive structures and practices. The construction of progressive politics is now affected by and must take account of globalization. Progressive social change relates to issues of what Nancy Fraser (1997) has called a politics of redistribution seeking to achieve a more equal society and to a politics of recognition, which works with a politics of respect for difference, as well as a politics of representation which enables marginalized voices to be heard. The first politics is concerned with equality and issues of poverty and social class, the second with matters of identity, while the third relates to global structures of power and democratic participation. The imaginative aspect of policy sociology is based on a set of normative principles, which encourages equality, respect for difference, and democratic participation in both the content of policy and in the manner in which policies are constructed and implemented.

Policy analysis cannot be value-neutral, involving a set of rational-instrumental techniques, as with much of the traditional policy sciences. These rational-instrumental techniques take the *status quo* for granted, as a given, as well as a policy's definition of the problem to which the policy is the intended solution. This type of policy analysis is circumscribed and does not confront larger questions relating to the changing structure and functioning of the state whose interests are represented in both decision-making and non-decision making in policy processes. In contrast, the position taken here is that policies not only embody a particular set of values, but that analysis of policy is also an inherently political activity.

This approach to education policy analysis then is at one level ecumenical, but at another it explicitly specifies the normative position adopted in analyzing texts which have policy effects. This position affects "how" we research and how we interpret "what we find," and how we suggest alternatives. Drawing on Kenway (1990) and Taylor, Rizvi, Lingard, and Henry (1997), policy sociology, as analysis of policy, involves a range of questions in respect of any given policy, situated against reflexive consideration of the positionality of the policy researcher. Critical social science theories and methodologies offer ways to research these questions, which can be categorized around contextual issues, textual issues, and implementation and outcomes issues, drawing on Taylor et al.'s framework for policy analysis of context, text, and consequences. Policy analysis need not, of course, address all of these issues at once, but may focus on a selected set: much depends on both the purpose of analysis, as well as the position of the analyst. For example, research might focus on the "origins" of policy, textual analysis of a policy, or policy outcomes through implementation. Trajectory and ecological approaches to education policy (Weaver-Hightower, 2008) are also concerned with policy across this cycle and its location in the broader context.

Within the broad spectrum of questions that can be asked in analysis of policy, various approaches have emerged, each defined by its focus. It is possible to focus exclusively, for example, on implementation and policy outcomes. Implementation studies in education have been highly influential, particularly in the United States (Honig, 2006). These studies are either top-down or bottom-up, with a "backward mapping" approach being a component of the latter type of studies (Elmore, 1979, p. 80). Backward mapping as a normative policy production approach looks at the site of practice which the policy wants to change, and then strategizes backwards to create the policy, structures, culture, and implementation strategy necessary to achieve such change. Top-down implementation studies are usually concerned with refractions, failures, or deficits in policy implementation, while the bottom-up studies recognize the inevitability of mediations by professionals. When professionals implement policies they inevitably take the specificities of the context into account.

Another common approach to policy analysis is concerned with the critical analysis of actual policy texts, including analyzing and documenting the discourses within which the texts are located (Taylor, 2004). This approach recognizes that policies are often as much about language as anything else (Fairclough, 2001) and that policies are often positioned within what Bourdieu and Passeron (1977) called "magisterial discourse," that is, language which is unidirectional and which commands and instructs. Such discourse attempts to constrain the possibilities for interpretation. Rizvi and Kemmis (1987) view policy implementation as "interpretation of interpretations," a situation which the magisterial nature of discourse seeks to limit.

An attempt to understand the problem to which a given policy is a putative solution represents yet another approach to policy analysis. This requires an appreciation of the problem, rather than simply taking the policy construction of the problem as given. As Gil (1989, p. 69) suggests, the first task of policy analysis is "to gain understanding of the issues that constitute the focus of the specific social policy which is being analyzed or developed. This involves exploration of the nature, scope and distribution of these issues, and of causal theories concerning underlying dynamics." Similarly, McLaughlin (2006, p. 210) points out that "assumptions about the nature of the policy problem determine the policy solutions pursued and the logic of action advanced by a policy. And notions about preferred solutions also determine how polices are formulated—the policy target, nature of policy implements, level of support and regulatory structures."

Traditionally, most policy problems and solutions were constructed within the nation-state. In recent decades however, policy gestation, especially for national, state-centric, top-down policies, can now increasingly be traced to international organizations and globalized education policy discourses. While there has always been policy borrowing and policy lending across nations (Steiner-Khamsi, 2004), these processes today have been speeded up with the emergence of a global field of education policy production, even if local factors remain important for nations. We also need to recognize that nations of the Global North and Global South are positioned differently in relation to these global pressures. But even for Global North nations measures of comparative educational performance on an international scale have become important. They take the measures of quality and equity outcomes in education on the OECD's PISA, for example, as a point of comparison, thus locating the national system within a global system. As Nóvoa and Yariv-Mashal (2003) suggest, the global eye works together with the national eye today in both education policy and governance. Policy analysis today needs to take account of this changed post-Westphalian optic.

Research and Policy Analysis

In 1990, commenting in a UK context, Stephen Ball (1990) observed that critical education policy analysis had the character of commentary and critique, which was not often supported by empirical evidence. The situation has changed over the past two decades. There have been two sets of pressures here: the first relates to the theoretical developments within the social sciences generally, while the second concerns the framing of policy research by government policies, which are located within the broader move to new public management and a desire for evidence-based policy. Research paradigms in education have become the focus of government policy, directly and indirectly (through funding priorities, output and impact emphases, encouragement of policy relevant research) and have sought to valorize certain theoretical and methodological frames over others (Ozga & Lingard, 2007, pp. 77–79) with effects on policy analysis.

Maguire and Ball (1994) classified qualitative approaches to education policy analysis into three kinds: elite studies ("situated studies of policy formation"), trajectory studies, and implementation studies. To this categorization, I would add policy text analysis. Elite studies usually involve interviews with the major policy players as a way of understanding policy texts and policy processes across the policy cycle, with a particular focus on the politics of policy text production. Such studies recognize the politics of relationships between politicians and policy makers and the politics involved inside the actual site of policy production itself. Elite studies can also be linked to policy histories, focusing on changing policies over time. From the argument to this point, it can also be seen that elite studies might stretch to interviews with policy makers in international organizations and to considerations of globalized policy discourses.

There is a range of methodological issues which are raised by the elite studies approach, because such research utilizes interviews with elite policy players and thus requires access to them. Such access is usually easier for seasoned academic researchers than emerging researchers, with the power relations between the researcher and the interviewees becoming highly problematic. Sometimes methodological issues of access can also provide important research evidence.

Trajectory studies deal with policy across the stages of the policy cycle, beginning with elite interviews, concerned with the gestation of a policy and the often internecine politics involved in the production of the actual policy text through to implementation and the reception and effects of the policy in practice. Similar to trajectory studies, policy ecology studies offer another way of locating policy in its broader ecological contexts. Weaver-Hightower (2008, p. 155) suggests that "a policy ecology consists of the policy itself along with all the other texts, histories, people, places, groups, traditions, economic and political conditions, institutions, and relationships that affect it or are affected by it." While trajectory studies trace policy across the policy cycle, policy ecology also locates the text and policy processes in a much broader context, as signified by the metaphor of "ecology" (Weaver-Hightower, p. 155). An anthropology of public policy takes a similar approach to that of policy ecology from within a different disciplinary framework (Wedel, Shore, Feldman, & Lathrop, 2005).

Implementation studies deal with the context of policy practice and use a variety of research methods including interviews, observations, document analysis, and sometimes ethnographic case study work. In trajectory studies there has been opposition to separating out policy production from policy implementation, with Cibulka (1994, p. 111) noting that "implementors have an explicit policy role, not merely a technical one." Those who use backward–mapping for policy production acknowledge that reality. Implementation studies have been a particularly strong focus of educational policy analysis in the United States, stretching from McLaughlin's (1987) earlier influential essay on changes in foci of implementation studies in the U.S. through Elmore and McLaughlin's (1988) Rand Corporation study and talk of "backward mapping" to the more recent collection edited by Honig (2006). In the United States a more policy relevant version of implementation studies is policy evaluation, usually commissioned by governments or state bureaucracies, and more limited in scope and responsive to the demands of those who commission such research.

Analysis of policy texts is another common approach to policy analysis. These studies often take a critical discourse analysis (CDA) approach to text analysis. These studies are located in the contention that the contemporary world of consumer capitalism and new global media has become text saturated and that text and language have become central to contemporary politics and policy making. In this context, Luke (2002, p. 98) has spoken of "semiotic economies" in which "language, text and discourse become the principal modes of social relations, civics and political life, economic behavior and activity." Regarding these economies, Fairclough (2000) has written at some length about the politics of the language used by the Blair Labour government in the UK. Focused analyses of specific policy texts usually emphasize either the linguistic features of the policy text or work with Foucauldian-inspired (and poststructuralist-inspired) accounts of texts in context, including discursive context. Fairclough's (2003) approach to CDA works across these two categories and is becoming more influential in this approach to policy analysis (e.g., Adie, 2008; Mulderrig, 2008; Taylor, 2004).

This is not the place to document the fine detailed types of analyses taken by CDA approaches, but suffice to say that Fairclough (2001, pp. 241–242) has suggested the following as features of texts which should be the focus of analysis: "whole text organization (structure, e.g., narrative, argumentative, etc.), clause combination, grammatical and semantic features (transitivity, action, voice, mood, modality), and words (e.g., vocabulary, collocations, use of metaphors, etc.)." So, for example, there have been analyses of the use of "we" in policy texts in education. Adie (2008), in a CDA analysis of Queensland "smart state" policies, for example, shows how "we" is used in the texts to mean both the government and the people, with slippages between the two. Fairclough's (2000) analysis of Blair's political language in the UK has also argued similarly with respect to usage of "we" and these dual and blended meanings.

Such textual analysis might also make us aware of what Fairclough (1992) called "overwording," the repetitive usage of certain words and types of words, for example "new," in attempts to justify the need for a policy. We also need to recognize the significance of the silences of a policy text; just as a politics of non-decision making can be important in relation to policy, so too can silences in policy texts tell us a lot about power. The postcolonial critic Edward Said (1983) speaks of reading (literary) texts contrapuntally, that is, reading their silences into them. This is equally necessary in policy analysis. Said has also talked about how spoken language carries its context with it, while this is not the case for a written text. To fully understand the written text the policy analyst has to "world" the text, situate it in its context.

Texts are positioned within discourses (Ball, 1994), which today are often globalized. Bourdieu's work is helpful to an analysis of policy texts and particularly those which circulate globally. Talking about the global circulation of texts, Bourdieu (2003) argues that policy and other texts are taken from their context of production and read in a different context of reception. This leads to multiple slippages across national borders and between sites of policy production and policy implementation, and can also be seen to work in relation to sub-national policy texts implemented in schools. Using Bourdieu's notion of fields, it can be argued that the context of the field of text production has particular logics, which are often different from those of the field of policy reception and of school and classroom practices, which have different logics and which thus ensure policy as "palimpsest," literally a new text written over a partly erased older text.

In Bourdieu's concept of social fields (one of the last additions to his theorizing), he suggested that the social arrangement consists of multiple quasi-autonomous fields with their own logics of practice, over-arched by a field of power linked to the economic field and a field of gender relations. Bourdieu's use of social field appears to refer to studies of social institutions, but rather than speak of politics, he talks of "the field of politics"; instead of the media, "the journalistic field"; in place of literature and the arts, "the field of cultural production"; and so on. Thus, instead of policy, Bourdieu would talk of the policy field. In the context of globalization, in addition to the national education policy field, we also need to recognize an emergent global education policy field (Lingard et al., 2005). The nature of relationships between fields or cross-field effects (Lingard & Rawolle, 2004), here for example the global and national education policy fields, then becomes an important task for contemporary education policy analysis.

Also important to explore in our media age are the ways in which policy texts are distributed—how their authority is allocated. Here the work of Fairclough (2000) is useful. In his analysis, Fairclough speaks of the "mediatization" of policy and politics. In some ways, this refers simply to the enhanced role of the media in contemporary politics and to the role of global media in the circulation of globalized education policy problems and discourses. However, it can have an even more specific meaning in relation to education policy production with implications for policy analysis. As Rawolle (2005) has demonstrated, today many policy texts are mediatized, that is, the logics of practice of journalism affect policy production processes. This sometimes involves journalists in the production of the actual policy text and the implied readership of the policy (the imagined policy community) becomes the public, rather than the professional community which will actually implement the policy in question, with implications for implementation. The media logic, including the proclivity to aphorism, alliteration, metaphor, and catchy phrases seeps into the wording of the policy and renders it less professionally relevant.

Globalizing Education Policy Analysis

Globalization has challenged theory and methodology within the social sciences. Thus globalization implies the need to challenge taken-for-granted assumptions of a society/nation homology in policy research. Today society is simultaneously local, national, regional, and global in terms of experience, politics, effects, and imaginaries. Further, these spaces are imbricated with unequal power relations which reflect both contemporary geopolitics and past political struggles. Residual, dominant, emergent, and contested geographies of power, including those of the colonial past and postcolonial present, are at play across these global spaces and manifest in vernacular ways in the local, national and regional. Fisher and Mosquera (2004, p. 5) have noted that Western "metaculture" relates to geographies of power, which include academic theories, epistemologies and research methodologies. For those researchers in the Global North, recognition of the researcher's positionality within Western universities and their relationships to these geographies of power is a central beginning for challenging the silent valorization of Western epistemologies in research of all kinds, including education policy research (Connell, 2007).

Such a challenge is central to what Arjun Appadurai (2001) calls the "deparochialization" of research and a strong internationalization of the Western academy, in the light of enhanced global flows of students and academics as part of the mobilities and networks of globalization. He argues for the need to deconstruct, in both an anthropological and pragmatic sense, the "taken-for-granted" assumptions of contemporary systems of research. In the context of increased flows of capital, people, ideas, images, and technologies, and disjunctions and related asymmetries of power, he specifically calls for a "deparochialization of the research ethic" (p. 15). He suggests a number of ways in which the research ethic might be challenged, including a reconnection with earlier pre-research paradigm thinking premised on a strong moral position; the promotion of the style of argumentation of public intellectuals; and paying greater attention to research linked to policy making and state functions in a range of nations, particularly those in the developing world.

Appadurai postulates that "epistemological diffidence" is necessary to the project of deparochialization of research—the need to move beyond the epistemological certainty of dominant forms of modernization theory of the 1950s and 1960s and their effects, particularly in the developing world. Modernization theory accepted without question that theory and research were metropolitan, modern, and Western, while the rest of the world was simply a research site to test and confirm such theory. Here relations of researcher and researched paralleled relations of colonizer and colonized, even within decolonizing and postcolonial politics and aspirations. Similarly, Linda Tuhiwai Smith (1999), in her *Decolonizing Methodologies*, a study of the relationships between research and indigenous peoples and knowledges in New Zealand, suggests that the term "research" is inextricably linked to European imperialism and colonialism. Raewyn Connell (2007) calls for acknowledgement of, and respect for, "Southern theory." We need to recognize then that relations of power and politics, in both macro and individual relations senses, distort even the most arcane theories to some extent. These theories are imbricated within global politics.

In rejecting an epistemological innocence characteristic of the dominant forms of social research, Appadurai, Smith, and Connell call for an "epistemological openness." Such a project, according to Appadurai, needs to be aligned with "grassroots globalization" or "globalization from below." We need to ask: whose globalization? And in doing so, issue a challenge to globalization from above as driven by leading international organizations and global cultural industries. In his book *Modernity at Large*, Appadurai (1996) speaks of "vernacular globalization" to refer to the ways in which local sites and their histories, cultures, politics, and pedagogies mediate to greater or lesser extents the effects of top-down globalization. This is an outcome of relations and tensions between the context-productive and context-generative effects of globalization; some local sites are more able to be context-generative and mediate global effects. The idea of globalization from below seeks to extend and strengthen this mediation and enhance global connections that resist globalization from above, read simply as neoliberal economics, what Bourdieu (2003) calls the performative construction of globalization. Policy is now increasingly located within this struggle, with implications for analysis.

Appadurai (2001) emphasizes the need for research to examine its own rhetoric and practices of "systematicity, prior citational contexts, and specialized modes of inquiry," replicability, along with "an imagined world of specialized professional readers and researchers" (p. 12), which taken together work to inhibit the deparochialization of research, its theories and methodologies. Prior citational contexts and an imagined world of specialized readers ensure the reproduction of more "parochial" Western- or Northern-dominated theories.

As already noted, the reality of *trans-* and supra-national processes labelled as globalization has challenged contemporary social theory. In sociology, Urry (2000) has argued the need to refocus from the social as society to the social as mobilities, indicating the weakened connectivity between society and nation-state and the stretching of networks across the globe. The spatial turn in social theory has been another response to the rescaling of experience. The spatial turn in social theory, exploring these relations between space and place as social constructions, reflects the new scalar politics. Brennan (2006, p. 136) has suggested that the centrality of space and place in contemporary globalization theory manifests the apparent "overcoming of temporality," with this new theoretical optic ushering in a transition from "tempo to scale," from "the chronometric to the cartographic."

Brennan (2006, p. 136) makes a distinction between space and place, suggesting "'space' is more abstract and ubiquitous: it connotes capital, history, and activity, and gestures towards the meaninglessness of distance in a world of instantaneous communication and virtuality." In contrast, place, he notes, connotes "the kernel or centre of one's memory and experience—a dwelling, a familiar park or city street, one's family or community." The necessary research disposition being argued for acknowledges this space/place distinction in relation to the conduct of education policy analysis. It is interesting to contemplate the significance of a conceptualization of the *space* of policy production and the *place* of policy implementation, and their differing logics, in relation to Brennan's argument.

Other theorists have demonstrated the implicit national space of much social theory and a complementary "methodological nationalism" (Beck, 2000). Bourdieu (1999), for example, has observed how "[i]ntellectual life, like all other social spaces, is a home to nationalism and imperialism" (p. 220) and that "a truly scientific internationalism" requires a concerted political project; this is another way of expressing the project in which Appadurai invites us to participate, namely the deparochialization of research and theory.

Bourdieu's theoretical stance and methodological disposition allow a way beyond such spatial and national constraints, a necessary position for analyzing and understanding global effects in contemporary educational policy and the emergence of a global policy field in education. Globalization has resulted in the compression of time and space, which has had the phenomenological effect of enhanced awareness amongst (privileged) peoples across the globe of the world as one place, evidenced in, for example, talk of the "world economy," "world recession," "global financial crisis," "global warming," "world heritage sites," "world policy," "global educational indicators," and so on. Castells (2000) speaks of flows and networks across the globe which render national boundaries more porous. He argues, somewhat like Appadurai (1996), that society is now organized around flows, namely, "flows of capital, flows of information, flows of technology, flows of organisational interaction, flows of images, sounds and symbols" (Castells, p. 442), with technology facilitating these flows via hubs and nodes located across the globe that are dominated by elites of various kinds. While the postnational accounts proffered by Castells and others perhaps overstate the "porousness" of national boundaries, particularly post-9/11, the suggestion that the world has become increasingly interconnected is now beyond doubt. This implies that the local and the national are now nested within regional, international, transnational, and global spaces. This implies the need to see the social relations of educational policy production as stretched out. It becomes the task of policy analysis to determine how, and with what effects. The policy cycle needs to be globalized with the consequent implications for policy analysis.

This task involves refusing to reify the concept of globalization, and requires us to historicize it and to recognize its potentially hegemonic role. The task needs to determine the asymmetries of power between nations, and attend to their colonial and neocolonial histories and postcolonial aspirations. Also important is the need to calibrate the differential national effects of neoliberal globalization. Bourdieu offers a way beyond such reification of globalization and allows for an empirically grounded account of the constitution of a global policy field in education, an example of globalization from above, and an account of global effects in national policy fields, globalization from below. In his later, more political work Bourdieu (2003) was concerned with the politics of globalization, read mainly as the dominance of a neoliberal approach to the economy. He was interested in exploring the ways in which global neoliberal politics have dented the relative autonomy of the logics of practice of many social fields, including that of the educational policy field, which has become more heteronomous, as a subset of economic policy. Bourdieu's approach allows for an empirical investigation of the constitution of the global economic market, as well as the ways in which the media field and its logics have affected the degree of autonomy of educational policy production.

In a homologous fashion, the global educational policy field is a political project and yet another manifestation of politics in the age of flows and diasporas of people and ideas across the boundaries of nation-states in both embodied and cyber forms. And just as a social imaginary of neoliberal globalization has been a central component in the creation of the global market, so it has been with the global field of educational policy. A global field of education policy is now established, certainly as a global commensurate space of measurement of educational performance. Such a field does not, of course, affect all nation-states in the same way, for they are positioned differently in terms of power and the strength of national capital within the global fields of the economy and governance and have to relate to these global fields in terms of their own economic, social and political conditions. While nation-states retain their significance for policy making in education, their capacity to set their policy priorities has become relativized, as they now have to refer to the global processes in a range of different ways, including their effects in specific nations.

Drawing on Bourdieu (2003, p. 91), it can be argued that the amount of "national capital" possessed by a given nation is a determining factor in the degree of autonomy for policy development within the nation. National capital in one articulation can be seen to consist of the economic, political, and cultural capital (evidenced in quantity and quality of education of a country's workforce) possessed by any given nation. Here the Global South is positioned very differently from the Global North in relation to the educational policy effects of the World Bank and other international agencies. National capital can be seen to mediate the extent to which nations are able to be context-generative in respect of the global field. Under globalization and the emergence of global fields, the sovereignty of different nation-states is affected in different ways. As Jayasuriya (2001, p. 444) suggests, "the focus should not be on the content or degree of sovereignty that the state possesses but the form that it assumes in a global economy."

The education policy field today is multilayered, stretched from the local to the global. Mann (2000) speaks of five socio-spatial layers, namely local, national, international (relations between nations), transnational (relations that pass through national boundaries), and global, which cover the globe as a whole. It is important to note, however, that these layers are inter-related, in ways that are affected by the processes of globalization.

If this is so, then education policy analysis demands an empirical and theoretical stretching beyond the nation, but in ways that do not overlook the importance of these layers. Bourdieu's notion of field is useful for examining the relations between these layers, suggesting that global, international, national, and local educational policy fields represent a different way to locate the practices and products of policy. This global educational policy field encompasses the contexts of the policy cycle, and offers some analytic gains in locating the effects of particular policies and reframes the contexts, texts, and consequences of policy. That is, it caters to these matters and also offers a particular way of utilizing Bourdieu's concept of field to discuss issues around the impact of different fields on one another within national fields of power, and of different scalar levels of fields also affecting one another. All three contexts of the policy cycle (Ball, 1994)—the context of policy text production, the context of influence, and the context of practice—are affected in different ways by globalization through both its policy mediation and its more direct effects.

Conclusion

This chapter has shown how globalization has given rise to a number of new theoretical and methodological issues for doing education policy analysis linked to globalization's impact within critical social science. Critical policy analysis has always required critical *reflexivity* and awareness of the *positionality* of the policy analyst. However, as demonstrated, both now need to be nuanced in different ways in the context of globalization. This is to ensure a deparochialized approach to education policy analysis, one which recognizes the layering of policy processes across local, national, regional, and global spaces and the globalization of many policy discourses in education. The disposition for critical education policy analysis in an era of globalization also demands that we recognize the *relationality* and *interconnectivity* of policy developments, given the contemporary rescaling of politics. This recognition is in response to the new spatial politics and interconnectivity within and across nations, evident in globalization. Critical policy analysis indicates how any given policy either supports or undermines the values of democracy, social justice, and difference, while also explicating its own imbrications in power/knowledge relationships. Beyond critique, another purpose of critical education policy analysis is to suggest how policy could be otherwise—to offer an alternative social imaginary of globalization to the neoliberal construction.

AUTHOR'S NOTE

This chapter has been developed from Chapter 3, "Globalizing Education Policy Analysis," in Fazal Rizvi and Bob Lingard's (2009) book, *Globalizing Education Policy*.

REFERENCES

Adie, J. (2008). The hegemonic positioning of "smart state" policy. *Journal of Education Policy*, *23*(3), 251–264.

Appadurai, A. (1996). *Modernity at large: Cultural dimensions of globalization*. Minneapolis: The University of Minnesota Press.

Appadurai, A. (2001). Grassroots globalization and the research imagination. In A. Appadurai (Ed.), *Globalization* (pp. 1–21). Durham, NC: Duke University Press.

Appadurai, A. (2006). *Fear of small numbers: An essay on the geography of anger*. Durham, NC: Duke University Press.

Ball, S. (1990). *Politics and policy making in education*. London: Routledge.

Ball, S. (1994). *Education reform: A critical and poststructuralist approach*. Milton Keynes: Open University Press.

Ball, S. (2008). *The education debate*. Bristol: Policy Press.

Beck, U. (2000). The cosmopolitan perspective. *British Journal of Sociology*, *51*(1), 79–105.

Bourdieu, P. (1999). The social conditions of the international circulation of ideas. In R. Shusterman (Ed.), *Bourdieu: A critical reader* (pp. 220–228). Oxford: Blackwell.

Bourdieu, P. (2003). *Firing back: Against the tyranny of the market 2*. London: Verso.

Bourdieu, P. (2004). *Science of science and reflexivity*. Cambridge: Polity Press.

Bourdieu, P., Accardo, A., Balazs, G., Beaud, S., Bonvon, F., Bourdieu, E., et al. (1999). *The weight of the world: Social suffering in contemporary society*. Cambridge: Polity Press.

Bourdieu, P., & Passeron, J.C. (1977). *Reproduction in education, society and culture*. London: Sage.

Brennan, T. (2006). *Wars of position: The cultural politics of left and right*. New York: Columbia University Press.

Brenner, N. (2004). *New state spaces: Urban governance and the rescaling of statehood*. Oxford: Oxford University Press.

Burawoy, M., Blum, J.A., George, S., Gillie, Z., Gowan, T., Haney, L., et al. (2000). *Global ethnography: Forces, connections, and imaginations in a postmodern world*. Berkeley: University of California Press.

Castells, M. (2000). *The rise of the network society* (2nd ed.). Oxford: Blackwell.

Cibulka, J.G. (1994). Policy analysis and the study of education. *Journal of Education Policy*, *9*(506), 105–125.

Connell, R. (2007). *Southern theory: The global dynamics of knowledge in the social sciences*. Sydney: Allen and Unwin.

Dale, R. (2006). Policy relationships between supranational and national scales: Imposition/resistance or parallel universes? In J. Kallo & R. Rinne (Eds.), *Supranational regimes and national education policies encountering challenges* (pp. 27–49). Turku, Finland: Finnish Educational Research Association.

Easton, D. (1953). *The political system*. New York: Knopf.

Elmore, R. (1979) Backward mapping: Implementation research and policy decisions. *Political Science Quarterly*, *94*(4), 601–615.

Elmore, R., & McLaughlin, M. (1988). *Steady work: Policy practice and the reform of American education*. The Rand Corporation, R-3574-NIE/RC.

Fairclough, N. (1992). *Discourse and social change*. Cambridge: Polity Press.

Fairclough, N. (2000). *New Labour, new language*. London: Routledge.

Fairclough, N. (2001). *Language and power*. Harlow, UK: Longman.

Fairclough, N. (2003). *Analysing discourse: Textual analysis for social research*. London: Routledge.

Fisher, J., & Mosquera, G. (2004). Introduction. In G. Mosquera & J. Fisher (Eds.), *Over here: International perspectives on art and culture* (pp. 2–9). Cambridge, MA: MIT.

Fitz, J., Davies, B., & Evans, J. (2006). *Educational policy and social reproduction: Class inscription and symbolic control*. London: Routledge.

Foucault, M. (1980). *Power/knowledge: Selected interviews and other writings*. C. Gordon (Ed.). New York: Pantheon Books.

Fraser, N. (1997). *Justice interruptus: Critical reflections on the "post-socialist" condition*. New York: Routledge.

Gale, T. (2001). Critical policy sociology: Historiography, archaeology and genealogy as methods of policy analysis. *Journal of Education Policy*, *16*(5), 379–393.

Gil, D. (1989). *Unravelling social policy: Theory, analysis, and political action towards social inequality*. Rochester, VT: Schenkeman Books.

Gordon, I., Lewis, J., & Young, R. (1977). Perspective on policy analysis. *Public Administration Bulletin*, *25*, 26–35.

Gregory, D. (2004). *The colonial present*. Oxford: Blackwell.

Honig, M.I. (Ed.) (2006). *New directions in education policy implementation: Confronting complexity*. Albany: State University of New York Press.

Jayasuriya, K. (2001). From political to economic constitutionalism. *Constellations*, *8*(4), 442–460.

Kenway, J. (1990). *Gender and education policy: A call for new directions*. Geelong: Deakin University Press.

Krasner, S. (2000). Compromising Westphalia. In D. Held and A. McGrew (Eds.), *The global transformation reader* (2nd ed., pp. 124–135). Cambridge: Polity Press.

Lingard, B., & Rawolle, S. (2004). Mediatizing educational policy: The journalistic field, science policy, and cross-field effects. *Journal of Education Policy*, *19*(3), 353–372.

Lingard, B., & Rawolle, S. (2009). Rescaling and reconstituting education policy: The knowledge economy and the scalar politics of global fields. In M. Simons, M. Olsen, & M. Peters (Eds.), *Re-reading education policies: Studying the policy agenda of the twenty-first century* (pp. 217–231). Rotterdam: Sense Publishers.

Lingard, B., Rawolle, S., & Taylor, S. (2005). Globalizing policy sociology in education: Working with Bourdieu. *Journal of Education Policy*, *20*(6), 759–777.

Luke, A. (2002). Beyond science and ideology critique: Developments in critical discourse analysis. *Annual Review of Applied Linguistics*, *22*, 96–110.

Maguire, M., & Ball, S. (1994). Researching politics and the politics of research: Recent qualitative studies in the UK. *International Journal of Qualitative Studies in Education*, *7*(3), 269–285.

Mann, M. (2000). Has globalisation ended the rise and rise of the nation state? In D. Held & A. McGrew (Eds.), *The global transformation reader* (pp. 136–147). Cambridge: Polity Press.

Massey, D. (1994). *Space, place and gender*. Cambridge: Polity Press.

McLaughlin, M. (1987). Learning from experience: Lessons from policy implementation. *Educational Evaluation and Policy Analysis*, *9*(2), 171–178.

McLaughlin, M.W. (2006). Implementation research in education: Lessons learnt, lingering questions and new opportunities. In M.I. Honig (Ed.), *New directions in education policy implementation: Confronting complexity* (pp. 209–228). New York: State University of New York Press.

Mulderrig, J. (2008). Using keywords analysis in CDA: Evolving discourses of the knowledge economy in education. In B. Jessop, N. Fairclough, & R. Wodak (Eds.), *Education and the knowledge-based economy in Europe* (pp. 149–169). Rotterdam: Sense Publishers.

Nóvoa, A., & Yariv-Mashal, T. (2003). Comparative research in education: A mode of governance or a historical journey? *Comparative Education, 39*(4), 423–438.

Ozga, J. (1987). Studying education policy through the lives of policy makers. In S. Walker & L. Barton (Eds.), *Changing policies, changing teachers: New directions for schooling?* (pp. 138–150). Milton Keynes: Open University Press.

Ozga, J., & Lingard, B. (2007). Globalisation, education policy and politics. In B. Lingard & J. Ozga (Eds.), *The RoutledgeFalmer reader in education policy and politics* (pp. 65–82). London: Routledge.

Rawolle, S. (2005). Cross-field effects and temporary social fields: A case study of the mediatization of recent Australian knowledge economy policies. *Journal of Education Policy, 20*(6), 705–724.

Rhodes, R.A.W. (1997). *Understanding governance: Policy networks, governance, reflexivity and accountability.* Buckingham, UK: Open University Press.

Rizvi, F., & Kemmis, S. (1987). *Dilemmas of reform: An overview of issues and achievements of the participation and equity program in Victorian schools 1984–1986.* Geelong: Deakin University Press.

Rizvi, F., & Lingard, B. (2009). *Globalizing education policy.* London: Routledge.

Roseneau, J.N. (1997). *Along the domestic-foreign frontier: Exploring governance in a turbulent world.* Cambridge: Cambridge University Press.

Said, E. (1983). *The world, the text and the critic.* Cambridge, MA: Harvard University Press.

Smith, L.T. (1999). *Decolonizing methodologies: Research and indigenous peoples.* New York: Zed Books.

Steiner-Khamsi, G. (Ed.) (2004). *The global politics of educational borrowing and lending.* New York: Teachers College Press.

Taylor, S. (2004). Researching educational policy and change in "new times": Using critical discourse analysis. *Journal of Education Policy, 19*(4), 433–451.

Taylor, S., Rizvi, F., Lingard, B., & Henry, M. (1997). *Educational policy and the politics of change.* London: Routledge.

Tickly, L. (2001). Globalisation and education in the post-colonial world: Towards a conceptual framework. *Comparative Education, 37*(2), 151–171.

Trowler, P. (2003). *Education policy* (2nd ed.). London: Routledge.

Urry, J. (2000). *Sociology beyond societies: Mobilities for the twenty-first century.* London: Routledge.

Weaver-Hightower, M. (2008). An ecology metaphor for educational policy analysis: A call to complexity. *Educational Researcher, 37*(3), 153–167.

Wedel, J.R., Shore, C., Feldman, G., & Lathrop, S. (2005). Towards an anthropology of public policy. *The Annals of the American Academy of Political and Social Science, 600,* 30–51.

Globalization as A System of Reason: The Historical Possibility and the Political in Pedagogical Policy and Research

THOMAS S. POPKEWITZ

Globalization is a word that flows through many different contexts. A Google search identifies over 20 million sites for its descriptions and prescriptions. It is a *topoi*, it is a word that everyone seems to know and which needs no author. Globalization is a contemporary industry that crosses academia, commerce, and governments. In a European study of educational governance and social inclusion, it travels in the narratives of politicians, ministries, school leaders, and teachers to describe the fate of humankind: globalization was the given fact of the world, and schools are to prepare children for this future-to-come (Lindblad & Popkewitz, 2001). The hope of globalization is also the darkness of present economic woes and the homogenizing of cultures and traditions.

My inquiry is about the historical principles of "reason" that enable "seeing," thinking, and acting as if globalization were an ontological object and subject that organizes modes of life. The chapter is first historical, providing a way to examine cultural theses generated in contemporary pedagogical policy and research about globalization. European and North American Enlightenment notions of cosmopolitanism are examined as making possible a particular linking of individuality and society that is inscribed in contemporary discourses of globalization. That linkage embodies "the homeless mind,"[1] the self and daily life placed, as a participant in social structures and imaginaries that appear without historical and cultural specificity and without geographical boundaries. Numbers are explored in this context, embodying categories of equivalence that appear outside of history. Ironically, I argue, the homelessness of cosmopolitanism and numbers simultaneously generate principles of collective belonging and "homes" in school policy, research, and programs. The inalienable rights and freedom of the citizen are examples of this irony of "homelessness" even as they inscribe homes in the nation.

The third and fourth sections inquire into the particular emergence of "globalization" in contemporary European Union and United States education policy and research. The third section addresses how globalization is (re)visioned as the "unfinished cosmopolitanism" of the lifelong learner who "thinks" and acts as a global individuality of the knowledge society—"homeless" but having particular qualities for governing conduct. The final and fourth section explores the globalizing qualities of cosmopolitanism as embodying their opposites—the child who does not have the global capabilities and is abjected, placed in spaces that "can never be of the average."

The analysis takes globalization as a noun and ontological condition of the present and turns it into an event to make visible its rules and standards of reason that order what is thought, hoped for, and acted on. Globalization, as a term about the present, then, is a fabrication that directs attention to the simultaneous practices of creating fictions to think about the things happening in the world that require attention, and that makes that world through theories, literatures, stories, and programs for ordering, dividing, and acting (see, e.g., Hacking, 1986). These two nuances of fabrication are intended to move away from the polarizations of comparative studies and globalization literatures that differentiate the "real"/context from the discourse/text.

Historicizing Reason: Time, Agency and the Entanglement of Distance and Immediacy

Globalization as a possibility of thought and action can be associated with modernity and particular principles of "reason" that have ordered individuality and society historically in Europe.[2] To consider this historicity in thinking about globalization, I compare briefly the systems of reason that order the classical Greek senses of past and present, the Medieval Church's notion of eternal time, and Northern European and American Enlightenment's notions of cosmopolitanism. The cosmopolitanism makes visible qualities of "the homeless mind" through the inventions of human agency, the linking of individuality to notions of society, and time as an irreversible process that can be regulated and planned for. These qualities overlap in research and schooling to form cultural theses[3] about such particular human kinds as the citizen who operates through a general "homelessness" that embodies transcendent values in projects of collective belonging. This cosmopolitan "reason," however, is a double gesture; its hope of the future instantiates a style of comparative thought that both divides and excludes. Globalization in today's narratives embodies cosmopolitan principles, but with different assembles and connections of individuality and society than in the past.

Historical Possibilities of "Reason": Space, Time and Distancing

Thinking globally and locally, to capture a prominent rhetoric, is a radical break in the principles governing how individuality locates and is located in the world. It is not that abstract categories did not exist before. Notions of salvation and redemption of the Church, for example, tied individuality to God and afterlife. The homeless mind, in contrast, brings those distant events to the City of Man [sic] where the collective belonging of the modern nation and society are dynamically bound to personal responsibilities, obligations, and good works.

A way to differentiate the reason of the homeless mind is through the Greek Stoic tradition. Two spatial orders were fused and merged into the cosmopolis: nature (the *cosmos*, recording the natural order of celestial events) and practical activities which depended on human experience and ability to command order (the *polis* or a community which gave coherence to its organization). The practical idea was linked with the natural order of things (Toulmin, 1990, p. 67). The structure of nature reinforced a rational social order.

The two orders, nature and practical life, were reasoned about by memory, which centered on the past and not the future. The subject was modified through the acts of memory that liberated one's own being. For the Greeks,[4] knowing oneself meant knowing the past that is drawn from the wisdom given by the gods. The primacy of memory was to "sing the hymn of gratitude and recognition to the gods" and "to grasp the reality of which we cannot be dispossessed and which makes possible a real sovereignty over ourselves" (Foucault, 2005, p. 468). Wars and distant places were defined through the oracles, and history as a chronicle of events and heroes.

One could locate oneself in distant places but not as implicating one's self in a logic of time and progress brought by human intentions. Humans were a natural part of the cosmos and origins of things embodied in that cosmos. The mind preoccupied with the future was consumed by forgetting, incapable of action, and not free. To speak of the future indicated hubris, as the future did not exist for people but for the gods. The Greeks saw the search for the future as destroying memory

and the person who forgets as "doomed to dispossession and emptiness-
. . . . [Individuals] are really no longer anything. They exist in nothing-
ness" (Foucault, 2005, p. 467). Reason, in its modern senses, did not
exist, as reason includes the possibility of human agency in controlling
the future and planning one's life.

Distant "things" that influenced life in time were cast in cycles.
People generally conceived of time as cyclical. The pre-Socratic philosopher Pythagoras depicted history as one world historical cycle in
which the sun, the moon, and all other planets return to their original
positions. There was no conception of a regularized and irreversible
time; nor was time a device to calculate and compare individuality and
societies for the future, as what was given was known by gods and
prophesies.

The medieval Christian church's claim to universality and questions of redemption in the afterlife mediated the conceptions of distance and the proximities of life (Pocock, 2003). There was no
"homeless mind" in the sense of inserting individuality in a sequence
of regularized time that spoke of human agency and progress as a
temporal quality that could judge and order the capacities of humanity. Time had a past, defined eternally, and told in the New Testament
that succeeded the Old. Reason disclosed the eternal, immemorial
ordering and hierarchies of nature and events in which people maintained their place in the cosmology of God. Philosophy, the highest
form of reason, contemplated the universal categories that rose above
the human and practical, earthly knowledge. The Church initially
rejected putting clocks on church steeples as God, not people, owned
time. Icons and frescos could not be signed by the painter, as God
owned knowledge as well. Reason for St. Augustine and Erasmus was
given by God, and thus distinguished the Christians who, by virtue of
the recognition, were civilized and divided from the infidels and non-
humans who could not recognize the sovereignty of God and his
earthly ministries.

In the later part of the sixteenth century, traveling through the new
French and American republican forms of nation comes a different way
of locating time and individuality through notions of human agency and
society, among others. This quality maintains a notion of the universal
tied to the City of People rather than to the gods. Global events of
"society" are given universal "homeless" values through which distances
and proximities are possible. Men and women in the landscape of a
universalized space of "humanity" assume center stage in an irreversible
conception of time that links past/present/future. Friedrich (2009)

argues, for example, that a particular temporalization is made visible that positions the individual as the citizen and subject-agent who is emancipated from given worlds of the aristocracy and the eternal time "owned" by the Church. That self-awareness of living in a "new" historical era has the double sense of distancing and belonging that I speak of here. The notion of historical consciousness embodies the production of memories and traditions to "see" the present. The present is indebted to the past yet different; it is possible to overcome its traditions through human agency. The temporalization embodied in comparative thought placed people into a continuum of time that differentiates "advanced" civilizations from those defined as the "primitive" and "antiquated."

The location in "thought" in time and distance is expressed in the different meanings of poetry in ancient Greece and modernity. Poetry functions as a metaphor of transportation and territorialization that brings distance and immediate life into a vision that makes possible new spaces for reflection and action. Individuality is simultaneously in a dual space, the qualities of which enunciate the reason of the homeless mind. Modern lyricism, the French philosopher Rancière (2004) argues, is a method that enables the individual to create a perceptual space that simultaneously enables individuality to be part of the immediate world written about and part of a remote and separate world that overlaps in poems. The "I" of the poem, Rancière argues, appears in relation to the remoteness of nature in the same way as, for example, the wind, clouds, or waves. The "I" is produced in echo with its act and also represents the subjectivity of a traveler who passes through a certain territory to make words coincide with things and utterances with visions (p. 12). This notion of the traveler (individual) whose life coincides with things and visions (society and nature), Rancière continues, is different from Greek poetry, where there is instead a conjunction between the ethos of the citizens which told about "a certain type of individual that should or should not be imitated and of a certain place of utterance that is or is not suitable for political experience of the *nomoi* of the city" (pp. 10–11).

The relation of the spaces of individuality and the social and natural world in modern poetry is homologous to the appearance of ideas of individuality and society, concepts presumed in the discourses of globalization. Prior to the seventeenth century, for example, society was an association or guild of people; individuality was not available as a concept of intentions and purpose. By the eighteenth century, society appears as a concept that refers to the anonymous forces and structures that influence life and which gave that individuality, ironically, its independent existence. Liberalism and capitalism were expressions that overlapped this new possibility of individuality and sociality. The seventeenth century Englishman John Locke's political theory linked the consciousness of the self to the knowledge gained in the experiences of society. The Swiss Jean-Jacques Rousseau's notion of the *social* contract placed the relation of government and individuality in determining "the general will." Adam Smith's notion of markets gave focus to the abstract forces through which the individual pursued self-interest in the promotion of the good of society. The invention of notions of society and individual made possible collective belonging as the abstract qualities of global principles about humanity, economy, and culture were brought into the reflexivity of daily life.

Cosmopolitanism and the Homeless Mind

I focus in this discussion on the European and North American Enlightenment cosmopolitanism as a particular cultural thesis about the relation of society and individuality. I am interested in cosmopolitanism as a way of seeing and acting rather than as a normative ideal about who people should be (Popkewitz, 2008). Cosmopolitanism embodies notions of human agency ordered and classified through relations to distant events and values in a calculated time designed to order the present for planning the future. The "homelessness" of agency given as a generalized and universalized quality of "all humanity" in fact acts to create "homes" expressed through such concepts as, for example, the freedom, happiness, and self-development of the citizen.

Cosmopolitanism embodies a radical cultural thesis in which human reason and rationality change the world and people. The cosmopolitan thesis expressed the hope of the world citizen whose commitments to reason and science transcended provincial and local concerns. The purpose of reason and science was to bring human progress, based on transcendent, universal human values and rights, with hospitality, to others.

Cosmopolitanism is a cultural thesis about a mode of living that connects individuality with the social. It places individuals as freely acting agents bounded by universal, global values that in turn bind a shared polity. Theories of agency (like contemporary theories of globalization) were expressed in terms of nature, social structures and forces, and institutions that functioned as actors in the sense of having capacities to act on others (Meyer & Jepperson, 2000). If the Anglo-Saxon, French, and German-speaking worlds are given attention, the individual was a citizen who could know and act in the world that allowed for the discovery of an autonomous, "homeless" social order subject to its own laws (Wittrock, 2000, p. 42).[5] Time was directed to the present and future as principles through which the world and the self could be realized. Citizenship was the major signifier of giving a "home" to the qualities of transcendent values perceived as "homeless."

The entanglement of distancing and immediacy was particularly evident in the constitution of humanness and humanity. Tröhler (this volume) describes, for example, the emergence of agency that (re)visions Calvinist notions of salvation into issues of individual liberty and personal realization, social betterment, and the rescue of those who have fallen from the grace of progress. Using the language of political theory, agency entails the movement of the objective order of institutions into the realm of subjectivity that is administered in the name of freedom (Pocock, 2003). Modern school pedagogy related, for example, George Herbert Mead's (1934) "generalized other" and Dewey's "community"—both of which re-signified the agentic qualities that ordered shared responsibilities and social obligations at the turn of the twentieth century.

Human agency, as enunciated by the Enlightenment, brought together the universal and the local that included epistemologies of diversity and difference. Eisenstadt (2000) argues, for example:

[First] there arises the bridging of the transcendental and mundane orders—of realizing through conscious human agency, exercised in social life, major utopian and eschatological visions. A second emphasized a growing recognition of the legitimacy of multiple individual and group goals and interests, [and] as a consequence allowed for multiple interpretations of the common good. (p. 5)

That notion of diversity and difference, as I argue later, reveals a double gesture that instantiated a comparative system of reason that enunciates and divides the capabilities of the child, who holds the emancipatory future from those feared as threatening the promise of the historically local inscriptions as that of a global of global progress.

The ordering of conduct through principles of the agentic individual embodied the classification of distant spaces intricately bound to

the time in which life is enacted. This linking of global spatial proximity with the intimacy of daily life was expressed by Marx in the
nineteenth century as the "annihilation of space by time" (cited in
Tomlinson, 1999). The here and now of family life and childhood, for
example, stood within a continuum of the past (traditions) to the
present that held the possibilities of being re-ordered for things to
come. It became possible to think of curriculum as the movement
of time and space organized through school grades. Curriculum is a
chronology of distancing through "expanding horizons" that flow
from the study of the family, to the community, the state, the nation
and the globe (international). The organization of the curriculum
is governed through psychologies of the child that carry cosmopoli-
tanist theses in ordering "proper" development as the mode of life
of choices, self-responsibility, motivation, problem solving, and
participation.

Science was the technology for creating ways to actualize or
realize distant qualities of the moral, social, and political world in
everyday life. Science carried a millennial belief in rational knowledge
as a positive force for action. Many Enlightenment thinkers, for
example, found the answer to the dilemma of progress in knowledge
provided by science. Its methods would bring an infinite progress in
the natural world and morally righteous and productive lives to the
civil world. The task of the liberal human sciences was to provide the
rules and standards of reflection and action that enabled the pursuit of
cosmopolitan values about social progress and individual liberty and
happiness.

The categories are only of science, whose descriptions provide an
ordering for possible actions. The categories "act" in the sense that
they loop back to (and into) immediate experiences and events to
judge, for example, the child's growth and development as not only
physical but emotional and cultural. The self becomes an object of
reflection that brings universals into the immediate site of what constitutes the objects made as "experience." Enlightenment "reason," it
was believed, aided by observation and experience, "tames" change in
a world seen as otherwise conditional, insecure, ambiguous, and
potentially dangerous.

Cosmopolitanism and its Comparative Style of Reason

To this point, I have argued that globalization embodies a grid of
practices that bring particular cosmopolitan principles into daily life to

order face-to-face relations with spaces beyond the immediate. The norms of conduct seem to have no home except as generalized qualities of all humanity. Locating and "seeing" one's life in broader historical and moral environments was placed in a continuum of values through stages of growth, development, and evolution. The comparative quality is expressed in the French Enlightenment's *philosophes* who narrated the idea of civilization as a story of the evolution of a universal humanity through the application of reason. People were placed in a continuum of universal values and a hierarchy to order and divide people, races, and their civilizations as differences in ethnicity, differences of language, and differences between savagery and barbarism (Foucault, 2003).

The comparative qualities and universal aspirations of cosmopolitanism brought forth double gestures of the hopes of future progress and fears of the dangers and dangerous populations to the future. Reason, it was thought in the formation of the American republic, was unequally distributed. Only some "people" were considered as possessing reason. The binding of people was to be organized through common moral sentiments about humanity. The founders of the republic saw government as promoting "happiness negatively by restraining vices, while society was to promote virtues positively by uniting our affections" (Wood, 1999, p. 42). When the leaders of the American Revolution in 1776 claimed "all men" had the same common nature, that claim about the social order had particular boundaries about who had instinctive capacity for moral judgments (p. 41).

The comparative inscriptions in human development as a global affair—of universally held values and fears of danger to progress—were evident in the international expositions and World's Fairs of the end of the nineteenth century and the beginning of the twentieth (Lawn, 2009; Sobe, 2007; and this volume). The World's Fairs were embodied narratives and images of modernity and the progress of science, with schooling a central feature of their expositions. As Sobe argues in this volume, the international exhibitions presented what was thought of as a comprehensive, encyclopedic survey of the world that "did much to construct the reality of a 'single world' as an all-encompassing, texturally even sphere within codified distinctions and standardized differences." Particular principles about global events and people in time circulated as though they had no home except as part of a singular global reality.

To summarize: science is a technology through which globalization is given intelligibility as opening up new possibilities and limits to life itself. "Things" are placed into systems whose qualities embody a continuum of time and space that enable comparisons. That continuum seems independent of history yet makes possible reform in governing the future. The World's Fairs expressed science in the name of modernity and progress, as Rancière (2004) argues, through examining the logic of philosophy and sociology, comparability in which the arbitrariness of differences is made into necessity and inevitability (p. 205).

Numbers in Grids of Intelligibility: Making Sense of How Educational Truth Is Told

The entanglement of the global and the immediate in cosmopolitan reason and science embodied the categories of equivalence that compared and differentiated large groups of people as it related to their characteristics and capacities. The notion of population, invention of nineteenth century state government, functioned as a category of equivalence from which to compare groups. To "see" and act through categories of equivalence in order to establish global qualities of differences as sameness required numbers as human "facts." The seeming rigor and uniformity of numbers, as transported across time and space, appear to summarize complex events and transactions in a manner that projects fairness and impartiality (Porter, 1995).

This insertion of uniform rules was important to the institution of democratic regimes in the nineteenth century (Poovey, 1998). A global space was created that embodied the idea of giving all an equal chance and representation. The standardized subject of measurement and the act of exchange were no longer seen as dependent on the personalities or the status of the individuals involved.

The objectivity lent to numbers constituted domains and rendered them as stable forms that can be calculated, deliberated about, and acted on. One can easily recognize the use of economic statistics in contemporary discourses of globalization as *inscription devices* that shape and fashion the field of "acting." The collection and aggregation of numbers participate in a "clearing" of space where thought and action can occur (Rose, 1999, p. 212).

This clearing of space for thought and action has particular qualities in schooling that relate to this discussion of "the homeless mind" and globalization. The particular clearing created by numbers produces categories of equivalence that serve as "maps" in structuring experience, ordering what is considered as practical and useful as people think of the choices within an apparatus created through the categories of equivalence (Rose, 1999, p. 203). For example, OECD's Program for International Student Assessment (PISA), a measurement program about children's knowledge, orders the responses of children in science, mathematics, and literacy into categories of equivalence that rank nations along a continuum about readiness for the globalized world of the knowledge society.

PISA performs as a technology project for the global world to come and for comparing the global, "homeless" qualities of knowledge linked to the psychology of the child. PISA's emphasis on psychological categories about "motivation to learn and learning," for example, is not merely about the child's solving problems that will "open life opportunities." The measures of curriculum knowledge embody implicit choices about "what to measure, how to measure it, how often to measure it and how to present and interpret the results" (Rose, 1999, p. 199). The idea of motivation as a quality of learning, as Danziger (1997) argues, is a technology of distance that historically concerns the design of the interior of the child's desire that is directed to norms and values considered as universal and globally applied for "all" children. This treatment of inner "thought," daily life and experience as qualities of motivation appeared in the early twentieth century as objects of administration that had nothing to do with learning science, mathematics, and literacy. Today motivation is a category of ordering conduct given focus through psychologies of the child through notions of self-esteem and efficacy in social and educational planning.

Numbers represent a technology of "the homeless mind." Numbers standardize and relocate the abstract systems of knowledge as the spaces of personal knowledge. The contemporary use of international ranking of children's achievement, for example, performs as a navigational tool (Lindblad, 2008). The measurements provide constant performance indicators in a continual process of locating one's self in the world that are analogous to global positioning inscribed in the assessments. The testing categories establish equivalences in different national settings in, for example, the European Union. The instantiation of comparative categories creates a space of consensus and cohesion through its categories of equivalences (Grek, 2009).

Numbers insert individuality simultaneously in the universality of time and in the particular time of daily life. The uniformity given by numbers enabled social life to bring unlike orders of magnitude into a system that regularized the relations among social and psychological components (Rose, 1999, p. 206). The continual placement in environmental feedback loops functions as a permanent "global positioning" that provides the criteria to judge the choices made (Simons & Maschelein, 2008).

The inscription of numbers makes difference into sameness; and the categories of magnitudes produce tools to manufacture and assess differences from the global spaces of unity. The categories of creating equivalence re-inscribe and (re)vision difference and divisions through the structuring of universal norms and values as objects of reflection and action.

Distancing in the Immediacy of the Present: A Cosmopolitan Modes of Life and the Lifelong Learner

Numbers as an element of "the homeless mind" are taken for granted in contemporary policy discourses and research about globalization.[6] The cultural thesis about the modes of life of the child is told as that of the lifelong learner in the knowledge society and the knowledge economy.[7] These categories, which bring together numbers and international assessments into a grid of practices about the individual and society, underlie the Turkish Ministry of Education's identification of teacher competences, European policy documents about educational reforms, and American reforms that are to prepare the child for the twenty-first century. The PISA description expresses, for example, the importance of national comparisons of curriculum in producing "the lifelong learner" for the globalization embodied in the knowledge society.

Who is this lifelong learner and how does he or she relate to the "homeless mind" of cosmopolitanism? The lifelong learner entails a never-ending mode of living through making choices, innovation, and collaboration. The life of choice is to maximize happiness through continual processes of rationally planning and organizing daily events for a better future. Personal responsibility and self-management of one's risks is tied to continually maximizing the correct application of reason and rationality.

The lifelong learner embodies qualities of "the unfinished cosmopolitanism" by (re)visioning Enlightenment hopes about reason and rationality through an agency directed to ordering the present and future. This agency generates particular principles about what is thought, hoped for, and done. The principles of the self stand in relation to the social expressed as global events and values from which the interpretation, planning, and altering of personal conditions are to occur.[8] This mode of life entails processes of making constant choice and innovation that has no finishing line or public values in view. The lifelong learner continually chases desire in paths never completed and filled with uncertainties, hence its unfinished qualities—the only thing that is not a choice is making choices! (Popkewitz, 2008)

Simons and Maschelein (2008) argue that this new individuality entails the shift from earlier notions of emancipation to empower- ment in which individual life becomes a continual learning process. Individuality subsists in learning as the capacity for appropriations that engage the uncertainties of the present. Virtue is managing effectively the limits and opportunities of the environment through steering one's performances in a continual feedback loop of self-assessment.

Whatever the merits of problem solving in the school curriculum, it is not merely descriptive of some natural reasoning of the child that research recoups. *The cultural thesis of a life of choices and problem solving appears to be a strategy that brings conditions of society and "globalization" into a mode of daily existence that is innovative and flexible.* The rules and standards of participation operate through particular principles of reflection and action that connect individuality to collective belonging. Problem solving is a quality that can be associated with the homeless mind, a practice of ordering life that is rationally ordering life to find paths to the future, a practice that is never complete and always defers the present for the salvation of the future.

The ubiquitous boundaries of globalism are naturalized in this pursuit of choice and future salvation. The life of choice and problem solving is bound to a universe of capabilities that has multiple iden- tities and different flows of time that emerge through collaboration in communities. Where knowledge has no particular roots or provincial values but provides paths to salvation and "happiness" through its social bearings, the lifelong learner appears to tackle problems glo- bally and universally. Mathematics education standards reform and its research, for example, are underwritten by constructivist pedagogies that stress the knowledge of mathematics as a universal and with no social mooring or provincial roots. That knowledge is to enable the child to order and judge actions in everyday life. But the ways of learning mathematics have less to do with mathematics than with cre- ating universal spaces that historically relate to political and social theories of liberalism in the formation of personal conduct. Brousseau (1997), for example, argues that effective instruction is about the order of conduct, that is, to have children "want to" as well as "be able to"

(Brousseau, p. 12). The autonomy assigned to the problem solver is generated through social and cultural narratives that position mathematics education as the " 'modern' social answer to enable children to become citizens—that is, members of a society who have access to both a shared culture and who are empowered with intellectual and emotional tools to face problems within the workplace and everyday life" (Sutherland & Balacheff, 1999, p. 2).

The lifelong learner is a category of a human kind that seems to be in a timeless time that, ironically, is to fulfill the present through actions that are to make the future. The regulation of time brings forth regulated spaces that have no difference, conflict, or uncertainty. Those regulated spaces, however, realign time through both speed of communications and compressions, such as spaces embodied in the communication technologies of computers that can create instant messages and video transmission, and handle mass data and locate patterns within micro-seconds and from multiple sources and sites around the world. The skills and knowledges to prepare the child for the "knowledge economy" and the future require shedding "outmodeled traditions" of the past in order to live a new existence.

The lifelong learner is inserted into the spaces that perform as an updating yet re-visioning of the distancing practices that bind individuality and sociality. The collective identities and universal norms embodied in the nation-building of the previous century are replaced with images of globalization of the knowledge society and knowledge economy. The space of the lifelong learner segregates the past (before the knowledge society) from a flow of time of present and future. Individuality is cast in a transcendental anonymous and homeless existence that requires participation in communities. If properly identified and administered, a stabilized space of individuality is processed through a regularized movement of time to enable security and harmony to change itself.

The lifelong learner recalibrates political aspirations and collective belonging. Agency is shaped and fashioned through problem solving and collaborating in multiple communities—communities of learning and discourse communities. Time is multiple and compressed. Yet the resignifying of spatial and temporal dimensions of globalization overlap with notions of community and collaboration that tell of the collective obligation to generalized global values of humanity. If conduct is ordered properly, the hope is of self-empowerment, happiness, and empowerment with socially defined values about progress in a changing and diverse world.

The lifelong learner and community embody categories of equivalences homologous to those of numbers. The categories are about human kinds created by the uniformity of unlike qualities, uniformity that regularizes conduct through making equivalences through different social and psychological components. European and U.S. policies express the individuality and sociality of the lifelong learner through cosmopolitan values about reason, science, and hospitality to "others."

The Child Not in the Space of "All Children": The Urban Child Left Behind

The distancing that enables contemporary European and U.S. pedagogical practices about globalization, I have argued, embodies a particular cosmopolitan cultural thesis about individuality and society that is expressed in the lifelong learner as a human kind that lives and finds happiness in the knowledge society and the knowledge economy. That happiness is shaped and fashioned as the cultural thesis about life as driven by self-motivation, self-direction, and self-responsibility in a community of collaboration, the latter connecting individuality with a notion of society. The reason and rationality of cosmopolitanism projects qualities and capacities that are placed in spaces of a globalized world, the noun qualities serving to instantiate both the hope and threats to the envisioned future into the rules and standards of conduct. That globalization that brings distant values and events into the proximity of daily life, however, creates differences in its categories of equivalence. The cosmopolitanism of the lifelong learner is jointly occupied with its "other," who is abjected into spaces of living among different capabilities and capacities.

To explore this, I want to return to the discussion of numbers as taking differences as sameness and simultaneously comparing difference through the magnitudes created. This construction of difference/sameness/difference is a quality of the commonplace of school reforms about equity in educational processes and outcomes through the term "all children"—"all children learn" and "education for all." The Education for All movement exemplifies this strategy of equity through creating a unity among difference. Education for All is stated by UNESCO as "a global commitment to provide quality basic education for all children, youth and adults" and is endorsed by major international agencies[9] to provide an "expanded vision of learning" that is "pledged to universalize primary education and massively reduce illiteracy by the end of the decade."[10]

The cultural thesis of "all children" and equity embodies an in-between place of the child who requires rescue by establishing difference. That recognition and inscription of difference, excluded and abjected as difference, can "never be of the average." The differences are embodied in the cultural thesis of the lifelong learner whose modes of life form a continuum of norms and values from which to locate the child and populations whose modes of life are dangerous to that future.

The in-between spaces of inclusion, abjection, and exclusion can be explored in policy and research foci about education for *all*. The *all* implies a unity that immediately creates a comparative system that introduces the child who does not fit into the spaces of "all children" who can and will participate in the knowledge society; that is, the "child left behind" used in U.S. policy and research. The child left behind who is recognized for inclusion is inscribed, however, as different. That difference is through achievement data linked to data about income, family characteristics, and ethnic and racial populations that become assembled through what I previously called categories of equivalence. One such category is that of the cultural thesis of the *urban child* in the United States and the UK, which combines statistical data with social and cultural distinctions about gender, poverty, race, and psychological notions of inadequate development (e.g., lacking self-esteem). The urban child is a child whose characteristics and qualities are recognized for inclusion but remains different from the category that inscribed the equivalences for the unity of all children. That difference orders programs of rescue, remediation, and redemption.

The distinctions and differentiations of the urban child cross geographical boundaries to produce a determinate category of equivalence ordered by psychologies of low expectations, lack of self-esteem and motivation, social categories of "dysfunctional families," and pedagogical distinctions of learning through "hands-on" experience rather than the *urban* flexible, problem-solving progress of the lifelong learner (Popkewitz, 1998). The urban and rural child occupy, discursively and programmatically, the same space in the sense of the characteristics and qualities; qualities different from yet embodied in distinctions that form the spaces inhabited by the lifelong learner.

The placing of the unfinished cosmopolitan and its "others"—children who are outside of the spaces signified by in the term "all"—is to recognize each as embedded in the other and as part of the same phenomenon of schooling. If I use the American notion of the urban child, it embodies a cultural thesis that has little to do with geographical place. American cities, for example, are spaces with great wealth and a cosmopolitan urbaneness that coexist with the spaces of poverty and racial segregation. Children who live in the high-rise apartments and brownstones of American cities appear as urbane and not urban. The "urban child" does not live only in the inner city. The cultural space of the urban child is a universal, globalizing practice that is "homeless" as it traverses geography to include suburbia and rural areas.

Distancing through the categories of equivalence and comparison reveals processes of inclusion, exclusion, and abjection. This inscription, as mentioned earlier, has a dual gesture. The cultural theses are gestures of individuality, belonging, and dividing. The distancing that produces the lifelong learner is given characteristics that are global, its unity defining the spaces of "all children" that differentiate "others." The inscription of differences is not of distinctions of the civilized/non-civilized that ordered nineteenth-century thought. Differences are generated by principles of literacy, gender, access, and achievement through which individuality is recognized in groups for inclusion by dividing. The simultaneous processes of producing the "other" in one's self are not intentional but occur under the banner of "helping" and rescuing. *The processes are instantiated in the very style of thought through which the distancing and immediacy are established.*

The comparative processes that abjects is embodied in the homeless mind. Distant things without history or authorship are produced as categories of equivalence from which difference is made into sameness that seems to have no "home." That unity in homelessness, however, inscribes difference in the proximities of daily life.

Conclusions

Globalization is not merely a thing to explain and plan for. I argued that it is a particular fabrication in which principles are generated about thought and action. In pursuing globalization in this manner, I sought to consider the particular historical grid that gives intelligibility to the particular distinctions, differentiations, and divisions governing what is said, thought, and acted on. Globalization, I argued, is a particular category of the present that can help make visible the structuring of experience and thinking about who "we" are, should be, and who is not enclosed in that space of the "we."

My excursions with globalization took the quality of "the homeless mind" in modernity to think about how distancing qualities and characteristics are given proximity in ordering reflection and action. The "homeless mind," I argued, brings into focus particular qualities of cosmopolitanism that are taken for granted in the various discourses about globalization: the idea of human agency, the irreversibility of time, and change that is guided through the rules and standards of reason and rationality (science). Globalization becomes both a perceived source of anonymous "forces" that have no historical "home" or author and something that enables planning for interventions in daily life. Numbers as the construction of categories of equivalence "act" to establish a globalness. Sameness becomes inscribed as difference that stands outside of history. The irony of the practices of globalization lies in its simultaneous relocation into practices that link the collective belonging qualities given to society with homes—the homeless quality of reason makes homes!

To explore the irony embodied in globalization as a quality of the homeless mind, I explored the entanglements of distant events and spaces with the immediacies of everyday life in European and U.S. policy and research concerned with cosmopolitan "reason" and the reasonable person in cultural theses about the lifelong learner in the knowledge society and the knowledge economy. The home in the homeless is embodied in the phrase "think globally and act locally." That individuality was not only about the cosmopolitan child-as-future-citizen but the in-between places and exclusions that cast the child who does not embody the characteristics and capabilities of "all children" into unlivable spaces. While I focused on the European and North American Enlightenment cosmopolitanism as an analytic of study, that analytic also entails recognition of other notions of cosmopolitanism outside of the West as they bear on the qualities of the homeless mind in ordering the entanglements of the "global" in daily life.

The strategy of inquiry into globalization as a system of reason also has implications for the study of schooling. My continually "seeing" opposites as part of the same phenomenon—inclusion with exclusion, homelessness with collective belonging, and homes/distance with proximity/unity from difference and the ordering of difference—was to go against certain analytic philosophical traditions that underlie social and educational studies. If I return to the notion of fabrication introduced in the beginning of this chapter, its different nuances overlap: globalization is a response to things happening in the world; it is a fiction for responding to those ontic "things," and involves processes of making that world. There are theories about globalization, school programs to teach children about participating in the global world. The different nuances of fabrication are captured in the phrase "think globally and act locally." Whether the metonym is adequate or not, the analysis speaks to some of the issues embedded in rethinking and (re)visioning the study of the political in social life that is shaped and fashioned around globalization in governing.

NOTES

1. The phrase is used differently from the conceptual apparatus offered by Berger, Berger, and Kellner's (1974) institutional theories of bureaucracy and technological production. My focus here is the systems of reason, that is, the historically generated distinctions, differentiations, and divisions that order what is seen, thought about, and acted on (see Popkewitz, 1991, 2008).

2. As referenced earlier, my use of European and United States literature is pragmatic and serves as a strategy to think about the study of the relation of distance and proximity.

3. There were multiple theses outside of Europe and North America, as well as within the latter in Germany, France, North America, and other spaces. For the purposes of exploring the entanglements of distance and immediacy embodied in notions of cosmopolitanism, I use the singular of cosmopolitanism.

4. As someone who studied Greek art, I recognize that I am historically merging nuances to make my general points.

5. Ironically, the cosmopolitan citizen was to hold values and commitments that extended beyond the local, provincial and nation. This distancing was quickly brought into the construction of political communities that called for new ways of relating individuality with participation in government as exemplified in the modern European republics, and in some ways the later Ottoman Empire that straddled corridors linking Europe and Asia.

6. Numbers as ways of telling the truth and as facts emerge from different historical processes that become visible between the eighteenth and the early twentieth century; thus the term "long nineteenth century."

7. I use these terms as interrelated and often embodying the same principles of conduct. When there is talk about the knowledge economy in education, the discussion relates to a cultural thesis about modes of life that folds into discussions about the knowledge society and the lifelong learner. That discussion is not about economy, per se, but about modes of living.

8. This notion emerged in discussions with Ruth Gustafson.

9. For example, UNDP, UNFPA, UNICEF, and the World Bank

10. See http://www.unesco.org/en/efa-international-coordination/the-efa-movement/.

REFERENCES

Berger, P., Berger, B., & Kellner, H. (1974). *The homeless mind: Modernization and consciousness*. New York: Vintage.

Brousseau, G. (1997). *Theory of didactical situations in mathematics [Didactique des mathematiques, 1970–1990]*. N. Balacheff, M. Cooper, R. Sutherland, & V. Warfield (Trans.). Dordrecht: Kluwer.

Danziger, K. (1997). *Naming the mind: How psychology found its language*. London: Sage.

Eisenstadt, S.N. (2000). Multiple modernities. *Daedalus, 129*(1), 1–29.

Foucault, M. (2003). Society must be defended: *Lectures at the Collège de France, 1975–1976*. D. Macey (Trans.). New York: Picador.

Foucault, M. (2005). The hermeneutics of the subject: *Lectures at the Collège de France, 1981–1982*. G. Burchell (Trans.). New York: Picador.

Friedrich, D. (2009). *Historical consciousness as a pedagogical device in the production of the responsible citizen*. Unpublished paper. Madison: The Department of Curriculum and Instruction, The University of Wisconsin-Madison.

Grek, S. (2009). Governing by numbers: The PISA effect in Europe. *Journal of Education Policy, 24*(1), 23–37.

Hacking, I. (1986). Making up people. In T.C. Heller, M. Sosna, & D.E. Wellbery (Eds.), *Reconstructing individualism: Autonomy, individuality, and the self in western thought* (pp. 222–236, 347–348). Stanford, CA: Stanford University Press.

Lawn, M. (Ed.). (2009). *Modelling the future: Exhibitions and the materiality of education* (pp. 15–30). Oxford: Symposium Books.

Lindblad, S. (2008). Navigating in the field of university positioning: On international ranking lists, quality indicators, and higher education governing. *European Educational Research Journal, 7*(4), 438–450.

Lindblad, S., & Popkewitz, T. (2001, November). *Education governance and social integration and exclusion: Studies in the powers of reason and the reasons of power (A Report from the EGSIE Project)*. Uppsala, Sweden: Department of Education, Uppsala University.

Mead, G.H. (1934). *Mind, self and society: From the standpoint of a social behaviorist*. Chicago: University of Chicago Press.

Meyer, J., & Jepperson, R. (2000). The "actors" of modern society: The cultural construction of social agency. *Sociological Theory, 18*(1), 100–120.

Pocock, J.G.A. (2003). The *Machiavellian moment: Florentine political thought and the Atlantic republican tradition*. Princeton, NJ: Princeton University Press.

Poovey, M. (1998). *A history of the modern fact: Problems of knowledge in the sciences of wealth and society*. Chicago: University of Chicago Press.

Popkewitz, T. (1991). *A political sociology of educational reform: Power/knowledge in teaching, teacher education, and research*. New York: Teachers College Press.

Popkewitz, T. (1998). *Struggling for the soul: The politics of education and the construction of the teacher*. New York: Teachers College Press.

Popkewitz, T. (2008). *Cosmopolitanism and the age of school reform: Science, education, and making society by making the child*. New York: Routledge.

Porter, T. (1995). *Trust in numbers: The pursuit of objectivity in science and public life*. Princeton, NJ: Princeton University Press.

Rancière, J. (2004). *The flesh of words: The politics of writing*. C. Mandell (Trans.). Stanford, CA: Stanford University Press.

Rose, N. (1999). *Powers of freedom: Reframing political thought*. Cambridge: Cambridge University Press.

Simons, M., & Maschelein, J. (2008). From schools to learning environments: The dark side of being exceptional. *Journal of Philosophy of Education, 42*(3–4), 687–704.

Sobe, N.W. (2007). Attention and spectatorship: Educational exhibits at the Panama-Pacific international exposition, San Francisco 1915. In V. Barth (Ed.), *Innovation and education at universal exhibitions, 1851–2010* (pp. 95–116). Paris: International Bureau of Expositions.

Sutherland, R., & Balacheff, N. (1999). Didactical complexity of computational environments for the learning of mathematics. *International Journal of Computers for Mathematical Learning, 4*, 1–26.

Tomlinson, J. (1999). *Globalization and culture*. Chicago: University of Chicago Press.

Toulmin, S. (1990). *Cosmopolis: The hidden agenda of modernity*. New York: The Free Press.

Wittrock, B. (2000). Modernity: One, none, or many? European origins and modernity as a global condition. *Daedalus, 29*(1), 31–60.

Wood, G.W. (1999). The American love boat. *The New York Review of Books, 56*(15), 40–42.

Global Mobility and the Challenges of Educational Research and Policy

FAZAL RIZVI

Introduction

Over the past few decades, we have witnessed ever-increasing levels of mobility facilitated not only by the revolutionary developments in communication and transport technologies but also by major shifts in the ways in which economic and political activity is conducted. A number of chapters in this volume have noted how educational ideas now move, circulating globally, and how there are now new modes in the production and dissemination of educational knowledge that are globally calibrated. There have been wide-ranging discussions about the forms and extent of global policy convergence in educational policy around a neoliberal social imaginary (Rizvi & Lingard, 2009). Authors such as Steiner-Khamsi (2004), have sought to provide an account of the politics of "policy borrowing." While circulation of policy ideas in education have of course been greatly facilitated by advances in information and communication technologies, equally significant has been the role of international organizations such as the World Bank and the OECD—as indeed has been the part transnational corporations have played in demanding from national policy makers a particular set of educational policy configurations. In this sense, policy ideas have become mobile in consort with shifts in global economic activity, resulting in new patterns and practices associated with the global mobility of capital.

Of course it is not only capital and finance and images, information and ideologies that have become more mobile; people have as well. Never before in history have there been more people moving across national boundaries. People are moving for a whole host of reasons: for migration, as refugees, for trade and business, for employment opportunities, as tourists, to attend international conventions and conferences, and for education. There are more international migrants—both documented and undocumented—than ever before, even more than after the Second World War, when a large number of displaced people sought residence and safer havens around the world (Cohen &

Kennedy, 2007). Despite declining instances of major wars, political conflict, and famines, there are now more people registered as refugees with the United Nations than any time in that organization's history (Marfleet, 2005). Refugees today are more globally aware of possibilities. While, on the one hand, they have better sources of information, advice, and support from government and non-government organizations, they are more subject to criminal exploitative practices of "people smugglers" on the other.

With the globalization of economic activity and trade, business executives are constantly on the move, as are workers recruited and employed by transnational corporations. Many people, both professionally educated and those who are not, no longer hesitate, as they once did, to take employment opportunities abroad, creating a large global remittances economy, now estimated to be over 800 billion dollars (Guarnizo, 2003). Waters (1995, p. 154) has noted that international tourism, measured in terms of arrivals from another country, expanded 17-fold between 1950 and 1990, and that this rate is likely to have doubled since then. International conferences and conventions have become commonplace, despite enhanced possibilities of online communication. And the number of international students is now more than 2.2 million, up from just 300 000 in 1970, and is expected to more than double by 2020 (Guruz, 2008).

This unprecedented level of people mobility, in its various forms and possibilities, is of course linked to the ways in which global economic and political systems work. But, in a manner that is equally significant, the movement of people is also driven by consumer desire and subjective awareness of global opportunities, and is, in turn, transforming social institutions, cultural practices, and even the sense of identity and belongingness. Global mobility has certainly transformed cities, creating urban conglomerates at the intersection of global flows of finance and capital (Sassen, 1991). It is in these "global" cities that most international migrants settle, raising major issues of security, sustainability, and adaptation to the new conditions of cultural diversity. In global cities, people from diverse backgrounds live across multiple time horizons, creating conditions not only of risk and vulnerability, but also of opportunities.

Among these opportunities, education is ranked highly. Education has become a major driver of the global mobility of people, especially from developing countries to developed English-speaking countries. As a growing phenomenon, global trade in higher education (Marginson, 2006) is arguably linked to mobility of capital, and to opportunities that are now available in the transnational labor market. Many governments are thus developing immigration and labor recruitment policies that are closely aligned with the neoliberal policy objectives of international education. The ensuing mobility of students has transformed university campuses in countries like Australia, Britain, and the United States, making them more diverse and creating new pressures for curriculum reform.

The sociologist John Urry (2000, p. 1) has shown how these changes—"the diverse mobilities of peoples, objects, images, information and wastes; and . . . the complex interdependencies between, and social consequences of, these diverse mobilities"—have led to multiple new cross-national, cross-cultural flows and networks that define the global world of the twenty-first century. Another social theorist, Nicholas Papastergiadis (2000) suggests these transformations require new ways of thinking about movement and new ways of accounting for migration, since the traditional push-pull and structural theories of distinctions between economic and forced migration, and of representations based on classic South-North flows, are no longer adequate. More recently, Steven Vertovec (2009) has argued that the increasing level of people mobility has "transnationalized" space, both the places to which people gravitate and the places they leave, since the two places become inextricably connected, not only culturally and economically but also politically.

In this chapter, I focus upon the global mobility of people and consider what some of its drivers are. I explore the consequences it has in transforming not only the demographic composition of communities, but also the ways in which global interconnectivities now define the terrain in which social, economic, political and formations take place. I want to discuss how global mobility is transforming spaces, making them transnational, and how transnational identities and cultural practices are forged out of long-distance, cross-border connections among people. Against the backdrop of this discussion, I want to explore in particular how transnationalization of space has given rise to a number of new challenges for conducting educational research and developing educational policy.

Re-Thinking Mobility

There is nothing new about movement of people, both within and across nations. Historically, people have moved as migrants and refugees in search of jobs, security, and other opportunities, for trade, as tourists interested in experiencing exotic locations and cultural "others," in search of new knowledge, and as part of colonial conquests and indentured labor. There have always been what migration theorists call "push" and "pull" factors. People are pushed out of their communities as a result of local politics, resulting sometimes in physical insecurity, and at other times for the lack of opportunities for particular groups. On the other hand, people have also been attracted to mobility for a whole host of reasons, such as education and business. The contemporary global architecture cannot be adequately understood without historical references to mobility, which include both long established patterns of "diasporization" of communities such as the Indians, Chinese, and Jewish, and more recent colonial settlements, such as the United States and Australia, which displaced indigenous peoples and imported others, often with the exercise of considerable force and brutality, establishing new patterns of economic, social and political relations., The contemporary dynamics of mobility is continuous with some of these processes, but is also much more complex. Not only has the number of mobile people increased significantly in recent years, so have the ways people think about and approach mobility. In the past, mobility was relatively permanent; now it is more contingent and flexible, with new information and communication technologies enabling people to keep their options open and retain links with their countries of origin. Aihwa Ong (1999) has sought to understand the changing nature of global mobility. She argues that, in the era of globalization, mobile individuals develop a flexible notion of citizenship often designed to accumulate capital and power. The logic of capital accumulation is to "induce subjects to respond fluidly and opportunistically to changing political-economic conditions" (Ong. p. 33). In the global era, powerful incentives exist for individuals to emphasize practices that favor "flexibility, mobility and repositioning in relation to markets, governments and cultural regimes."

Ong (1999, p. 37) illustrates her general thesis by referring to Hong Kong Chinese immigrants to the United States, who "seem to display an élan for thriving in conditions of political insecurity, as well as in the turbulence of global trade." The diasporic Chinese, she suggests, have been the forerunners of the mobile people, who are always "on the move" both physically and culturally. Similarly, Beck (2000) has used the phrase "place polygamy" to underscore the ways in which, under the conditions of global capitalism, people are able to live in more than one place at once. This problematizes the notion of citizenship, a notion that has traditionally linked each citizen to a singular national origin.

In the contemporary context, people are able to have multiple senses of belonging.

This mobility generates a range of transnational practices and imaginings, resulting in a re-alignment of political, ethnic, and personal identities more conducive to "navigating the disjunctures between political landscapes and the shifting opportunities of global trade" (Ong, 1999, p. 29). This is not to suggest arbitrary geographical and social positionings, but rather more creative articulations between subject positions and regimes of localities, the extended family, the nation-state and global capital. Ong's work places transcultural practices at the center of discussions of globalization, in the production and negotiations of cultural meanings within the normative framework of late capitalism. It needs to be noted, however, that such negotiations of meaning are accompanied by various dilemmas for mobile people who are pulled in the direction of cultural flexibility on the one hand and cultural uncertainty and confusion on the other, producing a wide variety of complex and dynamic social configurations that cut across national borders.

Traditionally, discussions of mobility were largely couched in terms of a range of realist distinctions, such as between home and abroad and between emigration and immigration. What this brief discussion suggests is that, in the current phase of globalization, such distinctions are becoming overwhelmed by cultural and technological innovations, as people are able to not only travel with greater regularity and ease than ever before but are also able to remain in touch with each on a daily basis, using new media and communication technologies such as e-mail and Skype. These changes have swept across frontiers, contributing to the declining capacity of the nation-states to maintain borders.

Even as nation-states seek to tighten physical borders with heightened security regimes, they simultaneously work hard to attract skilled workers, international students, and of course tourists. What is clear then is that cultural borders are becoming increasingly porous. James Clifford's (1997) idea of "traveling cultures" captures some of the fuzzy logic of interpenetration of cultural mobility, to which many people have became increasingly attracted, even if they do not physically move. This has led to the emergence of new cultural practices, competences and performances that link together places that are otherwise widely separated. Clifford prefers the term "travel" because it underscores contingency and dynamism in ways that such terms as "tourism," "displacement," "nomadism," "pilgrimage," and "migration" do not. The notion of "traveling cultures" suggests a two-way relation, an interactive dynamic process. It indicates that the contemporary cultures of mobility can not be bound by exclusionary national security regimes. Imagined constructions of nation-states tie "locals" to a single place, gathering people and integrating ethnic minorities. Global mobility disrupts this logic of national "belonging," as people are able to imagine the possibility of belonging to several places at once. Clifford (p. 137) uses the phrase "dwelling in travel" to refer to "the experiences of mobility and movement, through which people develop a range of new material, spatial practices, that produce knowledges, stories, traditions, comportments, musics, books, diaries and other cultural expressions." In this way, mobility has the potential to re-shape not only cultural expressions and practices but also their association with particular territories.

Mobile people, such as denizens, global business people, and international students, may be viewed as exemplary carriers of "traveling cultures," because they link cultural practices across vast distances, allowing for the emergence of a post-national politics. They establish a space of exchange and communication, not necessarily based on a one-way determinism, but rather on a set of multi-faceted cultural practices. We should, however, be cautious about generalizing from this valorization of mobility and *trans*-national dwelling. Admittedly, traveling cultures are not available equally to everyone, and are certainly inflected by gender, class, and race considerations. As bell hooks (1992) has remarked, mobility can often be unsafe and insecure for women. It is experienced differently by different racial groups, and its social consequences are unevenly distributed. Under the conditions of globalization, according to Bauman (1998), voluntary mobility is available largely to elites, a new global cosmopolitan class of people. In a challenge to Clifford, he euphemistically calls them "tourists," the mobile people who contribute in one way or another to the rapid development of the consumer economy. In a globalized era, for the mobile tourists—the *trans*-national businessmen, culture managers, and knowledge workers—the "state borders are leveled down, as they are dismantled for the world's commodities, capital and finances" (Bauman, p. 89).

This of course does not mean that those who are not physically mobile across national boundaries are not affected by the mobility of those who are. To begin with, the people who do not travel are equally implicated in the relations of global capitalism. Not only do the flows of capital across borders have the potential to reshape entire communities; so do the globally reconstituted labor processes, even in the poorest parts of the world. Communities in Africa, for example, live in the shadows of global capitalism, as Ferguson (2006) points out. Global capital flows have resulted in changes in the mode of production and consumption, which affects the structures of opportunity and the life chances of people, both mobile and immobile. In a period of economic globalization, rapid technological shifts, post-Fordism, and the hegemonic dominance of neoliberal policies, not only has the nature of work and of work conditions been transformed, but so have people's aspirations and desires and the calculations they are now able to make about their sense of strategic location. The new media has become an important source in the development of these aspirations and desires, as people have been able to access information and develop a new perspective on career and even citizenship possibilities. Global mobility has thus transformed most, if not all, localities, affecting most aspects of our lives, including our identities, social relations, and institutions such as schools.

It is clear then that the increasing level of global mobility of people we now witness is both driven by and aligned with other mobilities—of capital and finance, of ideas and images and media and technologies. Our perceptions, experiences, and desires are increasingly shaped by these intersecting mobilities, converting localities into transnational spaces. Our identities are increasingly elaborated and negotiated within and against a transnational spatial awareness. As Morley and Robins (1995) argue: because places are no longer internally homogeneous, bounded areas, identities are increasingly constructed out of material and symbolic resources that reach beyond local boundaries, and are forged in transnational spaces which are mediated and mitigated by cultural turbulence of globalizing forces, connections, and desires.

Transnationalization of Space

The concept of "space" is central to my argument. In the past two decades, an understanding of space as an objective phenomenon has been largely abandoned (Massey, 2005), and replaced with an idea that suggests a social grid within which objects are located, events occur, and relations are articulated. In this sense, space is no longer assumed to be natural, describable solely in terms of pre-existing physical laws. Recent critical geographers such as Pile and Thrift (1995) contend that the search for general spatial laws is futile, because such laws explain little about the interrelationships between people and place, and do no reveal anything about patterns of human settlement and relationships. Indeed, as Crang and Thrift (2000, p. 2) argue, absolute and essentialized conceptions of space have paradoxically reduced the world to "spaceless abstraction." In contrast, critical geographers now favor a more relational view of space, which seeks to provide an account of how it is constituted and given meaning through the various dynamics of social relations. In this way, space no longer represents a passive geometry, but is continuously produced through socio-spatial relations: it is better conceived as a product of cultural, social, political, and economic interactions. Space is something that is socially experienced and named. As Massey notes, space is constituted through both social relations and material practices.

It should be noted, however, that space is not merely a social construction. In a very helpful analysis, Soja (1989) makes a useful distinction between space and spatiality, suggesting that while not all space is socially produced, all spatiality is. His analysis is thus focused both on the symbolic construction of space at the level of social imaginary as well as its more concrete articulation in the landscape. In this way, while a university, for example, can be minimally represented as a spatial allocation that has a physical form, it is, more accurately, a complex phenomenon given meaning through rules, myths, language, and rituals that speak to its spatial form—it is defined by a set of social relations and cultural practices. Lefebvre (1991) argues that space is produced through three interrelated processes. First, any characterization of space involves a set of spatial practices through which flows and movements are identified in the realm of everyday routines. Second, space is produced through a set of "representations of space" in images, books, media, and so on. These serve to represent and make sense of space. Such representations have the capacity to reproduce space, working ideologically to legitimate or contest particular spatial practices. And, finally, space is a lived, felt, and experienced phenomenon we negotiate through the contingencies of everyday life, as we look back to our histories, describe our social relations, and express our aspirations. Space is thus imbued with ideological and political content. It involves dealing with broader structures, including various contrasting representations of space and spatial practices.

This complex relational view of space represents a most useful theoretical resource with which to understand the contemporary drivers, forms, and consequences of global mobility, and the challenges they pose for educational research and policy. Spatial analysis of mobility is useful not least because mobility is primarily a spatial notion. Moreover, spatial analysis is helpful not only because it underscores the importance of human agency, but also because it points to the connections between macroeconomic and geopolitical transformations and the patterns of social action. It suggests a need to account for the ways in which human agents interpret, engage with, and negotiate various generalized processes associated with globalization, at the level of their own constructions, intentionality, everyday practices, social relationships, and collective action. With respect to global mobility, a spatial analysis highlights the ways in which patterns of social interaction are changing, and now occur in spaces that are transnational. In this way, spatial analysis does not presuppose a transparent social process, but suggests the need to describe "the messiness of living and acting in the mediated world of today" (Morris, 1993, p. 39).

Transnationalism has emerged in recent years as a powerful new concept with which to understand how the world is now constituted by cross-border relationships; patterns of economic, political, and cultural relations; and complex affiliations and social formations that span the world. It names the multiple and messy proximities through which human societies have now become globally interconnected and interdependent. According to Vertovec (2009, p. 3), transnationalism describes:

> . . . a condition in which, despite great distances and notwithstanding the presence of international borders (and all the laws, regulations and national narratives they represent), certain kinds of relationships have been globally intensified and now take place paradoxically in a planet-spanning yet common—however virtual—arena of activity.

In this sense, the idea of transnationalism suggests that systems of ties, interactions, exchange, and mobility spread across and span the world.

Vertovec (2009) discusses what he calls three different "takes" on the transnational. First, he suggests, transnationalism may be viewed as a kind of social formation spanning borders. "Dense and highly complex networks spanning vast spaces are transforming many kinds of social, cultural, economic and political relationships," he suggests (p. 5), producing in a transnational public sphere that has rendered a strictly bounded sense of community obsolete. Second, Vertovec argues, transnational networks have produced a type of consciousness, marked by multiple senses of identification comprising ever-changing representations. Third, transnationalism involves a mode of cultural reproduction, associated with "a fluidity of constructed styles, social institutions and everyday practices" (p. 7). Fourth, transnationalism is linked to new practices of capital formations that arguably involve globe-spanning structures or networks that have largely become disconnected from their national origins. Thus, new global systems of supply, production, marketing, investment, and information management have become major drivers for much of the world's transnational mobility and practices. Fifth, transnationalism may be viewed as a site for political engagement where cosmopolitan anti-nationalists often exist alongside reactionary ethno-nationalists within various diasporas, representing the dynamism of the relationships between different sites of political activity. And finally, and perhaps most importantly for my argument, Vertovec suggests that transnationalism has reconstructed localities, regrouping, as a result of the mobility of both people and ideas, the practices and meanings derived from multiple geographical and historical points of origin. Transnationalism, he observes, has changed "people's relations to space particularly by creating transnational 'social fields' or 'social spaces' that connect and position some actors in more than one country" (p. 12).

Challenges of Educational Research

Now if this account is even partially accurate in describing how localities around the world are becoming "transnationalized," then its implications for educational research are profound. How do we, for example, research spaces that do not have any clear boundaries and where social relations potentially span vast distances? How do we take into account the distribution and dynamics of power whose contours potentially involve the entire globe? How do we provide accounts of social meaning when these are not linked to any specific community? How do we study social inequalities when their causes do not necessarily reside within the community that is the object of our research? In other words, how do we address the conceptual difficulties that inevitably arise in research concerning social phenomena such as education, when the very construction of "the social" cannot be easily defined?

Educational research has traditionally involved the collection and analysis of information about how people relate to each other, how they make social meaning, how education is positioned within a broader sets of social processes, how educational institutions work, and how pedagogy and curriculum should be organized. This is done within some specified locality or organization. This implies that educational research almost inevitably occurs within an assumed space, be it a social organization like a school or a community marked by deep, familiar and co-operative ties between its members and defined by its geographical borders. While research can, of course, have many purposes—to provide an account of identities, to understand how people make

meaning of their lives, to explain social, economic and political relations, to reveal patterns of inequality and power, to determine deep
structural barriers to the realization of objectives and so on—it always
takes place within a space. We cannot therefore ignore the issues of how,
in the era of globalization, space is constituted and how its boundaries
are drawn.

Of course, as we have already noted, space is never constituted in a
uniform and consistent manner. Not all spaces are transnationalized in
the same way or, indeed, to the same extent. Some spaces, like such
global cities (Sassen, 1991) as Chicago or London, have become transnationalized to a greater extent than isolated rural communities in
Africa, for example. In this sense, transnationalization may be viewed as
an ongoing dynamic social process affected by changing forms of connectivity between the global and the local, between a community's
interior and its exterior. At a conceptual level, however, the notion of a
transnational space would seem to undermine any meaningful distinction between the inside of a space and its outside, long regarded as
central to educational research. If such traditional naturalistic distinctions as the inside and outside of a community or an organization
cannot be easily maintained, then many new challenges emerge for
educational research.

In recent years, numerous ethnographers have pointed out, for
example, that, in the emerging global context, both the ideas of "ethno"
and "graphic" have become problematic. The relationship between
ethnographers and the people they studied was already complex, but in
transnational spaces new questions arise around such key terms as "oth-
ering" and "authorial" control, leading to what Wittel (2000, p. 1) calls
a "crisis in objectification." With respect to the idea of "ethno," a
culture can no longer be treated as a coherent entity that has a unique
form unaffected by its engagement with other cultures. Through
enhanced mobility of capital, people, and ideas, cultural contact has
become a norm, leading Clifford (1997) to suggest that human location
is now constituted by displacement as much as by stasis.

With deterritorialization, pluralization, and hybridization of cultures, the notion of "the field" as a geographically defined research area
has also become more complex. As Marcus and Fischer (1986) point
out, the transnational, political, economic and cultural forces that now
shape localities have undermined the traditional notion of "the field."
Gupta and Ferguson (1997) therefore suggest the need to redefine the
notion of "the field" by "decentering" it in ways that deny any clear-cut
distinction between "the here" and "the elsewhere." If people and

objects are increasingly mobile, then, Gupta and Ferguson argue, ethnography has to engage these movements and, with them, the ways in
which localities are a product of the circulations of meanings and identities in time-space. Research must become embedded self-consciously
within the world systems, changing its focus from single sites and local
situations to become multi-sited and multi-local, responsive to networked realities.

George Marcus (1998) has argued that multi-sited ethnography
makes it possible to research objects that are on the move. He argues
that social sites have never been silos with people of objects waiting to
be found, ethnographically or otherwise. Most ethnographers in the
field of education appear to assume boundedness with respect to the
field and object of their inquiry. However, as Nespor (1997, p. xi) points
out, "by looking at schools as somehow separate from cities, politics,
neighborhoods, businesses and popular culture," educational ethnographers "obscure how these are all inextricably connected to one another,
how they jointly produce educational effects." Once the realities of
transnational spaces are recognized, Nespor's point can now be
extended to underscore the need to also understand transnational relationalities, drawing attention to the ways in which different sites are
globally interconnected and may now be jointly produced

Castells (2000) has drawn our attention to the ways in which our
communities are becoming globally networked. A "network society"
for Castells is an open structure, able to expand without limits and in
ways that are dynamic. It consists of a set of nodes and connections
across the nodes, characterized by flows and movement. The Internet
is a good example of how its ubiquitous uses are re-shaping our everyday practices, affected, as they are, by the ways in which information
flows across various nodes of networks, in spaces that are highly mediated and interactive. These nodes are often transnational, and deeply
connect us to social networks that do not necessarily reside within a
specific territory.

What these attempts by Marcus, Castells, Gupta and Ferguson and
many others to craft a new way of approaching research in a world of
greater global interconnectivity show is that transnational spaces are
difficult to research because they are characterized by greater levels of
displacement, dynamism, contingency, plurality, and complexity. They
challenge some of the most taken-for-granted categories in educational
research, and potentially demand new theoretical and methodological
resources. One of the theorists who has written about the need for
developing a new way of thinking about social research is John Urry,

who has noted how various global processes "raise implications for most of the categories by which sociology and other social sciences have examined the character of social life" (2003, p. 2), transforming "many existing sociological controversies, such as the relative significance of social structure, on the one hand, and human agency, on the other." Urry insists that this disruption should not be viewed as merely an extra level or domain that can be "added" to existing sociological analyses that can carry on regardless (p. 3): a fundamental transformation is needed to explore the concepts of structure, flow, ideology, performance, and complexity that are associated with the dynamic character of transnationality.

Global mobilities have thus transformed the social fields and objects of education. They require a new understanding of time and space, and of the relationalities between them. Traditionally, space and time and have been interpreted against the backdrop of assumptions of linearity, regularity, and stasis. None of these assumptions can now be taken for granted. Urry (2003) has used recent developments in complexity theory to show how the social is in fact open-ended, uncertain, evolving, and self-organizing, and mobility unsettles the assumption of social order which has long been assumed to be the key problematic of social research. In the functionalist tradition in particular, the central issue for social research is how social order is secured and sustained (see, e.g., Parsons, 1960). The problematics of transnational mobility have rendered this issue obsolete, because the criss-crossings of social formations have resulted in complex interconnections with non-linear and unpredictable outcomes. This has meant that order and chaos are always intertwined.

This approach to understanding social phenomena as articulations of global complexity has major implications for education. Traditionally, nation-building has been one of the key tasks allocated to formal education. Each nation has been assumed to represent an apparently separate society, with its own ways of celebrating a "banal nationalism." Education has played a major role in securing and sustaining the presumed national order. But as Urry (2003, p. 107) points out, "the development of global complexity means that each such banal nationalism increasingly circulates along the global informational and communicational channels and systems." In the context of global mobility and the transnational processes to which it has given rise, nation-states have increasingly had to deal with, not a fixed and clear-cut national population, but a complex cultural diversity characterized by a fluid and dynamic set of relationships. This has posed a range of new policy challenges for nation-states, caught between the need to keep social order, on the one hand, and to work with recognition of complex diversity on the other. It is to a discussion of this policy dilemma to which I now turn.

Policy Challenges in Education

Cultural diversity has always existed in human societies. But in a globally mobile world, issues of diversity have become more complex. We have become increasingly aware of our interconnectivity and inter-dependence, and yet we confront conditions in which differences are exploited as communities increasingly define their identities against the encroaching forces of globalization and against each other. Touraine (2000) argues that although we desire diversity and mobility, we none-theless feel that our cultural distinctiveness is increasingly under attack by homogenized mass culture. Most nation-states now confront a dilemma of how to develop public policies which acknowledge the importance of cultural diversity within the context of a globalizing world, in which problems and their solutions are interconnected and transcend national boundaries, but insist upon the importance of social order based on a core set of values. A new policy understanding of intercultural relations is clearly needed, which uses "a new analytical optic which makes visible the increasing intensity and scope of circular flows of persons, goods, information and symbols" (Cagler, 2001, p. 607), on the one hand, and which addresses anxieties about these flows on the other.

These questions are of course not new. For many years, nation-states have struggled with issues of how best to interpret diversity and construct simultaneously a moral universe in which policies operate with a relatively stable understanding of society. In the context of extensive global mobility, these questions have clearly become more complicated. New patterns of mobility and resultant interconnectivities have contributed to a sense of urgency. In such a context, traditional institutions such as schools appear to have also lost their capacity to cope with the new modalities of cultural difference and social complex-ity. As we move rapidly from imagining nations-states as constituted by unitary cultures to spaces that are characterized by significant levels of cultural diversity and exchange, public policy struggles to define ways of both celebrating these new conditions and keeping them in check.

From the public policy point of view, it has been through the discourse of multiculturalism that many countries have sought to deal with these issues. Multiculturalism suggests that all citizens, no matter what their cultural background, should be able to contribute to a nation's cultural and economic development, and that it is the role of the state and its institutions, such as schools, to create conditions necessary for all citizens to be able to realize their potential. The policy discourse of multiculturalism, developed during the 1970s, has not, however, been without its problems. It is just as well to remember that in countries like Canada, Australia and the UK, multiculturalism emerged as a compromise formation designed to pacify increasingly volatile ethnic communities and their supporters on the one hand, and to allay the fears of the dominant cultural groups, alarmed by the changing demography of their cities, on the other. It turned out partly to be a strategy for managing inter-group relations and accommodating the interests of the ethnic middle class (Rizvi, 1985). At the same time, multiculturalism provided ethnic communities with symbolic resources around which they could organize themselves politically, utilizing a new politics of difference (Young, 1990).

As a policy construct, the idea of multiculturalism remains highly contested. This should not surprise anyone, because, like other politically contested ideas such as equality, democracy, and autonomy, it does not admit any clear-cut definition. There are a number of competing discourses of multiculturalism. Each definition seeks a new accommodation between and assemblage across competing values, and is often resisted by dominant groups unprepared to give up their privileges, on the one hand, and by the minority communities suspicious of compromise formulations on the other. The debates surrounding the educational implications of cultural diversity are located within this contested political terrain, either as part of popular discourses, as is the case in the United States, or as a state-sponsored policy, as has been the case in Australia and Canada.

Yet, despite opposition to its competing formulations, multiculturalism has proved to be a fairly flexible and dynamic concept, able to accommodate changing economic, political, and cultural conditions. For example, multiculturalism has been able to work simultaneously with a politics of redistribution embodied in its emphasis on access and equity, and a politics of recognition expressed in its support for the right of minority communities to maintain their cultural traditions. It has even been able to work with the neoliberal discourses of economic efficiency and market rationalism. It is assumed, for instance, that skills of intercultural communication are essential for global trade in services in particular. The idea of "productive diversity" (Cope & Kalantzis,

2002), for example, seeks to promote multiculturalism as a response to the requirements of the knowledge economy.

Flexible though the notion of multiculturalism clearly has been, I argue that it has remained trapped within a set of nation-centric assumptions. It continues to address issues of cultural diversity within a national framework. It thus appears divorced from the processes of cultural globalization that are increasingly affecting the ways in which many people think about their identity, their sense of belonging and the transnational spaces they inhabit. If multiculturalism is to survive as a useful policy concept, then it cannot remain tied exclusively to the agenda for managing inter-ethnic relations within the nation-state. For it to be useful in dealing with the transnational and transcultural spaces that have become central to attempts to deal with what Urry (2003) refers to as "global complexity," multiculturalism needs to interpret the local and the national within the wider global context. It has to deal, for example, with the diasporic spaces that enable many people to now belong simultaneously to more than one country, and to forge their identity within the context of economic, social, and political relations that span national boundaries (Cohen & Kennedy, 2007).

Globalization has encouraged new ways of thinking about cultural identities (Tomlinson, 2000). It is no longer useful to think about identities in terms of a set of closed cultural boundaries expressed in language, arts, and cultural traditions, bracketed as homogenized entities frozen outside history and contemporary interactive cultural relations, located within particular national spaces. Within a nation, the relationship between ethnic communities and their originating cultures can no longer be treated as a clear-cut one. This relationship is much more complex than can be captured by notions of nostalgia, of collective memory, or of desire for singular attachment (Ahmed, Castañeda, & Fortie, 2004).

The popular discourses of multiculturalism embrace a notion of culture that is inherently naturalistic and anthropological, conceptualized as a "way of life." Not surprisingly, therefore, in public policies this focus on "way of life" is reduced to cultural forms made most visible in language, habits and customs, and iconic objects. This reduction both appeals and lends itself to cultural essentialism. By ignoring and obscuring its historical and political construction, the discourse of multiculturalism runs the risk of reifying culture, and accords it an autonomous status. This essentialism implies that society is fundamentally constituted by an uninterrupted accord between diverse cultural traditions and that, as a consensual social site, it can accommodate differences in an impartial manner. However, as a number of critics (e.g., Papastergiadis, 2000) have pointed out, this pluralism ignores not only the workings of power and privilege but also the contemporary transnational spaces in which rights and responsibilities are negotiated. It presupposes harmony and agreement as natural states within which differences can co-exist without disturbing the prevailing norms.

The main problem with this view of intercultural relations is that it interprets difference as involving negotiations among culturally diverse groups against a backdrop of presumed homogeneity. There is a failure to recognize that identities are forged in histories of differentially constituted relations of power; that is, knowledges, subjectivities, and social practices, including practices of cultural negotiation, are established within asymmetrical and often incommensurate cultural spaces, even more so in transnational spaces. Identity is thus a dynamic relational concept, established by symbolic markings in relation to others. It is therefore a construct, maintained and developed in response to changing social and material conditions. It does not therefore so much frame intercultural relations as it is framed by them.

In transnational spaces, as Stuart Hall (1996) has argued, cultural identity needs to be understood in terms of a politics of location, positionality, and enunciation—not so much as a process of discovery of lost "roots," but as a construction of a "new" or "emergent" form of understanding of ourselves, linked to both contemporary social relations and prevailing relations of power. If this is so then public policy makers must accept the contemporary transnational condition to be necessarily complex and culturally "hybrid." It cannot be neatly packaged as a collection of ethnicities, for the purposes either of administrative convenience or hegemonic control. The idea of hybridity, with its connotations of mixture and fusion, applies unequivocally to the role of education in negotiating transnationalism as a space in which educational policy must learn to manage cultural uncertainties as it imagines and projects both the nation and the global condition..

If hybridity is a basic outcome of global mobility, then we need to remind ourselves that it has never been possible to know cultures in their pristine and authentic form. Instead, our focus must shift to the ways in which cultural forms become separated from existing practices and recombine into new forms, and into new practices in their local conditions set against global forces. In a world in which flows of information, media symbols and images, and political and cultural ideas are constant and relentless, how we understand and negotiate new cultural formations becomes a key educational challenge. In a world increasingly constituted by flows of finance, technology, and people, through tourism, education, and migration, hybridization has become a normal default condition of social existence, and is no longer something that can be regarded as exceptional.

Policy makers need to consider how, in transnational spaces, the idea of intercultural relations might be re-interpreted, for these relations are now appropriately viewed as complex and inherently unstable products of a range of historical factors, as well as of the contemporary experiences of the cultural economies of globalization. Such cultural economies are increasingly restructuring our established ways of looking and working across cultures, even if some policy makers and institutions appear reluctant to recognize this. And such is the pace of cultural change that the politics of looking and working across cultural differences involves inherent fluidity, indeterminacy, and open-endedness.

Recent theorists of cultural globalization use the notion of "deterritorialization" (Tomlinson, 2000) to suggest that the localities where we live our everyday lives have become imbricated in broader global relations. Néstor García Canclini (1998), for example, refers to "the loss of the 'natural' relation of culture to geographical and social territories." Similarly, Tomlinson suggests a "weakening or dissolution of the connection between everyday lived culture and territorial location." Tomlinson argues that increased global mobilities are deterritorializing forces that have the effect of re-shaping both the material conditions of people's existence and their perspectives on the world. He insists that this has led to "the gradual and constant alterations in the cognitive maps of people, in their loyalties and in their frames of social and cultural reference" (Tomlinson, p. 34). Global mobilities have enabled people to express cultural diversity as dynamic and creative, but they have also led to the homogenization of cultural practices and contributed to some people becoming dislodged from their communities, removed from their social links and obligations. Either way, Tomlinson argues, deterritorialization has been a powerful transformative agent in an era in which borders and boundaries are quickly eroding and becoming more porous.

If this is so, then should we not assume that the world will gradually become standardized through technological, cultural, and commercial synchronization? In my view, to assume that cultural globalization necessarily results in homogenization is to misread the complex processes involved. It is to assume, for example, that the West, however it is now characterized, remains unaffected by the processes of economic, political, and cultural globalization. While the local is always transformed as a result of engagement with others, this transformation is never uniform across cultural sites; globalization produces new hybrid formations that are highly context-specific and localized. As Piterese (2005, p. 87) puts it, the cultural uniformity and standardization argument "overlooks the counter-currents—the impact that the non-Western cultures have been making on the Western cultural practices. It downplays the ambivalence of the globalizing momentum and ignores the role of local reception of Western cultures, for example, the indigenization of Western elements." It overlooks the fact that different parts of the same community may in fact relate differently to the same social processes.

In the context of growing transnationalism, then, interculturality is always political; and it underlines the processes of fuzziness, cut-and-mix, and criss-cross and crossovers of cultural formations referred to as the processes of cultural hybridization. But this hybridization is never neutral; it involves a politics in which issues of economic and cultural power are central. As Shohat and Stam (1994) have argued, "A celebration of syncretism and hybridity *per se*, if not articulated with the issues of hegemony and neo-colonial power relations, always runs the risk of appearing to sanctify the *fait accompli* of colonial violence." As a theoretical idea, hybridity is indeed a useful antidote to cultural essentialism, but cannot in itself provide the answers to the difficult questions of how hybridity takes place, the form it takes in a particular context, the consequences it has for particular sections of the community, and when and how particular hybrid formations are progressive or regressive.

These political questions of hybridity need to be placed within a broader transnational politics that is helping to re-shape people's sense of themselves and others. As I have suggested, through accumulation strategies, mobility, and modern mass media, people are no longer linked just to one place, but through their transnational connections and imagination may identify with a number of locations. Globalization has engendered complex, shifting, and fragmented subjectivities that are at once local, yet also global. This demands new kinds of social organization that are equally deterritorialized, flexible, and mobile. At the same time, globalization has resulted in the proliferation of new commodity markets, which promote new life-styles and create consumers whose cultural identities are defined by their association with products rather than with their obligations to particular communities.

A new education policy agenda needs to take account of these changing conditions. But here too we confront further challenges.

While we might support initiatives that recognize shifting and hybrid cultural practices, we cannot afford to simply valorize difference and hybridity, allowing such processes to be simply framed by transnational cultural markets, media, and capital. In recent years, neoliberal states have indeed celebrated the emergence of global markets in the production, consumption and distribution of cultural diversity, consistent with the imperatives of what has been referred to as "globalization from above." But we need to pay attention equally to the realities of other practices of globalization: "globalization from below," which involves the criss-crossing transnational circuits of communication, the contested practices of place-making, the resistance of power differentials, and the making of new identities with their corresponding fields of difference.

Conclusion

In this chapter, I have shown how globalization has given rise to increasing levels of mobility, not only of capital and finance, images, information, and ideologies, but also of people. Focusing on the global mobility of people, I have argued that it has helped "transnationalize" most communities. This has rendered any strictly bounded sense of community obsolete. Transnationalism has given rise to new social formations that cut across national borders, leading to the emergence of certain kinds of relationships that are not only globally networked but also intensified. This account of global mobility and transnational social formations, I have argued, poses major new challenges for both research and policy in education. With deterritorialization, pluralization, and hybridization of cultures, the idea of a geographically bounded object and field of educational research has become hard to sustain. Educational research must therefore pay attention to the transnational spaces which are constituted by new relationalities that are necessarily non-linear, complex, open-ended, and evolving. This must involve a shift in focus from order and stasis to uncertainty and dynamism. With respect to educational policy, global mobility represents both opportunities and challenges. The opportunities relate to the possibilities of cultural creativity and a cosmopolitan future. The challenges involve a range of policy dilemmas: how to represent and deal with the cultural diversity that global mobility has enhanced, and how to develop a new policy optic which makes visible the increasing intensity and scope of circular flows of persons, goods, information, and symbols.

REFERENCES

Ahmed, S., Castañeda, C., & Fortie, A. (2004). *Uprootings/regroundings: Questions of home and migration*. Oxford: Berg Publishers.

Bauman, Z. (1998). *Globalization: The human consequences*. Cambridge: Polity Press.

Beck, U. (2000). *What is globalization?* Cambridge: Polity Press.

bell hooks (1992). *Teaching to transgress: Education as the practice of freedom*. New York: Routledge.

Cagler, A. (2001). Constraining metaphors and transnationalization of spaces in Berlin. *Journal of Ethnic and Migration Studies, 27*(4), 601–613.

Canclini, N.G. (1998). *Hybrid cultures: Strategies for entering and leaving modernity*. Minneapolis: University of Minnesota Press.

Castells, M. (2000). *The rise of the network society* (2nd ed.). Oxford: Blackwell.

Clifford, J. (1997). *Routes: Travel and translation in the late twentieth century*. Cambridge, MA: Harvard University Press.

Cohen, R., & Kennedy, P. (2007). *Global sociology* (2nd ed.). New York: New York University Press.

Cope, W., & Kalantzis, M. (2002). *Productive diversity*. Sydney: Pluto Press.

Crang, M., & Thrift, N. (Eds.). (2000). *Thinking space*. London: Routledge.

Ferguson, J. (2006). *Global shadows: Africa in the neo-liberal world order*. Durham, NC: Duke University Press.

Guarnizo, L.E. (2003). Economics of transnational living. *International Migration Review, 37*(3), 666–699.

Gupta, A., & Ferguson, J. (1997). *Culture, power and place: Explorations in critical anthropology*. Durham, NC: Duke University Press.

Guruz, K. (2008). *Higher education and international student mobility in the global knowledge economy*. Albany: State University of New York Press.

Hall, S. (1996). New ethnicities. In D. Morley & K.-H. Chen (Eds.), *Stuart Hall: Critical dialogues in cultural studies* (pp. 441–449). London: Routledge.

Lefebvre, H. (1991). *Critique of everyday life: Introduction*. London: Verso.

Marcus, G. (1998). *Ethnography through thick and thin*. Princeton: Princeton University Press.

Marcus, G.E., & Fischer, M.M.J. (1986). *Anthropology as cultural critique: An experimental moment in the human sciences*. Chicago: University of Chicago Press.

Marfleet, P. (2005). *Refugees in a global era*. Basingstoke, UK: Palgrave.

Marginson, S. (2006). Dynamics of national and global competition in higher education. *Higher Education, 52*, 1–39.

Massey, D. (2005). *For space*. London: Sage.

Morley, D., & Robins, K. (1995). *Spaces of identity: Global media, electronic landscapes and cultural boundaries*. London: Routledge.

Morris, M. (1993). Introduction. In J. From & M. Morris (Eds.), *Australian cultural studies: A reader* (pp. 3–24). Sydney: Allen and Unwin.

Nespor, J. (1997). *Tangled up in school: Politics, space, bodies, and signs in the educational process*. Mahwah, NJ: Lawrence Erlbaum.

Ong, A. (1999). *Flexible citizenship: The cultural logics of transnationality*. Durham, NC: Duke University Press.

Papastergiadis, N. (2000). *The turbulence of migration: Globalization, deterritorialization and hybridity*. Cambridge: Polity Press.

Parsons, T. (1960). *Structure and process in modern societies*. New York: Free Press.

Pile, S., & Thrift, N. (1995). Mapping the subject. In S. Pile & N. Thrift (Eds.), *Mapping the subject: Geographies of cultural transformation* (pp. 13–54). London: Routledge.

Piterese, J.N. (2005). *Globalization and culture*. London: Routledge.

Rizvi, F. (1985). *Multiculturalism as an educational policy*. Geelong: Deakin University Press.

Rizvi, F., & Lingard, R. (2009). *Globalizing education policy*. London: Routledge.

Sassen, S. (1991). *The global city: New York, London, Tokyo*. Princeton, NJ: Princeton University Press.

Shohat, E., & Stam, R. (1994). *Unthinking eurocentrism: Multiculturalism and the media*. London: Routledge.

Soja, E. (1989). *Postmodern geographies: The reassertion of space in critical social theory*. London: Verso.

Steiner-Khamsi, G. (Ed.). (2004). *The global politics of educational borrowing and lending*. New York: Teachers College Press.

Tomlinson, J. (2000). *Globalization and culture*. Chicago: University of Chicago Press.

Touraine, A. (2000). *Can we live together? Equality and difference*. Stanford, CA: Stanford University Press.

Urry, J. (2000). *Sociology beyond societies: Mobilities for the twenty-first century*. London: Routledge.

Urry, J. (2003). *Global complexity*. Cambridge: Polity Press.

Vertovec, S. (2009). *Transnationalism*. London: Routledge.

Waters, M. (1995). *Globalization*. London: Routledge.

Wittel, A. (2000). Ethnography of the move: From field to net to Internet. *Qualitative Social Research, 1*(1). Online journal. Retrieved October 1, 2009 from http://www.qualitative-research.net/index.php/fqs/article/view/1131/2518.

Young, I.M. (1990). *Justice and the politics of difference*. Princeton: Princeton University Press.

CURRICULUM INQUIRY

Editor-in-Chief:
DENNIS THIESSEN
Editors:
ELIZABETH CAMPBELL,
HEATHER SYKES, *and*
MARY KOOY

Ontario Institute for Studies in Education, University of Toronto

Curriculum Inquiry is dedicated to the study of educational research, development, evaluation, and theory. This leading international journal brings together influential academics and researchers from a variety of disciplines around the world to provide expert commentary and lively debate. Articles explore important ideas, issues, trends, and problems in education. Each issue also includes provocative and critically analytical editorials covering topics such as curriculum development, educational policy, and teacher education.